Fourth Canadian Edition

PRINCIPLES OF CLASSROOM MANAGEMENT

A PROFESSIONAL DECISION-MAKING MODEL

James Levin
Pennsylvania State University

James F. Nolan
Pennsylvania State University

James W. Kerr
Brock University

Anne E. Elliott
Brock University

Mirjana Bajovic
Brock University

PEARSON

Toronto

General Manager, VP Editorial: Jessica Mosher
Sr. Acquisitions Editor: Carolin Sweig and Lisa Rahn
Senior Marketing Managers: Loula March and
  Michelle Bish
Program Manager: Madhu Ranadive
Project Manager: Rohin Bansal
Developmental Editor: Tiffany McNeil,
  Electronic Publishing Services
Media Editor: Marisa D'Andrea

Production Services: Munesh Kumar, Aptara®, Inc.
Permissions Project Manager: Erica Mojzes
Photo Permissions Research:
  iEnergizer Aptara Ltd.
Text Permissions Research: Varoon Deo-Singh.
  Permission Specialist, Electronic Publishing
  Services, Inc.
Cover Designer: iEnergizer Aptara Ltd.
Cover Image: Fotolia

Credits and acknowledgments for material borrowed from other sources and reproduced, with permission, in this textbook appear on the appropriate page within the text.

If you purchased this book outside the United States or Canada, you should be aware that it has been imported without the approval of the publisher or the author.

Library and Archives Canada Cataloguing in Publication
Levin, James, 1946–, author
  Principles of classroom management : a professional decision-making model/James Levin, Pennsylvania State University, James F. Nolan, Pennsylvania State University, James W. Kerr, Brock University, Anne E. Elliott, Brock University, Mirjana Bajovic, Brock University.—Fourth Canadian edition.
  Includes bibliographical references and index.
  ISBN 978-0-13-308166-4 (bound)
  1. Classroom management—Canada—Problems, exercises, etc. 2. Teaching—Canada—Problems, exercises, etc. 3. Classroom management—Problems, exercises, etc. 4. Teaching—Problems, exercises, etc. I. Nolan, James F., 1950-, author II. Elliott, Anne E. (Anne Elizabeth), 1943–, author III. Kerr, James, 1949-, author IV. Bajovic, Mirjana, author V. Title.
  LB3013.L48 2014
  371.102'40971

C2014-906086-6

ISBN-10:   0-13-308166-4
ISBN-13: 978-0-13-308166-4

For Richard, Linda, Sinisa, and Doonia

BRIEF CONTENTS

CONTENTS

Chapter 5   PHILOSOPHICAL APPROACHES TO CLASSROOM MANAGEMENT   95

PREFACE

The central theme of the fourth Canadian edition of *Principles of Classroom Management* remains consistent with the first, second and third Canadian editions. We believe that teachers and students share responsibility for classroom behaviour, that teachers may have to modify their teaching style if they expect student behaviour to change, and that students in constructive relationships with adults are more likely to engage in positive social behaviour and to be successful academically.

In continuing to adapt the text for the Canadian educator, we acknowledge that Canadian society, culture, and education are distinct from those of our U.S. neighbours in several important ways. Our historical underpinnings, immigration policies, small population in a vast geographical expanse, as well as our provincially controlled educational systems make us distinct from our friends south of the border. In the officially bilingual (French and English) Canadian culture, there exists a deep tradition of tolerance in which diversity and multilingualism are valued. Canadians and Americans also differ in their views about security, nationalism, and relationships with other nations.

In order to reflect these Canadian differences, in this edition we continued to make structural changes and updates to the text by adding more recent Canadian references to reflect current research, recent responses to change, and best practices across the country. For instance, we added a new chapter about bullying, which has become a national focus for Canadian educators. We continue to emphasize differentiation of instruction as well as Marzano's work on assessment and feedback. Good and Brophy's body of work addressing the need to communicate high expectations to learners continues to be featured in this edition.

We have also reviewed the case studies and maintained those that contain perspectives from various points of view. The metaphor of the kaleidoscope refers to this type of case study because, in a kaleidoscope, as the lens is rotated, the same pieces realign in new ways to form a new image. In several of our cases, the case is described through the eyes of all of the participants who are engaged in the scenario, thereby providing the reader with a variety of perspectives that may offer broader insights into complex classroom issues.

We revisited our cases to ensure that they are typically Canadian in nature. Our kaleidoscope cases also reflect real issues in Canadian schools and show multiple viewpoints of a given situation. In order to make comprehension easier for the reader, the key ideas in each chapter have been emphasized in a number of ways. We placed pre-reading questions related to content at the beginning of each chapter. Key terms have also been highlighted throughout the text and defined at the conclusion of each chapter. Weblinks were updated, and questions for discussion were placed immediately after each classroom case study throughout the text.

Educators indicated that it would be helpful for teachers to acquire a list of strategies that have proven effective when dealing with various disruptive classroom behaviours. Therefore, we have developed and maintained a memorable model of sequential strategies for managing inappropriate classroom behaviours. To this model, we have aptly applied and further highlighted the following acronym: **CALM (consider, act, lessen, manage)**. This model provides a series of steps (Levels I through IV) that should serve to help teachers make logical decisions and avoid responding to problem classroom behaviours entirely from an emotional point of view. We have presented this model to several groups of beginning teachers and they have told us they find it credible and helpful.

As we considered the principles central to the text, we realized the critical nature of the language we chose. Rather than label students as "discipline problems" or "disruptive students," it was more consistent with our beliefs to separate the student from his or her problematic behaviour; therefore, we identified the situation, rather than the student, as being problematic. As a result, the onus was placed on teachers to modify either their behaviour or the situation that impinged on a student who exhibited disruptive behaviour. This is a subtle but critical difference that implies that teachers need to avoid negative personal labels and strive to maintain and build positive relationships with students who cause classroom disruptions. Another example of the evolving use of language in the teaching profession is found in Chapter 5 "Philosophical Approaches to Classroom Management." While we like the relevance of French and Raven's work from 1960 as they describe the four different types of power a teacher can employ, we reject the word "power." We believe that power is more aligned with control, whereas the word "authority" is more appropriate for today's classrooms as it includes respect. As a result, we chose to reconstruct the four types of "power" to four types of "authority" employed by teachers.

We would like to thank the following instructors for their feedback during the development of this text: Jerome G. Delaney, Memorial University of Newfoundland, Carla Di Nunzio, York University, Elaine Verchomin Harasymiw, University of Alberta, Andrea Holm-Allingham, Lakehead University, Kelly Young, Trent University.

SUPPLEMENTS

CourseSmart for Instructors

CourseSmart goes beyond traditional expectations—providing instant, online access to the textbooks and course materials you need. You can save time and hassle with a digital eTextbook that allows you to search for the most relevant content at the very moment you need it. Whether it's evaluating textbooks or creating lecture notes to help students with difficult concepts, CourseSmart can make life a little easier. See how when you visit www.coursesmart.com/instructors.

LEARNING SOLUTIONS MANAGERS

Pearson's Learning Solutions Managers work with faculty and campus course designers to ensure that Pearson technology products, assessment tools, and online course materials are tailored to meet your specific needs. This highly qualified team is dedicated to helping schools take full advantage of a wide range of educational resources, by assisting in the integration of a variety of instructional materials and media formats. Your local Pearson Education sales representative can provide you with more details on this service program.

PEARSON CUSTOM LIBRARY

For enrollments of at least 25 students, you can create your own textbook by choosing the chapters that best suit your own course needs. To begin building your custom text, visit www.pearsoncustomlibrary.com. You may also work with a dedicated Pearson Custom editor to create your ideal text—publishing your own original content or mixing and matching Pearson content. Contact your local Pearson Representative to get started.

Iterative Case Study Analyses

We describe four case studies of behavioural problems at different grade levels, and suggest that you analyze one or more of the case studies four times.

The first analysis should be completed before you read and study this text. This analysis will serve as the baseline from which to reflect upon your growth of understanding and ability to analyze complex student behaviours as you study the text and reanalyze the cases.

The second analysis should be completed after you have read and studied Part One, "Foundations," which includes Chapters 1 through 5.

The third analysis should incorporate the concepts discussed in Part Two, "Prevention," which includes Chapters 6 and 7.

The fourth and final analyses should use the concepts found in Part Three, "Interventions for Common Behaviour Problems," and Part Four, "Interventions for Chronic Behaviour Problems," which include Chapters 8 through 11.

For each reanalysis, consider what has changed and what has stayed the same from the previous analysis.

Iterative Case Study Analysis

1

The Foundations

FOCUS ON THE PRINCIPLES OF CLASSROOM MANAGEMENT

1. What is the single most important influence on the classroom learning environment?
2. What range of professional responsibilities do teachers need to accept in the classroom?
3. What ideas and strategies must teachers develop if they are to have a classroom characterized by a high level of on-task student behaviour?
4. If students are to display appropriate behaviour in class, what preplanning is necessary for teachers?

INTRODUCTION

In Canadian Faculties of Education, there are many courses that address issues critical to effective instruction. Provincial ministries of education require that the faculties provide courses that prepare teacher candidates in teaching methods, special education, educational psychology, history of education, and educational law. No course or program that focuses on instructional strategies can be complete without discussing the parameters of teaching—a topic that is closely tied to the topic of **classroom management**. Teacher candidates receive guidelines that help them plan meaningful learning experiences for students in all curriculum areas (e.g., language, mathematics, science and technology, arts, physical education). Teacher education programs include instruction for designing and writing effective student outcome expectations as a result of instruction. These also prepare teacher candidates for the task of creating lesson plans, unit plans, and long-term plans, and selecting supportive instructional material.

We have all taken and taught courses on classroom management at the pre-service, in-service, and graduate levels of education, but we, the authors, have noted a dearth of research on this issue, especially in Canada. The most thoroughly prepared and well-designed lesson has no chance of success if the instructor is unable to manage the classroom and her students' behaviour effectively.[1] In fact, extreme cases of poor management lead to poor learning;

[1]To foster equality without being cumbersome, gender pronouns will be alternated by chapter. Chapter 1 will have female pronouns; Chapter 2, male; Chapter 3, female; and so forth.

therefore, we begin by setting forth a definition of teaching and explaining how and why classroom management is such a critical part of the teaching process.

We have also developed a model of sequential strategies, which we have named **CALM** (see the four keywords—consider, act, lessen, and manage—in the levels outlined on the next page), for managing inappropriate classroom behaviours. The rationale for developing this model emerged from our discussions with educators who indicated that it would be helpful for beginning teachers, in particular, to acquire a list of strategies that have proven effective when dealing with various disruptive classroom behaviours. We believe that a layered method for analyzing and managing behavioural concerns is a superior approach to trying to anticipate all classroom challenges and providing methods for coping with each challenge separately. After carefully considering the types of questions that educators—from teacher candidates—to experienced classroom teachers—raise about classroom management, we have developed CALM as a flexible, hierarchical model for examining and managing challenges that may affect the classroom environment.

CALM will be discussed fully in Chapter 7, "Structuring the Environment," and we will refer to it throughout the text where appropriate. For now, we will provide the essential steps to the model.

The rest of this chapter presents a structural overview of the book. First, we present the principles of management that form the book's foundation. Second, we provide an explanation of the decision-making hierarchical approach to management. Last, we offer a flow chart of the knowledge, skills, and techniques that make up a management hierarchy and result in successful classrooms in which teachers are free to teach and students free to learn.

The CALM Model

The **CALM** strategy provides the following levels as a general guide for handling classroom-management issues. It can become automatic and be applied as needed. When these levels become an instinctive part of the teacher's repertoire of strategies, along with other components of the effective classroom-management approach (including the development of a positive rapport), the successful teacher should be able to determine quickly the suitable level to apply in order to avoid serious disruptions to the learning environment.

Level I—Consider

When a student's behaviour becomes disruptive, the teacher should **consider** the following question to initiate a response process. "Does the behaviour change, affect, or disrupt the classroom learning environment, teacher, or students?" If the answer to this question is "no," continue with instruction.

Level II—Act

Once the behaviour has become a "distracting" force for the teacher, the next level of intervention is introduced because it becomes necessary to **act**.

Level III—Lessen

Because it is important to minimize distraction and not give undue attention to inappropriate behaviour, it is best to **lessen** the use of invasive responses in dealing with a situation that requires action.

Level IV—Manage

Manage the milieu to quickly return to an effective learning environment.

DEFINING THE PROCESS OF TEACHING

Each year, universities educate and graduate thousands of teacher candidates who then enter the teaching profession. After completing their professional teacher education program, graduates enter the classroom and, in Canada, typically teach for 30 to 35 years. Many teachers, however, are unable to provide an adequate operational definition of teaching. Some argue that a formal definition is not necessary because they have been teaching for years and whatever they do seems to work; however, for a few of us who consider teaching a professionally sophisticated endeavour, experience—although invaluable in many teaching situations—is not the only thing that should be relied upon to develop and plan instruction. Furthermore, this "gut-reaction" approach is sorely limited when the old "proven methods" seem challenged, and there then arises a need for modifying the existing instructional or management strategies or for developing new ones. When asked, some people define teaching as the delivery, transference, or giving of knowledge or information. Definitions like these give no clue as to how knowledge is transferred and what strategies are used to deliver it; they limit teaching to the cognitive domain only, thus failing to recognize the extraordinary level of competence needed to make hundreds of daily decisions on the basis of content and pedagogical knowledge in complex and dynamic classroom environments. Teaching has always emphasized the cognitive domain; for instance, many educators currently adhere to Piaget's constructivist theory, which argues that individuals construct new knowledge from their experiences through assimilation and accommodation (Berk, 2014; Boudourides, 2003). However, when teachers view teaching as being concerned solely with cognitive development, they limit their effectiveness in managing students who exhibit disruptive behaviour. Troublesome students often need more encouragement and strategies to mature in the affective as well as cognitive domains; for instance, many require guidance to help develop essential interpersonal and societal skills, such as cooperating with peers, respecting others, and contributing positively to their community. Teachers who understand the critical nature of the affective domain are much better equipped to manage disruptive students (Miller and Pedro, 2006).

Vygotsky (1978) and Piaget (1975) have influenced educators with their belief that social interactions enhance children's cognitive development. Vygotsky asserted that social interactions need to include meaningful language opportunities that enable children to negotiate and experiment with new learning. This implies that teachers ought to structure and effectively manage children's social interactions to maximize learning. (Novak, 2010; Wessler and Preble, 2003).

Many exceptional teachers approach their work convinced students need teachers well equipped with effective classroom-management strategies because some young people exhibit behaviours that seriously interfere with teaching and learning (Horner, Sugai, Lewis-Palmer, and Todd, 2001; Vargas, 2013). Teachers with this conviction are better prepared to work effectively with disruptive students. They neither become frustrated easily nor feel as if they are wasting their time because they understand that strong teaching helps students to not only attain cognitive maturity but also develop emotional intelligence. Emotional intelligence has been recognized as a separate competency from cognitive aptitude (Lomas and Stough, 2012; Mayer, Salovey, and Caruso, 2004). Emotional self-awareness is an important skill for success in life, and this is an area where teachers have to help children grow stronger. Helping children develop this skill is central to good classroom management, and teachers

Group of businessmen to discuss the work plan.
© YURALAITS ALBERT/Shutterstock

who address emotional intelligence explicitly with their students are generally more successful in the classroom.

Teachers are likely to gain a clearer perception of the best practices for their profession when teaching is properly defined. Besides best practices awareness, teachers' self-efficacy is another key attribute essential for effective classroom management. Self-efficacy is teachers' confidence in their ability to promote student learning and to achieve instructional goals (Bembenutty and Chen, 2005). It is a teacher characteristic related to student achievement and has direct implications for classroom-management skills. Because teachers are more likely to engage in effective management behaviours when they believe they are capable of using those behaviours successfully, they need to possess an effective repertoire of management strategies for a huge variety of classroom scenarios. Moreover, one of the major tenets of Adlerian psychology (Sweeney, 1981) says that when we feel encouraged, we feel capable and appreciated and will usually connect and interact with others cooperatively. When we feel discouraged, however, we may act negatively by competing, withdrawing, or giving up. In finding ways of expressing and accepting encouragement, respect and social engagement, we are helped to feel optimistic and fulfilled (Prochaska and Norcross, 2013; Watts, 2003). In other words, teachers do not control student behaviour, students control their own behaviours. If this idea is accepted fully by instructors, it follows that they can change student behaviour only by influencing the change through modifications in their own behaviour, which is the only behaviour they can control directly. When actual student behaviour differs from an appropriate standard, teachers attempt to influence a change in the behaviour by changing their own behaviour. The behaviour the teacher decides to use should be one that maximizes the likelihood that student behaviour will change in the appropriate way.

Fortunately, most human behaviour is learned observationally through modelling—from observing others, a person can form an idea of how new behaviours are performed and then replicate them. This phenomenon, called *social learning theory* (Bandura, 1977; Zimmerman and Schunk, 2013), explains human behaviour in terms of interactions among cognitive, behavioural, and environmental influences. As it encompasses attention, memory, and motivation, social learning theory spans both cognitive and behavioural frameworks and is related to developing a series of classroom-management competencies. The probability of choosing the most effective behaviour increases when teachers have a **professional knowledge** (of instructional techniques, cognitive psychology, and child development) and when they use this knowledge to guide the modification of their own behaviour (Anderson, 2002; Zimmerman and Schunk, 2013).

With this background, we can define teaching as the use of preplanned behaviours—founded in learning principles and child development theory and directed toward both instructional delivery and classroom management—that increase the probability of effecting a positive change in student behaviour. The significance of this definition in trying to change any student's behaviour is threefold.

1. Teaching is concerned with what teachers are able to control—their own behaviour, which is preplanned. Teaching is not a capricious activity.
2. The preplanned behaviours are determined by the teacher's professional knowledge, which guides the teacher in selecting appropriate behaviours. It is the application of this specialized body of professional knowledge and knowing why it works that makes teaching a profession (Loughran, 2012).
3. Because many teaching behaviours are well founded in professional knowledge, the teacher's challenge is to select the best behaviours that change corresponding student behaviour. For this, the teacher must not only know students' initial behaviours but also have a clear picture of the desired student behaviours for any given instructional activity.

The emphasis on the use of professional knowledge to inform teacher behaviour is critical. If teachers are asked why they interacted with students in a particular manner or why they used a particular instructional strategy, their response should be based on pedagogical or psychological research, theory, or methodology.

Case 1.1, "Getting Students to Respond," illustrates how a teacher applies the definition of teaching to instructional delivery. Ms. Chong, a grade 10 teacher, was aware of the current student behaviour and, after questioning, had a clear picture of what she wanted the behaviour to become. To effect this change, she analyzed her behaviours and how they affected her students. Because changes in teacher behaviour influence changes in student behaviour, the former is often termed "affecting behaviour" and the sought-after student behaviour is termed "target behaviour" (Loughran, 2012). Using her professional knowledge, Ms. Chong modified her behaviour to improve her teaching practice to bring about the target behaviour. The behaviours she chose to employ were well founded in the educational literature on questioning methodology (see Chapter 6, "The Professional Teacher"). Ms. Chong performed as a professional.

CASE 1.1

Getting Students to Respond

Ms. Chong believes active student participation in class activities is necessary for learning to take place. She prides herself on her ability to design questions from all levels of the cognitive domain; she believes that students benefit from and enjoy working with questions that require analysis, synthesis, and evaluation. She is sorely disappointed, however, because very few students have been volunteering to answer questions, and those that did respond gave very brief answers.

Observation of Ms. Chong's class indicates a fairly regular pattern of behaviours during questioning. Standing in front of the class, she asks the first question: "Students, we have been studying the settling of the Canadian West in the late 1800s and early 1900s. Why do you think so many people picked up and moved thousands of miles to a strange land knowing that they would face incredible hardship and suffering during the long trip?" Two hands shoot up. Ms. Chong immediately calls on Judy. "Judy, why do you think they went?" "They wanted new opportunities," Judy answers. Ms. Chong immediately replies, "Great answer. Things where they lived must have been so bad that they decided it was worth the hardships they would face. In a new country, they would have a new beginning and be given free land. Another thing is that some of the pioneers might not have realized how difficult the trip would be. Do you think that the hardships continued even after the pioneers arrived in the Prairies? Ameer?"

After discussion, Ms. Chong realizes how her behaviours are affecting student behaviour. Instead of increasing participation, they actually hinder participation. After conducting further classroom discussions and reading about questioning strategies, Ms. Chong decides to change her approach. Instead of standing at the front of the class to ask questions, she begins to ask questions from different locations throughout the room. Initially, Ms Chong would select a student to answer as soon as a couple of hands went up, which gave the remaining students an opportunity to rely on the same students to answer while they directed their thoughts elsewhere. This time, however, Ms Chong waits at least three to five seconds before calling on any student. Also, after a student answers, she again waits at least three seconds and then points out the salient parts of the response, rephrases another question using the student's response, and directs this question to the class.

As before, her behaviours affect student behaviour; however, this time more students volunteer initially, responses are longer, and additional students are willing to expand on initial answers.

Questions to Consider

1. Why did Ms. Chong increase her wait time before accepting an answer to her question?
2. Which teacher behaviour encouraged student discussion?
3. Which behaviour inhibited student discussion?

Case 1.2, "Why Study? We Don't Get Enough Time for the Test Anyway," illustrates the relationship between teacher behaviour and targeted student behaviour in classroom management.

Like Ms. Chong, Mr. Casimir changed his behaviour to one that reflected a well-accepted educational practice. With this change came corresponding changes in student behaviour with his grade 6 class.

Although not as plentiful as the information available on effective teaching practices, there is now a body of knowledge concerning effective classroom management (Charles and Senter, 2004; Evertson and Weinstein, 2006; Holt, Hargrove and Harris, 2011; McLeskey, Rosenberg, and Westling, 2013). As stressed throughout this book, effective classroom management is inseparable from effective instruction. Without effective instructional practices, teachers are unlikely to be able to maintain successfully appropriate student behaviour; however, although absolutely necessary, effective instruction does not in itself guarantee classrooms free from disruptive behaviour. Even the best teachers may occasionally experience some disruptive behaviour.

PRINCIPLES OF CLASSROOM MANAGEMENT

As a result of the research on classroom management, a number of well-accepted principles governing teacher behaviour (to prevent and manage disruptive behaviour) have emerged. Some of these principles are quite specific to a particular philosophical underpinning (see Chapter 5, "Philosophical Approaches to Classroom Management"), whereas others are philosophically generic. This book presents the CALM model as well as 38 generic principles of classroom management developed through years of experience, research, and study. Each of the remaining ten chapters emphasizes this model, along with some of these principles, and discusses in detail how the teacher may incorporate them into effective management practices.

In the following section, we summarize the contents of each chapter and its relevant principles. These paragraphs are followed by an explanation of the decision-making hierarchical approach to managing classroom behaviour. Just as it is good classroom practice to provide the learner with an anticipatory set of expectations before in-depth instruction, these chapter summaries provide the reader with an indication of the scope, sequence, and structure of this text.

In Chapter 2, "The Nature of Behavioural Problems," we examine the details of behavioural problems. First, we review the limitations of trying to classify behaviours and their subsequent possible association with discipline problems. Offering a new operational definition of the term **behavioural problem** rectifies these limitations. This definition is then used to classify common classroom behaviours. Second, we analyze misbehaviour historically by frequency and type to provide an insight into schools today. Third, we present research concerning the effect of disruptive behaviour on both teachers and students. The related principles of classroom management are the following:

1. A problem exists whenever behaviour interferes with the teaching act, interferes with the rights of others to learn, is psychologically or physically unsafe, or destroys property.
2. For effective teaching to take place, teachers must be competent in managing student misbehaviour to maximize the time spent on learning.
3. Teachers who manage their classrooms effectively enjoy teaching more and have greater confidence in their ability to affect student achievement.

CASE 1.2

"Why Study? We Don't Get Enough Time for the Test Anyway"

Mr. Casimir has a rule that test papers will not be passed out until all students are quiet and in their seats with all materials, except a pencil, in the desk. He explains this to the class before every test. Without fail, he has to wait 5 to 10 minutes before everyone in the class is ready. Typically, some students complain, "Why do we have less time just because a few other kids are slow to get ready?" Sometimes, students will get visibly angry, saying, "This isn't fair"; "This is stupid"; or "Why study? We don't get enough time for the test anyway." He almost always resorts to arguing with the students. He is aware that his students begin their test in a negative environment, and he wonders if this negativity has a serious impact on test results. Mr. Casimir dreads test days.

During a discussion of this situation with another teacher, Mr. Casimir is introduced to the concept of logical consequences—in other words, allowing students to experience a logically related consequence of their behaviour. Employing this concept, Mr. Casimir announces to the class that he will pass out tests on an individual basis. "Once you are ready, you receive a test." He walks down the aisles giving a test paper to students who are ready and passing by, without comment, those who are not. As a result of his changed behaviour, student behaviour changes. Complaining stops, and in a few minutes, more students are ready to take the test.

Questions to Consider

1. Are there other ways Mr. Casimir could have solved this behavioural problem? Is there another approach that would give all students the same amount of time to write the test?

2. Would the students understand and accept the logical consequences in this situation?

3. What classroom routines do you think a teacher should establish to promote an effective test-writing environment for students?

In Chapter 3, "Understanding Why Children Misbehave," we explore the underlying complex causes of misbehaviour and provides multiple reasons for why children misbehave. Societal changes have created an environment vastly different from the one in which children of previous generations grew up. First, we examine how these out-of-school changes have influenced children's attitudes and behaviours.

Like adults, children have strong personal, social, and academic needs. At the same time, they undergo rapid cognitive and moral development. Schools today are ethnically diverse and students are technologically savvy. In the chapter, we also describe normal developmental behaviours as well as typical behaviours associated with children's attempts to meet their needs. We also detail behaviours that may appear when the home or school fails to recognize and respond to these needs and developmental changes. It is increasingly clear that some students attempt to meet their needs by bullying others either face-to-face or via the cyber world. This is a serious social concern because the long-term effects on both the bullied and the bully have lasting negative implications. This issue will be examined from both the bully and the bullied child's perspectives. Please refer to Chapter 4 "Bullying and Cyberbullying: Implications for the Classroom," for an in-depth discussion of bullying and cyberbullying.

It must be emphasized that teachers do not have control over the changes that are occurring in society and in children; however, they do have absolute control over their instructional competence. Excellent instruction and good classroom-management skills are a significant way to lessen the effects of uncontrollable factors and to prevent misbehaviour.

The following principles are endorsed in Chapter 3:

1. An awareness of the causes of misbehaviour enables teachers to use positive control techniques rather than negative ones that stem from erroneously viewing misbehaviour as a personal affront.
2. Basic human needs, such as food, safety, belonging, and security are prerequisites for appropriate classroom behaviour.
3. The need for a sense of significance, competence, virtue, and authority influences student behaviour.
4. Societal changes beyond schools' control greatly influence student behaviour.
5. Cognitive and moral developmental changes may result in transformations in student behaviour. These changes may produce positive or negative results in learning environments.
6. Instructional competence can lessen the effects of negative outside influences as well as prevent the misbehaviour that occurs as a result of poor instruction.

In Chapter 4, "Bullying and Cyberbullying: Implications for the Classroom," we describe bullying patterns, forms of bullying, and cyberbullying. While bullying and cyberbullying are prevalent in all societies, we focus on data and studies from Canada.

We identify the characteristics of bullies and victims as the indicators that a child is being bullied. We focus extensively on how a teacher can help all participants in the bullying process—the bully, the child being bullied, and the classroom bystanders. We make specific recommendations for classroom intervention that will help students understand the harmfulness of cyber bullying. Finally, we focus on both schoolwide and classroom prevention programs and classroom activities that can create an environment where bullying cannot flourish.

The principles of classroom management discussed in Chapter 4 are as follows:

1. What does a teacher need to know about bullying and cyberbullying?
2. What can a teacher do to help both the bully and the victim?
3. How can a teacher prevent bullying in the classroom and in the school?

In Chapter 5, "Philosophical Approaches to Classroom Management," we describe three theoretical models of classroom management. A series of nine questions helps teachers define their beliefs about the subject. These questions are then used to analyze, compare, and contrast the three models. It is a teacher's underlying belief about how children learn and develop and who has the primary responsibility for controlling a child's behaviour that determines which model provides the best fit.

Different management strategies are presented as either compatible or incompatible with certain schools of thought. When teachers employ behaviours that are inconsistent with their beliefs about children, they feel emotionally uncomfortable and usually do not see the desired change in student behaviour.

Teachers exert influence through the use of five different social authority bases. In the chapter, we place each authority base along a continuum, which begins with those authority bases that are most likely to engender students' control over their own behaviour, and proceeds to those bases that foster increasing teacher management over student behaviour. The chapter concludes with a discussion of teacher behaviours that are congruent with the various authority bases.

The following principles of classroom management are discussed in Chapter 5:

1. Theoretical approaches to classroom management are useful to teachers because they offer a basis for analyzing, understanding, and managing student and teacher behaviour.
2. As social agents, teachers have access to a variety of authority bases that can be used to influence student behaviour.
3. The techniques a teacher uses to manage student behaviour should be consistent with the teacher's beliefs about how students learn and develop.

In Chapter 6, "The Professional Teacher," we explore the effective instructional techniques used by professional teachers. Effective teaching prevents most discipline-related problems. Our discussion here is divided into two parts. The first part, "The Basics of Effective Teaching," gives an overview of the knowledge that the experts have gained from research on teacher effects. This research focuses on teacher behaviours that facilitate student achievement in lower-level cognitive tasks as measured by paper-and-pencil tests. The second section of the chapter, "Beyond the Basics," covers more recent conceptualizations of teaching and learning that focus on student cognition and higher-order cognitive learning tasks.

Chapter 6 foregrounds the following two principles:

1. Student learning and on-task behaviour are maximized when teaching strategies are based on what educators know about student development, how people learn, and what constitutes effective teaching.
2. Understanding and using the research on effective teaching enhance the teacher's instructional competence and help to prevent classroom-management problems.

In Chapter 7, "Structuring the Environment," we detail how to structure the environment to minimize disruptive behaviour. Many classroom-management problems arise because students are either unaware of or unclear about what types of behaviours are expected of them or why certain procedures must be followed in the classroom. This lack of awareness usually occurs when teachers are ambiguous about how they want their students to behave; thus, developing meaningful classroom guidelines is a key to success.

We present the procedures for designing classroom guidelines with emphasis on the importance of having both a rationale and stated consequences for each rule. We also offer techniques to communicate guidelines to students in a way that maximizes understanding and acceptance.

In the chapter, we also discuss the influence of cultural background on teacher and student values, norms, and expectations for appropriate behaviour. We also advocate using cooperative learning activities and teaching social skills to create classroom group norms that support prosocial behaviour and engage students in learning activities.

The principles discussed in Chapter 7 include the following:

1. When environmental conditions are appropriate for learning, the likelihood of disruptive behaviour is minimized.
2. Students are more likely to follow classroom guidelines if the teacher models appropriate behaviour and explains the relationship of the guidelines to learning, to mutual respect between student and teacher, and to protection and safety of property and individuals.
3. Clearly communicating guidelines to students and obtaining their commitment to following them enhances appropriate classroom behaviour.
4. Enforcing teacher expectations by using natural and logical consequences helps students learn that they are accountable for the consequences of their behaviour and hence responsible for controlling their own behaviour.
5. When classroom guidelines and rules match the culture of students' homes and communities, the likelihood that students will behave appropriately is increased.
6. When the teacher creates group norms that are supportive of engagement in learning activities, the students are more likely to behave appropriately.

In Chapters 8, "Managing Common Misbehaviour Problems: Nonverbal Interventions," and 9, "Managing Common Misbehaviour Problems: Verbal Interventions and Use of Logical Consequences," we explore the management of common misbehaviours through the use of a three-tiered hierarchical decision-making model of nonverbal and verbal behaviours called "coping skills." Research reviewed in Chapter 8 reveals that the majority of misbehaviours are verbal interruptions, off-task behaviour, and disruptive physical movements. The frequency of these surface disruptions can be greatly reduced with proper planning, instructional strategies, environmental structure, and verbal and nonverbal teacher behaviours.

In Chapter 8, we outline the first tier of the decision-making hierarchy. We discuss the appropriate use and limitations of three nonverbal coping skills: planned ignoring, signal interference, and proximity interference. The chapter includes an intervention decision-making model that hierarchically orders nonverbal behaviours teachers can use to manage student behaviour. The hierarchy begins with those nonintrusive techniques that give students the greatest opportunity to control their own behaviours and proceeds to intrusive strategies that give the teacher more responsibility for managing student behaviour. We also present five implementation guidelines.

The following principles are the focus of Chapter 8:

1. Classroom-management techniques need to be consistent with the goal of helping students to become self-directing individuals.
2. Use of a preplanned hierarchy of remedial interventions improves the teacher's ability to manage misbehaviour.
3. The use of a hierarchy that starts with nonintrusive, nonverbal teacher behaviours gives students the opportunity to exercise self-control, minimizes disruption to the

teaching/learning process, reduces the likelihood of student confrontation, protects students' safety, and maximizes the teacher's management alternatives.

In Chapter 9, we discuss in detail the second and third tiers of the decision-making hierarchy: verbal intervention and the application of logical consequences. Twelve verbal-intervention techniques are presented, along with nine guidelines for their appropriate use as well as their limitations. Once again, these techniques are ordered along a continuum that ranges from nonintrusive student control to intrusive teacher management of behaviour. The use of verbal intervention is founded on the assumption that teachers do have effective alternatives to angry, personal, sarcastic confrontations with students. Such alternatives typically defuse rather than escalate misbehaviour. The third tier of the decision-making hierarchy, the use of logical consequences, is a powerful technique in managing student behaviour. The concept of logical consequences is explained in detail, along with the guidelines teachers use to develop effective logical consequences for a wide range of misbehaviour. We also discuss the assertive delivery of logical consequences.

These are the principles dealt with in Chapter 9:

1. When nonverbal teacher intervention does not lead to appropriate student behaviour, the teacher should employ verbal intervention to deal with the misbehaviour.
2. Some forms of verbal intervention defuse confrontation and reduce misbehaviour, whereas other forms escalate misbehaviour and confrontation.
3. When verbal intervention does not lead to appropriate student behaviour, the teacher needs to apply logical consequences to the student's misconduct.

In Chapter 10, "Classroom Interventions for Chronic Problems," we look at classroom interventions for students with chronic problems. We present two long-term problem-solving strategies—relationship building and disrupting the cycle of discouragement—along with three techniques for managing behaviour. Most strategies used with chronic **behavioural problems** involve referral outside the classroom; however, there are three effective, field-tested, in-classroom techniques: self-monitoring, behaviour contracting, and anecdotal record keeping. The effective use of these three techniques assumes that the teacher's classroom behaviours have met the prerequisites discussed in previous chapters and outlined in this one. We explain the step-by-step implementation of these techniques and present a detailed discussion of the critical communication skills that can make the difference in successful management of chronic misbehaviour. Lastly, we explain teacher-controlled exclusion from the classroom, an interim step between in-classroom management and outside referral.

The following principles are discussed in Chapter 10:

1. When dealing with students who pose chronic behavioural problems, teachers should use strategies to resolve the problems within the classroom before seeking outside assistance.
2. Finding positive qualities in students who have chronic behavioural problems and building positive relationships with those students increase the possibility that the problems can be resolved within the classroom.

3. Breaking the cycle of discouragement in which most students with chronic behavioural problems are trapped increases the likelihood of in-classroom problem solving.

4. When teachers conduct private conferences and use effective communication skills with students who have chronic behavioural problems, these problems are more likely to be resolved within the classroom.

5. Interventions that require students to recognize their inappropriate behaviour and its impact on others increase the likelihood of the problems being resolved within the classroom.

6. Interventions that require students with chronic behavioural problems to be accountable for trying to control their behaviour on a daily basis increase the possibility of in-classroom problem resolution.

7. Interventions that call for gradual but consistent improvement in behaviour better the chances of resolving chronic problems within the classroom.

In Chapter 11, "Seeking Outside Assistance," we offer outside-the-classroom advice. When in-classroom techniques have been exhausted and have not resulted in appropriate student behaviour, it is necessary to seek outside assistance. We offer teachers guidelines to follow when deciding whether or not outside consultation is warranted. We also explain the concept of a success–failure ratio, and discuss how this ratio contributes to persisting misbehaviour.

Some students may need outside referral even though they do not display any forms of chronic misbehaviour. These students may exhibit signs of emotional stress or family dysfunction. We discuss six warning signs of these problems. We offer a referral process that stresses multidisciplinary team consultation as an effective means of working with these students. We present the roles of the counsellor, parents, administrator, and school psychologist along with the legal issues that must be considered when making outside referrals.

Parental support and cooperation with the school is critical when working with students who misbehave chronically. We have set out specific guidelines that teachers can use to decide when parents need to be contacted; we also discuss techniques on how to conduct parent conferences to facilitate and enhance parental support and cooperation.

These are the classroom-management principles underlined in Chapter 11:

1. Professional teachers recognize that some chronic behavioural problems are not responsive to treatment within the classroom or are beyond their expertise and necessitate specialized outside assistance.

2. When outside assistance must be sought to manage a chronic misbehaviour problem adequately and appropriately, the use of a multidisciplinary team is the most effective approach.

3. Parental support and cooperation with the school is critical when attempting to manage a student who chronically misbehaves. Careful planning and skilled conferencing techniques are essential in developing a positive working relationship between home and school.

PROFESSIONAL DECISION-MAKING HIERARCHY

In the teaching profession, hierarchies, taxonomies, and classification systems are used to organize vast amounts of isolated bits of data into manageable, comprehensible bodies of knowledge. Hierarchies may be used for more than just organizing information. They may also be used to guide professional decisions. The advantages of using a hierarchical approach are threefold: (1) it allows for the systematic implementation of the knowledge that informs the practice of a given profession, (2) it provides the practitioner with a variety of approaches rather than a limited few, and (3) it offers an overarching methodology that may be applied to specific cases. Thus, the hierarchical approach increases the likelihood of successful outcomes. The hierarchical strategies are based on professional knowledge, and if early strategies are ineffective, there are numerous other strategies that may produce positive results.

Applying a hierarchical approach to classroom-management decisions allows teachers to employ knowledge effectively in order to understand, prevent, and manage

CASE 1.3

The Vice-Principal Wants to See Whom?

Ms. Iannizi decides that one way to maintain discipline in her grade 8 class is to be firm and consistent with the enforcement of classroom rules and procedures, right from the beginning of the school year. One of her rules is that students must raise their hands to be called on before answering questions. She explains this rule to the class: "By grade 8, I'm sure you all understand that everyone has an equal chance to participate. For this to happen, all students must raise their hands to be called on. I hope I will have to tell you this only once."

During the year's first question-and-answer session, Jill calls out the answer. Ms. Iannizi reminds her, "Jill, you must raise your hand if you want to answer. I do not expect this to happen again." However, it isn't much longer until Jill calls out again in an enthusiastic and energetic manner. This time Ms. Iannizi says, "Jill, please leave the room and stand in the hallway. When you feel that you can raise your hand, come back and join us."

In a few minutes, Jill returns to class and, as before, calls out an answer. This time Ms. Iannizi says, "Go to the office and speak with the vice-principal." Within minutes, Jill is sent back to class and apologizes to Ms. Iannizi, saying that she keeps forgetting because her previous teacher never commented on this behaviour. Later that day, Ms. Iannizi receives a message in her mailbox requesting her to set up a meeting with the vice-principal to discuss the matter.

Questions to Consider

1. Why was Ms. Iannizi's attempt to be consistent problematic?
2. What new problems did she create for herself and for her students by removing Jill from the classroom?
3. What could she have done when Jill called out the second time? The third time?
4. How can Ms. Iannizi help Jill develop appropriate answering behaviours?
5. What message do you think that Ms. Iannizi is attempting to send to her students? How do you think they are interpreting that message?

student behaviour. When such an approach is not used, teachers may find themselves with few alternatives for managing student behaviour. Consider, for example, Case 1.3.

Needless to say, Ms. Iannizi's approach to managing a common student behaviour was a gross overreaction. It not only led to an administrator-initiated meeting, but also would probably result in increased student misbehaviour as students recognize the discrepancy between the minimal student behaviour and the maximal teacher response. Furthermore, Ms. Iannizi's approach left her with few, if any, alternatives in managing other students who called out answers in the future. It is highly unlikely that parents, students, administrators, or other teachers would support this approach. The technique of exclusion from class is usually reserved for use after many less-intrusive strategies have been attempted. In other words, classroom management is best accomplished when the teacher employs management strategies in a hierarchical order; for example, the CALM model incorporates the principles outlined in Chapters 2 through 11 and provides a step-by-step strategy to effectively manage the classroom environment.

When teachers use a professional body of knowledge to make decisions, the decisions are usually professionally acceptable and defendable, and result in desired changes in students' behaviours. When teachers make "gut" or emotional decisions, sometimes called reactions, the decisions more often than not result in unexpected and undesirable student behaviours, as Ms. Iannizi discovered. The principles of classroom management and the decision-making hierarchy of coping skills presented in this book have served many educators well in making effective decisions concerning the management of student behaviour.

An additional two hierarchies are presented in this book. The first is a summary of how classroom management should be viewed. The chapters are grouped into four parts that represent this hierarchy (see the Contents on pages v–viii). Part One, "Foundations"—Chapters 1 through 5—presents the foundational knowledge base. "Prevention"—Chapters 6 and 7—examines the prevention of management problems. Part Three, "Interventions for Common Behaviour Problems"—Chapters 8 and 9—deals with the management of common misbehaviour problems. Part Four, "Interventions for Chronic Behaviour Problems"—Chapters 10 and 11—addresses the issues related to managing chronic misbehaviour problems.

The second hierarchy, which is a subset of the **CALM model**, includes the introduction and implementation of management strategies once the teacher determines that it is necessary to proceed to Level III. This hierarchy is a decision-making model that uses specific techniques called coping skills. Entering the decision-making model, the teacher finds a variety of nonintrusive coping skills that provide students with the opportunity to manage their own behaviour while at the same time curbing the common forms of classroom misbehaviour efficiently and effectively (Shrigley, 1985). As the teacher moves through the coping skills, the techniques become more and more intrusive, with the teacher playing an increasingly larger role in managing student behaviour.

The overall hierarchy of *Principles of Classroom Management* is illustrated in Table 1.1.

TABLE 1.1   A Hierarchical Approach to Successful Classroom Management

Conceptualizing the process of teaching	Developing effective teaching strategies	Using proactive coping skills	Relationship building
Understanding classroom-management principles	*Lesson design*	Using preplanned, remedial nonverbal intervention	Disrupting the cycle of discouragement
Understanding the decision-making hierarchical approach	*Student motivation: teacher variables*	*Planned ignoring*	Using self-monitoring
Defining a behavioural problem	*Teacher expectations*	*Signal interference*	Using anecdotal record procedure
Understanding the extent of behavioural problems in today's schools	*Classroom questioning*	*Proximity control*	Using behavioural contracts
Understanding how behavioural problems affect teaching and learning	*Time-on-task*	*Touch control*	Understanding the nature of persisting misbehaviour
Understanding societal change and its influence on children's behaviours	Teaching for understanding	Using preplanned verbal intervention	Recognizing when outside assistance is needed
Recognizing student needs	Authentic instruction	*Adjacent reinforcement*	Making referrals
Understanding developmental changes and accompanying behaviours	Thinking and problem-solving skills	*Calling on the student*	*Counsellors*
Recognizing the importance of instructional competence	Creating learning communities	*Humour "I message"*	*Administrators*
Understanding and employing different authority bases of teachers	Teaching for multiple intelligences	*Direct appeal Positive phrasing "Are not for"*	*School psychologists*
Referent	Student motivation: student cognition	*Reminder of rules Glasser's triplets*	Working with parents
Expert	Designing the physical environment	*Explicit redirection*	Protecting student rights
Legitimate	Establishing classroom guidelines	*Canter's "broken record"*	
Reward/Coercive	*Determining procedures*	Applying logical consequences	
Understanding theories of classroom management	*Determining rules*		
Student-directed	*Determining consequences* natural • logical • contrived		
Collaborative	*Communicating rules*		
Teacher-directed	*Obtaining commitments*		
	Teaching rules		
	Understanding cultural embeddedness of behaviour		
	Creating positive group norms		
	The CALM model		

Summary

In this chapter, we first discussed a critical premise concerning successful classroom management that the reader should understand clearly before continuing: Teaching (which is defined as "the use of pre-planned behaviours—founded in learning principles and child-development theory and directed toward both instructional delivery and classroom management—that increase the probability of effecting a positive change in student behaviour") and classroom management are really the same process. By deliberately changing their own behaviour, therefore, teachers can help to bring about positive changes in students' behaviours. We then explained the principles and the decision-making hierarchical approach to classroom management on which this entire book is based. These serve as the foundation on which specific management techniques are developed throughout the rest of the book.

Key Terms

behavioural problem (or inappropriate behaviour): in the opinion of the teacher, when a student interferes with the act of teaching or with the rights of others to learn, or causes psychological or physical harm, or destroys property.

CALM model: a flexible, hierarchical model for examining and managing challenges that may affect the classroom environment.

CALM Level I—Consider: when a student's behaviour becomes disruptive, the teacher should consider the following question to initiate a response process. "Does the behaviour change, affect, or disrupt the classroom learning environment, teacher, or students?"

CALM Level II—Act: once the behaviour has become a "distracting" force for the teacher, the next level of intervention is introduced because it becomes necessary to act.

CALM Level III—Lessen: because it is important to minimize distraction and not give undue attention to inappropriate behaviour, it is best to lessen the use of invasive responses in dealing with a situation that requires action.

CALM Level IV—Manage: manage the milieu to quickly return to an effective learning environment.

classroom management: a teacher's ability to establish and maintain an environment that is suited to teaching and learning. The teacher possesses a repertoire of procedures to ensure optimal learning for all students.

professional knowledge: pedagogical and practical knowledge related to teaching and learning.

Exercises

1. Many teachers define teaching as the delivery of knowledge or the giving of information. In your opinion, are these definitions adequate? If so, why? If not, what are the limitations?
2. What problems may arise when teachers base most of their decisions on "gut reactions"? Give specific examples.
3. In recent years, there has been much discussion over whether teaching is a profession. In your opinion, is teaching a profession? If yes, explain why. If no, why not and what must occur to make it a profession?
4. Review the definition of teaching presented in this chapter. Do you agree with the definition, or should it be modified? If you agree, explain why. If not, explain what should be changed.
5. The definition of teaching in this chapter focuses on teachers changing their behaviour to manage discipline problems because that is the only behaviour over which

they have control. Given this, how might you reply to a principal who believes that teachers should be able to control their students' behaviour?

6. We discuss in Chapter 1 how teacher behaviours (affecting) influence changes in student behaviour (targeted). For each targeted behaviour that follows, suggest an appropriate affecting behaviour and explain why such a behaviour would increase the likelihood of a positive change in the student's behaviour.

7. Suggest some ways that busy teachers can keep up with the latest research on effective teaching.

8. This book offers principles of classroom management. Principles are usually very broad statements. How can teachers use these principles to guide their teaching practices and specific management techniques?

9. The authors of this book support the use of a decision-making hierarchical approach to classroom management. Discuss the advantages as well as the disadvantages to such an approach.

Situation	Targeted Behaviour	Affecting Behaviour
calling out answers	raising hand	
not volunteering	volunteering	
daydreaming	on task	
forgetting textbook	prepared for class	
short answers to questions	expanded answers	
few students answer	more participation questions	
passing notes	on task	
walking around room	in seat	
noisy during first five minutes of class	on task from start of class	

Weblinks

Health Canada

www.hc-sc.gc.ca

The federal government's health site, designed to help Canadians maintain and improve their health, with advice and resources for issues like bullying.

The Learning Disabilities Association of Canada

www.ldac-taac.ca

The LDAC is a nonprofit voluntary organization founded in 1963 that acts as a voice for persons with learning disabilities and those who support them.

The Ontario College of Teachers

www.oct.ca

The OCT licenses, governs, and regulates the practice of teaching in Ontario.

California Department of Education

www.cde.ca.gov/ls/ss

This website provides information about safe schools and violence-prevention programs in California.

CanTeach: Classroom Management

www.canteach.ca/elementary/classman1.html

This webpage takes a positive approach to classroom management by listing ways to encourage good behaviour.

TeacherVision

www.teachervision.fen.com/classroom-discipline/resource/5806.html

The site offers suggestions for Behaviour Management Resources.

2

The Nature of Behavioural Problems

FOCUS ON THE PRINCIPLES OF CLASSROOM MANAGEMENT

1. When does a behaviour become a problem?

2. For teaching to be effective, what skills must teachers possess?

3. What are the benefits to both students and teachers when classrooms are well managed?

INTRODUCTION

When educators, public officials, or parents with school-age children discuss schooling, the topic of classroom behaviour inevitably arises. Behaviour and classroom management are topics that have been widely discussed by both professionals and the public for a considerable period of time. Researchers recently reported that more of a classroom teacher's time is spent managing behavioural and social problems than actually teaching, with beginning teachers being particularly stressed by these management demands (Darling-Hammond, 2012; Palumbo and Sanacore, 2007; Romano and Gibson 2006). One-quarter of teacher respondents to a survey in Nova Scotia said they had faced physical violence in their schools (Highbeam Business, 2003).

The general assumption is that everyone knows what **behavioural problem** means and that inappropriate behaviour poses major problems for some educators; however, when pre- or in-service teachers are asked "What is a behavioural problem?" there is no overall agreement in their responses. Contrary to popular belief, there seems to be no professional consensus about which behaviours negatively affect teaching and learning in the classroom. Some teachers suggest that behavioural problems in schools and classrooms are not only increasing but also assuming a more severe magnitude, whereas others disagree.

Almost everyone agrees that it is important for students to behave properly in classrooms. What are the actual effects of misbehaviour on students and their learning and on teachers and their teaching? In this chapter, we will (1) develop a working definition of what constitutes a behavioural problem in a classroom; (2) assess the magnitude of behavioural problems in Canadian schools today; and (3) determine the effect of misbehaviour on both students and teachers.

DEFINING A BEHAVIOURAL PROBLEM

Teachers often describe students who have behavioural problems as lazy, unmotivated, belligerent, aggressive, angry, or argumentative. These words at best are imprecise and judgmental. After all, a student can be unmotivated or angry and yet not be a disruptive factor in the classroom. Furthermore, attribution theory (Ahles and Contento, 2006; Weiner, 1980; Winzer, 2002) tells us that our thoughts guide our feelings, which in turn guide our behaviour; therefore, when teachers use negative labels to describe children and react to children negatively, these same children may seek to continue this type of response because a negative reaction is better than no reaction (Seligman, 2011; Yoon, 2002). Also, negative teacher reaction is ineffective in helping children learn appropriate behaviour (Allen, Murray and Simmons, 2013; Martin, Dworet, and Davis, 1997); thus, for a definition of a behavioural problem to be useful to a teacher, it must clearly differentiate student behaviour that requires immediate corrective action from that which does not.

Surprisingly, recent literature has rarely considered the most basic question— "What types of student behaviours constitute classroom problems?" Having a clear understanding of which behaviours are inappropriate in the classroom is a prerequisite for effective classroom management. Without this understanding, it is impossible for teachers to design rational and meaningful classroom guidelines and communicate them to their students, to recognize misbehaviour when it occurs, or to employ management strategies effectively and consistently (Reupert and Woodcock, 2011).

It should be clear from this discussion that any definition of the term "behavioural problem" must provide teachers with the means to determine instantly whether or not any given behaviour requires discipline or intervention. Once you have identified this, you can then decide on which specific **teacher intervention** to use. Please refer to the CALM model. The first level is *Consider*; that is, "Does the behaviour change, affect, or disrupt the classroom learning environment, teacher, or students?" The CALM model, described in Chapter 1, provides an easy-to-remember method for making strategic decisions.

Consider the following six scenarios. For each one, ask yourself the following questions:

1. Is there a behavioural problem?
2. If there is a behavioural problem, who is exhibiting it?
3. Does the behaviour require discipline or intervention? Refer to CALM to determine which level(s) applies.

Scenario 1: Marisa quietly enters the room and takes her seat. The teacher requests that students take out their homework. Marisa does not take out her homework but instead takes out a magazine and begins to flip quietly through the pages. The teacher ignores Marisa and involves the class in reviewing the homework.

Scenario 2: Marisa quietly enters the room and takes her seat. The teacher requests that students take out their homework. Marisa does not take out her homework but instead takes out a magazine and begins to flip quietly through the pages. The teacher publicly announces that there will be no review of the homework until Marisa puts away the magazine and takes out her homework.

Scenario 3: Marisa quietly enters the room and takes her seat. The teacher requests that students take out their homework. Marisa does not take out her homework but instead takes out a magazine and begins to flip quietly through the pages. The teacher begins to involve the class in reviewing the homework and at the same time moves closer to Marisa. The review continues with the teacher standing in close proximity to Marisa.

Scenario 4: Marisa quietly enters the room and takes her seat. The teacher requests that students take out their homework. Marisa does not take out her homework but instead takes out a magazine and begins to show the magazine to the students who sit next to her. The teacher ignores Marisa and begins to involve the class in the review of the homework. Marisa continues to show the magazine to her neighbours.

Scenario 5: Marisa quietly enters the room and takes her seat. The teacher requests that students take out their homework. Marisa does not take out her homework but instead takes out a magazine and begins to show the magazine to the students who sit next to her. The teacher does not begin the review and, in front of the class, loudly demands that Marisa put the magazine away and get out her homework. The teacher stares at Marisa for the two minutes that it takes her to put the magazine away and find her homework. Once Marisa finds her homework, the teacher begins the review.

Scenario 6: Marisa quietly enters the room and takes her seat. The teacher requests that students take out their homework. Marisa does not take out her homework but instead takes out a magazine and begins to show the magazine to the students who sit next to her. The teacher begins the homework review and, at the same time, walks toward Marisa. While a student is answering a question, the teacher, as privately as possible, assertively asks Marisa to take out her homework and put the magazine away.

If you are like many of the teachers to whom we have given these same six scenarios, you probably have found answering the questions that preceded them difficult. Furthermore, if you have taken time to discuss your answers with others, you undoubtedly have discovered your answers differ from theirs.

Much of the difficulty in determining an appropriate teacher response can be avoided using our preferred definition of the term "behavioural problem," which recognizes that classroom problems are multifaceted: "A behavioural problem is behaviour that (1) interferes with the teaching act, (2) interferes with the rights of others to learn, (3) is psychologically or physically unsafe, or (4) destroys property." This definition not only covers calling out, defacing property, or disturbing other students but also other common behaviours that teachers confront every day. Note, however, that the definition does not limit behaviour to student behaviour. This is very important, for it means teachers must consider their own behaviour as well as their students' behaviour (Reinke, Lewis-Palmer, and Merrell, 2008; Sharma, Loreman, and Forlin, 2012).

Using our definition, review the six scenarios again and compare your analysis with ours. In Scenario 1, there is no need for discipline or intervention because neither Marisa's nor the teacher's behaviour is interfering with the rights of others to learn. The teacher has decided to ignore Marisa for the time being and focus on involving the class with the homework review.

In Scenario 2, the teacher has caused a problem because he has interrupted the homework review to reprimand Marisa, who isn't interfering with any other student's learning. In this situation, it is the teacher who is interfering with the rights of the students to learn.

In Scenario 3, there is no evident problem. Neither Marisa's nor the teacher's behaviour is interfering with the other students' right to learn. The teacher has not decided to ignore Marisa but has wisely chosen an intervention strategy that allows the homework review to continue.

In Scenario 4, both Marisa and the teacher are displaying problematic behaviours. Marisa is interfering with the other students' right to learn, and, by ignoring her, the teacher also interferes with the other students' right to learn.

In Scenario 5, Marisa and the teacher are again displaying problematic behaviour. Marisa's sharing of the magazine is disruptive, but the teacher's choice of intervention is also a problem. In fact, it is the teacher's behaviour—not Marisa's—that is actually interfering more with learning.

In Scenario 6, Marisa's behaviour is distinctly problematic; however, the teacher's intervention strategy enables the class to continue to learn and simultaneously manages Marisa's behaviour.

Most misbehaviour can be managed at some later time, after the other students have begun their work, during a break, or before or after class. When a behaviour becomes problematic for the **learning environment**, however, the teacher must intervene immediately because, by definition, there exists a behaviour that is interfering with other students' rights or safety. When teachers inappropriately or ineffectively use management strategies that result in interference with the learning of others, they themselves, in fact, become the disruptive factor.

Let's examine Case 2.1. Did Tobias's late opening of his book interfere with teaching or his classmates' learning? Was it unsafe or did it destroy property? Was it not Mr. Karis's behaviour that caused the escalation of a minor problem that would have corrected itself? Using our definition, Mr. Karis's behaviour escalated the problem. It is doubtful that any teacher intervention was necessary at all. See Chapter 8 "Managing Common Misbehaviour Problems: Nonverbal Interventions," for a full discussion of when teacher intervention is appropriate.

Problem Student Behaviour Outside the Definition

By now, some readers have probably thought of many student behaviours that are not covered by our definition; for example, students who refuse to turn in homework, or who are not prepared for class, or who are daydreaming, as well as those who give the teacher "dirty looks." A careful analysis of these behaviours will reveal that under the terms of the definition, they are not problems that require teacher intervention. Rather, they may be **motivational problems**.

Motivational problems can occur because of low levels of self-confidence, low expectations for success, lack of interest in academics, lost feelings of autonomy, achievement anxieties, fears of success or failure, or health or relationship issues (Alderman, 2013; Novak and Purkey, 2001; Yang, 2009). Thus, working with students who have motivational problems often involves long-term individualized intervention and/or referrals to professionals outside the classroom.

Although in-depth coverage of motivational problems is beyond the scope of this book, we must recognize that some of the very strategies used to manage these

CASE 2.1

Can a Teacher's Behaviour Be the Disruptive Factor?

Usually when the bell rings, the students in Mr. Karis's grade 9 class have their books out and are quietly waiting to begin work. Today, when Mr. Karis finishes taking attendance and is asking a few questions to review the previous day's work, he notices that Tobias is just starting to get his book out and appears to be unmotivated and lethargic. Mr. Karis feels annoyed and asks abruptly why he isn't ready. Tobias replies in a somewhat surly manner that he has a lot on his mind. Mr. Karis then reminds Tobias in a strong tone that when the bell rings he is to be ready to start. Tobias replies in a way that makes it very clear that he, too, is annoyed, "Look, you don't know what my morning's been like!" Mr. Karis feels embarrassed and that his authority is being threatened in front of the other students. He tells Tobias sharply that he "is not to be spoken to in that tone of voice."

The rest of the students are now either talking or laughing quietly among themselves and are deeply involved in the outcome of the confrontation. By the time Tobias decides it probably is not in his best interest to continue the escalating conflict, at least five minutes of class time have elapsed, no teaching or learning has taken place, and the rest of the class is unfocused. Mr. Karis is left feeling disempowered.

Questions to Consider

1. Describe the scenario from Tobias's perspective.
2. What has the class learned about Mr. Karis? About Tobias?
3. How could Mr. Karis have avoided this loss of instructional time?
4. Using the CALM model, identify at least two strategies Mr. Karis might have used to avoid the confrontation with Tobias.

---

problems—problems which themselves generally do not interfere with other students' learning—actually disturb the learning of others or reduce the time spent on learning. It is, therefore, best to work individually with students who have motivational problems, *after* involving the rest of the class in the day's learning activities. Doing so allows the teacher to protect the class's right to learn and to maximize the time allocated for learning.

Even though the strategies presented later in this book are generally used to manage behavioural problems, some of them, particularly coping skills and anecdotal record keeping, can be used quite successfully for motivational problems (Alderman, 2013). We cannot stress enough, however, that motivational problems must be properly addressed, usually by focusing on students' expectations of success and the value students place on the learning activity, so that they do not develop behavioural problems (see Chapter 6, "The Professional Teacher"). Case 2.2 illustrates how one teacher ensures that this does not occur.

Ms. Polinski recognized that Rahul's behaviour did not interfere with the teaching and learning act and so did not need immediate action (CALM, Level 1). She used effective strategies that protected the class's right to learn. The strategies were the beginning of a long-term effort to build up Rahul's interest and confidence in mathematics and to have him become an active, participating member of the class. Probably, many readers have witnessed similar situations in which the teacher, unfortunately, chose to deal with the student's behaviour in ways that were disruptive to the entire class.

CASE 2.2

Solving a Motivational Problem

Ms. Polinski teaches grade 4. She believes that she is a good teacher and spends a great deal of time preparing interesting units of study and motivational activities to enhance her students' learning experiences. She is concerned about one of her students, Rahul, who rarely participates in class and often is the last one to begin classwork. She has observed him closely and believes that he is shy and lacks self-esteem. He is not a problem in class, and the other students treat him with respect, although he is often ignored when plans are made for recess and after-school activities.

One day, the class is assigned math problems for seatwork. After a few minutes, Ms. Polinski notices that Rahul has not started. She calmly walks over to Rahul, kneels down beside his desk, and asks him if he needs any help. This is enough to get Rahul to begin his math problems. Ms. Polinski waits until three problems are completed; she then tells Rahul that since he understood them so well, he should put them on the board. Rahul complies and neatly presents his work on the board but accomplishes the task with little enthusiasm. After the class has finished the assignment, Ms. Polinski begins to review the answers, stressing the correct procedures Rahul used to solve the problems and thanking him for his board work. There is little reaction from Rahul.

Questions to Consider

1. Describe Rahul's feelings about this incident.
2. What do you think Rahul's behaviour will be a week later?
3. What is Ms. Polinski's belief about behavioural problems in her class?
4. How can Ms. Polinski build on this beginning without being too obvious and thus risking embarrassing Rahul?

EXTENT OF THE PROBLEM

When Canadians were asked how they felt about their education system, 57 percent said that they were satisfied with it in their province. The most satisfied were residents of the Prairies (72 percent), Quebecers (68 percent), and 18- to 24-year-olds (74 percent). Except in British Columbia (45 percent), more than 50 percent of residents of other regions said they were satisfied with the education system in their province: Alberta (59 percent), Atlantic provinces (55 percent), and Ontario (52 percent) (Leger, 2002). According to Statistics Canada (2009), however, Canadians had concerns about student violence and behavioural problems in the public school system. To some extent, these concerns may reflect current fears resulting from the high media coverage of school shootings in both Canada and the United States in the last few years. Recent shootings in Toronto high schools have prompted the Ontario government to issue new school health and safety initiatives (e.g., Ontario Ministry of Labour, 2010,).

Certainly, Canada has not escaped from the headlines associated with severe violence in schools. One of the most serious incidents was in December 1989, when Marc Lépine killed 14 women engineering students at l'École Polytechnique in Quebec. In 2006, a gunman entered Dawson College in Montreal and began a shootout with the police. In 2007, 14-year-old Jordan Manners was shot and killed at a secondary school in Toronto, and in August 2013 two teens were arrested in for allegedly cyberbullying a 17-year-old girl who committed suicide. Although these were shocking, high-profile cases of extreme violence, they are, fortunately, relatively uncommon in Canada.

According to Statistics Canada, in 2011, the overall national crime rate was down 6 percent over the previous year and was the lowest it had been in over 25 years. At the same time, youth crime has been declining over the past decade. Youth crime and the youth crime severity index (CSI) fell by 10 percent between 2010 and 2011.

We are hopeful that these numbers lead to a long-term trend because, in contrast, in 2006, about 1 in 10 youth crimes happened on school property, with assaults being most common at 27 percent followed by drug offences at 18 percent. Weapons were present in about 7 percent of crimes committed on school property with less than 1 percent of these weapons being firearms. The most common weapon was a knife or a blunt object. According to police, about 73 percent of all youth crime reported as occurring on school property was during school hours with the remaining occurring after school. These rates gradually increase among 12- to 17-year-olds, touch a high among 18-year-olds, and then decreases thereafter. Continued concerns related to bullying and violence among students make these statistics of great interest to educators.

Since charges are laid in less than one-half of the cases where youth are accused, it is important to recognize that, in Canada, youth from 12 to 17 years are governed by a justice system that is different from that for those 18 years and older (Statistics Canada, 2012). Even though well-behaved students greatly outnumber those who exhibit inappropriate behaviour, educators require skills to help them deal with serious behaviour challenges. Numerous authors argue that school boards should establish and implement policies and provide programs that help teachers develop strategies to manage behaviours not appropriate for the classroom (e.g., Benn, 2002; Bonta and Hanson, 1994; Crux, 1993; Holt, 2007; James, 1993; MacDougall, 1993; Ontario Ministry of Education, 2012; Patus, 1993; Roy, 1993). This is an important professional issue, because the reasons teachers give for exiting early from the profession are that they have become dissatisfied with student behaviour or the working environment (Canada Education, 2013; Canadian Teachers' Federation, 2002).

Since the early 1980s, researchers have made a concerted effort to distinguish between crime (violence and vandalism) and common misbehaviour (off-task and disruptive classroom behaviours). Such a distinction is essential because crime and routine classroom misbehaviour are inherently different challenges that require different solutions administered by a variety of professionals both inside and outside the school. Even though teachers are responsible for managing routine classroom misbehaviour, crime often must come under the control of the school administration and outside law-enforcement agencies.

In the mid-1980s, Wayson stated that "most schools never experience incidents of crime and those that do seldom experience them frequently or regularly" (1985, 129), but disruptive behaviour of "the kinds that have characterized schoolchildren for generations . . . continue to pose frequent and perplexing problems for teachers" (1985, 127).

These conclusions were supported by numerous studies reporting that teachers and administrators consistently ranked common classroom misbehaviours (excessive talking, failure to do assignments, disrespect, lateness) as the most serious and frequent disturbances, whereas they ranked crime (vandalism, theft, assault) as the least serious disturbances to their teaching or the least frequently occurring (Huber, 1984; Thomas, Goodall, and Brown, 1983; Weber and Sloan, 1986).

The schools of the late 1980s and early 1990s were perceived as experiencing less crime than the schools of the 1970s, and even though classroom misbehaviour continued to be a major problem, it too was perceived as lessening in frequency. By the late 1990s, however, there were indications that these trends were reversing, and students agreed that violence in school was increasing (Angus Reid Group, 1999).

Students themselves are usually aware of the frequency of disruptive behaviour. According to a national poll of teenagers, conducted just prior to the Littleton, Colorado and Taber, Alberta school shootings, one-third of Canadian teens said that violence had increased in their schools over the previous five years (Angus Reid Group, 1999; Taylor-Butts and Bressan, 2006).

The form of violence that is causing great concern among parents and in Canadian schools is bullying and cyberbullying. Bullying runs counter to the UN Convention of 1990 on the rights of children, which determined that a child has the right to feel safe at home, in school, and in the community. More recently, cyberbullying has been increasingly prevalent mainly among adolescents (Hong and Espelage, 2012), with males being more likely to be bullies and female victims being more likely to report the incident to adults (Li, 2006, 2007). Bullying Canada.ca identifies four kinds of bullying: (1) Verbal bullying, which includes name calling, teasing, threatening, spreading rumours, making negative comments about one's culture, region, sexual orientation, race, or gender; (2) Social bullying, which includes mobbing, excluding others from a group, scapegoating, and making humiliating gestures in public that are designed to put others down; (3) Physical bullying, which includes hitting, punching, pinching, chasing, shoving, destroying or stealing personal belongings, and unwanted

Male student working at desk in Chinese school classroom.
© Monkey Business Images/Shutterstock

sexual touching; and (4) Cyberbullying, which is using the internet or text messaging to put someone down, to spread rumours, to intimidate, or to make fun of someone (Li, 2007; Pepler and Craig, 2011).

Please refer to Chapter 4 "Bullying and Cyberbullying: Implications for the Classroom," for an in-depth discussion on bullying and cyberbullying.

Of equal concern are the findings of a Canadian study (Janosz, Archambault, Pagani, Morin, and Bower, 2008), which revealed the serious detrimental effects of witnessing school violence. Students who witness violence can feel anxiety and depression, which can result in either aggression or feelings of victimization. These feelings, which include a sense of powerlessness, fear, and insecurity, often manifest as a dislike of school. In addition to the negative effects of witnessing violence, there has also been an increase in the incidence of verbal abuse, students threatening others, and older students harassing younger ones (Lomas and Stough, 2012).

The Canadian federal government's National Strategy on Community Safety and Crime Prevention was established in 1998 to help people deal with crime and victimization. This program placed particular emphasis on children, youth, women, and Aboriginal people. The strategy supports schools' efforts to encourage resilience in children and build healthy learning environments. Specifically, the program is raising the consciousness of teachers and children alike to establish grassroots initiatives to combat bullying. This strategy also supports the current belief that if schools are to provide a safe place for learning, the issue of bullying needs to be addressed explicitly. A more recent deterrent has been established by PREVNet (Promoting Relationships & Eliminating Violence Network, www.prevnet.ca) as a way to address the high incidence of bullying. The PREVNet mandate is to provide understanding, assessment tools, intervention, and prevention strategies for adults, children, and youth where they live, work, and play (Craig and Pepler, 2007; Pepler and Craig, 2011). Currently in Canada, schools are adopting clear policies regarding bullying and are applying consequences consistently. For many school boards, this means adopting a zero-tolerance policy.

As the new millennium progresses, therefore, every successful teacher will have to be able to recognize the genesis of potentially violent situations and manage disruptive classroom behaviours properly. Teachers must be proficient in defusing such situations and directing students toward more prosocial means of conflict resolution (Novak and Purkey, 2001).

THE EFFECT OF CLASSROOM-DISRUPTIVE BEHAVIOUR ON TEACHING AND LEARNING

When classrooms are characterized by disruptive behaviour, the teaching and learning environment can be adversely affected. The amount of interference in the teaching and learning environment is related to the type, frequency, and duration of the disruptive behaviour. Disruptive behaviour also affects students' psychological safety, readiness to learn, and future behaviours.

In the course of the last decade, we have had the opportunity to interact with thousands of teacher candidates as well as with many in-service teachers and school administrators who want to improve their classroom-management skills. One of the first questions we always ask is, "Why do students have to behave in a classroom?" At first, we were somewhat embarrassed to ask such a basic question because we felt

CASE 2.3

Discipline: A Costly Waste of Time

Mr. Kay, a grade 9 science teacher and head of the science department in the high school, teaches four classes a day. Sometimes, his departmental duties cause him to be a couple of minutes late for class. He is content to allow his students, on entering the room, to stand around and talk rather than prepare their materials for class. As a result, each time the class convenes, it usually does not begin until five minutes after the bell has rung.

Questions to Consider

1. Provide some reasons that Mr. Kay might give for not starting on time.
2. Why is punctuality an important issue for teachers?
3. What routines should Mr. Kay establish with his students to avoid wasted time when he is occupied elsewhere?

there was a universally obvious answer. To our surprise, however, the answer was not obvious to others. The answer, of course, involves the widely accepted learning principle: more learning time (time on task, or engaged time) equals more learning (Brophy, 1988; Fang and Dvorak, 2013; Winzer, 2002). In other words, disruptive, off-task behaviour takes time away from learning.

Case 2.3 touches on a very common problem in classrooms, namely, the tremendous amount of time that can be wasted over the course of a school year by some very minor off-task behaviours. Over a period of a week, 25 minutes that could have been directed toward learning are wasted. Over the 40-week school year, 1000 minutes are consumed by off-task behaviour. This amounts to more than 22 class periods, or approximately one-ninth of the school year, that could have been directed toward learning goals. If the calculations also consider the 120 students Mr. Kay teaches per day, 2640 "student class periods" were not spent on learning science.

Certain reports suggest that some teachers spend as much as 30 to 80 percent of their time addressing discipline problems (Skaalvik and Skaalvik, 2010; Walsh, 1983). This figure simply highlights a previously mentioned basic fact of teaching: to be successful, teachers must be competent in managing student behaviour to maximize the time spent on learning.

Case 2.4 shows how disruptive behaviour can result in a *ripple effect*. In other words, students learn misbehaviour from observing misbehaviour in other children (Baker, 1985; Pepler and Craig, 2011). The off-task behaviours of Rebecca's friends draw her off task. This type of observational learning is often accelerated when a student notices the attention a disruptive student gains from both the teacher and his classmates.

Ripple effects are not limited to the initial misbehaviour. The methods the teacher uses to curb the misbehaviour and the targeted student's resultant behaviour can cause a second ripple effect (Kounin, 1970; Wheatley et al., 2009). Research has shown that threatening teacher behaviour can lead to student anxieties; these anxieties can cause additional disruptive behaviours. Students who see disruptive classmates comply with the teacher's management technique and who tend to rate their teacher as fair are less

CASE 2.4

The Ripple Effect

Rebecca is a well-mannered, attentive grade 5 student. For the first time since starting school, she and her two best friends are in the same class. Unlike Rebecca, her friends are not attentive and are interested more in each other than in class activities. The teacher often has to reprimand them for passing notes, talking to each other, and giggling excessively during class.

One day, Rebecca is tapped on the shoulder and is handed a note from her friend across the room. She accepts the note and sends one back. With this, her friends quickly include her in their antics. The teacher, who has been observing this increasingly distracting

behaviour decides that it is necessary to remove Rebecca from her friends' influence in the classroom and to reduce the off-task behaviours of the other two girls.

Questions to Consider

1. Based on the levels in the CALM model, the teacher has already identified a concern. Discuss this case from the perspective of the next three steps in the model.

2. How might this teacher reduce Rebecca's off-task behaviour?

3. How can a teacher effectively prevent friends in the same classroom from letting their friendship interfere with their learning?

distracted from their class work than when they observe unruly students defying the teacher (Lomas and Stough, 2012; Smith, 1969). Clearly, the dynamics that come into play with even minor classroom disruptions are quite complex.

Common day-to-day off-task student behaviours such as talking and leaving seats without permission exist in all classrooms to some degree. Although less common, some classrooms, indeed some entire schools, are plagued by threats, violence, and vandalism. In Ontario, a survey conducted by the Ontario English Catholic Teachers' Association (OECTA) in 1992 revealed an increase in biting, kicking, and the use of weapons, and a 50 percent increase in minor incidents, such as verbal abuse, over a three-year period (Johnson, 2012; Roher, 1993). Much of this aggression was perpetrated against students, although teachers and other adults in the school also had fallen victim. The OECTA survey also reported that the number of verbal assaults increased 6.1 percent and 20.5 percent in elementary and secondary schools, respectively. In terms of student-to-teacher incidents, verbal assaults were more likely to occur with less experienced teachers (Department of the Solicitor General of Canada, 2002; James, 2010). This same report indicates that there are a number of initiatives at the board and school levels to identify and implement effective solutions to school-based violence. A large majority of school boards have policies or programs to address these issues. School boards also generally delegate to administrative staff and teachers responsibilities related to communicating policy information and promoting a positive school climate. Unfortunately, staff members are often not provided with the support needed to familiarize themselves with these policies and programs.

Teachers are also identifying the need for well-defined policies and programs in the increasingly used communication technologies. In 2012, 85 percent of households in Canada had access to the internet, which had grown from 79 percent in 2010 (Statistics Canada, 2013). The digital divide, however, does still exist to some extent, largely being affected by geography, income, gender, education levels, age, disability, and aboriginal status.

The ubiquitous internet and the use of email and text messaging have led to many benefits and some potential behavioural problems for those who have access to new media technologies. Advantages include almost instantaneous access to information and contact with colleagues, friends, and family. Some of the less serious, but still troubling, issues involving the internet, email, and text messaging occur during instructional or assigned work periods during school hours when the students log on to chat with virtual friends. Teachers are not always able to monitor a large class of students to make sure that they are on task; therefore, increasingly, many schools are setting up filters to limit access to the internet as well as inappropriate uses of communication technology.

In conclusion, minor *and* major misbehaviour reduces learning time for both disruptive students and their peers. And less learning time equals less learning. Although not a clear cause-and-effect relationship, there is a positive correlation between poor grades and all types of misbehaviour (Arum, 2003; Holt, 2007; Lomas and Stough, 2012).

Classroom behavioural problems also have a negative impact on teacher effectiveness and career longevity. We believe that the overwhelming majority of teachers choose to enter the profession because they enjoy working with children and are intrinsically motivated when they know that their efforts have contributed to children's academic growth; therefore, teachers are emotionally vulnerable to behavioural problems. They put long hours of preparation into what they hope will be interesting, motivating, and meaningful lessons. When uninterested, off-task students undermine these efforts, teachers begin to feel discouraged and often "burnt out." The result is that, currently, 20 to 25 percent of Canadian teachers quit in their first five years of teaching. In urban settings, closer to 50 percent of all teachers who initially enter the profession quit within their first three years of teaching (Canadian Teachers' Federation, 2002; Skaalvik and Skaalvik, 2011).

No matter how carefully teachers control their personal biases, it is inevitable that some of these will influence their interactions with disruptive students. Indeed, studies have shown that teachers interact differently with disruptive students than they do with nondisruptive ones (Jina, 2002; Skaalvik and Skaalvik, 2011; Winzer, 2002). Such differential treatment is fuelled by the negative beliefs many teachers have about disruptive students, the negative feelings many teachers harbour toward them, and the disparaging labels they often assign to these students (Brendtro, Brokenleg, and Van Bockern, 1990). Unfortunately, differential treatment serves only to escalate inappropriate student behaviour. Even the most chronic disruptive student spends *some* time showing appropriate behaviour; however, teachers may sometimes become so angry with certain students that they overlook the appropriate behaviour and focus only on the disruptive conduct. When this occurs, teachers miss the few opportunities they have to begin to change disruptive behaviours to acceptable ones. Studies have concluded that teachers are much more likely to reprimand inappropriate behaviour than to acknowledge appropriate behaviour when interacting with disruptive students (Bear, 2010). As a result, students soon learn that when they behave appropriately, nothing happens; but when they misbehave, they are the centre of both the teacher's and other students' attention.

Any teacher can attest that students easily realize when rules and expectations are not consistently enforced or obeyed by either the teacher or the students. Even so, because teachers are so emotionally tied to the disruptive students, they often set and enforce standards for these students that are different from those for the rest of the class. Often, these standards are so inflexible and unrealistic that they actually reduce the chances of the disruptive students' behaving appropriately.

Because disruptive students have a history of inappropriate behaviours, they must be given the opportunity to learn new behaviours. The learning process is usually best accomplished in small, manageable steps that enable problem students to achieve a high probability of success. This process requires setting realistic behavioural standards that are the same as those set for the rest of the class. The teacher must recognize and encourage what at first may be infrequent and short-lived appropriate behaviours. A teacher risks losing the confidence and support of even the non-disruptive students, when he sets behavioural standards for some students that are stricter than for the rest of the class. When this occurs, the disruptive student gains peer support. In such circumstances, all students view the teacher as being unfair.

Teachers, when they begin to experience more and more discipline problems, will sometimes lose their motivation to teach and assume a laissez-faire attitude. If conditions do not improve, this attitude may develop into a "get-even" approach. A get-even attitude overrides a teacher's motivation to assist students in learning, replacing supportive and effective teacher behaviours with vengeful behaviours. Once a teacher operates from a basis of revenge, teaching effectiveness ceases and power struggles between teachers and students become commonplace. Such power struggles often further fuel and escalate disruptive behaviour and place the teacher in a no-win situation (Dreikurs, 1964).

Teachers should be aware that when children display disruptive behaviours, the classroom environment becomes a less effective conduit for teaching and learning. The time and energy needed to cope with some disruptive students can be both physically draining and emotionally exhausting. Stress related to classroom management is one of the most influential factors in

Portrait of a happy teacher explaining something to a pupil in a classroom.

© Wavebreakmedia/Shutterstock

failure among novice teachers (Clement, 2010; Housego, 1990) and a major reason why they leave the profession (Canter, 1989; Skaalvik and Skaalvik, 2011). Those instructors who do persist through their first few years of teaching report that students who continually misbehave are the primary cause of job-related stress (Feitler and Tokar, 1992; Rieg, Paquette, and Chen, 2010).

Teachers who manage their classrooms effectively, on the other hand, report that they enjoy teaching and feel a certain confidence in their ability to affect student achievement (Bear, 2010). Such feelings of efficacy lead to improvements in the teaching–learning process and job satisfaction, which ultimately result in gains in student achievement.

Summary

This chapter has answered three questions that are critical for an understanding of discipline and classroom management: Is there a behavioural problem? If there is a behavioural problem, who is exhibiting it? Is the behaviour a discipline problem or is it another kind of problem?

After a discussion of the contemporary definitions of the term *behavioural problem* and their shortcomings, an operational definition was provided: A behavioural problem is any behaviour that (1) interferes with the teaching act; (2) interferes with the rights of others to learn; (3) is psychologically or physically unsafe; or (4) destroys property. According to this definition, teachers as well as students are responsible for ensuring appropriate behaviour.

In response to the second question ("If there is a behavioural problem, who is exhibiting it?"), we explored the belief that today's schools are plagued by violence, crime, and disruptive classroom behaviour. Recent Canadian studies indicate that schools since the late 1990s may have experienced not only an increase in disruptive classroom behaviour but also an increase in student violence. However, as noted earlier in this chapter fewer students are charged. This is likely because of the effect that the Youth Criminal Justice Act introduced in 2003. Youth aged between 12 and 17 are governed by a separate justice system than those 18 years and older (Statistics Canada, 2012).

Finally, we showed that disruptive behaviour reduces the time spent on learning, encourages misbehaviour in on-looking students because of a ripple effect, and may cause fear in other students, with a resultant decrease in school attendance and academic achievement. Teachers are also adversely affected by disruptive behaviour; they often suffer through reduced in-class effectiveness, a rise in job-related stress, and decreased career longevity.

Key Terms

behavioural problem: an action that distracts from an effective learning environment.

learning environment: a setting in which teaching and learning can occur.

motivational problems: student difficulty in initiating, participating in, and/or persevering with learning or classroom activities.

teacher intervention: teacher actions—which may include verbal response, proximity, or silence—that lead to desired student behaviour.

Exercises

1. Is it important that all teachers have a consistent definition of what types of student behaviours constitute behavioural problems? Why or why not?

2. Do you agree with the definition of a behavioural problem stated in this chapter? If so, why? If not, how would you modify it?

3. Give several examples of teacher behaviour that would cause a classroom-management problem.

4. Using the definition of a behavioural problem stated in this chapter, categorize each of the following behaviours as a behavioural problem or a non-behavioural problem and explain your reasoning.

Behaviour	Non-behavioural Problem	Behavioural Problem	Rationale
a. A student consistently tries to engage the teacher in conversation just as class is about to begin.			
b. A student continually comes to class one minute late.			
c. A teacher stands in the hallway talking to fellow teachers during the first three minutes of class.			
d. A student does math homework during social studies class.			
e. A student interrupts a lecture to ask permission to go to the washroom.			
f. A student often laughs at answers given by other students.			
g. A student doesn't wear safety goggles while welding in industrial arts class.			
h. A grade 1 student continually volunteers to answer questions but never has an answer when he is called on.			
i. A grade 4 student refuses to wear a jacket during recess.			
j. A grade 7 student constantly pulls the hair of the girl who sits in front of him.			
k. A boy in grade 8 spends half of the time allotted for group work encouraging a girl to go out with his friend.			
l. A grade 9 student consistently uses the last two minutes of class for hair combing.			
m. An unkempt student can't get involved in group work because all students refuse to sit near him.			
n. A student continually asks good questions, diverting the teacher from the planned lesson.			
o. A student eats a candy bar during class.			
p. A student flirts with the teacher by asking questions about his clothes and personal life during class.			
q. A student consistently makes wisecracks that entertain the rest of the class.			

5. At this point in your reading, how would you handle each of the 17 behaviours listed in question 4? Why?

6. For each of the 17 behaviours in question 4, give at least one type of teacher behaviour that might escalate the student behaviour.

7. Think back to your days as a student. To what extent would you say that behavioural problems were rampant in your school? What types of behavioural problems were most common?

8. Do you feel that behavioural problems in schools have increased or decreased since you attended high school? On what evidence or information do you base your opinion?

9. Considering what teachers' jobs entail and their relationship with students, why would they be prone to take behavioural problems personally?

10. What are the dangers of personalizing student behaviour? How might doing so affect the instructional effectiveness of a teacher?

11. How can teachers protect themselves from personalizing misbehaviour?

12. Think back on your days as a student. Can you recall instances in which classroom behavioural problems prevented you and others in the class from learning? How did you feel about the situation at the time?

13. When students disrupt a class and take away the right of others to learn, do those students forfeit their right to learn? If you believe they do, what implications does that have for teacher behaviour? If you believe they don't, what implications does that have for teacher behaviour?

14. Do you think that youth violence is on the increase, or is this just a common misperception brought about by the increased coverage of this topic by the media?

15. What would you do as the teacher if a student told you that a member of your class had brought a gun to school?

Weblinks

Canadian Teachers' Federation
www.ctf-fce.ca
A site dedicated to showing and preserving the work of teachers.

Canadian Child Care Federation
www.cccf-fcsge.ca
Provides valuable resources on children and families.

Ipsos Canada
www.ipsos.ca
Latest research and results.

Statistics Canada
www.statcan.gc.ca
Produces and reports statistics on Canada's population, resources, economy, society, and culture.

3

Understanding Why Children Misbehave

FOCUS ON THE PRINCIPLES OF CLASSROOM MANAGEMENT

1. How does an awareness of the causes of misbehaviour enable teachers to avoid viewing misbehaviour as a personal affront and select positive rather than negative intervention strategies?

2. What basic human needs are prerequisites for appropriate classroom behaviour?

3. How does the need for a sense of significance, competence, virtue, and power influence student behaviour?

4. What societal changes beyond schools' control greatly influence student behaviour?

5. How do cognitive and moral developmental changes result in student behaviour that, while normal, often is disruptive in learning environments?

6. How can instructional competence minimize misbehaviour?

INTRODUCTION

> Kids aren't the way they used to be. When I went to school, kids knew their place. Teachers wanted to teach, and students wanted to learn. The students respected their teachers, and, believe me, they sure didn't fool around in school like they do today.

Adults frequently make statements like this one as they remember the "way it used to be." But are such statements true? Not entirely.

There have always been some behavioural problems in our schools if only because of students' normal developmental changes. There also have always been some schools and homes that have been unable to provide adequately for children's needs. Even so, rapid societal changes have caused new behavioural problems and have compounded existing ones. Significant shifts in the family structure, the pervasiveness of media in children's lives, the cultural and racial makeup of the population, stressful world economies that seem to increasingly widen the rich–poor divide, and fast-paced advances in technology have made huge impacts on students' thoughts, attitudes, and behaviour. Nonetheless, students still are intrinsically motivated toward skill acquisition and competency (Brophy, 2010; Stipek, 1993), and teachers still want to teach (Czubaj, 1996; Hord, 1997).

If, however, teachers want to maximize their teaching time, they must minimize the effect of societal changes on student behaviour. Teachers must (1) not expect students to think and act the way they did years ago; (2) not demand respect from students solely on the basis of a title or position; (3) understand the methods and behaviours young people use to find their place in today's society; and (4) understand the ongoing societal changes and the influence these changes have on students' lives (Fullan, 1993, 2001; Ng, 2006). To assist teachers in reaching these goals, we describe in this chapter some of the factors that have influenced students to change and provide an explanation of why students now behave as they do.

SOCIETAL CHANGES

For over 100 years now, schools have been recognized as microcosms of the larger society (Banks, 2008; Dewey, 1916; Kindsvatter, 1978; "Ontario: where everyone . . .," 1999). Therefore, discipline problems in the schools reflect the problems that face society. The social climate of the nation, city or town, and the community that surrounds each school has profound effects on students' perceptions of the value of education and on their behaviour in school (Kuperminc, Leadbeater, and Blatt, 2001; Muscott and Mann, 2010).

Our society is plagued by the ills of drug and alcohol abuse, crime, violence, unemployment, child and elder abuse, and adolescent suicide. It is no coincidence that as these problems increase, so do a school's behavioural problems. This clear relationship between social problems and school behavioural problems demonstrates that many factors that contribute to behavioural problems are beyond the schools' control (Barton and Coley, 2007; Hord, 1997). Even if there were no societal problems, disruptive behaviour could still be expected because a school brings together many of the conditions that facilitate misbehaviour. Large numbers of young people, many of whom are still learning socially acceptable behaviours and would rather be elsewhere, are concentrated in one place for long periods of time. Currently, according to Statistics Canada, immigration is responsible for two-thirds of Canada's growth in population (Mahoney, 2007). The three largest census metropolitan areas (CMA), Toronto, Montreal, and Vancouver have grown to include 35.2% of all Canadians. The country's non-CMAs grew by 0.3% (Statistics Canada, 2014). This increasingly important demographic has implications for schools, the curriculum, and the way teachers interact with students.

Young people in our schools now come from a wide range of backgrounds, with different ethnic, racial, and parental attitudes and expectations concerning education. A school exposes all students to **off-task/norm-violating behaviours** and makes failure visible (Gilbert and Gilbert, 1998; Salmivalli, 2001).

Children no longer grow up in a society that provides them with constant, consistent sets of guidelines and expectations. The intense, rapid technological advancements in mass communication of the last several decades have exposed young people to a multitude of varying viewpoints, ideas, and philosophies (Elliott, Bosacki, Woloshyn, and Richards, 2001). With this exposure, the direct influence of parents, community, and school has begun to wane. Role models have changed. Now schools are faced with children who are exposed to a greater variety of information than ever before. As a result, these children think and act differently than earlier generations.

THE KNOWLEDGE EXPLOSION

Erosion of Respect for Authority

Since the 1950s, when the Soviet Union launched Sputnik, the first satellite, there has been an unabated explosion in scientific knowledge and technological advancements. This explosion has resulted in products only dreamed of previously: Digital and satellite phones, DVDs, iPods, tablets, iPhones, satellite dishes, CD-ROMs, powerful personal computers and laptops, fax machines, the internet, email, PDAs, and other telecommunication devices provide instantaneous, worldwide personal communication. And today, we have access to an ever-expanding array of databases.

To understand how great the explosion of knowledge has been, consider this: In the early 1970s, less than 20 years after Sputnik's launch, it was estimated that by the time children born in 1980 reached the age of 50, the world's knowledge would have increased by a factor of 32 times from what it was when they were born (Toffler, 1970). With the advances that have been made in as few as the last 10 years, these estimates are probably much too low. Nothing illustrates this better than the emergence of the internet. The internet provides any user of a personal computer with instantaneous access to an almost limitless range and quantity of global information. Such high-speed growth in technology, information, and, hence, knowledge appears to create a widening gap between those who "stay current" with these advances and those who do not; for example, by the end of elementary school, many children possess knowledge that their parents only vaguely comprehend. This is poignantly clear in such areas as personal computing, information retrieval, ecology, biotechnology, and astronomy. In addition, because of the almost instantaneous telecommunication of national and world events, children are keenly aware of the state of the present world. They see famine, terrorist attacks, political corruption, drug busts, street violence, and chemical/oil spills on a daily basis.

Such knowledge has caused many young people to consider past solutions to life's problems as irrelevant to their present world and to perceive adults as ineffective managers of this world. As a fallout of this perception, adults, who traditionally commanded respect for their worldliness and expertise, no longer have the kind of influence they once had on the young (McMillan and Morrison, 2006; St. Thomas University, 2013). When talking to adolescents, we commonly hear such statements as, "My parents don't understand"; "Why do we have to do it by hand when there are calculators that can do it for us?"; and "Why do I have to be honest when government officials and politicians are always lying?"

As the world becomes a more complex and frightening place, and as young people perceive their parents and teachers to be less relevant providers of solutions, the future for these young people becomes more remote, uncertain, and unpredictable. Over 50 years ago, Stinchcombe (1964) demonstrated a direct relationship between adolescents' envisioned images of the future and their attitudes and behaviours. Those adolescents who saw little or nothing to be gained in the future from school attendance were likely to exhibit rebellious, alienated behaviour. Unfortunately, there are even more young people today with this pessimistic view of the future. Clearly, then, a teacher's ability to maximize student success and demonstrate the present and future usefulness of the material to be learned plays an important role in students' perceived value of education (Leithwood, Day, Sammons, Hopkins, and Harris, 2006).

Teacher and Student Frustration and the Relevancy of Schooling

Students are not alone in their feelings of frustration. Teachers, too, perceive many school curricula to be irrelevant to today's world. They are frustrated because of the almost impossible task of keeping up with the expansion of knowledge and the new technologies (Graham, 2011; McMillan and Morrison, 2006). Changes in school curricula occur at a snail's pace compared to the daily expansion of information and technological advances. The advent of standardized testing for numeracy and literacy has served to focus teachers' attention on these two subject areas.

Many teachers have said that they find it impossible to keep abreast of developments in their content areas and the rapidly expanding array of new pedagogical models, many of which support the use of new technologies. In addition, many teachers have found it difficult to integrate the new material into an already overloaded curriculum. Although they truly desire to restructure their curricula in meaningful ways and to integrate technologies into their **instructional practices** (and **strategies/techniques/methodology**), they often find that their schools lack the necessary resources or commitment to invest in the latest technologies, training, or teacher release time for curriculum development. Their feelings of frustration lead to job dissatisfaction and poor morale, which can foster less-than-ideal interactions between teachers and students. However, when schools are able to invest in the new technologies and teachers are properly trained in their use, powerful changes can occur for both teachers and students, as illustrated in Case 3.1.

CASE 3.1

"This Is the Greatest Thing That Has Happened to Me in 20 Years of Teaching"

About five years ago at a national education conference, one of the authors met Mr. Lee, a 20-year veteran high school earth sciences teacher. Clearly somewhat distressed, Mr. Lee said that he felt he was no longer reaching his students—they were uninterested, distracted, and turned off learning in his class. In his opinion, each day was an endless hassle that left him tired and frustrated. This frustration was following him home, and he felt he was making his family unhappy, too. As a result, he was not sure he wanted to return to the classroom the following year.

A couple of years later, surprisingly, the author met Mr. Lee again at another national conference. When pressed, Mr. Lee said that not only had he remained in the classroom but that he had regained his enthusiasm for teaching, and it was currently as high as it had ever been. When he was asked what had prompted the rejuvenation, he replied that he had challenged himself to restructure his course to better reflect contemporary earth sciences.

Specifically, he had used his yearly allotment for resources to purchase a high-speed internet connection to enable his students to access a real-time meteorological–oceanographic database that allowed them to examine the same up-to-the-minute data that scientists used. He said it was the best strategy he had ever implemented. He was delighted to observe that his students responded to this opportunity with interest and enthusiasm. For the first time in many years, visitation night was crowded with parents who had come to see what was going on in their children's earth sciences class. Mr. Lee was gratified to hear that many of his students were going home and talking with their parents about the neat things they were doing in class for the first time ever.

Mr. Lee went on to say that he was so impressed by the educational impact of technology that he had decided to study instructional technology at the graduate level and recently had enrolled in a doctoral program. He was eagerly anticipating learning more about how to motivate his students.

Questions to Consider

1. Describe the steps in Mr. Lee's transformation.
2. What was the most significant component of Mr. Lee's new way of teaching?
3. What do you think was more important: Mr. Lee's new-found enthusiasm or the technology that he introduced into his classroom?

Just as students are positively affected by contemporary and innovative educational programs that meet their needs, they are also negatively affected by those that do not. Frustration is a natural outcome when instructional methodology does not change, and students are expected to learn more in shorter periods of time. Using uniformly traditional instructional practices to deliver outdated content is meaningless and boring to youths who are growing up in a world significantly different from that of their parents. What teachers often label as a lack of motivation may actually have more to do with the students' inability to feel any affiliation with what is going on in the classroom (Brown, Higgins, Pierce, Hong, and Thoma, 2003). Lack of affiliation leads to boredom and off-task, disruptive classroom behaviours (Green, Campbell, Stirtzinger, DeSouza, and Dawe, 2001).

Teaching just "the facts" is not sufficient. To prepare them for their futures rather than our past, students must be instructed in ways that facilitate their *learning how to learn* (see Chapter 6, "The Professional Teacher"). Case 3.2 illustrates how students respond to a type of educational experience, depending on its relevancy.

CASE 3.2

Who Really Cares?

Over the winter holidays, a group of adults and their children played a newly unwrapped board game that involved facts about Canada. The question that would win the game seemed simple: *What is the capital of the territory of Nunavut?* Even so, none of the adults who were playing could remember the answer. Don said, "I'm sure I never saw this

(Continued)

(Continued)

in the paper—the place must be very small and unimportant. That's what bothers me about these games; I always end up feeling frustrated and stupid." He turned to his two daughters and said, "Hey, one of you answer this question. I'm sure you said you learned the provincial and territorial capitals in grade 5. So, what's the capital of Nunavut?" Amy, now in grade 7, replied by saying, "I hated that stuff. Our teacher made us memorize all 10 provincial capitals for a test. I did it and passed the test, but I have never needed to know the city names again, so I've forgotten them, and I'm not sure I ever learned the capital of Nunavut in the first place. Anyway, who really cares about capitals of places?

What's the point?" Ashley, who was in grade 6, said, "I don't remember Nunavut's capital either, although I am sure we had to learn it along with the other territories. It's not hard to find out, though. I can go and look it up on the computer now. I'll google it! Just wait one minute while I go to Google and then we'll know.

Questions to Consider

1. What do you consider more important: the content knowledge or the skill to locate it? How can we teach to emphasize the most important learning?
2. What could a teacher do to motivate Amy?
3. Can teachers influence parental attitudes? If so, how?

Obviously, Ashley has a much better attitude than Amy about learning capitals. Although neither sister knew the answer to the Nunavut question, Ashley knew one way to find the capital of that territory and was willing to follow through. Could it be that the sisters' different attitudes are related to varying instructional strategies that had been used in the girls' respective classrooms? Unlike Amy, Ashley had an opportunity to use appropriate instructional technology and was taught a skill that facilitates her ability to be a self-learner. In other words, Ashley was learning how to learn.

Media and Violence

Unlike any previous time in human history, people today have instant access to incredible amounts of information and entertainment through the media. As an example of this phenomenon, according to a 2009 Statistics Canada survey, 93 percent of Canadians used the internet for email (Statistics Canada, 2010). A recent study conducted by Active Healthy Kids Canada (2012) showed that children and youth on average spend almost 8 hours per day in front of a screen. In 2012, 12 million households had a basic television service subscription. While more than half of Canadians owned a smartphone, over a quarter of them owned a tablet. In the same year, as many as 27.9 million Canadians had wireless subscriptions and over three-fourth of the 13.9 million households in the country had an Internet subscription (CRTC, 2013). It would also be no surprise to anyone then that 83 percent of Canadians 16 and overuse the internet personally from various locations (Statistics Canada, 2013).

One concern is about the inhabitants of the television world and the characters in electronic games, who often act and think in ways that contrast sharply with the conventional attitudes, behaviours, beliefs, and values of society in general. As a result, many parents and educators feel helpless in trying to convey appropriate behavioural messages in the face of such stiff opposition from the passive and interactive media that dominate so many children's lives (Rosenberg and Barbara, 2007). The widespread worry is that children who watch violence on television and in movies, and who are exposed to violent behaviours and attitudes while playing pervasive electronic games, will become more aggressive and desensitized to the horror of violent acts. A more recent study of 1,492 Canadian students from the ages of 8/9 to 17/18 showed that those who played violent video games over a longer stretch of time may show increased propensity for aggressive behaviours. (Willoughby, Adachi, Paul, and Good, 2012). Violent shows on television have become not only more frequent, but also more violent in recent years (Parents Television Council, 2007). Researchers have consistently identified three problems associated with heavy exposure to media violence: children may show less empathy to the suffering of others; they may be more fearful in general; and they may develop aggressive behaviour toward others (Anderson, Gentile, and Buckley, 2007; Huesman, 2002).

These concerns are not new. Many of the same worries surfaced in the 1950s with the advent of mainstream television viewing.. On average, there are 26 acts of violence per hour on children's programming, with some cartoons having more than 80 acts of violence per hour (American Psychiatric Association, 2002). Although these are US statistics, given the format for most television shows—brief sequences of fast-paced action with frequent interruptions for unrelated commercial messages—and given that most Canadians watch a great deal of US-made television and movies, it is no surprise that Canadian viewers are exposed in more violence as the number of violent acts per hour on television is increasing (Paquette, 2004).

All children may not be equally vulnerable to adopting aggressive behaviour; however, research has found that children, including Canadian children, who watch violent television programs involving characters to whom they can relate and those who view these programs as authentic may have a greater chance of becoming physically aggressive young adults (Canadian Press, 2003; Kirsh, 2011). Another study found that children who play violent video games are more likely to have engaged in a physical fight in the past year than children who play fewer violent electronic games (Thompson, 2005). Violent video games allow players to solve problems using violence, and once the violent acts occur in these games, the player is typically reinforced by gaining more ammunition, gaining points, or progressing to the next highest levels. This repeated exposure to positive reinforcement of aggressive problem-solving tactics can be related to the formation of acceptable aggressive scripts and structures that can create an aggressive personality (Gentile and Gentile, 2008). It has also been noted that the rise in bullying activities in the schoolyard has coincided with the rise in violent representations in the media (Alphonso, 2003; Rosenberg and Barbara, 2007), and that players of violent electronic games are more likely to perform poorly in school than children who play fewer of those types of games (Gentile, Lynch, Linder, and Walsh, 2004). Another related concern is that regular heavy gaming may inhibit a child's ability to distinguish real life from simulation (Subrahmanyam, Kraut, Greenfield, and Gross, 2000).

Although in the 1950s some psychologists suggested that TV violence had a cathartic effect and reduced a child's aggressive behaviours, by the 1980s, laboratory and field studies had cast serious doubt on the cathartic hypothesis (Pearl, Bouthilet, and Lazar, 1982). A poignant statement on the relationship between television viewing and real-life violence was made by the American Psychological Association (APA): "There is absolutely no doubt that higher levels of viewing violence on television are correlated with increased acceptance of aggressive attitudes and increased aggressive behavior" (1993, 33). Psychologists now suggest that the effects of TV violence may extend beyond causing viewers' increased aggressive behaviours to the *bystander effect*, or the desensitization/callousness of people toward violence directed at others (Morgan, Shanahan, and De-Guise, 2001).

Some researchers have proposed that violence on TV produces stress in children. Exposure to too much violence over too long a time, they say, creates emotional upset and insecurity, leading to resultant disturbed behaviour (Rice, 1981). A 1984 study indicated that heavy television viewing is associated with elementary school children's belief in a "mean and scary world" and that poor school behaviour—restlessness, disruptiveness, inattentiveness, aggressiveness—is significantly correlated with the home television environment: the number of sets, hours of viewing, and types of programs Anderson et al., 2010; Singer, Singer, and Rapaczynski, 1984).

Of course, there have been many theories about the relationship between TV viewing and children's behaviour (Pearl, 1984). The observational modelling theory, which is now over 30 years old, is the most widely accepted. This theory proposes that aggression is learned from the models and real-life simulations portrayed on TV and is practised through imitation (Bandura, 1973; Cantor, 2002). In more recent years, researchers found a correlation between television coverage of violence and our perception of how much violence exists in the world around us (Kirsh, 2011; "Seeds of Violence," 2001). In trying to explain the effects of TV on children's behaviour at school, Rice, Huston, and Wright (1982) hypothesized that the stimuli of sound effects, exciting music, and fast-action images generate an arousal reaction, with an accompanying inability to tolerate the typically long conversations, explanations, and delays characteristic of the real world of school. This hypothesis has been supported by more recent research (e.g. Swing, Gentile, Anderson, and Walsh, 2010).

An overview to this issue is difficult to state definitively, as research is conflicting. Certainly, children view a great deal of violence on television, and young people of this era have been called the "gaming generation" because electronic games have become such a major source of leisure-time entertainment (Olson Kutner, Warner, Almerigi, Baer, and Nicholi, 2007). As mentioned earlier, many of these games are very violent. According to some researchers, though, the problems may be overstated, as most children still prefer to meet their friends face to face and participate in their favourite activities; for instance, the Canadian Teachers' Federation (2003) found that while boys in higher elementary grades state electronic games as a favoured activity, they still prefer to play sports either in organized leagues or more informally with their friends. The bottom line appears to be that a small portion of children may be at risk for losing sight of reality in the gaming world, but the vast majority return to real life unscathed (Turkel, 1996; Willoughby, Adachi and Good, 2012). The debate continues, however, and parents and educators need to remain vigilant.

The Media and Alternative Role Models

Television, the internet, music, videos, and magazines, and also the commercials contained in all of these media, directed at children, influence their behaviours by presenting a wide range of alternative models and lifestyles. At the same time, they are presenting uniform images about the most desirable attitude, body image, and fashion, putting pressure on young people to conform to these "norms," often dismissed or denigrated by adults; for instance, Canada's popular Much Music Television broadcasts 24 hours a day the audio and video imagery of the latest popular music. What once were often indecipherable lyrics have been replaced by visual depictions, many concerning drug and alcohol use, sexual promiscuity, hopelessness, and distrust of school and teachers. Often, these songs become components of other forms of questionable "entertainment" such as video games. Rosenberg and Barbara (2007) argue that "like the worst television shows, the worst video games teach children to associate violence and killing with pleasure, entertainment, and feelings of achievement."

The proliferation of talk shows and reality shows presents children with a glamorized view of oftentimes dysfunctional lives—and at a critical point in the formative years of such young viewers as they attempt to determine who they are, what they can do, and how far they can go in testing the limits of their parents' and teachers' authority. In addition, the news media's propensity to cover war, violence, and natural disasters with intensive 24-hour saturation-coverage desensitizes immature viewers. The television coverage of the war in Afghanistan, Ukraine, and Gaza, for instance, tends to depict this deadly conflict in a manner that often parallels video-game formats. The media have the power, therefore, to communicate pluralistic standards, changing customs, and shifting beliefs and values. Although behavioural experimentation is both a prerequisite for, and a necessary component of, the cognitive and moral developmental growth of young people, today's world is more complicated than it once was, and parents and teachers need to have a working knowledge of the alternative models with which they compete.

Media messages possibly have the most detrimental effects on children who live in poverty. These children usually are aware that they do not possess the things most others have. They also know they lack the opportunities to obtain them in the near future; thus, television's depiction of the "good life" may compound their feelings of hopelessness, discontent, and anger. Such feelings, coupled with the fact that many of these children feel they hold no stake in the values and norms of the more affluent society, lays the foundation for rage, which is often released in violent or aggressive behaviours directed at others (Anderson, Gentile, and Buckley, 2007). It is imperative for teachers to be aware of these outside influences on student behaviours in order to work constructively with, and be supportive of, today's youth.

THE FAILURE TO MEET CHILDREN'S BASIC NEEDS

The Home Environment

Educators have long recognized the significant influence of home life on a child's behaviour and on academic progress. As Case 3.3 illustrates, the home's ability to meet students' basic needs is particularly crucial.

CASE 3.3

Hanging on the Corner

Teresa, a grade 5 student, is on the school playground at 7:45 every morning, even though school doesn't start until 9:00. Often, she is eating a bag of potato chips and drinking a can of soda. On cold, snowy mornings, she huddles in the doorway wearing a spring jacket and sneakers, waiting for the door to be unlocked. She brags to the other students that she hangs out on the corner with the teenagers in her neighbourhood until 12:00 or 1:00 A.M. The home and school coordinator who has investigated her home environment has confirmed this.

Teresa is the youngest of four children. Her father left the family before she started school. Her mother works for a janitorial service and leaves for work by 7:00 A.M. When she returns home in the evening, the mother either goes out with her boyfriend or goes to sleep early, entrusting Teresa's care to her 16-year-old brother, who has recently quit school.

Teresa is two years below grade in both reading and mathematics. She is never prepared for class with the necessary books and materials, never completes homework assignments, and usually chooses not to participate in learning activities. Her classroom behaviour is clearly attention seeking, as she is generally off task, characterized by moving noisily both in and out of her seat, calling out, and disrupting other students by talking to them or physically touching them. Occasionally, Teresa becomes abusive to her fellow students and her teacher, using a loud, challenging voice and vulgarities.

Questions to Consider

1. In your opinion, does Teresa's home situation explain and excuse her disruptive behaviour in class?
2. Discuss three specific things a teacher might do to help Teresa academically and personally.

When considering Teresa's home environment, is it surprising that she has academic and behavioural problems in school? Abraham Maslow's theory of basic human needs predicts Teresa's behaviour. According to Maslow (1968), basic human needs align themselves into a hierarchy of the following levels:

1. *Physiological needs:* hunger, thirst, breathing
2. *Safety and security needs:* protection from injury, pain, extremes of heat and cold
3. *Belonging and affection needs:* giving and receiving love, warmth, and affection;
4. *Esteem and self-respect needs:* feeling adequate, competent, worthy; being appreciated and respected by others
5. *Self-actualization needs:* self-fulfillment by using one's talents and potential

If lower-level (physiological, safety and security, and belonging and affection) needs are not met, an individual could experience difficulty, frustration, and a lack of motivation in attempting to meet the higher-order (esteem and self-respect and self-actualization) needs.

Maslow's hierarchy also represents a series of developmental levels. Although the meeting of these needs is important throughout an individual's life, a young child spends considerably more time and effort meeting the lower-level needs than does an older child. From preadolescence on, assuming the lower-level needs are met, emphasis shifts to the higher-order needs of esteem and self-actualization. (Further discussion of self-esteem is found in the "Children's Pursuit of Social Recognition and Self-Esteem" section, later in this chapter.)

Academic achievement and appropriate behaviour are most likely to occur when a student's home environment has met her physiological, safety, and belonging needs. This enables her to begin to work on meeting the needs of esteem and self-actualization both at home and at school. Let's now examine Teresa's home environment in light of Maslow's hierarchy of basic needs. Her breakfast of potato chips and soda, her clothing (a light jacket and sneakers) on cold days, the absence of a father, and the inconsistent presence of her mother at home are strong indications that her physiological safety and belonging needs are not being met. Because of her inadequate home environment, Teresa has attempted to meet her need for belonging and esteem by bragging about hanging out with teenagers and by using loud, vulgar statements in class and disturbing other students. Given her situation, it is surprising that Teresa still attends school on a regular basis. If Teresa's home environment remains the same, and if she persists with below grade expectations academically, and exhibits social and emotional difficulties, she probably will quit school at an early age, still unable to control her behaviour. This might be disastrous for her, as school may be her only stable and predictable environment.

The results of a longitudinal study of students in grades 3, 6, and 9 (Feldhusen, Thurston, and Benning, 1973) provided clear evidence of the importance of the home environment on school behaviour. Persistently disruptive students differed substantially from persistently prosocial students in a number of home and family variables:

1. Parental supervision and discipline were inadequate, being too lax, too strict, or erratic.
2. The parents were indifferent or hostile to the child. They disapproved of many things about the child and handed out angry, physical punishment.
3. The family operated only partially if at all, as a unit, and the marital relationship lacked closeness and equality of partnership.
4. The parents found it difficult to discuss concerns regarding the child and believed that they had little influence on the child. They believed that other children exerted bad influences on their child (Feldhusen,Thurston, and Benning, 1973).

In its 1993 publication, *Violence and Youth*, the American Psychological Association offered examples of the family characteristics of children with antisocial behaviours that were quite similar to the Feldhusen et al. findings (1973). The examples included parental rejection, inconsistent and physically abusive discipline, and parental support of their children's use of aversive and aggressive problem-solving approaches. The study found that lack of parental supervision was one of the strongest predictors of children's later conduct disorders. Case 3.3, Feldhusen's longitudinal study and the APA's summary describe homes that could be considered abusive or at least neglectful; however, many nonabusive or non-neglectful home environments also create situations that are quite stressful to children (Sylva, Melhuish, Sammons, Siraj-Blatchford, and Taggart, 2010). This stress may manifest itself symptomatically as behavioural problems. Consider the example of Seth in Case 3.4.

CASE 3.4

Marital Conflict

Seth was a typical grade 11 student from a middle-class suburban home who attended the local high school. He was friendly by nature and enjoyed school activities, particularly sports. Although he was not an outstanding student, he was motivated and attentive enough, and his teachers seldom had any real problems with his in-class behaviour. Occasionally, he had to be reminded to stop talking and to take his seat when class started. His grades were typically Bs with a few Cs. Seth had discussed his future with his guidance counsellor and his parents and it was decided that he would attend a small university and major in liberal arts. According to his teachers, they liked Seth and enjoyed having him in their classes.

Now, at the end of grade 11, something is different, and Seth appears to have changed. He frequently fails to hand in his homework and is regularly off task in class. It is evident that his usual motivation has disappeared. When questioned, Seth says that he has changed his plans about attending university and now he wants instead to get a job right out of high school. His teachers begin to discuss the observable changes in Seth's behaviour and aspirations; his counsellor

reveals that Seth shares the information that his parents have been discussing divorce.

As the oldest of the three children in the family, Seth is being included in the discussions about how the family will manage in the future. The counsellor also discerns that both of Seth's parents are now asking him for assistance in fulfilling family responsibilities—they are not minimizing the ramifications of the marital breakup for the young man. Clearly, the situation is putting a great deal of stress on Seth and causing him to be distracted from his schoolwork; however, of greater concern is the fact that his aspirations for a university degree, which is well within his academic reach, are also being affected negatively. In addition, the counsellor identifies that Seth is considerably less outgoing with fellow students and appears distracted and unhappy when talking with them.

Questions to Consider

1. What role, if any, should the school play in cases of family breakdown when the child is being affected very negatively?
2. How could a counsellor or teacher help Seth without interfering in matters beyond her control?

While Seth's home environment is significantly different from Teresa's, it, too, has a detrimental effect on behaviour in school. Seth's situation is one that an increasing number of children face.

What changes have occurred in the home environment of Canadian children? The Divorce Act was revised in 1985, which resulted in the increase in the number of divorces by more than 20 percent between 1986 and 1987. For three consecutive years leading up to 2000, the divorce rate went up (Statistics Canada, 2002). The divorce rate rose from 5.1% in 1981 to 11.5% in 2011 by 3.0 percent (Statistics Canada, 2011). Remarriage often creates additional problems for children (Amato, 2000). Any form of marital conflict increases the likelihood that children will develop some type of behavioural problem (Bornstein, 2003). In a Canadian study, 92 percent of children who had lived with both parents from birth to 15 years of age reported that they had enjoyed a very happy childhood. Of those who had lived through a change in parental structure before age 15, however, only 72 percent said that they had happy memories of their early years (Williams, 2001). In another study, Jenkins, Simpson, Dunn, Rasbash, and O'Connor (2005) found that not only did marital conflict predict a change in children's behaviour but children's behaviour also predicted an increase in marital conflict.

Divorce not only changes the family structure but it also frequently results in a decrease in the family's standard of living, with an increasing number of children and their single mothers moving into poverty status (Bornstein, 2003). The 1995 General Social Survey reported that 96 percent (22.5 million) of Canadians who were age 15 and older were born into families with two parents. A significant number of children (87 percent) lived with both parents until they were at least 15 years old. Before age 15, however, there was a change in family composition for approximately 1.9 million Canadians, or 13 percent (Williams, 2001).

Canadian Council on Social Development (CCSD) research shows that 15 percent of Canadian residents were living in poverty in 1990. This percentage had increased to 16.2 percent by 1999 representing 4,886,000 persons. Of these, 1,298,000 were children under the age of 18 (Canadian Council on Social Development, 2002). These children are at greater risk than others of developing academic and/or behavioural problems (Gelfand, Jenson, and Drew, 1982). "Education is a fundamental human right and the cornerstone in the battle against poverty. It is critical that bilateral and international institutions work together more closely to ensure that support is increased to national education programs for the poor" ("Canada Says Education Is Key . . .," 2001). A slight improvement was noted in 2011. In that year, 12.9 percent Canadians was in low income before tax (Statistics Canada, 2013).

The School Environment

PHYSIOLOGICAL NEEDS. Students are in school to learn. They are continually asked to demonstrate their new understanding and skills. In asking them to do so, schools are attempting to aid students in a process that Maslow calls *self-actualization*. When students successfully demonstrate new learning, they usually are intrinsically and extrinsically positively reinforced, which leads to the development of self-esteem and self-respect. Positive self-esteem motivates students to learn, which results in the further development of self-actualization. The cycle of self-esteem, learning, and self-actualization can be maximized only if the home and schools create environments in which the lower-level needs—physiological, safety and security, and belonging and affection—are met (Brophy, 2010; Novak and Purkey, 2001). Consider Sari's reaction in Case 3.5 when the teacher unintentionally stifles her enthusiasm.

Case 3.5 illustrates how a young child attempts to meet the physiological need of movement and activity. For some young children, no school activity takes more energy than sitting still. When the teacher demanded that Sari sit and then eventually removed recess, her physiological need was no longer being met. This resulted in Sari's excessive movement around the room. When Sari's needs were met, the disruptive behaviours stopped.

CASE 3.5

Forgetting to Sit Down

Sari, a grade 2 student, is a bright, happy, active child. She is always the first one ready for recess and the last one to stop playing. When going to or from school, she is often seen skipping, jumping, or doing cartwheels.

Sari's desk is second from the front. When given seat work, she either stands at her desk or half-stands with one knee on the chair. Her teacher always reminds Sari to sit, but no sooner has she sat down than she is back up on her feet.

After a good number of reminders, Sari is kept in from recess. When this occurs, she begins to walk around the room when class is in progress. This leads to further reprimands by her teacher. Finally, her parents are notified.

Sari's parents inform her teacher that at home Sari is always jumping rope, playing catch, dancing, and even standing rather than sitting for piano lessons and practice. She even stands at the table at mealtimes. It is decided that Sari's seat will be moved to the back of the room so that her standing doesn't distract the other students. After this is explained to Sari, she agrees to the move. The reprimands stop. Sari continues to do excellent work, and by the end of grade 2, she is able to sit in her seat while working.

Questions to Consider

1. Do you consider Sari's active behaviour to be a problem? Why? Why not?
2. Why did this solution succeed with Sari?
3. Which teacher behaviours could have led to Sari becoming a behavioural problem?

The importance of meeting students' physiological needs as a prerequisite to learning should be evident to everyone. Ask any teacher how much learning occurs on the first cold day of fall before the heating system is functional or on the first hot day of early spring before the heating system has been turned off. At a minimum, every classroom in every school should have adequate space and proper lighting and ventilation.

Somewhat less evident, but no less important, than a school's environmental conditions are concerns about poverty, overcrowding, noise, and frequent interruptions. Teachers have long known that students are less attentive in classes held just before lunch. When schools are overcrowded and/or lunch facilities are inadequate, some students may eat lunch before 11:00 A.M., whereas others may not eat until after 1:00 P.M. This can produce a group of students whose long wait for lunch leaves them inattentive to learning tasks. In an attempt to improve learning environments and nutritional practices, many boards of education are experimenting with alternative scheduling in their schools. One of the current timetabling implementations is called the *balanced day* (Wagner, 2007). The timetable is designed to provide longer periods in each class, two nutritional/activity breaks that replace the structure of two recesses and a lunch break (McNamara, 2013). "Schools that piloted this new schedule have reported an increase in concentration levels of students, more positive play time, more physically active students, and better opportunities for learning through uninterrupted blocks of teaching/learning time" (Waterloo Region District School Board, 2007).

Regardless of students' ages, the interruptions, noise, and overcrowding can produce emotional uneasiness that may result in nervousness, anxiety, a need to withdraw, or overactivity. In these cases, emotional uneasiness interferes with on-task behaviour and reduces the effectiveness of the teaching–learning environment (Brophy, 2010; Marini, Spear, and Bombay, 1999). Consider, for example, Cases 3.6 and 3.7. Schools must pay particular attention to minimizing distractions if they want to reduce student off-task behaviour.

CASE 3.6

"There Must Be a Better Way"

One university requires its secondary student teachers to follow a student's schedule of classes for an entire day. Teacher candidates must record their reactions to this experience. What follows are a couple of common reactions:

*No sooner were we in our seats in the first-period class than the VP was on the intercom system. She spent at least five minutes with announcements mostly directed at the teachers. The speaker was loud and very annoying. After the announcements, most of the students were talking among themselves. By the time we got down to work, 15 minutes had passed. Halfway through the period, a student messenger interrupted the class when he brought the morning office notices to the teacher. And believe it or not, five minutes before the end of class, the VP was back on the intercom with additional announcements. It was quite evident to me that these interruptions were a direct cause of inattentiveness and reduction in effective instruction. Much time was wasted during the announcements and in obtaining student **on-task behaviour** after the interruptions. There must be a better way.*

Probably the most eye-opening experience I had was remembering how crowded and noisy schools can be. This was most evident to me when we changed classes. We had three minutes between classes. The halls were very crowded, with frequent pushing, shoving, and just bumping into each other. The noise level was so high that it really bothered me. On arriving at the next class, all I really wanted to do was sit quietly for a few minutes before starting to work. The changes from hallways to classrooms are dramatic. I can see why it is difficult for some students to settle down and get on task at the beginning of class. As bad as the hallways were, it didn't prepare me for lunch. The lunchroom was even noisier. By the time I waited in line, I had only 15 minutes to eat and then back to the hallways to class. By the end of the day, I was drained.

Questions to Consider

1. "A noisy, crowded school is a fact of life, and students and teachers just need to accept it!" Comment on this statement.
2. How can a classroom teacher minimize the effects of disruptions and noisy hallways?

CASE 3.7

Too Much Noise

Karen is a quiet, well-behaved grade 3 student who does her work conscientiously and achieves well academically. She sits near the front of the class and seldom interrupts or offers answers to questions. She is always responsive to her teacher Ms. Gray's instructions and Ms. Gray recently told Karen's parents that "she is a pleasure to have in the class."

One day, all the grade 3 classes are taken to the all-purpose room to watch a well-known film on environmental issues. As the class has been studying this topic for the past week, interest and excitement are unusually high. The teacher has encouraged this excitement by giving the children a sheet of questions that can be answered by watching the film.

All the grade 3 classes happen to enter the hall on the way to the all-purpose room simultaneously, and the children in the hallway are very noisy because of increased excitement and expectation about the break in the usual routine to see the movie.

Ms. Gray notices Karen walking down the hall, not interacting with her peers, and holding her hands over her ears. Curiously, Ms. Gray watches Karen enter the all-purpose room heading right for the back corner of the room and sitting down against the wall. Going over to Karen, Ms. Gray asks her what the problem is. Karen replies quietly that the noise hurts her ears and she feels like crying. Clearly distressed, she adds that she doesn't want to be there if the noise is going to be loud.

Ms. Gray quickly moves to the front to quiet the students, and Karen appears to relax and enjoy the film. Ms. Gray, though, is troubled by the obvious distress that Karen displayed, so she contacts Karen's parents and suggests a consultation with an ear specialist. Some weeks later, the parents contact Ms. Gray and report that the specialist has confirmed Karen has no problems with her hearing or her ears. They are all baffled by the strange behaviour Karen exhibited on movie day.

Questions to Consider

1. What steps should Ms. Gray take to ensure that Karen does not have a recurrence of this issue?
2. What can be done to help Karen cope when her classmates become noisy and excited?

SAFETY AND SECURITY NEEDS. For the most part, schools create environments in which students feel safe from physical harm. There are, however, occasions when students, like Keith in Case 3.8, fear for their physical safety (Bender, and Lösel, 2011; Marini, Fairbain, and Zuber, 2001; Marini, Spear, and Bombay, 1999). Students in troubled schools are sometimes assaulted, coerced, bribed, or robbed. Violence such as that observed in US schools is becoming increasingly evident in Canadian schools and has been the subject of serious study (Jull, 2000; MacDonald, 1997). This may not be surprising, as more weapons are brought to schools each day, and the presence of street gangs at schools is increasing (Kirsh, 2011; Ruck and Wortley, 2002). Also, in all schools there are students who occasionally experience anxiety about walking to and from school, going to the restroom, dressing in locker rooms, or changing classes (MacDonald, 1997). In Canada, studies suggest that about 6 percent of students aged 12 to 19 report bullying others on a weekly basis. Furthermore, 8 percent report that they are the victims of bullying weekly and 1 percent report that they are both victimized and bully others weekly (Volk, Craig, Boyce, and King, 2003). Surveys also indicate that many more boys than girls are involved in bullying (Kaltiala-Heino, Fröjd, and Marttunen, 2010; Totten, Quigley, and Morgan, 2004). The more students feel insecure about their physical safety, the less likely they will exhibit the on-task behaviours necessary for learning.

CONCENTRIC CASE STUDY KALEIDOSCOPE

CASE 3.8
Afraid of Going to School

Keith, a grade 8 student, achieves at an average level in his classes. He does best in social studies, which is scheduled for the last period of the day. Keith is generally attentive and has never caused any disruption in class. Approximately midway through the year, Keith's behaviour in social studies begins to change. He goes from being a student who is attentive and participates freely to one who rarely is engaged in the discussion. The teacher notes that he seems distracted and is clearly not paying attention. When asked a specific question that he would normally have been able to answer, Keith appears not to have heard and has to ask the teacher embarrassedly to repeat the question. When the teacher does so, Keith mumbles that he doesn't know the answer. Mystified, the teacher begins to notice that Keith is often watching the clock nervously and is the first to leave his seat and rush through the door at the end of class.

After a few days of observing this behaviour, the teacher asks Keith to stay behind for a few minutes after class to discuss his distracted behaviour. Keith appears upset at being asked to stay and, when questioned, tells the teacher that he has to leave early because his schoolmate Greg will beat him up if he sees him on the street. Keith is fearful of the boy because Greg has threatened him for telling the gym teacher that he

was the one throwing Keith's clothing around the locker room after gym class.

Keith's Perspective

I used to like social studies class, but now I can't concentrate on it. I just can't! I keep watching the clock so that I can get my books away and get out the door before Greg does. Then I can run all the way home and avoid getting trapped by him. He is really mad at me and has told everyone that he intends to beat me up. He is bigger than me and much tougher and can easily do it. I bet he could really hurt me. I know that the kids will gather around and some of my friends will feel bad for me, but I also know that they will not be able to help me. I just have to get home before he catches me.

I know he is really mad at me for telling the teacher that he was the one throwing my clothes around the locker room last month. I just wasn't thinking when the teacher asked me who had made a mess, and I was really stupid not to have lied. I should have said that I didn't know who had done it. Now I'm in trouble.

I could tell my parents, but they will come over to the school and there will be a big fuss. I don't want them to know. The other day when I got home from school all hot and sweaty and out of breath, Mom asked me why

(Continued)

(Continued)

I had run so hard. I lied and told her that I wanted to get home so I could watch a program on TV. Also, I don't want the other kids to call me a sissy. I could tell the teacher, but that's what got me into this mess in the first place.

The problem is that this is all I think about. I know my marks are going down and I will get zero for participation this term, but I am so afraid of being beaten up and made to look like an idiot. I just have to get out of class quickly and run home as fast as I can. I hope he forgets about me soon. I wish someone else would offend him so he would lay off me.

Things could get really bad now because the teacher asked me to stay late and I did not know what to say when he asked me why my classroom behaviour had changed. I told him about Greg's bullying. I am not sure what he will do now, but I am really afraid Greg will find out that I snitched on him again and get even madder. I am really scared—I wonder if I should tell my parents or call the police. I feel desperate…

Greg's Perspective

That little creep Keith keeps leaving class early so he can avoid getting what he deserves. I can see that I have frightened him, though, as he seems to run all the way home. Good! He should have known better than to be a snitch about me throwing the clothes around—it was really only a joke. I hate it when people don't treat me with respect and I'm going to show everyone what happens when I get mad. I can't wait to get my hands on him and I know that he can't escape me forever. It's just a matter of time— I can wait until he drops his guard.

One thing that does bother me is that today the teacher asked him to stay after class. I bet the creep told him why he leaves early and runs home. Little snitch! I'll make him pay for that, too.

Teacher's Perspective

I wonder what is happening to Keith these days. He seems like a different student, and his marks are going to reflect his non-participation in class. I feel sorry about that because I have always enjoyed and valued his input. He looks distracted and inattentive throughout the class, gathers his books up in a hurry, and darts out of the class before I can talk to him. I wonder if I should call his parents or talk to him first.

I have decided to talk to Keith first and managed to hold him back after class, although he was clearly very agitated about not leaving in a hurry. After some persistent questioning, he finally told me that Greg was bullying him by threatening to beat him up for tattling. I am not surprised, as I have noted for some time that Greg appears to be a bully in the classroom. The other kids treat him very carefully, and he makes threatening comments quite openly. I wasn't sure whether he was a real threat or just acting like one, but clearly to Keith the threat of violence is very real. Now I have a real issue that I must deal with.

Questions to Consider

1. How can the teacher help Keith cope with being the victim of bullying?
2. How can the teacher help Greg stop being a bully?
3. What is the first step that should be taken by the teacher?

BELONGING AND AFFECTION NEEDS. While these needs are most often met by family at home or the students' peers in and out of school, there must be elements of caring, trust, and respect in the interpersonal relationships between teachers and students.

In other words, there should be a caring, supportive classroom climate (Bender, and Lösel, 2011; Novak and Purkey, 2001). Such a climate is more likely to be created by teachers who subscribe to a referent authority base in the classroom. The development of various teacher authority bases will be studied in Chapter 5, "Philosophical Approaches to Classroom Management."

Withall (1969) has stressed that the most important variables in determining the climate of a classroom are the teacher's verbal and nonverbal behaviours. Appropriate student behaviour can be enhanced when teachers communicate the following to the learners:

Trust: "I believe you are able to learn and want to learn."

Respect: "Insofar as I try to help you learn, you are, by the same token, helping me to learn."

Caring: "I perceive you as a unique and worthwhile person whom I want to help to learn and grow." (Withall, 1979)

For students to learn effectively, they must participate fully in the learning process. This means they must be encouraged to ask and answer questions, attempt new approaches, make mistakes, and ask for assistance; however, learners engage in these behaviours only in settings in which they feel safe from being ridiculed or made to feel inadequate. Study Case 3.9. As the year progressed, Ms. Barrie failed to demonstrate her trust, respect, and caring for her students; thus, her students were discouraged from fully participating in the learning process.

CASE 3.9
Turning Off Students

Ms. Barrie, a high school science teacher, is quite concerned over what she perceives to be a significant decrease in student participation throughout the year. She views the problem as follows: "I ask a lot of questions. Early in the year, many students volunteer, but within a few weeks I find that volunteering has almost ceased and the only way I can get students to participate is to call on them."

Arrangements are made to observe the class to determine the causes of the problem. Teacher questions, student responses, and teacher feedback are recorded. An example of one such interaction follows:

TEACHER QUESTION: "We know that man is in the family of Hominidae. What is man's taxonomic order?"

STUDENT RESPONSE: "Mammals."

TEACHER FEEDBACK: "No, it's not mammals. We had this material last week; you should know it. The answer is primates."

Further observation reveals that about 70 percent of Ms. Barrie's feedback is totally or partially negative. Students note that they don't like being put down because their answers aren't exactly what Ms. Barrie wants. One student states, "I answer only when I know I'm correct. If I don't understand something, I often just let it go rather than be drilled."

Questions to Consider

1. Describe a learning situation that you have been in that has made you reluctant or nervous about answering/asking questions.
2. Reword the teacher's feedback so that the student will be encouraged to contribute again.

CASE 3.10

"I'm Going to Be Sorry When Grade 5 Is Over"

One afternoon last May, I was acting as a parent volunteer with my daughter's grade 5 class to supervise at a track and field meet. While we were sitting around waiting for the final event, I overheard a group of grade 5 students talking. I paid very little attention until I heard one of them say, "I'm going to be sorry when grade 5 is over." I observed that the other students appeared to be in agreement, what with the nodding of heads and mutterings of, "Yeah, me too." Interested, I interrupted the conversation and asked if they would be willing to explain to me why they felt this way. Their comments follow.

"She lets us give our opinions."

"If we say something stupid, she doesn't say anything."

"She lets us decide how we are going to do things."

"She gives us suggestions and helps us when we get stuck."

"You can say how you feel."

"She gives us choices."

"She tells us what she thinks, but doesn't want us to think like her. Some teachers tell us their opinions, but you know that they really want you to think the same way."

"We learn a lot."

Questions to Consider

1. Describe this grade 5 teacher's philosophy of education.
2. What were these children learning?
3. Given the teacher's skill, what do you think would be the response from children at the primary level, the intermediate level, or the senior level to such teaching?

Comments such as, "Why do you ask so many questions?"; "You should know this; we studied it last week"; or "Everyone should understand this; there should be no questions" serve no useful purpose. Indeed, they hinder learner participation, confidence, and motivation and lead to off-task behaviour. Glasser (1978) sees failure as the root of misbehaviour, noting that when students don't learn at the expected rate, they get less "care" and recognition from the teacher. As the situation continues, students see themselves as trapped. Acceptance and recognition, it seems to them, can be gained only through misbehaviour. In sharp contrast to the feelings of Ms. Barrie's students are those of the grade 5 students in Case 3.10.

CHILDREN'S PURSUIT OF SOCIAL RECOGNITION AND SELF-ESTEEM

Social Recognition

Alfred Adler, the renowned psychiatrist, and Rudolph Dreikurs, Adler's student and colleague, believed that behaviour can be best understood using three key premises (Adler, 1966):

1. "People are social beings who have a need to belong, to be recognized, and to be accepted.

2. Behaviour is goal-directed and has the purpose of gaining the recognition and acceptance that people want.
3. People can choose how they behave; they can behave or misbehave. Their behaviour is not outside their control."

Putting these key ideas together, Adler and Dreikurs theorized that people choose to try a wide variety of behaviours to see which behaviours gain them the recognition and acceptance they want. When socially sanctioned behaviours do not produce the needed recognition and acceptance, people often choose to misbehave in the mistaken belief that socially unacceptable behaviours will produce the recognition they seek.

Applying these premises to children's conduct, Dreikurs, Grundwald, and Pepper (1982) identified four goals of disruptive behaviours: attention getting, power seeking, revenge seeking, and the display of inadequacy. According to this theory, these goals, which are usually sequential, are strongest in elementary-aged children but are also present in adolescents.

Attention-seeking students make up a large part of the misbehaving population in the schools. These students may ask question after question; use excessive charm; continually need help or assistance; and continually ask for the teacher's approval, call out, or show off. In time, the teacher usually becomes annoyed. When the teacher reprimands these children, they temporarily stop their attention-seeking behaviour. In Case 3.11, Kayer is a child who feels that he is not getting the recognition he desires. He sees no chance of gaining this recognition through socially accepted or constructive contributions. He first channels his energies into gaining attention. Like all attention-seeking students, he has the notion that he is important only when others take notice of him and acknowledge his presence. When attention-getting behaviour no longer gives the students the recognition they want, many of them seek recognition through the next goal—power—which is exactly what Kayer does when he begins to confront the teacher openly.

CASE 3.11
Seeking Faulty Goals

Kayer is a grade 6 student of average academic ability. On the first day of class, when students are asked to choose seats, Kayer chooses the one next to the window in the back of the room. Between classes, he rarely interacts with classmates. Instead, he either bolts out of the class first or slowly swaggers out last.

During instructional times, he either nonchalantly leans back in his seat or jumps up and calls out answers. During seat work, he often has to be reminded to begin, and once finished, he taps his pencil, wanders around the back of the room, or noisily moves his chair and desk.

Kayer's behaviour often improves for short periods of time after excessive teacher attention, ranging from positive reinforcement to reprimands. These periods of improvement are followed by a return to disruptive behaviours. Kayer's attention-seeking behaviour continues throughout the first half of the school year.

As time goes on, the teacher usually yells at Kayer, sends him to the principal, or

(Continued)

(Continued)

makes comments in front of the class that reflect her extreme frustration.

Eventually, the teacher's behaviour is characterized by threats, such as, "You will stay after school longer every day until you begin to behave," or "Every day that you don't turn in your homework, you will have 20 more problems to do." Kayer sees immediately the impossibility of some of the threats and boldly says, "If I have to stay longer after school each day, in two weeks I'll have to sleep here." There are tremendous amounts of laughter from his classmates at such comments; however, after a week or two, Kayer says, "I'm not coming for your detention," and "You can't make me do homework if I don't want to." The teacher no longer feels annoyed but now feels threatened and challenged.

Whenever problems arise in the classroom, the teacher and students are quick to blame Kayer. Occasionally, he is accused of things that he has not done, and he is quick to shout, "I didn't do it; I'm always the one who gets blamed for everything around here." His classmates now show extreme annoyance with his behaviours, and Kayer resorts to acts directed against individuals. He kicks students' chairs and intentionally knocks over others' books as he walks down the aisles.

One day, one of the boys in the class accuses Kayer of taking his book. Without warning, Kayer flips the student's desk. The student falls backward, lands on his arm, and breaks it. As a result, Kayer is suspended.

When Kayer returns from his suspension, he is told that he will be sent to the office for any violation of a classroom rule. He is completely ignored by his classmates.

For the rest of the year, Kayer comes in, goes to the back of the room, does no work, and bothers no one. At first, the teacher tries to get Kayer involved, but all efforts are to no avail. The teacher thinks to herself that she has tried everything she knows. "If he wants to just sit there, let him. At least he isn't bothering anyone anymore," she says.

Postscript: Teachers should be very aware of student behaviour and act quickly to provide feedback that will redirect inappropriate behaviours. In Kayer's case, the teacher could have determined that Level II in the CALM model—act—applied in this scenario. Once it has been decided that acting is necessary, do not hesitate. It is important to realize that prompt action at Level III may have defused the situation without further complications; however, the teacher chose to ignore the situation until it became more confrontational.

Questions to Consider

1. Describe all the strategies used by this teacher to deal with Kayer's negative behaviour.
2. In light of the CALM model, describe what other strategies the teacher might have employed.
3. Should a teacher modify expectations for an exceptional student like Kayer? What impact might modifications have on the rest of the class?

Students who seek power through misbehaviour usually feel that they can do whatever they want. By challenging teachers, they often gain social acceptance from their peers. Power-seeking students argue, lie, ignore, become stubborn, throw temper tantrums, and become disobedient in general to show that they are in command of the situation. Some teachers feel threatened or challenged by these children and often feel compelled to force them into compliance. Once teachers enter into authority struggles with power-seeking students, the students usually "win." Even if these students do not succeed in getting what they want, they succeed in getting the teacher's attention. If a teacher "wins" the power struggle, the winning reinforces the student's idea that power is what really counts.

With a power-seeking student, reprimands from the teacher result in intensified challenges or temporary withdrawal before new power-seeking behaviours reappear. As power struggles develop between a teacher and a student, both teacher-controlling and student-power-seeking behaviours usually become more severe and the student–teacher relationship deteriorates further (Levin and Shanken-Kaye, 2002). If students see themselves as losing the power struggle, they often move to the next goal—seeking revenge.

When students perceive that they have no control over their environment, they experience an increased sense of inferiority and futility. They feel that they have been treated unfairly and are deeply hurt by what they consider to be others' disregard for their feelings. They may seek revenge by bullying and occasionally hurting others indiscriminately; for instance, Kayer sought his revenge on random individuals who happened to be sitting along his aisle. Revenge-seeking children destroy property, threaten other students and sometimes the teacher, engage in extremely rough play, and use obscenities.

When working with these students, teachers feel defeated and hurt and have a difficult time focusing on what is best for the student. Teacher reprimands usually result in an explosive display of anger and abusiveness from the student. Over time, the teacher may feel a strong need to "get even." The teacher may falsely believe that retribution will help regain control.

Unfortunately, revenge-seeking behaviours elicit dislike and more hurt from others. Revenge-seeking students continually feel a deep sense of despair and worthlessness. Their interactions with other people often result in negative feelings about themselves, which eventually move them to the last goal—the display of inadequacy. These students cannot be motivated and refuse to participate in class activities. Their message is clear: "Don't expect anything from me because I have nothing worthwhile to give." They are often heard saying, "Why don't you just leave me alone—I'm not bothering anyone"; "Mind your own business"; "Why try, I'll just get it wrong"; or "I can't do it."

Teachers often feel that they have tried everything with these students. Further attempts usually result in very little, if any, change in the students' refusal to show interest, to participate, or to interact with others. Kayer's teacher actually felt somewhat relieved that he no longer was a disturbing influence in class; however, if the teacher had been able to stop his progression toward the display of inadequacy, Kayer would have had a much more meaningful and valuable grade 6 learning experience, and the teacher would have felt much more professionally competent.

Most of the goals of misbehaviour are pursued one at a time, but some students switch back and forth between goals. Goal-seeking misbehaviours can also be situational. The CALM model, which is the decision-making hierarchical approach to classroom management presented in this book, offers many strategies for working with children seeking these four mistaken goals. In addition, specific management techniques for each goal are discussed in detail in Charles, Senter, and Barr (1995); Dreikurs, Grundwald, and Pepper (1982); Dubelle and Hoffman (1984); and Sylva, Melhuish, Sammons, Siraj-Blatchford, and Taggart, 2010.

Self-Esteem

Self-esteem, or a feeling of self-worth, is a basic need that individuals continually strive to meet. Without a positive sense of self-esteem, a child is vulnerable to a variety of social, psychological, and learning problems (Gilliland, 1986; Orenstein, 2013).

In his definitive work on self-esteem, Stanley Coopersmith (1967) wrote that self-esteem is made up of four components:

Significance: a learner's belief that she is liked, accepted, and important to others who are important to her.

Competence: a learner's sense of mastery of age-appropriate tasks that have value to her.

Power: a learner's ability to control important parts of her environment.

Virtue: closely akin to significance, a learner's sense of worthiness to another person's well-being because of the care and help she provides to the other person.

If families, teachers, or communities fail to provide prosocial opportunities that allow students to experience a sense of significance, competence, power, and virtue, students are likely to express these four components in negative, distorted ways (Levin and Shanken-Kaye, 2002).

It is possible to express the concept of self-esteem as an equation. Manifested in this way, the equation offers an explanation of why students choose to be disruptive:

$$\text{Self-Esteem} = \text{Significance} + \text{Competence} + \text{Power} + \text{Virtue}$$

Chronically disruptive students have low levels of significance because they feel they are not liked or accepted by their teachers, peers, and sometimes even their parents. Their levels of competence are depressed because they rarely achieve academically, socially, or in extracurricular activities. In addition, because these students rarely choose or are rarely selected by the teacher to interact responsibly with others, their sense of virtue is low; therefore, as the self-esteem equation indicates, the only component left to build a chronically disruptive student's self-esteem is *power*. It is exactly this striving for power, or control of the environment, that is operating when students choose to behave disruptively. In fact, the chronically disruptive student can be viewed as the most powerful individual in the classroom. How she behaves often determines the amount of time spent on learning in the classroom and whether the teacher leaves the classroom with a headache, or, in some cases, leaves the profession. It is, however, important to note that this is not pro-social power but distorted power. The display of such power provides the student with a distorted sense of significance and competence that is evident in this type of mindset: "The other kids know that they can count on me to get Mr. Beal to go ballistic, which would liven this class up a bit."

As Case 3.12 illustrates, when teachers interact with students without considering the students' self-esteem, they increase the likelihood that students will use distorted power to preserve self-esteem. If a student's self-esteem is publicly threatened in front of peers, the likelihood of the young person using distorted power increases.

CASE 3.12

Just Can't Get Respect!

Rob, Justin, Ami, Tanya, and Miya, who are all grade 10 students, are talking in the hallway outside their last-period class. They are animated and excited about an upcoming weekend event. Ms. Wertz, who teaches across the hall and knows Rob from last year, comes out of her classroom to see who is making the noise. She raises her voice to a very high level and says, "Rob, get into your class immediately. A struggling student like you should never be standing around wasting time like this. You need all the time in class you can get." Rob replies in a respectful calm tone, "Ms. Wertz, my class is right here and we have another two minutes before we . . .." Before he can finish, Ms. Wertz interrupts, "Don't give me your feeble excuses—you always have excuses." There is a silence among the students in the hall, and then Rob replies again in a calm, respectful manner, "Ms. Wertz, this is not an excuse, this is my class and these are the rules in this class. We are allowed to stay in the halls and talk with our friends until the teacher is ready to start." Rob's friends in the hall are angry on his behalf and talk about ways of telling the principal about what they see as inappropriate behaviour on the part of Ms. Wertz.

Questions to Consider

1. What previous events prompted Ms. Wertz's behaviour?
2. How are both Ms. Wertz and Rob damaged by this encounter?
3. What, if anything, do you think the student bystanders should do in response to what they see as an injustice? Do you think that their actions would help or harm Rob?

STAGES OF COGNITIVE AND MORAL DEVELOPMENT

Jean Piaget's work in the area of cognitive development has shown that children move through distinct stages of cognitive and moral development. At each stage, children think about and interpret their environment differently than children at other stages. For this reason, a child's behaviour varies as she moves from one stage to another. An understanding of the stages of development enables a teacher to better understand student behaviour patterns.

Cognitive Development

Throughout his life, Piaget studied how children interacted with their environment and how their intellect developed. To him, knowledge was the transformation of an individual's experience with the environment, not the accumulation of facts and pieces of information. His research resulted in the formulation of a four-stage, age-related cognitive development theory (Piaget, 1970), which has significantly influenced the manner in which children are educated.

Piaget called the four stages of development the *sensory-motor, the preoperational, the concrete operational*, and *the formal operational* stages. The sensory-motor stage occurs from birth to approximately 2 years of age. It is characterized by the refinement of motor skills and the use of the five senses to explore the environment. This stage, obviously, has little importance for teachers working with school-age children.

The preoperational stage occurs from approximately 2 to 7 years of age and is the stage when most children begin their school experience. Children at this stage are egocentric—they are unable to conceive that others may see things differently than they do. Although their ability to give some thought to decisions is developing, the great majority of the time they act only on perceptive impulses. Their short attention span interacts with their static thinking, resulting in an inability to think of a sequence of steps or operations. Their sense of time and space is limited to short duration and close proximity.

The concrete operational stage occurs from approximately 7 to 12 years of age. Children are able to order and classify objects and to consider several variables simultaneously as long as they have experiences with "concrete" content. These children need step-by-step instructions if they are expected to work through lengthy procedures. What can be frustrating to teachers who do not understand the characteristics of this stage is that these children do not attempt to check their conclusions, have difficulty thinking about thinking (how they arrived at certain conclusions), and seem unaware of and unconcerned with inconsistencies in their own reasoning.

At about the age of 12, at the earliest, children begin to move into the formal operational stage. They start to develop independent critical-thinking skills, plan lengthy procedures, and consider a number of possible answers to problems. They no longer are tied to concrete models but instead are able to use symbols and verbal examples. These children, who are adolescents, begin to think about their own and others' thought processes, which leads them to consider motives; the past, present, and future; the abstract; the remote; and the ideal. The methodological implications for teaching students at each stage are straightforward and have been researched and written about extensively (Adler, 1966; Egan, 2012; Karplus, 1977).

Moral Development

Piaget related his theory of a child's cognitive development directly to the child's moral development. Through his work, Piaget demonstrated that children are close to or at the formal operational stage of cognitive development before they possesses the intellectual ability to evaluate, consider, and act on abstract moral dilemmas; thus, an elementary schoolchild's perception of what is bad or wrong vastly differs from that of an adolescent's (Piaget, 1965).

Using Piaget's work as his basis, Laurence Kohlberg proposed that moral development progresses through six levels of moral reasoning: *punishment–obedience*, *exchange of favours*, *good boy–nice girl*, *law and order*, *social contract*, and *universal ethical principles* (Kohlberg, 1969, 1975).

Between the ages of 4 and 6, children have a punishment–obedience orientation to moral reasoning. Their decisions are based on the physical consequences of an act: Will they be punished or rewarded? Outcomes are paramount, and there is very little comprehension of a person's motive or intention. Children's egocentrism at this stage limits their ability to see other points of view or alternatives.

Between the ages of 6 and 9, children move into the exchange-of-favours orientation. At this level, judgments are made on the basis of reciprocal favours: "You do this for me and I will do this for you." Fulfilling one's own needs comes first. Children are just beginning to understand the motives behind behaviours and outcomes.

Between the ages of 10 and 15, children move into the good boy–nice girl orientation. Conformity dictates behaviour and reasoning ability. Peer review is strong, and judgments about how to behave are made on the basis of avoiding criticism and pleasing others. The drive to conform to peer pressure is so strong that it is quite common for children to follow peers unquestioningly; at the same time, these children always ask *why* when adults make any requests.

The law-and-order orientation dominates moral reasoning between the ages of 15 and 18. Individuals at this stage of development are quite rigid. Judgments are made on the basis of obeying the law. Motives are understood but not wholeheartedly considered if the behaviour has broken a law. At this stage, teenagers are quick to recognize and point out inconsistencies in expected behaviour. It is quite common to hear them say to adults, "Why do I have to do this? You don't." It is at this stage that adolescents begin to recognize the consequences of their actions.

According to Kohlberg (1969 and 1975) few people reach the last two levels of moral reasoning. The social-contract orientation is reached by some between the ages of 18 and 20. At this level, moral judgments are made on the basis of upholding individual rights and democratic principles. Those who reach this level recognize that individuals differ in their values and do not accept "because I said so" or "that's the way it is" as rationales for rules.

The highest level of moral reasoning is the universal-ethical orientation. Judgments are based on respect for the dignity of human beings and on what is good for humanity, not on selfish interests or standards upheld by authority.

As in cognitive development, the ages mentioned earlier for any of the moral development stages are approximations. Individuals continually move back and forth between stages, depending on the moral situation at hand, especially at transitional points between stages.

Behaviour: The Interaction of Cognitive and Moral Development

In order to understand how children perceive what is right and wrong, what cognitive skills they are able to use, and what motivates their social and academic behaviour, teachers must know the stages of moral and cognitive growth. They must also recognize common developmental behaviours that are a result of the interaction of the cognitive and moral stages through which the children pass. Although this interaction does not and cannot explain all disruptive classroom behaviours, it does provide a basis on which we can begin to understand many disruptive behaviours. Table 3.1 summarizes the cognitive and moral stages of development, their characteristics, and associated behaviours.

At the beginning of elementary school, students are in the preoperational stage cognitively and the punishment–obedience stage morally. Their behaviour is a result of the interplay of such factors as their egocentricity, limited sense of time and space, little comprehension of others' motives, and short attention span. At this stage, children become frustrated easily, have difficulty sharing, argue frequently, believe that they are right and their classmates wrong, and tattle a lot.

From roughly grades 4 to 9, children are in the concrete operational stage cognitively and somewhere between the exchange-of-favours and the good boy–nice girl stages morally. Early in this period, students form and re-form cliques, act on opinions based on a single or very few concrete characteristics, and tell secrets. They employ many annoying attention-seeking behaviours to please the teacher. Later in the period, the effects of peer conformity appear. Students are often off task because they are constantly in conversation with their friends. Those who do not fit into the peer group are excluded and ridiculed.

TABLE 3.1 Cognitive and Moral Development with Common Associated Behaviours

Cognitive Stage (age in yrs)	Cognitive Abilities	Moral Stage	Moral Reasoning	Common Behaviours
Sensorimotor (0–2)	Use of senses to "know" environment			
Preoperational (2–7)	Difficulty with conceiving others' points of view (egocentric) Sense of time and space limited to short duration/ close proximity Difficulty thinking through steps or decisions Acts impulsively	Punishment– obedience (4–6)	Actions based on physical outcome Little comprehension of motives Egocentric	Inattentiveness Easily frustrated Difficulty sharing Arguments during day
Concrete Operational (7–12)	Limited ability to think about thinking Often will not check conclusions Unaware of and unconcerned with their own inconsistencies	Exchange of favours (6–9)	Actions based on reciprocal favours Fulfilling one's own needs comes first Beginning to understand motives	Cliques Attention-getting behaviour Exclusion of certain classmates Inattentiveness during periods of discussion "Know-it-all" attitude
Formal Operational (12+)	Able to think about thinking Can use independent critical thinking skills Can consider motives; the past, present, and future; the abstract; and the ideal	Law and order (15–18)	Rigid judgments based on following the law Motives and consequences recognized	Point out inconsistencies between behaviours and rules Challenge rules and policies Demand rationale behind rules Will not unquestioningly accept authority Argumentative
		Social contract (18–20)	Actions based on upholding individual rights and democratic principles	Refuse to change even in face of punishment
		Universal ethical (few people reach this level)	Actions based on respect for human dignity	Refuse to change even in face of punishment

Students still have little patience with long discussions and lengthy explanations. They are unaware of, or unconcerned about, inconsistencies in their own thinking. They are closed-minded, often using such phrases as, "I know!"; "Do we have to discuss this?"; or "I don't care!" with a tone that communicates nonchalance.

By the time students are leaving grade 8 and entering high school, most of them are in the formal operational stage cognitively and moving from the good boy–nice girl stage to the law-and-order stage morally. By the end of high school, a few of them have reached the social-contract level.

At this stage, students can deal with abstractness and conceive of many possibilities and ideals, as well as the reality of their environment. Although peer pressure is still strong, they begin to see the need and rationale for rules and policies. Eventually, they see the need to protect rights and principles. They are now attempting to discover who they are, what they believe in, and what they are competent in.

Because students at this stage are searching for self-identity and are able to think abstractly, they often challenge the traditional values taught in school and home. They need to have a valid reason for why everything is the way it is. They will not accept "because I said so" as a legitimate reason to conform to a rule. Some young people will hold to a particular behaviour, explanation, or judgment—even in the face of punishment—if they feel that their individual rights have been challenged or violated. Unfortunately, many of these behaviours are carried out in an argumentative format.

There have been a number of studies supporting the idea that normal developmental changes can lead to disruptive behaviour. Jessor and Jessor (1977) found that the correlates of misbehaviour in school are "(1) growth in independence; (2) decline in traditional ideology; (3) increase in relativistic morality; (4) increase in peer orientation; and (5) increase in modelling problem behaviours." They concluded that the normal course of developmental change leans toward a greater probability of problems; however, Clarizio and McCoy (1983) have found problem behaviours that occur as a developmental phenomenon have a higher probability of being resolved with increasing age. A study of 400 famous 20th-century men and women concluded that four out of five had experienced difficulties and problems related to school and schooling (Goertzel and Goertzel, 1962), which appears to support Clarizio and McCoy's findings.

INSTRUCTIONAL COMPETENCE

At first glance, it would seem that the teacher has little or no control over the five influences of misbehaviour that have been discussed thus far. Although it is true that a teacher cannot significantly alter the course of most of these societal, familial, and developmental events, she can control her instructional competence. Excellent instructional competence can minimize the negative effects that could be triggered by these ongoing events, maximize the learning potential in the classroom, and prevent misbehaviour caused by poor instructional methodology. Case 3.13 describes the difficult consequences for a teacher who did not understand the *art* of teaching.

In Case 3.13, why does Ms. Cook, who is knowledgeable and enthusiastic about her subject matter and enjoys working with young people, have such management problems? Why do otherwise well-behaved students misbehave to such an extent in

CASE 3.13

Not Being Able to Teach

Ms. Cook loves mathematics and enjoys working with young people, which she often does in camp and youth organizations. After graduating with a B.Sc. in mathematics, she goes on to earn a master's degree in math and becomes certified to teach at the secondary level. She obtains a teaching position at a progressive suburban junior high school.

Ms. Cook conscientiously plans for all of her algebra and geometry classes and knows the material thoroughly. Within a few months, however, her classes are characterized by significant discipline problems. Most of her students are out of their seats, talking, throwing paper, and speaking out. They come in unprepared and, in a few instances, openly confront Ms. Cook's procedures and competence. Even though she is given assistance, supervision, and support from the administration, Ms. Cook decides not to return for her second year of teaching.

In an attempt to understand the class's behaviour, the students are interviewed at the end of the school year. The following are the most common responses concerning Ms. Cook's methods:

1. Gave unclear explanations.
2. Discussed topics having nothing or little to do with the subject at hand.
3. Kept repeating understood material.
4. Wrote things on the board but never explained them, and her board work was sloppy.
5. Would say, "We already did this" when asked for help.
6. Did not involve the whole class and called on the same people.
7. Had difficulty giving clear answers to questions.
8. Didn't explain how to apply the material.
9. Always used her note cards.
10. Could not determine why the class was having difficulty understanding the material.
11. Either gave the answers to the homework or didn't go over it, so no one had to do it.

Questions to Consider

1. What is the common theme among Ms. Cook's students' complaints?
2. Describe Ms. Cook's beliefs about teaching.
3. What three suggestions would you have for Ms. Cook?

one particular class? The students' responses indicate a reasonable answer: the teacher's lack of skill in basic instructional methodology.

Because of Ms. Cook's instructional skill deficiencies, her students did not accord to her *expert power*, the social authority and respect a teacher receives because she possesses special knowledge and expertise (French and Raven, 1960). This and other authority bases are discussed in depth in Chapter 5, "Philosophical Approaches to Classroom Management." Her inability to communicate content clearly, evaluate and remediate student misunderstandings, and explain the relevancy of the content to her students' lives caused Ms. Cook's students to fail to recognize her expertise in the field of mathematics.

Happy teacher teaching her two students inside the school.
© Racorn/Shutterstock

A teacher's ability to explain and clarify is foremost in developing authority. Kounin (1970) and Wentzel (2010) have found that teachers who are liked are described by students as those who can explain the content well, whereas those who are disliked leave students in some state of confusion. They also noted that when students are fond of their teachers, they are more likely to behave appropriately and are more motivated to learn. As Tanner has stated, "Teacher effectiveness, as perceived by pupils, invests the teacher with classroom authority" (1978, 67). To students, teacher effectiveness translates to "explaining the material so that we can understand it." When this occurs, students regard the teacher as competent, and the teacher is invested with authority.

RESILIENCY

This chapter summarizes many of the ills of society and how such environments can negatively affect students' behaviour (Health Canada, 2013). These negative influences are often called risk factors. Many of these risks are beyond the control of teachers and schools and include social and economic disadvantages, dysfunctional child-raising practices, family discord and divorce, mental health issues, antisocial peer group, and trauma. These factors are cumulative; the risk for poor life outcome rises sharply as the number of risk factors increase (Schunk and Mullen, 2012; Ungar, 2012). However, many children rise above the risks in their lives to become competent people. When this occurs, it is said that they are resilient and have adapted successfully to overcome severe stressors and risks in their daily lives (Zolkoski, and Bullock, 2012). Resilience is a life skill that is developed through handling stress using positive coping patterns that buffer children and reduces the odds that they will develop negative behaviours. It has been shown repeatedly that it is the strong affectionate relationships in the child's life that provide a buffer and bolster resiliency (Cameron, Lau, Tapanya, 2009; Legault, Anawati, and Flynn, 2005; Robinson, McIntyre, and Officer, 2005). Additionally, some gender differences have emerged with boys being more vulnerable and less likely to be resilient because they tend to form fewer close relationships and thus are more likely to display antisocial behaviours. Additional resilience factors include having good teacher role models, the ability to use humour, creativity in the arts, education as a priority, and good nutrition (Cameron, Lau, and Tapanya, 2009).

Resiliency is not a finite characteristic, however, as it is a complex dynamic process reflecting the interactions among cognitive, social, and genetic factors, and teachers should avoid the temptation to generalize or stereotype their students who live in trying circumstances. Most importantly, there are characteristics of the family, school, and community that can aid students in circumventing risks in their lives and being able to display resilient behaviours. Protective factors can be grouped into three main categories: (1) caring and supportive relationships, (2) positive and high expectations, and (3) opportunities for meaningful participation.

Caring supportive teachers are the most frequently encountered positive role models outside the family (Noddings, 1988; Wentzel, 2010). Meaningful student–teacher rapport that is built on trust, care, and respect is motivational for students in jeopardy (Levin and Shanken-Kaye, 2002).

Schools and teachers that establish high academic and behavioural standards help students—provided support is available to help them to achieve these standards. Also, providing opportunities for involvement in meaningful class, school, and community responsibilities and projects helps students find a sense of purpose and meaning in their lives that makes them resilient against less positive aspects of their existence. Overall, the research suggests that teachers do not need a series of strategies to help their students develop resiliency, rather, they need to be positive and encouraging, and should serve as role models from the beginning of the school experience until the final grade.

Summary

Although there are numerable influences on students' behaviour in schools, this chapter has focused on some of the major ones. Societal changes, most notably the effects of the knowledge explosion and the media revolution, have created an environment that is vastly different from the one that children of previous generations grew up in. More children now than ever before live in single-parent homes. Also, more children today are living at or below the poverty level than in previous generations. Because of these and other factors, some children's basic needs, including the need for self-esteem, are not met by the home. Such out-of-school experiences are much more significant predictors of school behaviour than children's in-school experiences. When a child's basic need for self-esteem is not met at home and/or is not met at school, discipline problems frequently result.

Throughout the school year, children's cognitive and moral development, as well as their continual need for social recognition, are reflected in their behaviour. Teachers have little or no control over many of these developments. What they can control is their own instructional competence. Excellent instruction can ameliorate the effects of outside influences and prevent the misbehaviour that occurs as a direct result of poor instruction. Effective teaching techniques are covered in detail in Chapter 6, "The Professional Teacher."

Key Terms

instructional practices/strategies/techniques/methodology: procedures that instructors use to deliver lesson materials.

off-task/norm-violating behaviours: conduct that is deemed inappropriate in the current environment.

on-task behaviours: conduct that is deemed appropriate and productive in the current environment.

Exercises

1. Look back on your own school experiences. What are some instructional techniques your teachers used that had the potential to change disruptive student behaviours?
2. What, if anything, can schools and classroom teachers do to help students meet the following basic human needs: (a) physiological, (b) safety and security, and (c) belonging and affection?
3. Self-esteem can be conceptualized mathematically as follows:

$$\text{Self-Esteem} = \text{Significance} + \text{Competence} + \text{Power} + \text{Virtue}$$

How does the self-esteem equation help to explain why students behave disruptively inside and outside the classroom?
4. How does the self-esteem equation provide insight into the types of interventions that can lead to decreasing a student's disruptive behaviour?
5. How does self-esteem or lack of self-esteem relate to success or failure?
6. Even though they are beyond the school's control, changes in society can influence student behaviour in school. What changes in society during the last 15 years do you feel have had negative influences on classroom behaviour?
7. In your opinion, can television programs and films cause students to misbehave in the classroom? If so, list some specific examples to support your opinion. If not, explain why.
8. Explain why some educational researchers believe that cognitive development is a prerequisite for moral development.
9. Considering students' cognitive development, how might an instructor teach the following concepts in grades 3, 7, and 11?
   a. volume of a rectangular solid = L H W H H
   b. civil rights and equality
   c. subject–predicate agreement
   d. gravity
10. How might inappropriate teaching of these concepts for the cognitive level of the students contribute to classroom discipline problems?
11. Considering students' moral development, what can we expect as typical reactions to the following events in each of the following grades?

Event	One	Four	Seven	Twelve
a. A student from a poor family steals the lunch ticket of a student from a wealthier family.				
b. A teacher gives the entire class a detention because of the disruptive behaviour of a few.				
c. A student destroys school property and allows another student to be falsely accused and punished for the vandalism.				
d. A student has points subtracted from her test score for talking after her test paper was already turned in.				

12. What are some normal behaviours for elementary students or high school students (considering their developmental level) that can be disruptive in a classroom?

13. What might a teacher do to allow the normal behaviours (listed in your answer to question 12) to be expressed, while at the same time preventing them from disrupting learning?

14. Disruptive students often rationalize their inappropriate behaviour by blaming it on the teacher: "I'll treat Mr. Lee with respect when he treats me with respect." Unfortunately, teachers often rationalize their negative behaviour toward a student by blaming it on the student: "I'll respect Nicole when she respects me." Using the levels of moral development, explain why the student's rationalization is understandable but the teacher's is not.

Weblinks

Behavioural Planning

www.edu.gov.mb.ca/k12/specedu/beh
Helps educators develop a range of responses to students with behaviour problems.

Media Smarts

http://mediasmarts.ca/
"Canada's Centre for Digital and Media Literacy"—A Canadian website that provides "Resources and support for everyone interested in media literacy and digital literacy for young people."

Canadian Council on Social Development

http://www.ccsd.ca/
"CCSD will help build and fortify the needed collaborator circles to address the real world issues that plague us today, and build a stronger, more resilient society for all of us."

Government of Saskatchewan

http://www.education.gov.sk.ca/
Provides many valuable educational documents and resources. For example, in the search box enter "*challenging behaviour*". There are 75 items from that site alone. (e.g http://www.education.gov.sk.ca/search?c=education&q=challenging+behaviour&x=10&y=5)

TeacherNet

Archived at http://webarchive.nationalarchives.gov.uk/*/http://www.teachernet.gov.uk/
Also, the Department for Education can be found at http://www.education.gov.uk/schools
The above two sites from the UK are packed with resources designed to help teachers in the many aspects of teaching.

Active Healthy Kids Canada

http://www.activehealthykids.ca/ReportCard/SedentaryBehaviours.aspx
See also: http://dvqdas9jty7g6.cloudfront.net/reportcards2012/AHKC%202012%20-%20Report%20Card%20Long%20Form%20-%20FINAL.pdf
A site designed to "get kids moving."

4

Bullying and Cyberbullying: Implications for the Classroom

FOCUS ON THE PRINCIPLES OF CLASSROOM MANAGEMENT

1. What does a teacher need to know about bullying and cyberbullying?

2. What can a teacher do to help both the bully and the victim?

3. How can a teacher prevent bullying in the classroom and in the school?

INTRODUCTION

Bullying is one of the most prevalent forms of violence and has become a great concern in Canadian schools, especially with recent media coverage of tragic teen suicides and the introduction of provincial anti-bullying bills. Teachers often feel as though they are on the front lines observing acts of bullying and seeing the pain they can cause. These situations are among the most challenging ones for teachers as they search for appropriate responses and actions that can address the needs of all parties. This increasing concern is timely because, along with the tragic suicide cases, Canada was recently identified as possessing the ninth highest rate of bullying in the 13-years-old category on a scale of 35 countries (Statistics Canada, 2013). The issue of bullying also frequently resonates with teachers at a personal level because it is not uncommon for many adults to have an unpleasant memory related to bullying, either when they were the **victim** of bullying and felt humiliated or ostracised or when they themselves acted as the **bully**. Adults often also have bad memories of having observed acts of bullying. Such memories are deeply affecting, and they often remain in individual psyches as important elements in personal growth and development (Bazelon, 2013). For all these reasons, understanding how to prevent bullying and using appropriate **intervention** techniques and strategies when bullying occurs are part of managing a positive classroom and school environment.

Today, bullying is the most common form of violence experienced by young people with at least 1 in 3 adolescent students in Canada reporting that they have been bullied recently, and 47 percent of Canadian parents reporting having a child who is a victim of bullying (Statistics Canada, 2013). Frequently experienced at school, it is identified by students as a bigger problem than drugs, alcohol, or racism (Hirsch, Lowen, and Santorelli, 2012). Bullying in schools is also receiving a great deal of media attention and concern because it has an enormously detrimental effect on schools as safe learning environments. Once bullying occurs in a person's life, a number of undesirable outcomes are possible, including drug and alcohol abuse, anxiety, low self-esteem and social withdrawal, insecurity, and aggressive reactions. There is, thus, a professional obligation for teachers to understand and recognize bullying in all its manifestations and implications, and it is imperative that they establish some explicit plans for counteracting it when it inevitably raises its ugly head in their classrooms or schools. Carefully watching students' interactions in their classrooms and on the playground is also a teacher's responsibility, as bullying in its various guises can either be extremely obvious or cleverly hidden.

Whatever its manifestation, at its core, bullying is a systematic form of violence that is cruel, devious, and harmful, and which can never be dismissed as benign (Mason, 2013). One of the consequences of bullying in schools is that it infringes on the victims' basic right to human dignity, their sense of freedom and security, and their right to privacy.

CASE STUDY

Joel is an 11-year-old in grade 6 who has recently transferred from his old school to a new one in a new neighbourhood. This transition is a difficult one for him, causing him to feel withdrawn and uncomfortable in this new environment. Joel has noticed that a boy in his class, Mark, has many friends and appears to be a leader and is always the centre of activities. To compound Joel's feelings of insecurity in his new classroom, Mark seems dismissive of any tentative overtures Joel makes to be included.

One day, during recess, Mark approached Joel and said, "Why did you have to come here? I bet nobody liked you in your old school because you are stupid."

Joel could not think of anything to say in response so he just started to walk away.

Mark moved quickly to confront him and pushing his hands into Joel's chest aggressively yelled, "Where do you think you are going? I am talking to you, you little creep!"

A few of the students quickly became interested, gathering around the boys saying, "You tell him Mark!", "Go back where you came from!" and then continually calling Joel "little creep." Other students expressed disgust with Mark's aggression saying, "Leave him alone." Still others said nothing but watched to see what would happen next.

At that moment, Joel started to cry and ran from the school yard, going straight home. While he was tearfully telling his mother about his experiences, the phone rang. It was the teacher, Miss Aldecott, inquiring about Joel. Sounding very upset, Joel's mother reiterated Joel's story about the incident. Miss Aldecott attempted to defuse the situation by saying, "Boys will be boys," and assuring Joel's mother that she would speak to Mark, assuring her that all would be forgotten by the next day.

The next day, Joel felt reluctant about going to school but his mother promised him that everything would be fine. Joel felt very nervous about going on the school yard at recess, fearing a repetition of the previous day's bullying; however, everyone was acting as though nothing had happened—but then Joel began to notice that several students were looking at their cell phones, glancing at him, and laughing. He pulled his phone from his pocket and checked his messages. Sure enough, there was a message from Mark with a picture of Joel attached with the label, "Only cry-babies run home." Mark's closest friends began to laugh and to fake crying and rubbing their eyes. Joel felt miserable but tried to hide his feelings to avoid further humiliation.

Mark continued to harass Joel by pushing or punching him in the hallways when no one was watching. This behaviour continued for a couple of weeks off and on and Joel became increasingly insecure and unhappy. He did not confide, however, in his parents until his mother noticed a bruise on his arm. When his parents probed, Joel first hesitated but finally told them everything that he was enduring. Remembering the ineffective response of the teacher, his parents decided to call the police.

That same day, the police arrived and Joel told them the entire sequence of events. The police then went directly to Mark's house and asked to speak with him in the presence of his parents. They gave him a strong warning about his bullying behaviour and told him to desist unless he wanted them to take further action. Mark's parents were horrified and reinforced the police position but began to question why Mark had chosen to be a bully.

The police had really frightened Mark, and his parents' reaction had made him feel ashamed. The next day he went to school and discovered that everyone knew the police had been at his house discussing his behaviour toward Joel. His normal group of friends avoided him, and he began to feel isolated and depressed. Over the next few weeks, his parents grew increasingly worried about his absolute refusal to go back to school. The situation became so extreme that they sought professional medical help for Mark. Mark was not able to attend school for a number of months and when he did return, his parents transferred him to another school.

Questions to Consider

1. Is there something Miss Aldecott could have done to help Joel integrate into his new school more successfully?
2. What actions warranted calling Mark a bully?
3. What did the bystanders do in this case? What could they have done to defuse the situation?
4. What, if anything, could Miss Aldecott have done the first day to have ensured the bullying was not continued?
5. Why did Joel not confide in anyone as the bullying continued?
6. Did Joel's parents do the right thing by calling the police? What other options might have been more effective?
7. In your opinion, which is more common currently: direct bullying or cyberbullying? Which do you believe has the most harmful effects for those involved?
8. At what point did Mark become a victim, too?

BULLYING PATTERNS

It is important to recognize bullying patterns and, to that end, here are three characteristics that describe bullying.

1. The bullying action is repeated again and again. It is not a one-time occurrence.
2. The bullying is intentional. The bully wants to cause fear, distress, or even actual physical harm to the victim. The behaviour is not an accident in any way. Additionally, the bully takes pleasure in the negative impact the behaviour has on the victim.
3. Bullying does not occur when people are evenly matched. There is always an imbalance in power or control between the victim and the bully. Bullies are generally one or more of the following: stronger, older, more popular, or wealthier; possess better technological skills; know something embarrassing about the victim; are homophobic; or focus on a person's limitations.

FORMS OF BULLYING

Bullying can take a variety of forms that are all extensions of the previously mentioned characteristics. First, bullying can be physical, with either a person or his property being harmed or damaged in some way. Physical bullying, which is most obvious to an onlooker, can take the form of hitting, punching, slapping, pushing, pinching, chasing, or kicking. It also take more subtle forms of physical violation, such as locking a person in a confined space or touching a person in an unwelcoming or threatening way or destroying or stealing personal belongings.

Second, bullying can be verbal. In verbal bullying, a person is intentionally hurt through insults or name-calling, threats, or hurtful teasing or taunting, sometimes with the intent of providing amusement to those nearby. A more insidious form or verbal bullying involves the use of racial or homophobic comments. This common form of bullying is particularly devastating, but is not always observed by others, especially by adults, even when they are in the vicinity. Verbal bullying may also take the form of spreading rumours or gossip about others, regardless of whether the information is accurate. This form of verbal bullying is especially prevalent among adolescents.

A final common type of bullying takes the form of social actions. In these cases, a person can be ostracized from a social group. The ostracization is often accompanied by threatening or taunting notes, negative social media messages, and/or threatening telephone calls. Social bullying can manifest itself through mobbing: humiliating or threatening gestures made in public that are designed to put the victim down. Social bullying can also take the form of prominently displaying insulting or threatening graffiti in a variety of places.

A more recent and equally disturbing type of bullying that can be found in isolation or in combination with the methods already mentioned is cyberbullying, which uses online social media—often in the form email or text messaging—to threaten, put down, spread rumours, intimidate, or make fun of someone (Li, 2007).

Cyberbullying

The term *cyberbullying* is a relatively new word the definition of which evolves at about the same pace as the technology that acts as a conduit for this type of abuse, degradation, insult, and rumour generation. Cyberbullying refers to the posting of usually anonymous, mean-spirited messages about a person (often a student) through a variety of social media and electronic devices (Bolton & Graeves 2005).

The last word of the definition, *anonymously*, also includes being invisible, which are aspects that set face-to-face bullying and cyberbullying apart. In this case, the target is always accessible, the abuse is replicable easily, and the audience for the bullying tactics can be limitless. Many young people who are being harassed online also endure simultaneous face-to-face bullying (Sontag, Clemans, Grabe, and Lyndon, 2011), and the combined damage can be particularly harmful (Hinduja and Patchin, 2010). The hurt that these bullies inflict may have effects that can lead to disastrously extreme results. Recently, there have been several cases where victims of cyberbullying have become so depressed that they ended their own lives.

Another factor that sets cyberbullying apart from traditional bullying is that it is not necessary for the **cyberbully** to have a physical advantage over the person at the "receiving end" of the attack(s). It is also not compulsory for the electronic tormenter to have a mastery of the English language. They have the luxury of composing their insults behind closed doors and taking as much time as they need to tweak their e-insults for maximum injury. Also, children's digital messages can be edited by others to change the meaning and then forwarded to other children to embarrass, intimidate, and insult— often in an attempt to create humour at the expense of the original message creator.

The electronic nature of cyberbullying allows the virtual perpetrator to abuse the victim but remain hidden behind the technology. In fact, not only is proximity unnecessary, the cyberbully may execute the assaults from anywhere on the planet, thereby allowing a high degree of anonymity; however, the results of the harassment are no less devastating than face-to-face bullying (Limber, 2012). In fact, cyberbullies are not necessarily the same ones who conduct face-to-face bullying. Many young people who are not otherwise aggressive may be perpetrators of cyberbullying because technology grants a sense of safety and distance from the victim (Tokunaga, 2010). Cyberbullies report that they bully online because it makes them feel funny, popular, and powerful—although many reported feeling guilty afterward. Victims of cyberbullying have reported feeling, angry, sad, and depressed after being bullied online. Unfortunately, most young people who are cyberbullied believe they have little recourse when they are targeted in this way. Most of those who admitted to being cyberbullied did not tell anyone about it (Hargrove, 2013; Mishna, Cook, Gadalla, Daciuk, and Solomon, 2010).

A number of different kinds of cyberbullying have been identified (Canadian Red Cross, 2014). These include:

Harassment—repeatedly sending offensive, rude and insulting messages to an individual.

Denigration—distributing derogatory and often untrue information about someone else by posting it on a webpage, or sending it through email or instant messaging, or posting or circulating photos of someone in a compromising position or pictures that are digitally altered.

Flaming—online "fighting" using electronic messages with angry and vulgar language.

Impersonation—hacking into an email or social networking account and using that person's online identity to send or post vicious or embarrassing material to others or about others.

    Outing or Trickery—sharing someone's secrets or embarrassing information or tricking someone into revealing secrets or embarrassing material about themselves, which is then forwarded to others.

    Cyber Stalking—repeatedly sending threatening or highly intimidating messages to the receiver, or engaging in online activities that make a person afraid for his personal safety.

Sometimes cyberbullies combine the previously mentioned methods to humiliate publically the victim; for instance, a cyberbully posts a derogatory message about a fellow student on Facebook and others "gang up" on that student and bombard him with flaming emails. Those who participate in such actions are more likely to be supportive of cyberbullying without realizing the pivotal role they are playing in harming the victim.

SOCIETAL INFLUENCES ON BULLIES

Before considering causes and effects of bullying, it is worth reflecting upon the bigger societal picture that may be related to this issue. Among adult Canadians, 38 percent of males and 30 percent of females reported having experienced occasional or frequent bullying during their school years. Sadly, the bullying experiences of adults are more than memories, as 40 percent of Canadian workers experience bullying on a weekly basis (Statistics Canada, 2013). Children do not learn their behaviour simply by trying new behaviours and either succeeding or failing; rather, they depend strongly upon the replication of the actions of others. Children are often exposed to adults who bully at all levels, including home life, social interactions, the political arena, and frequently in the evening news. They are also often exposed to violent movies and television shows that have bullying embedded and frequently celebrated in the action.

    According to Social Cognitive Theory, children learn by observing others, with the environment, behaviour, and cognition as the chief factors that combine to influence development (Bandura, 1991; 2001; 2011). For instance, through observational learning, children may adopt certain values by which they may begin to judge the behaviour of others, and later internalize that behaviour as their own. Bandura (2011) identified that observational learning does not limit itself only to the adoption of new, presumably good moral values and behaviours, it also may enforce or weaken existing values; thus, parents and educators need to be especially cognizant of the role model they are providing for young people in their social relationships. When we consider the various forms of bullying that permeate society and serve as potential role models for children and young people's behaviour, perhaps it should not be surprising that many children think it is permissible to bully or be mean to others in order to elevate themselves in the eyes of their peers or to feel superior.

A WORLD-WIDE PROBLEM

Bullying behaviours know no limits and can be found in all countries at all levels of society. Wherever it is found and whatever form it takes, bullying runs counter to the UN Convention of 1990 on the rights of children, which determined that any child has the right to feel safe at home, in school, and in the community. As awareness grows of this antisocial behaviour, many countries have identified bullying as a critical public health issue. For more than 20 years, the World Health Organization has been involved in research studies with international researchers from over 30 countries and has concluded that bullying is a health issue that knows no boundaries (Canadian Council on Learning, 2008). Wherever it occurs, the behavioural patterns and the consequences are the same. Although bullying occurs everywhere in the world, the data is particularly strong for North America, Europe, and Russia, while it appears slightly less prevalent in the Scandinavian countries. We also know that bullying of any kind in any country does not go away without direct intervention. In fact, without intervention, it often gets worse (Larochette, Craig, and Murphy, 2010).

BULLYING AND CYBERBULLYING IN CANADA

Data on bullying has been collected by Canadian researchers since the early 1990s and they have concluded that bullying exists as a serious social problem in schools of all levels in Canada, including the earliest months of schooling, to a degree that it cannot be ignored or discounted (Pepler and Craig, 2011). It is startling to note that among Canadian youth in grades 6 through 10, between 17 and 25 percent report having been bullied once to twice in the past few months. Among adolescents, 1 in 3 students report having been bullied recently (Statistics Canada, 2012). The result of bullying is that the victims often suffer from severe anxiety, intimidation, and chronic fear (Battey and Ebbeck, 2013; Marini, Spear, and Bombay, 1999; Smokowski and Kopasz, 2004). Systematic observations of children on playgrounds note that some type of bullying occurs every 7 minutes. When children are in the classroom, bullying occurs once every 25 minutes (O'Connell, Pepler, and Craig, 1999). Males are more likely to be bullies and females are more likely to be victims and are more likely to report the incident to adults (Li, 2007). More recently, 10 percent of adults who live with adolescents report the occurrence of cyberbullying (Statistics Canada, 2012). Girls tend to be more involved in cyberbullying and are more frequently bullied than are boys. Boys are more likely to both experience and get involved in direct, physically aggressive forms of bullying (Mason, 2013). It should then come as no surprise that Canadian children spend a considerable chunk of their time using communication gadgets. Canadian children between 8 and 18 years old spend an average 6 hours per day using laptops and smartphones for communication, entertainment and as an information source (Rubin, 2014).

According to a Canadian study by Janosz, Archambault, Pagani, Morin, and Bowen (2008), there are equally concerning and serious detrimental effects to merely witnessing school violence. Students who witness violence can feel anxiety and depression, which can result in either aggression or feelings of victimization whether they were the recipient of the violence or not. These feelings, at their root, manifest a sense of powerlessness, fear, and insecurity—none of which are readily acknowledged by youth but which they often articulate as a dislike of school. Over 50 percent of students also report that they hear verbal abuse at least several times a week and often every day in their lives. Over 20 percent of students have heard threats to others and about one in six students reported observing older students harassing younger ones and 12 percent reported having been bullied themselves once a week or more.

It is important to note that there is increasing recognition that this most important topic needs to be viewed in new ways if we are to be successful in creating safe environments for all students. There is an instinctive approach of feeling sorry for the victim and a desire to provide the victim with help or to punish the bully so that justice appears to be served. Additionally, there is a tendency to identify bystanders and shower them with guilt. This traditional thinking and accompanying actions are questionable because they are largely unsuccessful at having any significant impact (Mason, 2013). Bullies are part of the equation, as are impassive bystanders. If the problem is to be remedied and relationships restored so the community becomes safe for all members, each participant in the bullying situation needs to be addressed so that violation of rules and moral integrity can be repaired for everyone's well-being. It is vital to elevate the repairing of community relationships above the desire for revenge and punishment.

According to the Canadian Teachers Federation (2008), 34 percent of Canadian teachers surveyed knew of students in their community who had been victims of cyberbullying during the past year and additionally, one respondent in five was aware of teachers who had been cyberbullied. In this same survey, 89 percent of teachers ranked cyberbullying as their issue of highest concern. Surveys of Canadian teachers confirm that teachers believe that bullying and violence are serious problems in Canadian schools (Mishna et al., 2010). In 2011, another research project reported that cyberbullying is most rampant on social networking platforms as young people abandon email in favour of text and instant messaging (Knighton, 2012). About half of all victims of cyberbullying report that they know their perpetrators and that they do not reveal their names to adults (Tokunaga, 2010).

Nova Scotia's Cyberbullying Task Force Online Survey in 2011 found that 75 percent of respondents said they believe that cyberbullying is a serious problem in that province's schools. Additionally 60 percent of student responders indicated that they had been cyberbullied (MacKay, 2012).

A Statistics Canada report from 2009 found that girls are more often involved in cyberbullying incidents than boys are (86 percent compared to 55 percent) and that cyberbullying incidents are slightly more prevalent in students between those aged 8 and 12 years old (Hargrove, 2013). Nevertheless, it is a fact in the lives of many young people between the ages of 8 and 18.

In one large study of 7313 grade 6 to grade 10 students, depression was associated with four forms of bullying (Wang, Nansel, and Iannotti, 2011). This study is one of a growing number of studies that examines depression and the association with various forms of bullying and victimization. The forms are identified as physical, verbal, relational, and cyber. These researchers also observe increased depression levels among bullies, victims, and bully-victims (a person who is both a bully and a victim of bullying). It is important to note that higher depression was found in cyberbullying victims than in bullies or bully-victims in face-to-face encounters. Results suggest that more research is needed on this very critical issue that is emerging and evolving with the technology.

CHARACTERISTICS OF BULLIES

Bullies share some common characteristics including the possibility that they may witness physical or verbal violence or aggression at home. As a result, they often see this behaviour through a biased lens that reinforces aggression toward others. It is what they know! They have not been taught to view their actions in relation to how those actions make others feel. Physically they are usually strong, think highly of

8

themselves, and may be popular with their peers. As they thrive on creating fear, they are constantly teasing or laughing at those around them as a sort of test. They are looking for a victim who does not retaliate or report the incident but rather one who shows weakness and fear. The bully usually establishes a victim after the first interaction when the imbalance of power becomes evident to both the bully and the victim. This pattern explains why children who are targeted usually find themselves in the same situation over and over again even when they change schools.

Bullies are of concern to educators because they have certain characteristics that need modifying as they mature to become productive citizens.

1. They generally lack empathy and concern for others and tend to demonstrate a strong need to dominate or even subdue others.
2. Quick to anger, they are frequently defiant, oppositional, and aggressive toward intervening adults.
3. As they mature, they are at increased risk of becoming involved in criminal activities and often become engaged in illegal drug use and other antisocial behaviours (Beran, Hughes, and Lupart, 2008).

CHARACTERISTICS OF VICTIMS

Victims of bullying are usually people who are perceived to be vulnerable or different in some way. They tend to dress differently, often being part of an under-represented group. Those who learn more slowly or who are unskilled in technological or other skills can also become targets for bullying. Conversely, in some cases high achievers can also be targeted by bullies. Basically, weaknesses or differences of any kind make a person vulnerable to aggressive bullies. Three characteristics have been identified in recognizing exploitable weaknesses in victims.

1. They may have poor social skills that create difficulty interacting with their peers and "fitting in" or in picking up appropriate social cues. These deficits may make the persons appear odd or different from the majority of their peers at an age where "sameness" is valued.
2. They have few or no friends and thus lack a social network to help when harassment occurs. Newcomers to a school may undergo a period of vulnerability in the process of adjustment before they make friends and may become easy targets for bullies.
3. They may be shy and have nonconfrontational personalities, generally failing to assert themselves against their aggressors. Rather, victims may respond by crying, giving in to demands, begging to be left alone, or merely carefully avoiding the bully by changing routes from school or practicing careful avoidance on the playground (Gini, 2008).

Alternatively, some victims may be proactive when attacked by a bully but are socially unskilled, and their actions may irritate their peers and bullies further. They are not accomplished fighters, either physically or verbally, and at times, their behaviour may allow other children or even adults to feel that the attacks are justified. It has also been suggested that this irritation to others can sometimes be caused by hyperactivity disorders in victims (Toblin, Schwartz, Hopmeyer Gorman, and Abou-ezzeddone, 2005).

CHARACTERISTICS OF BYSTANDERS

Most young people have been in the role of bystanders of a bullying incident at some time in their lives where their presence has had the potential to influence both the bully and the victim (Mason, 2013). Bystanders can choose to play a positive role in the bullying situation by trying to make the bully stop, by reporting the incident to someone in authority, or by comforting the victim. Conversely, they can choose to encourage the bully by actively joining in the bullying, by cheering and encouraging, or by laughing during or after bullying incidents. Finally, bystanders can simply remain neutral by choosing not to become involved and by merely observing in silence while providing a passive audience for the bully. The decision to do nothing may actually serve to reinforce the bullies in their actions (Hirsch, Lowen, and Santorelli, 2012). During cyberbullying incidents, which also take place in a public forum with a potentially unlimited audience, bystanders are more inclined to remain passive (Holfeld, 2014). After initially observing the bullying online, however, if the recipients either support negative messages directly or forward them, they join the bullying process (Affan, 2013).

The factors that influence the choices made by bystanders are numerous and include their relationships with the bully or with the victim (Hirsch, Lowen, and Santorelli, 2012). According to Pozzoli and Gini (2012), the context in which the bullying occurs is critical to determining bystander reaction. The contextual environment includes the nature of the peer group, the school, and the parents as well as whether any assertiveness training or bullying intervention has been undergone. Nevertheless, certain general characteristics are common to many bystanders. A primary reason for people remaining passive is the fear of becoming victims themselves by finding themselves as new targets for the bully. Some bystanders feel that if they intervene, they will make the situation worse; therefore, they remain indecisive not knowing what to do. Reporting the incident to authority figures is sometimes viewed negatively as accusations of being a "snitch" or a "tattle tell" can result. They also may feel that adults will not do anything to help the situation. If a culture of respect has been established and a reporting procedure encouraged, however, bystanders are more likely to trust an adult with the bullying information.

While bullies and victims both clearly experience negative effects of the bullying experiences, there are negative effects for the bystanders as well. Bystanders may be afraid to associate with the victim for fear of becoming an additional target. They may also feel guilt and helplessness for not doing anything to stop the bullying. Most concerning is that the power allocated to the bully may become appealing to the bystanders, and they may begin to find bullying acceptable and emulate the bullying activities (Mason, 2013). Teaching bystanders to recognize bullying when they see it, to respond appropriately to it, and to report it to an adult helps alleviate some of the possible negative outcomes for the bystander.

INDICATORS THAT A CHILD IS BEING BULLIED

Although children who are being bullied often remain silent, they do project certain clues to an observant teacher or parent. They may complain in nonspecific terms of being treated poorly by their peers and appear uncharacteristically sad or depressed.

Additionally, there may be physical factors that indicate bullying is occurring; for instance, some children may suffer from lack of sleep and nightmares, or may feel sick, especially in the morning before they go to school. Eating habits may change with children either having no appetite and losing weight or overeating and gaining a large amount of weight. They may also have angry outbursts or become unusually aggressive toward younger children or siblings. Parents may report that their child is unwilling to go to school or that the child changes the route to school or even feigns sickness in order to skip school. A bullied child may come home with torn clothes and unexplained bruises or have inexplicably lost money. Children's relationships and friendships may change. It is likely that both parents and teachers will notice a distinct drop in school performance (Beran, Hughes, and Lupart, 2008).

Studies have shown that children who are bullied or even those who have served as bystanders to bullying generally have higher overall anxiety levels (Carney, Hazler, Hibel, and Grander, 2010). Even more concerning is the fact that research studies have found that a major impact of bullying victimization can be found in an increased incidence of depression up to 35 years later, and the younger the child was at the time of the bullying, the stronger the effect was (Ttofi, Farrington, Losel, and Loeber, 2009). Statistics Canada (2012) points out that any participation in bullying increases the risk of suicidal ideas in youth. Canada has recently had a number of highly public cases where bullying has led to teenage suicide. These deaths have served to further raise public awareness and have resulted in concerted preventative actions at the school and board levels as well as at provincial and federal government levels.

In addition to the immediate impact on the victim, research has also established a relationship between childhood and adolescent bullying and criminal offending in later life (Piquero, Connell, Piquero, Farrington, and Jennings, 2013). Researchers unanimously promote the implementation of anti-bullying programs that could be viewed as a form of early crime prevention (Ttofi, Farrington, Losel, and Loeber, 2011).

HOW TO HELP A CHILD WHO IS BEING BULLIED

First, it is imperative for teachers to be alert and observant regarding the behaviours in his class that may indicate bullying. Remember that the victim is not only hurt and fearful but also usually embarrassed and humiliated, all of which leads to reluctance to tattle for fear of further retribution. Children will only talk to you about their bullying experiences if they feel you will listen and help them. For them, this is a crisis situation and you initially need to remember the three S's of crisis management.

1. *Safe and Secure:* Let children know that you will ensure that they are safe and that you will protect them from any harm. Thank them for sharing and ask them to tell you more about it.
2. *Stability:* Keep the current routines and maintain the status quo in the classroom environment. This can provide comfort to a scared child. Avoid appearing upset or angry yourself. This is another instance of the appropriateness of applying the CALM model and remaining in control of your emotions.
3. *Support:* Validate their fears and experiences in the bullying situation and be reassuring that eventually this crisis will pass (Mason, 2013). Avoid being an

interrogator. Instead, ask them to tell you more about it and validate their feelings and their fear during their description (i.e., "I know you feel worried."; "I see you are distressed.").

Follow these steps in order to write down what happened. Avoid editorializing and suggesting how they could have reacted differently.

1. What happened.
2. Where and when it happened.
3. Names of those involved.
4. Names of witnesses.
5. Nature of the tactics used by the bully.
6. How the victim reacted.
7. How the bully and bystanders responded (Mason, 2013).

An intervention can be set up by a caring and knowledgeable teacher who remains calm, is supportive and reassuring, and reassures by offering to help. An example of one such intervention that can be used by a caring teacher is the Five-Step Technique.

The Five-Step Technique "It's All About Me (and You)"

The Five-Step Technique is a first step in solving a bullying issue. This process brings the bully and victim together for a discussion and explanation of the events in the presence of the teacher. This technique is effective when a teacher becomes aware of a case of bullying, and it provides a chance for resolution and perspective taking. Both victim and bully have a chance to express their rationale, feelings, and interpretations of the incidents. If the bullying persists, parents should be informed.

Three elements are necessary for the success of this technique.

1. The victim prepares a list of "I statements"; for example: "I don't like it when…." and "It makes me feel…."
2. The bully must be the ringleader and be recognized by all as the leader of the bullying.
3. The facilitator must be able to guide the two participants through the five steps.

   Step 1: A meeting is held with the facilitator and the victim to review the victim's concerns. The victim prepares the list of "I" statements and practices saying the list aloud. The facilitator coaches for eye contact, body language, voice tone, and such.

   Step 2: Without prior knowledge, the bully is asked into the room and is seated across from the victim. The facilitator sits to form a triangle of chairs.

   Step 3: The facilitator goes over the rules first. The rules include the following:
   a) Be honest with yourself.
   b) Be honest with each other.
   c) Check any bad attitudes at the door.

   Step 4: The facilitator starts by looking at the bully and says, "(bully's name), I understand you have been paying a lot of attention over the past (give time frame) to (victim's name), and I would like you to hear the results of your actions."

Step 5: The facilitator looks at the victim and has him read the first concern. Once it is read, the facilitator looks at the bully and says, "I would like you to respond to that." (The bully may want to avoid eye contact with the victim, but the facilitator should prompt him to do so.) This process continues until the victim's list is complete with the bully answering each one of the concerns separately.

Ending the Meeting: The victim is excused and the facilitator addresses the bully. "Did you like this meeting today?" Listen to the bully's answer, and then say, "If you do not want to have another meeting then go back and tell your friends there will be no more bullying of (victim's name). If I or anyone else hears of you or your friends continuing the bullying, you will be called back for another meeting."

Note: The bully at this point may try to take on the role of victim, and the facilitator must emphasize that the bully will be brought back in if the bullying does not stop. It might help to suggest the leadership qualities the bully possesses and the fact that others look up to him and the influence he has over the attitudes of others. Finally, make it very clear that this meeting will not be discussed outside the room.

Also: Either the victim or the bully (or both) may shed tears, in which case the facilitator should merely carry on (Michael, 2007).

HOW TO HELP A CHILD WHO IS A BULLY

When you decide to confront a child who is bullying for a one-on-one discussion, and to let him know that while you dislike the behaviour, you like many other qualities you have observed in him. It is, however, vital to make it clear that bullying behaviour is not acceptable and will not be tolerated. Point out that it is harmful to others. Hold the bully accountable for his actions and do not accept any rationalizations made in self-defence. Remember also that some children bully because they have been bullied themselves, so it may be important to watch for this possibility as you are trying to form a picture of what is occurring (Raising Children Network, 2014).

The message to the bully is:

- Stop bullying immediately.
- Bullying will not be tolerated in any form.
- Everyone in every role—bully, bullied, and bystanders—are harmed.
- Bullying sets a bad example for others, especially younger observers.
- Bullying can cause the bully to lose friends.
- Everyone deserves to be treated with dignity and respect.
- Everyone is different and has a right to be different.
- There are other ways to resolve conflict (Mason, 2013).

The discussion could include asking for their side of the story (everyone deserves to be heard). You could also ask about what he was thinking at the time. Contrast that response to what are you feeling now? How do you think the victim is feeling now? What have you been thinking about since the bullying incident(s)? The most important question to which you need to arrive is "What do you need to do to put things right?"

PROTECTING YOUNG PEOPLE FROM CYBERBULLYING

Interventions from teachers and parents may be necessary in some circumstances, but it is increasingly important to try and establish a school or classroom environment where bullying is less likely to occur. Many schools are becoming more proactive about creating policies and pledges to address the issues and have open discussions with students about how they can monitor their own online actions and reputation. It is useful to share all such policies with parents and community partners. Many schools are also training teachers on preventing and responding to cyberbullying.

Students need to understand the harm that cyberbullying causes, and there are plenty of disastrous examples in the news of victims whose parents have shared their stories in the public forum in order to help counter the cyberbullying trend. It is also important that students understand that, generally, whenever there is an online bully and a victim, there are also silent observers (bystanders). A teacher should point out the differences between humour and teasing and hurtful behaviour and taunting, and that the line between them is very fine. They should also identify what is acceptable and what is not.

On the large scale of character development, teachers should model and teach empathy, especially in the context of internet communications. The practical steps of dealing with cyberbullying such as blocking users whose messages are hurtful or threatening should be taught as a first step. Other recommendations include establishing a bullying prevention committee to whom students can report incidents of cyberbullying, either as victims or observers/bystanders. The principal should be informed of these incidents, and he should act upon them. There is also general agreement that there needs to be a national consensus about what constitutes cyberbullying, and similar consequences should apply across the provinces.

Cyber or online bullying concept with two young women students or teenager girls shocked at the text they are reading on their cell phone, perfect for awareness.

© Sylvie Bouchard/Shutterstock

Bring Parents into the Solution

There may already be a policy in place in your school about keeping parents informed, but it is important that teachers make every attempt to ensure that parents understand the full story and become partners in trying to help the bully move past the need to intimidate. Talk about the need to build the bully's self-esteem as well as to provide positive attention both at home and at school. In some cases, a "behaviour contract" may be appropriate. The contract is most effective when it is made with the school, the child, and the parents.

Applying Consequences

If the bully is resistant or repeats the offense, it will be necessary to apply logical and forewarned consequences that are consistent with the policy of the school. It is best to consult with the administration and the parents prior to applying the consequences to gain their support. The key to successfully applying consequences is to avoid punishment for its own sake and rather focus on a discipline that helps the bully learn that his behaviour is inappropriate and harmful (McCready, 2012). Lecturing is not helpful!

Asking how the bully felt while bullying is useful, and follow up by asking how the bully thinks the victim felt. A simple act of kindness to the victim can be effective learning for the bully. For instance:

- For destroying personal belongings: Replace them.
- For physically harming a classmate: Write a note poem or story about what's great about the person (best applied when the victim is a former friend).
- For starting a rumour: Write a letter about how the rumour hurt the person and tell the truth to those who heard the rumour.
- For blaming the victim for something the bully did: Publicly acknowledge and take responsibility (McCready, 2012).

Preventing Bullying in Schools

"No one is born hating another person because of the color of his skin, or his background, or his religion. People must learn to hate, and if they can learn to hate, they can be taught to love, for love comes more naturally to the human heart than its opposite." (Mandela, 1995 p. 622)

Given the prevalence of bullying in its various forms and the accompanying enormously destructive results combined with the fact that so much bullying occurs at school, educators have both a professional and moral obligation to understand the phenomenon and to know the best ways to intervene. The nature of intervention and its effectiveness has been under much debate over the years; however, there is agreement that the "Let them work it out" approach or similar ignoring techniques are insufficient. Thus, as the new millennium progresses, every successful teacher will need to be able to recognize the genesis of potential bullying situations and manage these behaviours properly. Teachers must be proficient in defusing such situations and directing students toward more prosocial means of conflict resolution (Durlak, Weissberg, Dymnicki, Taylor, and Schellinger, 2011; Novak and Purkey, 2001). Some educators have suggested that given the prevalence of bully activities, teachers should not wait for bullying to occur but rather assume that it is happening and behave accordingly (Hirsch, Lowen, and Santorelli, 2012). There are several practices and programs that have been designed to reduce and hopefully prevent bullying and cyberbullying. Many schools are becoming more proactive about creating policies and pledges to address the issues and have open discussions with students about how they can monitor their own online actions and reputation. It is useful to share all such policies with parents and community partners. Many schools are also training teachers on preventing and responding to cyberbullying.

Many governments have implemented "safe school" legislation to enable schools to become free of violence and fear so that learning can be the focus. In the following pages, several proactive prevention methods, interventions, and school programs will be discussed.

WHAT TEACHERS NEED TO LEARN ABOUT BULLYING

Before embarking on any program of intervention or prevention, teachers need to consider the existing anti-bullying legislation from the province, policies of their school board and the school, as well as any existing local initiatives. They should also review current and accurate data on bullying behaviours and victimization. Consideration needs to be given to the population or composition of students and parents including such factors as race, religion, and culture. It is also useful to consider the rates and nature of hate crimes committed by minors in the area. Hate crimes are defined as criminal offenses motivated by hate toward an identifiable group. Unfortunately, hate crimes in Canada are on the rise, with most people aware that the number of hate crimes reported differs sharply from the actual number of incidents as many such crimes go unreported (Dauvergne and Brennan, 2009). Sadly, many hate crimes are perpetrated by 12- to 17-year-olds, with the majority of the hate crimes reported listing race or ethnicity as the reason for the incident (Dauvergne and Brennan, 2009). With the increased discussion of religious differences and the growing intolerance in some provinces for immigrants of other cultures and religions, this issue is becoming more relevant to Canadians. Statistics indicate that issues of ethnicity, religion, and sexual orientation are taken seriously by young people today. Perspectives on these issues are learned primarily from the media, from their parents, and from each other. For this reason, young people benefit from a conscious consideration of their personal perspective through the use of anti-bullying programs.

The reality is that most effective anti-bullying programs require engagement beyond the school, and require cooperation among parents, teachers, and the entire community (Mitchell, 2012). Adults in the school need to be models of respectful and caring behaviour toward students, each other, and the school administration. An example of good modelling occurs when adults avoid being passive bystanders and respectfully and quickly intervene when bullying does occur. Once the prior information and behaviour has been consulted, considered, and acted upon, there are a number of different ways to proceed. It is important to remember that when selecting an anti-bullying program of any kind, due diligence needs to be exercised so that the selected program that has evidence of effectiveness around areas of concern for your school or class. Then, the program must be implemented well and monitored judiciously in order to ensure successful outcomes (Jones, Weissbourd, and Ross, 2012).

SCHOOLWIDE ANTI-BULLYING PROGRAMS

More and more schools are establishing programs that help students develop the skills they will need to successfully handle life's challenges and thrive in their learning and social environments. When social and emotional skills and an understanding of moral standards become the focus of the school or classroom, the resulting climate helps prevent or reduce bullying (Bosaki, Marini, and Dane, 2006; Knoff, 2007).

One such program is called Social and Emotional Learning (SEL). Through this program, students acquire the knowledge, skills, and attitudes that need to successfully identify their emotions so they can exercise the control to demonstrate concern and caring for others, build strong interpersonal relationships, make good decisions, and handle challenging social situations positively and constructively (Hirsch, Lowen, and Santorelli, 2012). The five components to attaining these social and emotional skills are:

1. *Self-awareness:* Being able to accurately assess one's feelings and strengths, which contributes to a sense of self-confidence.
2. *Self-management:* Being able to regulate one's emotions to handle stressful situations and control negative impulses and instead express emotions constructively. Also, to learn to set goals and monitor progress toward achieving those goals.
3. *Social awareness:* Developing the ability to take the perspective of and empathize with others; identifying and following societal standards of conduct; and using family, school, and community resources.
4. *Relationship skills:* Establishing and maintaining strong relationships based on cooperation. Being able to resist inappropriate social pressure and resolving interpersonal conflict and knowing when to seek help.
5. *Responsible decision-making:* Possessing the ability to make decisions based on an understanding of ethical standards, safety issues, respect for others, and possible consequences.

There are many excellent SEL curricula and programs available online that provide sequential and developmentally appropriate instruction in these skills (i.e., http://www.casel.org/social-and-emotional-learning/ and http://www.edutopia.org/sel-research-evidence-based-programs).

Olweus Bullying Prevention Program

One of the most influential anti-bullying programs is the Olweus Bullying Prevention Program, developed in 1993 by Dans Olweus of Norway. It is considered to be the one of the most researched and well-known anti-bullying programs in the world. It has also been evaluated several times and employed in over 12 countries, including Canada. It is comprehensive and schoolwide and can be used in elementary or high schools. The elements of this program include:

- Form a Bullying Prevention Coordinating Committee.
- Conduct committee and staff training.
- Assess the nature and prevalence of bullying by administering the Olweus Bullying Questionnaire schoolwide.
- Hold staff meetings for discussions and invite parents.
- Hold a school kick-off event to launch the program.

- Increase adult supervision in known "hot spots" where bullying occurs most frequently.
- Establish class rules against bullying that are enforced consistently.
- Hold meetings with students involved in bullying.
- Hold meetings with parents of students involved in bullying.
- Intervene with students who are either bullies or victims of bullying.
- Provide disciplinary methods in a warm and loving framework rather than in a punitive, zero tolerance atmosphere for the best outcomes (Smith, Salmivalli, and Cowie, 2012).

When followed consistently, this program has resulted in a reduction of 50 percent or more in reported incidents of bullying as well as a significant reduction in the number of reports about anti-social behaviour such as vandalism, fighting, theft, and truancy. These results are accompanied by students' reports of more positive social relationships and more positive attitudes toward school in general (Centre for the Study and Prevention of Violence, 2006).

In Canada, the Education Ministries of most provinces have explicit information for educators about how to prevent bullying in their schools and classrooms by using particular programs (i.e., Ontario: Abuse, Bullying and Violence Prevention—Beyond the Hurt; Alberta: Safe and Caring Schools and Communities; New Brunswick: It Hurts It's Wrong; Quebec: Action Plan to Prevent and Deal with Violence in the Schools; Saskatchewan: Anti-bullying Action Plan; Newfoundland and Labrador: Bullying Intervention Protocol). There is an emerging consensus in the bullying prevention literature that the whole-school approach is the most effective and long-lasting approach to bullying in schools. The foundation of such programs is the creation of an anti-bullying policy and anti-bullying initiatives that are consistently applied. This means that everyone understands the initiative—from teacher and staff roles and responsibilities, to the code of conduct for students and the clear consequences for bullying incidents. Successful whole-school programs have the following elements:

1. Strong teacher leadership.
2. Strong student-teacher bonds.
3. Clear and consistent norms for behaviour.
4. Use of both positive and negative consequences, with problematic behaviours being identified quickly and just as quickly reprimanded.
5. Parental awareness and involvement.
6. Focused and intense supervision before and after school and during lunch and recess breaks, including awareness of "hot spots" for bullying in the past.
7. Support from all stakeholders including, teachers, staff, administrators, parents, and students themselves.
8. Student involvement at all levels of the program. [This critical element can include regular class meetings to discuss aspects of bullying, including students on the committee overseeing the program and also including them in the implementation of the strategies in use.]
9. An ongoing long-term commitment to the program, with the understanding that the problems cannot be solved in a few months or even during a single year.
10. A focus that is as positive as possible and centres on developing strong social skills, including interpersonal skills, assertiveness, empathy and compassion, and conflict resolution skill. (Public Safety Canada, 2014).

Magical Anti-Bullying Presentation Program

In Ontario, the Reportbullying.com team has created a program that focuses on behavioural solutions to bullying behaviour. In this approach, everyone is considered a **bystander**, so the program focuses on the bystanders' behaviour and outlines their roles in taking a stand by speaking to someone in authority. The program adapts to all levels of schooling from primary to high school and offers action-packed assemblies, audience participation, and "magic." In addition, each school will receive ballot boxes, stickers, instructions on how to report cyberbullying, character education exercises, and a post-program survey. Keynotes for teachers and parents are also offered because maintaining a safe school environment requires a community effort.

Beyond the Hurt

The National Red Cross in Canada has several excellent resources for schools and teachers under their RespectED programs. The *Beyond the Hurt* program is designed to help a school prevent bullying while building empathy and respect among students. It is based on the idea that everyone—bullies, victims, and bystanders—all have a critical role to play in preventing bullying. For adults, there is a four-hour bullying prevention online course, and Red Cross Training Partners can deliver a three-hour Beyond the Hurt workshop to youth. These resources can be found at http://www.redcross.ca/what-we-do/violence–bullying-and-abuse-prevention/educators.

Roots of Empathy

As most bullies victimize those they perceive to be weaker than themselves and lack empathy for their victims, the *Roots of Empathy* program attempts to enhance emotional literacy through helping students learn to take the perspective of others (Berkowitz and Bier, 2005). This program is suitable for students from Kindergarten to Grade 8. In Canada, the program can be delivered in English and French and can be administered in urban and rural settings, including Aboriginal communities. It is also delivered internationally. The Roots of Empathy program strives to educate both heart and mind by raising social and emotional competence and thus increasing empathy. Essentially, it identifies a willing parent and infant who come to the classroom every three weeks over the school year. A person trained by Roots of Empathy accompanies the parent and infant and coaches students to observe the baby's development over the first year and to discuss the baby's feelings after each visit. The baby is actually the instructor! The accompanying adult instructor can help students identify and reflect upon their own feelings as well as those of others as a function of watching the baby grow and change. As a result of the program, children learn to challenge cruelty and injustice. Social inclusion and consensus-building activities are also a part of the program, and are designed to build a culture of caring in the classroom to which each student contributes.

The program has been researched extensively and has had consistently positive results; for instance, there has been an increase in social and emotional knowledge and a decrease in aggression (Nagin and Tremblay, 2001). Results have also shown an increase in prosocial behaviour, and perceptions that the classroom is a caring environment. Most importantly, the results have been shown to be lasting (Santos, Chartier, Whalen, Chateau, and Boyd, 2011).

CLASSROOM BULLYING PREVENTION ACTIVITIES

Teachers can create a "Bully-Free Zone" in their classrooms by employing the Crucial Cs to meet their students' basic needs. These Cs are *Connected, Capable, Count, and Courage*. *Connected* means helping all students feel like they belong, fit in, and are secure. *Capable* means providing all students with the opportunities to take responsibility and demonstrate competence in a variety of activities. *Count* refers to ensuring that every child feels significant and impactful within the group and *Courage* refers to fostering the ability for students to handle themselves in difficult situations and overcome their fear (McCready, 2012). Anti-bullying activities and ideas can be explored by students when a teacher adapts and integrates a variety of such activities into many areas of the curriculum. For example:

Drama

Whether or not bullying has been an issue in the class, skits or small-group student improvisations can be created to illustrate the emotional aspects of bullying. The skits can be created by the students from a teacher-selected scenario (can be as short as a sentence) and be filmed or presented to the class or even to the whole school. Follow-up discussion or deconstruction of the experience is useful.

Background Music

Creating a positive classroom environment can reduce the instances of bullying among students. Although not an absolute panacea, it has been found that calming background music can have an effect on mood and create a pleasant atmosphere where bullying is less likely to occur. The addition of music has been helpful in combination with other intervention programs in reducing aggressive behaviour (Ziv and Dolev (2011).

Writing

Writing activities can be adapted to any type of assignment (i.e., essays, newspaper reports, poetry, narrative, reflective journals or persuasive arguments) at any grade level, and these fit easily into the curriculum. The strength of this approach to bullying lies in the need to formulate ideas thoughtfully enough to write them down, and then to share them with peers and discuss various perspectives. The topic is current and meaningful to most students.

Bulletin Boards

Bulletin board messages (preferably created by students) are an effective and creative way to spread a message, especially in Kindergarten to Grade 8 schools; for instance, the use of words such as *Courage, Confidence,* and *Conscience* can illustrate the role of a bystander and help eliminate bystander apathy and fear. Such boards can also illustrate the importance of *Respect* and *Responsibility* to the community. These should be positive messages that empower and promote integrity.

The Power of Words

The activity could start with a circle discussion with the whole class. The circle is important because it signals that everyone's words matter and can make a difference.

The teacher could introduce the topic of bullying and discuss the characteristics of a bully and responsibilities of bystanders. Students could write a journal entry at the conclusion of the discussion or draw a picture about a time when they were bullies or a time when they observed bullying and did nothing. It is important to stress that the picture and writing activities should share the emotions felt by the bully, bullied, and bystander. The following day, the circle could be resumed and those students who wished to do so could share their writings or pictures. It is important for the teacher to recognize that this issue may be very painful for some students and they may not wish to share. On a subsequent day, the class could generate positive words that reflect the group's ideas about how to prevent bullying in the classroom or school. The words could be posted on a bulletin board and would have additional meaning because they came from the experiences of the students involved in this process.

Bullying Awareness Rallies

A single class could take responsibility for staging a *Bullying Awareness Rally* and thus engage the entire school in committing to attributes such as *Courage, Conscience, Integrity, Responsibility*, and *Respect* for everyone in the school environment. There could be follow-up comments over the course of the year through PA announcements and reminders during Pep rallies before school athletic events. One class could take the lead role on this initiative and monitor how the school environment becomes more positive (Hamilton and Reati, 2010).

List of Books That Address Bullying

The following list contains examples of books that could help teachers use a read-aloud program or novel study to raise the topic of bullying for discussion and critical analysis. Remember to pre-read any book that is shared with a class to determine its appropriateness.

Ages 4–8

Bradley, K.B. *Ballerino Nate* (2006). Dial.

D'amico, C. and D'amico, S. (2004). *Ella the Elegant Elephant*. Arthur A. Levine Books.

Dewdney, A. (2013). *Llama Llama and the Bully Goat*. Viking.

Geissel, T. (Dr. Zuess) (1961). *The Sneetches and Other Stories*. Random House.

Jenkins, E. (2008). *The Little Bit Scary People*. Hyperion Books for Children.

Lovell, P. (2002). *Stand Tall, Molly Lou Melon*. Scholastic.

Sornson, B. and Dismondy, N. (2011). *The Juice Box Bully: Empowering Kids to Stand Up for Others*. Ferne Press.

Steiner, H. (2010). *This Is Gabriel Making Sense of School*. Tefford Publishing.

Ages 8–13

Blume, J. (1974*). Blubber*. Yearling

Fox, A. (2009). *Real Friends vs. the Other Kind*. Free Spirit Publishing.

Ludwig, T. (2006). *Just Kidding*. Tricycle Press.

Madonna. (2003). *Mr. Peabody's Apples*. Callaway.

Olson, G. (2007). *Call Me Hope*. Little Brown and Company.
Rowling, J.K. *The Harry Potter series*.
Spinelli, J. (2002). *Loser*. Joanna Colter Books.
Woodson, J. (2007). *Feathers*. Putnam Juvenile.

Ages 12–17

Anderson, L. H. (2008). *Twisted*. Speak
Asher, J. (2007). *Thirteen Reasons Why*. Penguin Group.
Brown, J. (2010). *Hate List*. Little, Brown and Company.
Collins, S. (2008; 2009; 2010). *The Hunger Games Triology*. Scholastic Press.
Howe, J. (2003). *The Misfits*. Athenuem Books for Young Readers.
Howe, J. (2007). *Totally Joe*. Athenuem Books for Young Readers.
Spinelli. J. (2000). *Stargirl*. Alfred A Knopf.
Wihelm, D. (2011). *The Revealers*. RR Donnelley & Sons Company.

Summary

In this chapter, we have identified and discussed two major issues for classrooms and schools: bullying and cyberbullying. We outlined the multiple ways that bullying can manifest itself and clarified that, whatever its manifestation, it is a systematic form of violence that is cruel, devious, and harmful. We identified the three basic characteristics of all acts of bullying, which are: (1) The bullying action is repeated again and again; (2) the bullying is intentional with the goal of causing fear, distress, or physical harm; and (3) bullying does not occur when people are evenly matched. There is always an imbalance in power or control between the victim and the bully.

We discussed the prevalence of bullying around the world with particular reference to Canadian statistics as well as the detrimental effects to both victims and bystanders who passively witness the bullying events. We also explored the multiple and negative effects on victims, including severe anxiety, feelings of intimidation, chronic fear, diminished self-esteem, decreased marks at school, and even suicide.

In order to help teachers identify patterns of behaviour related to bullying among their students, we outlined the characteristics of both bullies and victims. We pointed out that victims seldom discuss the issues with adults and, therefore, we included a series of behaviours that may indicate that a child is being bullied. These behaviors include, but are not limited to sadness or depression, feeling sick, gaining or losing a large amount of weight, angry outbursts, and unusual aggression toward siblings or younger children.

Cyberbullying is a unique form of bullying that we addressed separately as it is a growing and often hidden type of intimidation and victimization. Canadian statistics show that 34 percent of teachers knew of a child who had been cyberbullied and one in five were aware of a teacher who had been cyberbullied as well. The key element of this type of bullying is that it is frequently anonymous with the target victim always being accessible—allowing the bullying to occur repetitively. Another daunting aspect is that the audience can be limitless. Different kinds of cyberbullying were addressed including harassment, denigration, flaming, impersonation, outing or trickery, and cyber stalking.

As teachers learn to deal with bullying, we stressed that victim, bully, and bystander all need intervention. We stressed the importance of the three Ss of crisis management, which are (1) safety and security, (2) stability, and (3) support. Procedures for helping victims, as well as stopping the bullying and helping the bully were outlined. Finally, the consequences that are appropriate for repeated bullying were shared.

As schools work together to establish anti-bullying policies and bullying prevention programs, we outlined steps and sources for both schools and individual classrooms. We identified specific activities such as drama activities, use of background music, writing activities, effective use of bulletin boards, using words effectively, and conducting bullying awareness rallies. Finally, we included a list of books that could support both curriculum objectives and raise the issue of bullying for classroom awareness and discussion.

Key Terms

bully: a person who shows a pattern of aggressive behaviour meant to hurt or cause discomfort to another person.

bystander: a person who is neither the bully nor the victim but who witnesses the bullying behaviour.

cyberbully: a person who bullies anonymously through online social media in order to harm or humiliate another person.

intervention: an action that is undertaken, generally by an adult, to stop and/or prevent bullying behaviour.

victim: a person who is verbally or physically tormented or who is tormented through social media and who displays insecurity and vulnerability and is unable and unwilling to challenge his tormentors.

Exercises

1. Think of a time when you were bullied or acted as a bully. Describe the situation and discuss the feelings associated with both points of view. What actions, if any, were taken by teachers or parents?

2. Think of a time when you were cyberbullied or acted as a cyberbully. Discuss the situation and the feelings associated with both points of view. What actions, if any, were taken by teachers or parents?

3. A Social and Emotional Learning (SEL) program suggests 5 components for developing social and emotional skills as a form of preventing bullying. List these 5 skills and discuss their implementation.

4. You are a teacher who has noticed that one particular child in your class is acting in an unusual manner. What are the signs that indicate that this child might be being bullied?

5. You have noticed that there is a child in your class who is being systematically bullied. What actions would you take with the child, the bully, and with the class as a whole? How would you apply the 3 S's of crisis management to protect this child?

6. An older sibling of a student in your class has confided in you that his sister is being flamed and cyber stalked. What is he trying to tell you? What steps should you take now that you have this information with regards to the student, the parents, and the school administration?

7. Identify the various types of cyberbullying and provide an example for each. Use your experience or the experience of others to describe each type in detail.

8. Discuss recent examples of cyberbullying discussed in the media. In your opinion, how has the media contributed to awareness, prevention, perpetuation, and legislation of cyberbullying?

Weblinks

Define the Line

http://definetheline.ca/dtl/

A Canadian site that is "clarifying the blurred lines between cyberbullying and digital citizenship."

PromotePrevent / Preventing Bullying

http://preventingbullying.promoteprevent.org/cyberbullying/understand-cyberbullying?gclid=CNbL1fznqLwCFQxo7AodRRMAaw

This website provides valuable information to help understand different types of bullying and the effects of bullying.

The Olweus Bullying Prevention Program

http://kids-can.ca/program

The Olweus Bullying Prevention Program is designed to improve peer relations and make schools safer, most positive places for students to learn and develop.

Abuse, Bullying and Violence Prevention— Beyond the Hurt

http://www.redcross.ca/what-we-d-/violence-bullying-and-abuse-prevention/courses

Online training and adult workshops for administrators, teachers, volunteers, bus drivers, school council members, and parents.

Magical Anti-Bullying Presentation Program

http://www.reportbullying.com

This program focuses on the bystanders' behaviour and their role in speaking up to someone in authority.

5

Philosophical Approaches to Classroom Management

FOCUS ON THE PRINCIPLES OF CLASSROOM MANAGEMENT

1. How are theoretical approaches to classroom management useful to teachers as they manage their own and their students' behaviour?

2. What are the authority bases that teachers can access in order to influence student behaviour?

3. Why is it important that the techniques a teacher employs to manage student behaviour be consistent with the teacher's beliefs about how students learn and develop?

INTRODUCTION

Teaching can be a threatening and frustrating experience, and all of us at some time entertain doubts about our ability to maintain an effective classroom learning environment. For many teachers, however, these normal self-doubts, which are especially common early in a teaching career (Klassen and Chiu, 2010; Reupert and Woodcock, 2010), can lead to a frantic search for gimmicks, techniques, or tricks that they hope will allow them to survive in the real classroom world (Beltman, Mansfield, and Price, 2011). This is indeed unfortunate, as Case 5.1 illustrates. When classroom-management problems are approached with a frenetically sought-after bag of tricks instead of a carefully developed systematic plan for decision-making, teachers are likely to find themselves behaving in ways they later regret. The teachers who are most successful at creating a positive classroom atmosphere that enhances student learning are those who employ a carefully developed plan for classroom management. Clearly, any such plan must be congruent with their basic beliefs about the nature of the teaching and learning process. When teachers use this type of plan, they avoid the dilemma that Ms. Knepp encounters in Case 5.1.

CASE 5.1

The Tricks-of-the-Trade Approach

Judy Knepp is a first-year teacher at Armstrong School. Although most of her classes are going well, she is having a great deal of difficulty with her grade 6 developmental reading class. Many of the students seem uninterested, lazy, immature, and rebellious. As a result of the class's continuous widespread chattering, Ms. Knepp spends the vast majority of her time yelling at and reprimanding individual students. She has considered using detention to control students, but there are so many disruptive students that she doesn't know whom to give detentions to first. The class has become such a battlefield, that she finds herself hating to go to school in the morning.

After struggling on her own for a couple of long weeks, Ms. Knepp decides that she had better ask somebody for help. She is reluctant to go to any of the administrators because she thinks that revealing the problem will result in a low official evaluation for her first semester's work. Finally, she decides to go to Ms. Hoffman, a veteran teacher of 14 years with a reputation for striking fear into the hearts of her grade 6 students.

After she tells Ms. Hoffman all about her horrendous class, Ms. Knepp waits anxiously for some words of wisdom that will help her to get the class under control. Ms. Hoffman's advice is short and to the point: "I'd just keep the whole class in for detention. Keep them until about 4:30 P.M. for one day, and I guarantee you won't have any more trouble with them. These kids think they're tough, but when they see that you're just as mean and tough as they are, they'll melt pretty quickly."

Ms. Knepp is dismayed. She immediately thinks, "That's just not fair. What about those four or five kids who don't misbehave? Why should they have to stay in, too?" She does not voice her objections to Ms. Hoffman,

fearing the veteran teacher will see her as rude and ungrateful. She does ask, "What about parents who object to such punishment?" Ms. Hoffman assures her that she has never had any trouble from parents and that the principal, Dr. Kropa, will support the disciplinary action even if any parents do object.

Ms. Knepp feels trapped. She knows that Ms. Hoffman expects her to follow through, and she fears that her colleague will tell the other veteran teachers if she doesn't take the advice. Like most newcomers, Ms. Knepp longs to be accepted.

Despite her misgivings, then, Ms. Knepp decides to follow the advice and to do so quickly before she loses her nerve. The next day, she announces that one more disruption—no matter who the culprit is—will bring detention for the entire class. For five minutes, silence reigns and the class actually accomplishes some work. Ms. Knepp has begun to breathe a long sigh of relief when suddenly she hears a loud "You pig!" from the back corner of the room. She is positive that all the students have heard the epithet and knows that she cannot ignore it. Ms. Knepp also fears that an unpoliced barb will mean disaster for her reading class.

"That does it. Everyone in this class has detention tomorrow after school." Immediately, the air is filled with "That ain't fair"; "I didn't do nothing"; "You wish"; and "Don't hold your breath." Naturally, most of these complaints come from the biggest troublemakers; however, several students who never cause trouble also complain bitterly that the punishment is unfair. Deep down, Ms. Knepp agrees with them, but she feels compelled to dismiss their complaints with a fainthearted, "Well, life just isn't always fair, and you might as well learn that now." She stonewalls it through the rest of the class and is deeply relieved when the class is over.

When Ms. Knepp arrives at school the next morning, there is a note from Dr. Kropa in her box stating that the Palmers are coming in during her free period to talk about the detention vis-à-vis their son, Fred. Fred is one of the few students who rarely cause trouble. Ms. Knepp feels unable to defend her action. It contradicts her beliefs about fairness and how students should be treated. The conference is a disaster. Ms. Knepp begins by trying to convince the Palmers that she is right but ends by admitting that she, too, feels Fred has been dealt with too harshly. After the conference, she discusses the punishment with Dr. Kropa, who suggests that it is best to call it off. Ms. Knepp drags herself, half in tears, to her class. She is going to back down and rescind the punishment. Ms. Knepp believes that the kids will see this as a sign of weakness, and she is afraid of the consequences.

Questions to Consider

1. What might Ms. Knepp have done to avoid her dilemma with regard to following Ms. Hoffman's advice?
2. Why did the detention idea fail?
3. Should Ms. Knepp have rescinded the punishment? What should she have said to the class?
4. Most important, what can Ms. Knepp learn from the experience?

There are multiple models or systems of classroom management and hundreds of techniques for promoting positive student behaviour within these models. Most of these techniques are effective in some situations, but not others; for some students, but not others; and for some teachers, but not others. What is frequently forgotten is that the efficacy of any strategy or technique depends upon the context. The teacher's personality and the nature of the group being taught combine to indicate what strategies or techniques are likely to be most effective when addressing complex management issues (Clunies-Ross, Little, and Keinhuis, 2008). Because every technique is based implicitly or explicitly on some belief system concerning how human beings behave and why they behave the way they do, classroom teachers must reflect upon and determine their personal belief system and then find prototypes of classroom management that are consistent with their beliefs and use them under appropriate circumstances.

How can teachers ensure that their behaviour in dealing with classroom-management problems will be effective and will match their beliefs about students, teachers, and learning? First, they can understand their own basic beliefs about classroom management. Second, they can develop, based on their beliefs, a systematic plan for promoting positive student behaviour and dealing with inappropriate behaviour. Chapters 7 through 10 in this text, which provide multiple options for dealing with any single classroom-management problem, are designed to help teachers develop a systematic plan. We provide numerous options to allow teachers to develop a personal plan for encouraging appropriate student behaviour and for dealing with unacceptable behaviour in a manner that agrees with their own basic beliefs about management. Because there are numerous options, teachers can prioritize them in a hierarchical format.

To help teachers and future teachers lay the philosophical foundation for their own classroom-management plan, we offer in this chapter an overview of a variety of philosophical approaches to classroom management. So that they may be considered in a more systematic and orderly fashion, the approaches are grouped under two major headings: *teacher authority bases* and *theories of classroom management*. In the first section, we discuss the four authority bases—the types of authority or influence that are available to teachers to promote appropriate student behaviour. In the second, we explain three theories of classroom management and their underlying beliefs; we also include models and techniques for each of the theoretical approaches.

It is important to be aware of the inherent connection between the four authority bases and the three theories. Each of the three theories relies on the dominant use of one or two authority bases. Teachers can examine the foundations on which their own classroom-management plans rest by comparing their beliefs with those inherent in each of the various teacher authority bases and theories of classroom management.

It is appropriate here to emphasize that teachers should reflect on the levels that the CALM model recommends for dealing with issues of classroom management which applies to all theoretical approaches. For a more detailed description, please refer to Chapter 1, "The Foundations," of this book.

The CALM model comprises the following four levels:

Level I: Consider the question of whether student behaviour has become disruptive in your classroom.

Level II: Act only when it becomes necessary.

Level III: Lessen your invasive responses to deal with the disruptive situation.

Level IV: Manage the milieu to quickly return to an effective learning environment.

TEACHER AUTHORITY BASES

After fifty years, the foundational work of French and Raven (1960) remains relevant for teachers (Elias, 2008). They have identified four different types of authority that teachers, as social agents, may use to influence student behaviour. Although we accept the relevance of these ideas for today's teachers, we prefer to use the term "authority" rather than "power." For us, although the terms can be used interchangeably in some contexts, "power" is more aligned with control whereas "authority" also implies respect and expertise; thus, we will refer to authority bases rather than power bases. An additional rationale for using the term "authority" is reflected as well in differing teaching styles including *authoritative, authoritarian* and *permissive*, which are discussed later in this chapter. The effective teacher is aware of the type of authority she wants to use to influence student behaviour and is also aware of the type of power that is implicit in each of the techniques available. It cannot be emphasized enough that when teachers' beliefs and behaviours are consistent, they are more likely to be successful than when a teacher functions inconsistently. The CALM model promotes consistency through providing a pattern of thinking prior to acting. When beliefs and behaviours are congruent, teachers usually follow through and are consistent in dealing with student behaviour. Students usually perceive such teachers as genuine and fair; they practise what they preach. As you read the descriptions of the four types of authority bases, ask yourself which type or types fit your beliefs and which ones you could use comfortably. Although teachers likely use each of the four types of authority at some time or other, most tend to have a dominant authority base.

The four teacher authority bases are presented in a hierarchical format, beginning with those more likely to foster student control over their own behaviour and moving toward those that bring forth increasing teacher dominance. If teachers believe, as we do, that one of the important long-range goals of schooling is to encourage student self-direction, then their frequent use of those authority bases at the top of the hierarchy becomes paramount. For teachers who do not share the goal of achieving student self-direction, the hierarchical arrangement of authority bases will not be as important. Whatever teachers believe about the long-range goals of education, they must understand the four teacher authority bases—no single one is effective for all students, all classrooms, or all teachers. Thus, effective classroom management requires the use of a variety of authority bases.

Referent Authority

Consider Case 5.2. The type of authority Mr. Emig uses to influence student behaviour has been termed *referent authority* by French and Raven (1960). When a teacher has **referent authority** students behave as the teacher wishes because they like the teacher as a person. Students view the teacher as a good person who is concerned about them, cares about their learning, and demands a certain type of behaviour because it is in their best interests.

CASE 5.2

The Involved Teacher

Mr. Emig is a grade 8 teacher in Prince Philip School, which has a reputation of being a rough inner-city school where it is difficult to teach because so many students are unruly. Mr. Emig teaches English to all the grade 8 students, and his classes are admired by administrators and teachers alike because he never sends misbehaving students to the principal's office, never gives detentions, and never needs to call parents to discuss student behaviour. Rather, Mr. Emig is able to concentrate on his lessons and spend his time pinpointing novels to study that will engage his students in discussions of issues related to social justice. Other teachers, who often have problems with the very same students who participate quite enthusiastically in Mr. Emig's lessons, are openly envious of the fact that Mr. Emig seldom suffers any behavioural problems with his students—they actually enjoy his classes.

The principal, Mr. Karr, and the vice-principal have most of their days filled with the behavioural problems of students in other classes. They begin to wonder if other teachers could learn something from Mr. Emig's teaching style and techniques. Accordingly, Mr. Karr decides to ask some of the students why they behave so well in Mr. Emig's class. The students are willing to share their reasons openly. They agree that they like Mr. Emig because he is often involved in extracurricular school activities with them. They point out that he sponsors the school newspaper, goes skiing with the ski club each Friday night in the winter, always shows up at their athletic events, chaperones school dances on a regular basis, and is the staff advisor to the student council. He is friendly and encouraging in all these situations, and the students say they know him well and like him. Students also say they feel Mr. Emig is "real" and that he never

(Continued)

(Continued)

talks down to them. One of the boys adds that Mr. Emig respects them as people. They do not see him just as a teacher, but also as a well-rounded and really good person who is interested in them and their activities. "He really seems to care about kids." They add that, as a result, no one ever feels like hassling him in class, they actually do their homework, and class members enjoy some good discussions about the novels they're reading for assignments.

Questions to Consider

1. How important is it to be liked by your students?
2. Should students view their teachers as "cool"? Why or why not?
3. Explain which is more important in the student–teacher relationship: being respected or being liked? How are these two qualities related?
4. Describe the responsibilities and role of teachers in student activities beyond the classroom.

There are two requirements for the effective use of referent authority:

1. Teachers must perceive that the students like them
2. Teachers must communicate that they care about and like the students.

They do this through positive nonverbal gestures; positive oral and written comments; extra time and attention; and displays of sincere interest in students' ideas, activities, and, especially, their learning. Teachers with referent authority are able to appeal directly to students to act a certain way. Examples of such direct appeals are, "I'm really not feeling well today. Please keep the noise level at a minimum," and "It really makes me frustrated when you hand assignments in late. Please have your assignments ready on time." These teachers might handle Ms. Knepp's problem with a statement such as, "You disappoint me and make me very angry when you misbehave and disrupt class time. I spend a great deal of time planning activities that you will enjoy and that will help you to learn, but we lose so much time to misbehaviour that we don't get to them. I would really appreciate it if you would stop the antics."

Referent authority must not be confused with attempts to be the students' friend. Usually teachers who want to be friends with students are dependent on students to fulfill their personal needs. This dependency creates an environment in which students are able to manipulate teachers. Over time, teacher and students become equals, and the teacher loses the ability to influence students to behave appropriately. In contrast, teachers who use referent authority do make respectful demands on students. Students carry out the teacher's wishes because they like the teacher as a teacher, not as a friend.

It is neither possible nor wise to use referent authority all the time with all students. In any classroom, it may be difficult to establish referent authority with some students. In these cases, a different technique must be selected because the foundation for using referent authority cannot be built; however, when students make it clear, through their general reactions before, during, and after class, that they like the teacher, and when the teacher has communicated caring and concern to students, the use of referent authority can make classroom management easier and create classrooms where mutual respect is evident (Glick, 2011).

Expert Authority

Ms. Sanchez in Case 5.3 is a teacher who uses **expert authority** to influence student behaviour. When a teacher enjoys expert authority, students behave as the teacher wishes because they view that teacher as someone who is strong and knowledgeable and who can help them to learn. This is the authority of professional competence. To use expert authority effectively, two important conditions must be fulfilled:

1. Students must believe the teacher has both special knowledge and the teaching skills to help them acquire that knowledge.
2. Students must value learning what the teacher is teaching. Students may value what they are learning for any number of reasons—the subject matter is inherently interesting, they can use that knowledge in the real world, they want good grades, or they want to reach some personal goal, such as college or a job.

CASE 5.3

Her Reputation Precedes Her

Ms. Sanchez is a chemistry teacher at Lakefront High School. Each year, she teaches an academic chemistry course for university-bound students. For the past five years, none of her students has failed the final chemistry exam. All failing students have studied in one of two other classes with different chemistry teachers. This fact has become obvious to students, parents, administrators, and other teachers in the school. They've all noticed that students in Ms. Sanchez's class not only habitually pass the final exam in the course relatively easily but they also have a strong foundation for achieving a university credit in chemistry as well.

Because of her reputation as an excellent teacher, students who are serious about their academic futures, strive to get into Ms. Sanchez's classes. They recognize that she knows a lot about chemistry and also has a large repertoire of teaching skills and strategies. In addition, Ms. Sanchez has a reputation for really caring about the success of

each student and is available for extra help early in the morning before class starts. She treats each student as an individual learner and encourages all of them to seek help when they feel they need it.

When people walk past Ms. Sanchez's classroom or when administrators enter it, they consistently notice the same thing: students are thoroughly engaged in class activities with very little off-task behaviour. The administrators have noted for five years that Ms. Sanchez almost never needs to send behaviourally challenged pupils to the office.

Questions to Consider

1. What did Ms. Sanchez likely do over the past five years to build such a positive reputation?
2. How could Ms. Sanchez's skills and attitudes be useful for other staff members?
3. Imagine a new student attempting to undermine Ms. Sanchez. How do you think the teacher would respond?

Teachers who use expert authority successfully communicate their competence through mastery of content material, the use of motivating teaching techniques, clear explanations, and thorough class preparation. In other words, such teachers use their professional knowledge to help students learn. When expert authority is employed successfully, students make comments similar to these: "I behave because he is a really good teacher"; "She makes biology interesting"; and "He makes you really want to learn." A teacher with an expert authority base might say to Ms. Knepp's disruptive class: "I'm sure you realize how important reading is. If you can't read, you will have a rough time being successful this year. You know that I can help you learn to read and to read well, but I can't do that if you won't behave as I've asked you to behave."

As is the case with referent authority, a teacher may be able to use expert authority with some classes and some students but not with others. A math teacher may be able to use expert authority with an academic calculus group but not with a remedial math group; an auto mechanics teacher may be able to use expert authority with the vocational-technical students, but not with students who take auto mechanics to fill up their schedules.

One final caveat concerning this type of authority: Whereas most primary teachers are perceived as experts by their students, expert authority does not seem to be effective in motivating these students to behave appropriately; thus, unlike the other three authority bases, which can be employed at all grade levels, the appropriate use of expert authority seems to be confined to students beyond the primary grades.

Legitimate Authority

The third type of authority identified by French and Raven (1960) and utilized by Mr. Kumar in Case 5.4 is **legitimate authority**. The teacher who seeks to influence students through legitimate authority expects students to behave appropriately because the teacher has the legal and formal authority for maintaining appropriate behaviour in the classroom. In other words, students behave because the teacher is the teacher, and inherent in that role are a certain authority and power.

CASE 5.4

"School Is Your Job"

Mr. Kumar looked at his grade 4 class noting that many of them were talking to friends or staring into space rather than doing the assignment that he had just passed to them. He felt a surge of anger coupled with frustration. He said, "You are really disappointing me as you sit there wasting precious time. School is not a place for wasting time. School is your job just as your parents have jobs. It is *my* job to see that you work hard and learn something during my classes." As he continued, Mr. Kumar noticed some students were listening intently while others appeared bored. "Your parents pay taxes so that you'll have the chance to come to school and learn. You and I both have a responsibility to do what we are supposed to do. Now, cut out the daydreaming and talking and do your math." When he finished, there was a silence in the class and most students did appear to be doing their math assignment.

Questions to Consider

1. How long do you think Mr. Kumar's rant will keep the students focused on the math assignment?

2. Explain the effectiveness of this strategy.
3. What else could Mr. Kumar have said that might have been more effective in keeping his students focused?

4. Using your own "rant" technique and words, try role-playing to emulate the actual classroom scenario where one of the players is the teacher and the others are the students.

Teachers who wish to use a legitimate authority base must demonstrate through their behaviour that they accept the responsibilities, as well as the authority, inherent in the role of teacher. They must be viewed by students as fitting the professional image of a teacher (e.g., in dress, speech, and mannerisms). Students must believe that teachers and school administrators are working together for the common good. School administrators help teachers gain legitimate authority by making clear, through words and actions, that students are expected to treat teachers as legitimate authority figures. Teachers help themselves gain legitimate authority by following and enforcing school rules and by supporting school policies and administrators.

Students who behave because of legitimate authority make statements such as, "I behave because the teacher asked us to. You're supposed to do what the teacher says." A teacher who employs legitimate authority might use a statement in Ms. Knepp's class such as, "I do not like the way you people are treating me. I am your teacher. I will not put up with disrespectful behaviour. I am responsible for making sure that you learn, and I'm going to do that. If that means using the principal and other school authorities to help me do my job, I'll do just that."

Because of the societal changes that we discussed in Chapter 3, "Understanding Why Children Misbehave," most teachers rightly believe that today's students are less likely to be influenced by legitimate authority than students of 30 or 40 years ago were; however, it is still possible to use legitimate authority with some classes and some students.

Reward and Coercive Authority

Notice how the teacher in Case 5.5 is using **reward and coercive** authority to influence student behaviour. Although they may be considered two separate types of teacher authority, reward and coercive authority are really two sides of the same coin. They are both based on behavioural notions of learning, they both foster teacher control over student behaviour, and they are both governed by the same principles of application.

CASE 5.5

Going to Recess

"Okay, grade 2s, it's time to put your mathematics books away and get ready for recess. Now, we must all remember that we get ready by putting all our books and materials neatly and quietly in our desks and then we fold our hands on the desk and look quietly at me. Let's see which row is ready first." There was a pause and a flurry of activity and then the class began to settle down. The teacher said, "I see that Tammy's row was ready first. Okay, Tammy's row can get their coats and boots and go quietly out to the playground." As everyone in

(Continued)

(*Continued*)

Tammy's row rose to leave, the teacher spoke sharply, "Oh, no, wait a minute. Where are you going Joe? You're not to enjoy recess this week because of your poor behaviour on the bus. Instead, you are to go to Mr. Li's room and do an additional math assignment. I will be in to check it after recess."

Questions to Consider

1. Name three strategies being used by this teacher.

2. Explain why you agree or disagree with Joe's punishment and the teacher's reminder to him in this context.

3. If Joe had misbehaved on the bus, what other penalty could the teacher choose for the student?

4. Describe how the consequences might be different if Joe's misbehaviour happened when the teacher was
   a) on the bus, too.
   b) not on the bus.

There are a number of requirements for the effective use of this authority base:

1. The teacher must be consistent in assigning and withholding rewards and punishments.
2. The teacher must ensure that students see the connection between their behaviour and a reward or punishment.
3. The rewards or punishments must be perceived as rewards or punishments by the student (many students view a three-day, out-of-school suspension as a vacation, not a punishment).
4. The students must see the application of the rewards or punishments as fair and reasonable.

Teachers using the reward and coercive authority base rely on a variety of rewards (e.g., oral or written praise, gold stars, free time, "good news" notes to parents, and release from required assignments) and a mix of punishments (e.g., verbal reprimands, loss of recess or free time, detention, in-school suspension, and out-of-school suspension).

Students who behave appropriately because of reward and coercive authority are apt to say, "I behave because if I don't, I have to write out a stupid 'I will not . . .' line 50 times and get it signed by my parents." A teacher using reward and coercive authority to solve Ms. Knepp's problem might say, "I've decided that for every five minutes without a disruption this class will earn one point. At the end of each week, for every ten points it has accumulated, the class may buy one night without homework during the following week. Remember, if there are any disturbances at all, you will not receive a point for the five-minute period." This point system is an example of a behaviour-modification technique. You can obtain more information on the use of behaviour modification in the classroom from many sources (e.g. Alberto and Troutman, 2012; Davis, Fredrick, Alberto, and Gama 2012; Martella, Nelson, Marchand-Martella, and O'Rilley, 2011; Poduska, Kellam, Wang, Brown, Iolongo, and Toyinbo, 2008).

As is true for the other three authority bases, reward and coercive authority cannot be used all the time. As students become older, they often resent obvious attempts to manipulate their behaviour through rewards and punishments particularly if it has been overused by previous teachers. It is also difficult to employ this method with older students and to find rewards and punishments that are under the classroom teacher's control, and also are powerful enough to motivate the students (see Chapter 7, "Structuring the Environment"). Still, some teachers have found that their control of student time during school has allowed them to use reward and coercive authority successfully with some students and some classes at all levels of schooling.

It should be noted that there are some inherent dangers in the use of reward and coercive authority. Research has indicated that when students are rewarded for engaging in an activity, they are likely to perceive the activity as less inherently interesting in the future and are less likely to engage in that activity without external rewards (Ng, et al., 2012; Guay, Ratelle, and Chanal, 2008). Also, overuse of punishment is likely to engender negative attitudes toward school and learning in students. Finally, this approach runs counter to encouraging and developing self-directive learners.

It is important for a teacher to recognize what authority base she uses to influence students in a given situation and to recognize why that base is appropriate or inappropriate. It is also important for the teacher to recognize the authority base she uses most frequently as well as the authority base she is comfortable with and would like to use. For some teachers, the two things may be quite different. Examining your beliefs about teacher authority bases is one important step toward ensuring that your beliefs about classroom management and your actions are congruent. Table 5.1 offers a brief comparison of the four authority bases on several significant dimensions.

TABLE 5.1 Teacher Authority Bases

	Referent	Expert	Legitimate	Reward/Coercive
Motivation to behave	Student likes teacher as a person	Teacher has special knowledge	Teacher has legal authority	Teacher can reward and punish
Need for teacher management of student behaviour	Very low	Very low	Moderate	High
Requirements for use	Students must like the teacher as a person	Teacher expertise must be perceived and valued	Students must respect legal authority	Rewards and punishments must be effective
Key teacher behaviours	Communicates caring for students	Demonstrates mastery of content and teaching skills	Acts as a teacher is expected to act	Has and uses knowledge of student likes and dislikes
Age limitations	Useful for all levels	Less useful at primary level	Useful at all levels	Useful at all levels but less useful at senior high level
Caveats	Teacher is not the student's friend	Heavily dependent on student values	Societal changes have lessened the usefulness of this authority base	Emphasizes extrinsic over intrinsic motivation

Of course, most teachers use a combination of authority bases in the classroom, depending on the types of classes and students they tend to have. They may even need to use a variety of authority bases with the same students. This approach may, indeed, be the most practical and effective one, although combining certain authority bases—for example, coercive and referent—can be difficult to do.

THEORIES OF CLASSROOM MANAGEMENT

In this section, we will describe three basic theories of classroom management. In order to make the differences clear among the three theories, we will describe each one as if it were completely independent of the others. In reality, however, the theories are more like three points on a continuum, moving from student-directed toward teacher-directed practices. On such a continuum, collaborative models represent a combination of the two end points. Of course, the classroom behaviour of most teachers represents some blending of the three theories. As always, there can be a significant difference between theory and practice when a theory is applied to classroom situations and where teacher decision-making must be immediate (Martin, Sugarman, and Hichinbottom, 2009). Teachers are charged with the dual task of building strong teacher–student relationships while simultaneously establishing relational boundaries (Aultman, Williams-Johnson, and Schutz 2009). This necessity requires establishing and maintaining a balance among various theories of management and may fluctuate during a career depending on experience (Riley, 2009). Still, if a teacher's behaviour is examined over time, it is usually possible to classify her general approach to working with students and goals for classroom management into one of the theories on a fairly consistent basis.

Before reading the specific theories, determine your answers to the following nine basic questions about classroom management. Inherent in each theory are answers, either implicit or explicit, to these questions. If you are aware of your own beliefs about classroom management before you begin, you will be able to identify the theory that is aligned most closely with those beliefs.

1. Who has primary responsibility for managing student behaviour?
2. What is the goal of classroom management?
3. How do you view time spent on management issues and problems?
4. How would you like students to relate to each other within your management system?
5. How much choice will you give students within your management system?
6. What is your primary goal in handling misbehaviour?
7. What interventions will you use to deal with misbehaviour?
8. How important to you are individual differences among students?
9. Which teacher authority bases are most compatible with your beliefs?

Readers of other versions of this text will recognize that the labels of the three theories have changed from *noninterventionist* to *student-directed*, from *interventionist* to *teacher-directed*, and from *interactionalist* to *collaborative*.

We believe the new labels describe the theories more clearly than the former labels, which were taken from Wolfgang and Glickman (1995). Because the student-directed approach is used less frequently in schools than the other two approaches and may be unfamiliar, more specific details are provided for it. Additional information about these management theories can be found in Charles (2007) and Wolfgang (2008).

Student-Directed Management

Advocates of the **student-directed classroom management** theory believe that the primary goal of schooling is to prepare students to live in a democracy, which requires citizens who are able to control their behaviour, to care for others, and to make wise decisions. Previously, student-directed models of classroom management were drawn primarily from counselling models. Gordon's (1989) teacher-effectiveness training, Berne's (1964) and Harris's (1969) transactional analysis, and Ginott's (1972) communication model relied to a large extent on one-to-one conferencing between teacher and student to deal with behaviour issues. Such models were difficult to implement in the reality of a classroom filled with 25 to 30 students, each with a variety of talents, needs, interests, and problems. As a result, **teacher-directed management** models dominated most classrooms. In recent years, however, there has been considerable progress in developing student-directed management models that can be employed effectively within classrooms. Ruth Charney (2002); Martin, Sugarman, and Hichenbottom (2009); Sumerall and Schillinger (2004); and Schwartz and Pollishuke (2002) have provided a variety of practical strategies that classroom teachers can use effectively. More recent literature refers to **person-centered classroom management** (Doyle, 2009; Freiberg and Lamb, 2009). Person-centered classrooms seek to attain high achievement and positive learning environments with strong teacher–student relationships while de-emphasizing teacher-directed discipline. This approach consists of four prosocial learner aspects: (1) a social emotional emphasis, (2) school connectedness, (3) positive school and classroom environment, and (4) student self-discipline.

The student-directed or person-centered theory of classroom management, which Ms. Koskowski in Case 5.6 uses to handle David's behaviour, rests on two key beliefs:

1. Students must have the primary responsibility for controlling their behaviour.
2. Students are capable of controlling their behaviour if given the opportunity to do so.

Given these beliefs, student-directed models of management advocate the establishment of classroom learning communities, which are designed to help students become more self-directed, more responsible for their own behaviour, more independent in making appropriate choices, and more caring toward fellow students and teachers. The well-managed classroom is one in which students care for and collaborate successfully with each other. They need to use problem-solving and consensus-building skills to make good choices, and continuously strive to do high-quality work that is interesting and important to them.

CONCENTRIC CASE STUDY KALEIDOSCOPE

CASE 5.6

Handling Disruptive David

Ms. Koskowski, Ms. Sweely, and Mr. Green teach grade 4 at Longmeadow School. Although they work well together and like each other, they have very different approaches to classroom discipline. To illustrate their differing approaches, let's examine their behaviour as each one deals with the same situation.

In the classroom, there are three students at the reading centre in the far right-hand corner and two students working quietly on insects at the science interest centre near the chalkboard located at the front of the room. Five students are correcting math problems individually, and ten are working with the teacher in a reading group. David, one of the students working alone, begins to mutter out loud, "I hate this math. It's too hard to do. I never get fractions right. Why do we have to learn about them anyway?" As his monologue continues, David's voice begins to get louder and clearly becomes a disruption for the other students.

Ms. Koskowski

Ms. Koskowski recognizes that David, who is not strong in math, is really frustrated by the problems on fractions. She walks over to him and quietly says, "You know, David, the other night I was trying to learn to play tennis, and I was getting really frustrated. It helped me to take a break and get away from it for a minute, just to clear my head. How about if you do that now? Go get a drink of water; when you come back, you can get a fresh start." When David returns to his seat and begins to work, Ms. Koskowski helps him to think through the first problem and then watches and listens as he does the second one on his own.

Ms. Sweely

As soon as she sees that David is beginning to interrupt the other students, Ms. Sweely gives the reading group a question to think about and walks toward David's desk. She quietly approaches David until she is right beside him, but the muttering continues. She says, "David, you are disrupting others; please stop talking and get back to math." David stops for about five seconds but then begins complaining loudly again. "David, since you can't work with the group without disrupting other people, you will have to go back to the castle [a desk and rocking chair partitioned off from the rest of the class] and finish your math there. Tomorrow, if you believe that you can handle it, you may rejoin your math group."

Mr. Green

As soon as David's muttering becomes audible, Mr. Green says, "David, that behaviour is against our class rules. Stop talking and concentrate on your math." David stops talking momentarily but begins again. Mr. Green walks calmly to David's desk and removes a small, round, blue chip. As he does, he says, "Well, David, you've lost them all now. That means no more recess for the rest of the week and no good-news note to your mom and dad."

Questions to Consider

1. Whose approach would likely receive the best learning response from David? Why?
2. What would the other students be learning by observing each of the teachers interact with David?

When viewed from a student-directed perspective, time spent on management is seen as time well-spent on equipping students with skills that will be important to them as adult citizens in a democracy. "Democracy as a way of life emphasizes that people grow as they learn to bring their individuality and intelligence to the many communities they inhabit" (Novak, 2005 p.115). Thus, teaching for democratic under-standing of life means modeling the belief that everyone has a role in the classroom relationships and activities that lead to growing and learning. In attempting to develop a student-directed learning environment in which students develop self-regulation skills, collaborative social skills, and decision-making skills, the teacher relies heavily on several major concepts: *student ownership, student choice, community building,* and *conflict resolution and problem solving.*

Student ownership is established in several ways. Although the teacher takes responsibility for the arrangement of the classroom and for the safety of the environment, students are often responsible for deciding how the room should be decorated, and for maintaining the room. In fact, sharing the responsibility of establishing a positive learning environment can empower students to take control of their own learning (Schwartz and Pollishuke, 2002). Throughout the school year, students rotate through committees (the art supplies committee, the plants and animals committee, the cleanup committee, and so forth) that are responsible for various aspects of the class's work. Often, these committees are structured so that students gain experience in planning, delegating, and evaluating their own work in a fair and equitable manner.

Students are also given a great deal of responsibility for determining classroom environment. Typically, the teacher and students hold a class meeting to discuss classroom behaviours. Students are asked to think about the ways they are treated by others that make them feel good or bad. These experiences are then used as a springboard for a discussion about how the students want to treat each other in the classroom. The students' words and ideas provide the guidelines for classroom behaviour.

Choice plays a key role in student-directed learning and person-centered environments because it is believed that a student can learn to make good choices only if she has the opportunity to make choices (Deci and Ryan 2012; Earl, 2013). In addition to making choices about the physical environment of the room and the expectations for behaviour, students are given choices about classroom routines and procedures, learning activities, and the assessment of their learning—including assessment options and criteria. Creating rubrics together, prior to a learning task, is a good example of providing students with meaningful choices about their own learning (Brookhart, Moss, and Long, 2008). Classroom meetings, which are viewed as important vehicles for establishing and maintaining a caring classroom community, provide more opportunities for choices. Agendas for the meetings, which may be planning and decision-making meetings, check-in meetings, or problem-solving and issues-oriented meetings, are often suggested by the students. Employing social media activities to enhance learning can provide multiple options that add new dimensions to the learning process and simultaneously provide choice and student-directed learning opportunities (Wodzicki, Schwammlein, and Moskaliuk, 2012).

Through the physical arrangement of the room, class meetings, and planned learning activities, the teacher attempts to build a community of learners who know and care for each other and work together productively. Doyle (2009) calls this type

Happy students learning with teacher in university class.
© Robert Kneschke/Shutterstock

of approach to person-centered management "Situated Practice" because teaching and learning are inextricably situated in concrete activities and the context for these activities needs to be jointly constructed. He also stresses that the establishment of durable contexts requires that the students possess a solid unalienable belief that they are respected and valued. To achieve this goal a great deal of time is spent at the beginning of the year helping students to get to know each other through get-acquainted activities, meetings, and small group activities. Throughout the year, the teacher uses co-operative learning activities stressing individual accountability, positive interdependence, face-to-face interaction, social-skill development, and group processing (see Chapter 7). These types of activities are emphasized because student-directed theorists believe that students learn more in collaborative activities. Theorists say that when students know and care for those in their classroom community, they are more likely to choose to behave in ways that are in everyone's best interest.

Student-directed teachers see interpersonal conflict as a teachable moment. They realize that conflict is inevitable when individuals are asked to work closely together. In fact, the absence of conflict is probably a good indication that individuals are not working together very closely; thus, these teachers believe that helping students deal with interpersonal conflict productively is an important goal of classroom management. They should also remember that these skills are not intuitively or automatically developed but rather must be taught explicitly with patience (Remember CALM!); therefore, conflict resolution, peer mediation, and interpersonal problem-solving skills are taught just as academic content is taught. Students are prompted to use these skills when conflicts arise. Issues that concern the class as a whole—conflicts concerning the sharing of equipment, class cliques, and relationship problems—become opportunities for using group problem-solving skills during class meetings. Some teachers even use class meetings to involve the entire class in helping a particular student improve her behaviour. It is important to note that encouraging caring relationships and teaching ways to deal with conflict productively go hand in hand; and if students do not know or care about each other, conflict is hard to resolve. Conversely, if students do not acquire the ability to resolve conflict productively, they are unlikely to build caring relationships with each other.

Student misbehaviour is seen by the teacher not as an affront to authority but rather as an opportunity for learning. In response to misbehaviour, the teacher tries to determine what motivates the child and to find ways to meet the unmet needs by learning new skills. A student-directed teacher would view the behaviour problems in Ms. Knepp's class, in Case 5.1, as a clear indication that the learning activities and curriculum were not meeting the student needs. The teacher probably would hold a class meeting to address the problem behaviours in the classroom. She would articulate her feelings and reactions to the class and would elicit student feelings about the class as well. Through a discussion of their mutual needs and interests, the teacher and the class would develop a solution to the problem that would probably include some redesign of the tasks that students were asked to perform.

Kohn (2006) suggests that the first questions the teacher should ask when a child is off task are (1) What is the task? and (2) Is it really a task worth doing? Many teachers find it helpful to try to identify with the child. Strachota (1996) calls this "getting on their side." This strategy seems especially appropriate when coping with students who seem out of control and unable to behave appropriately. If a teacher can identify experiences in which *she* has felt out of control, she is usually more empathetic and helpful (see Chapter 10, "Classroom Interventions for Chronic Problems"). In Case 5.6, Ms. Koskowski employs this strategy with David.

Student-directed teachers also believe in allowing students to experience the consequences of their behaviour. Natural consequences (consequences that do not require teacher intervention) are the most helpful because they allow the student to experience the results of her behaviour directly; however, sometimes the teacher must use logical consequences. The teacher's role in using consequences is neither to augment nor to alleviate the consequences but rather to support the child or the class as the consequences are experienced. According to the theorists, students learn to make wise choices by recognizing that their behaviour inevitably has consequences for themselves and others.

Some student-directed theorists also believe that restitution is an important part of dealing with misbehaviour when behaviour has hurt other students. In order to emphasize that the classroom is a caring community and that individual behaviour has consequences for others, a student whose behaviour has hurt others is required to make amends to those harmed. One strategy used by some teachers is called "an apology of action" (Forton, 1998; see Chapter 9, "Managing Common Misbehaviour Problems: Verbal Interventions and Use of Logical Consequences"). In this strategy, the student who has been hurt is allowed to decide what the offending student must do to make restitution. The strategy not only helps students to recognize that inappropriate behaviour hurts others but also can be a powerful way to mend broken relationships.

Referent and expert teacher authority bases seem most compatible with student-directed management theory. Each authority base emphasizes students' control over their own behaviour. At the same time, the student-directed perspective adds a new dimension to the notion of expert authority. Students must recognize the teacher's specialized knowledge and her ability to build a caring classroom community in which students are given the opportunity to make choices and take responsibility for directing their own behaviour. Putting this philosophy into practice demands highly competent and committed teachers. Such teachers truly believe that enabling students to become better decision-makers who are able to control their own behaviour is an important goal of schooling. These teachers must be committed to establishing more democratic classrooms that are true caring communities (Doyle, 2009; Novak, 2005). A teacher who is not committed to these beliefs will be unwilling to invest the time and effort needed to establish a student-directed learning environment. Long-term commitment is one key to success.

It is important to note that student-directed classrooms are not laissez-faire situations or classrooms without standards. In fact, the standards for student behaviour in most of these classrooms are exceptionally high. When student efforts fall short of meeting agreed-upon standards for behaviour and work, the teacher plays the role of encourager, helping students identify ways to improve. The teacher's role is not to punish the student who has behaviour or academic problems but rather to find ways to help the student overcome the problems and develop new collaborative and social skills.

Student-directed strategies can be effective in all teaching situations but are especially well-suited for self-contained early childhood and elementary settings—for several reasons. First, students and teachers in these settings typically spend a large portion of the day together, which gives them the opportunity to build close relationships with each other. Second, because the classes are self-contained, it is possible to build a community in which students really know and care about one another. Finally, teachers in these settings have greater control over the allocation of time during the day than most secondary teachers. Because they are not "bell bound," they are free to spend more time dealing with classroom-management issues with individual students or the class as a whole. Secondary schools would seem to be well-served by adopting similar structures to personalize the environment and make it more student-directed; that is, by using an integrated curriculum (Drake, 2012). At present in many secondary schools, students and teachers spend about 80 minutes together per day, and an individual teacher may teach 120 students or more per day. In such environments, although it may be more difficult, it is still possible to get to know each other personally, to understand each other's needs, in order to establish a caring community.

Collaborative Management

The collaborative theory of classroom management is based on the belief that the control of student behaviour is the joint responsibility of the student and the teacher (Gootman, 2008). Although those who adopt the collaborative approach to management often believe in many of the tenets of the student-directed and person-centered theory, they also believe that the number of students in a class and the size of most schools make it too hard to put a purely student-directed philosophy into practice. With the current provincial trends toward standardized testing and prescriptive and extensive curriculum, the time required to work collaboratively with students under this model is becoming more difficult for teachers to attain (Volante, 2010). In fact, many secondary teachers feel that the size of their classes and the limited time they have with students make it imperative for them to place the needs of the group above the needs of any individual student. Under the collaborative theory, then, students must be given some opportunity to control their own behaviour because long-range goals of schooling are to enable students to become mature adults who can control their own behaviour and value on-going learning; but the teacher, as a professional, retains primary responsibility for managing student behaviour because the classroom is a group learning situation.

In Case 5.6, Ms. Sweely represents the **collaborative management** theory in action. Note that she tries to protect the reading group activity and, at the same time, deal with David. While the group is occupied, she uses proximity interference (see Chapter 8, "Managing Common Misbehaviour Problems: Nonverbal Interventions") to signal to David that he should control his behaviour. When he cannot, she emphasizes the effect of his behaviour on others and separates him from the rest of the group to help him recognize the logical consequences of being disruptive in a group situation; thus, the teacher oriented toward the collaborative theory promotes individual control over behaviour but sometimes subordinates this goal to the right of all students to learn. From the collaborative perspective, the goal of classroom management is to develop a well-organized classroom in which students are (1) engaged in learning activities, (2) usually successful, (3) respectful of the teacher and fellow students, and (4) co-operative in following classroom guidelines because they understand the rationale for the guidelines and see them as appropriate for the learning situation. From the collaborative point of view, then, students become capable of controlling their own behaviour not by simply following rules but, rather, by understanding why rules exist and then choosing to follow them because they make sense. Neither blind obedience to rules nor complete freedom in deciding what rules should exist is seen as the best route toward self-regulated behaviour.

In collaborative classrooms the teacher and students develop rules and procedures jointly. Some teachers begin with a minimum list of rules, those that are most essential, and allow students to develop additional ones. Other teachers give students the opportunity to suggest rules but retain the right to add rules or veto suggested rules. Both of these techniques are intended to help the teacher maintain the ability to use her professional judgment to protect the rights of the group as a whole (Gootman, 2008).

Teachers who adopt a collaborative approach to classroom management often give students choices in other matters as well. Typically, the choices are not as open-ended as those provided by student-directed advocates; for example, instead of allowing students to develop the criteria for judging the quality of their work, a collaborative teacher might present a list of ten potential criteria and allow students to choose the five criteria that will be used. Thus, the students are provided with choices, but the choices are confined to some degree by the teacher's professional judgment. This same system of providing choice within a given set of options may be followed in arranging and decorating the classroom or selecting topics to be pursued during academic units.

Advocates of a collaborative approach see time spent on classroom-management issues as potentially productive for the individual but not for the class as a whole unless there is a major problem interfering with the learning of a large number of students. Thus, collaborative teachers, whenever possible, do not take time away from group learning to focus on the behaviour of an individual or a few students. Interpersonal conflicts are treated in a similar way. They are not dismissed, but collaborative teachers usually do not use classroom time to deal with them unless they involve many students. When an interpersonal conflict arises, the teacher deals with the individuals involved when there is a window of time to do so. Class meetings are used to deal with management issues or conflicts involving large numbers of students. Collaborative teachers tend to view a class meeting as a means for solving problems and for maintaining the classroom community.

While collaborative management advocates believe that outward behaviour must be managed to protect the rights of the group, they also believe the individual's thoughts and feelings must be explored to get at the heart of the behaviour; therefore, collaborative teachers often use *coping skills* (see Chapter 8) to manage student behaviour in a group situation and then follow up with a conference with the student. Because collaborative theorists believe that relating behaviour to its natural or logical consequences helps students learn to anticipate the consequences of their behaviour and thus become more self-regulating (see Chapters 7 and 9 for discussions of consequences), they advocate consequences linked as closely as possible to the misbehaviour itself. A student who comes to school five minutes late, for example, might be required to remain five minutes after school to make up work.

The teacher authority bases that are most compatible with collaborative management theories are the expert and legitimate bases. Each of these authority bases rests on the belief that the primary purpose of schools is to help students learn important processes and information. A collaborative teacher running Ms. Knepp's class might decide to hold a class meeting to review the classroom expectations and the rationale for them, to answer any questions or concerns regarding those expectations, and to remind students that the expectations will be enforced through the use of logical consequences. The teacher might also allow the class to make some choices concerning upcoming activities and events from a presented list of options. Well-known collaborative-management models come from the work of Kohn (2006); Dreikurs, Grundwald, and Pepper (1998); Glasser (1992); Soller, Martinez, Jermann, and Muehlenbrock (2005); and Murray, Ma, and Mazur (2009).

Teacher-Directed Management

Advocates of the teacher-directed management theory believe that students become good decision-makers by internalizing the rules and guidelines for behaviour that are given to them by responsible and caring adults. The teacher's task, then, is to develop a set of guidelines and rules that will create a productive learning environment, to be sure that the students understand the rules, and to develop a consistent system of rewards and punishments that make it likely that students will follow the guidelines and rules. The goal of the teacher-directed theory is to create a learning environment, in which management issues and concerns play a minimal role, to discourage misbehaviour and to deal with it as swiftly as possible when it does occur. (The CALM model works well to this end.)

In this theory, the teacher assumes primary responsibility for managing student behaviour. Time spent on management issues is not seen as productive because it reduces time for teaching and learning as well as the time spent on management issues can negatively impact the entire environment. The well-managed classroom is seen as one in which the management system operates efficiently and students are co-operative and consistently engaged in learning activities. The primary emphasis in teacher-directed classrooms is on academic content and processes. Current Canadian trends are prompting more teachers to adhere to this model of management in light of increased curriculum expectations and standardized testing. Pressure from the public— exerted through the media and parent groups—as well as from provincial ministries of education for increased teacher accountability, is also contributing significantly to this trend (e.g., Alberta Department of Education, 2010; Newfoundland and Labrador Department of Education, 2010; Ontario Ministry of Education, 2006).

More recently, a debate is emerging across Canada about the benefits and detriments of employing standardized testing (Volante, 2004). (Manitoba is currently the only province not using standardized testing (2014). In Alberta the issue was raised when a teacher gave students a zero for failing to do assignments. In British Columbia questions are emerging from the Teachers union and principals about a possible conflict between standardized tests and the government's new B.C. Education Plan. Action Canada has called for a review of standardized testing in Ontario to ascertain whether educational goals as outlined in its Education Act are being met. The declared objective is to share insights from the review with other provinces (Depres, Kuhn, Npirumpatse, and Parent, 2013).

In teacher-directed environments, the teacher makes almost all of the major decisions, including room arrangement, seating assignments, classroom decorations, academic content, assessment devices and criteria, and decisions concerning the day-to-day operation of the classroom. Students may be given a role to play in implementing teacher decisions—for example, they could be asked to create a poster—but they are usually restricted to implementing the teacher's decisions. Advocates of teacher-directed models view the teacher as a trained professional who understands the students as well as the teaching and learning process, and who, therefore, is in the best position to make such choices.

Usually, the teacher presents rules and a system of consequences or punishments for breaking those rules to students on the first or second day of school. Often, students are asked to sign a commitment to obeying the rules, and frequently their parents are asked to sign a statement declaring that they are aware of the rules. Punishments for misbehaviour are typically not directly related to the misbehaviour itself but rather are universal consequences that can be applied to a variety of transgressions; for example, the student's name may be written on the board, a mark may be made in the grade book, or a call may be made to the student's parents. Teachers may also establish a set of rewards that are provided to the class as a whole if everyone follows the rules consistently. Punishments and rewards are applied consistently to ensure that the management system and rules are internalized by all and are perceived as fair. Although teachers who follow teacher-directed approaches do use co-operative learning strategies, their management techniques usually are not focused on the creation of a democratic classroom community in which caring is a primary motivator for choosing to behave appropriately. In a teacher-directed classroom, the primary relationship is usually the one between the teacher and individual students. Students tend to be seen as a collection of individuals who should not interfere with each other's right to learn or with the teacher's right to teach. Self-control is often viewed as a matter of will. If students want to control their own behaviour, they can.

Given this, conflict is seen as threatening, nonproductive, and disruptive of the learning process. The teacher deals swiftly with any outward manifestations of a conflict, but usually not with the thoughts and feelings that have led to the conflict. Students have a right to feel upset, it is argued, but not to act in inappropriate ways. Using the predetermined list of punishments or consequences, the teacher redirects the misbehaving student to appropriate behaviour by applying the appropriate consequence. For the most part, punishments are sequenced so that second or third offences bring more stringent consequences than first offences. While individual differences may play an important part in the academic aspects of classroom work, they do not play a major role in the management system. This rather mechanistic approach to classroom management has recently been challenged by Walker (2009) who believes that nurturance and control, similar to an effective parenting model, must interact if student engagement and learning are to be effective. Basically teachers need to know when to "lighten up" and when to "tighten up" as these two dimensions interact constantly in most classrooms. Consider the actions of Mr. Green in Case 5.6. As an advocate of teacher-directed management, he moves quickly to stop the misbehaviour, emphasizes classroom rules, employs blue chips as rewards, and uses punishments in the form of loss of recess privileges and good-news notes.

Clearly, reward and coercive authority is the teacher authority base that is most compatible with the teacher-directed theory. Advocates use clear, direct, explicit communication, behaviour contracting, behaviour modification, token economy systems, consistent reinforcement of appropriate behaviour, and group rewards and punishments. A teacher following this theory might handle Ms. Knepp's dilemma by setting up a group management plan in which the group earns points for appropriate behaviour. The points could then be exchanged for meaningful rewards. At the same time, the teacher uses a predetermined set of punishments for any students who misbehave.

The teacher who wants to use a teacher-directed approach should be aware of some important considerations. A thorough understanding of the principles of behavioural psychology is necessary in order to apply a behaviour-modification approach appropriately. Individual student differences do play a role in the management system because they must be considered in developing rewards and punishments. After all, a reward to some individuals may be a punishment to others. Thus, most teacher-directed theorists are concerned with students' thoughts and emotions; however, the primary goal in dealing with misbehaviour is management of the student's outward behaviour. Therefore, individual differences do not play a strong role in determining which behaviours are acceptable. Some well-known authors of classroom-management systems derived from the teacher-directed perspective are Alberto and Troutman (2012); Canter and Canter (2007); Cangelosi (2008); and Martella, Nelson, Marchand-Martella, and O'Rilley (2011).

Table 5.2 provides a summary of the three theories of management in terms of their answers to the nine basic questions about classroom management introduced at the beginning of this section.

TABLE 5.2 Theories of Classroom Management

Question	Student-Directed	Collaborative	Teacher-Directed
Primary responsibility for management	Student	Joint	Teacher
Goal of management	Caring community focus and self-direction	Respectful relationships, academic focus	Well-organized, efficient, academic focus
Time spent on management	Valuable and productive	Valuable for individual but not for group	Wasted time
Relationships within management system	Caring, personal relationships	Respect for each other	Noninterference with each other's rights
Provision of student choice	Wide latitude and freedom	Choices within teacher-defined options	Very limited
Primary goal in handling misbehaviour	Unmet need to be explored	Minimize in group; pursue individually	Minimize disruption; redirect
Interventions used	Individual conference, group problem solving, restitution, natural consequences	Coping skills, natural and logical consequences, anecdotal recordkeeping	Clear communication, rewards and punishments, behaviour contracting
Individual differences	Extremely important	Somewhat important	Minor importance
Teacher authority bases	Referent, expert	Expert, legitimate	Reward/coercive
Theorists	Charney, Faber and Mazlish, Gordon, Kohn, Strachota, Putnam and Burke	Curwin and Mendler, Dreikurs, Glasser	Axelrod, Cangelosi, Canter and Canter, Valentine

Summary

In the first section of the chapter, with the CALM model in mind, we provide an explanation of the four teacher authority bases: referent, expert, legitimate, and reward and coercive. Each base is presented in terms of the underlying assumptions about student motivation to behave, the assumed need for teacher control over student behaviour, the requirements for employing the base effectively, the key teacher behaviours in using the base, and limitations and caveats concerning its use.

In the second section, we discuss nine basic questions that are useful for articulating beliefs about classroom management:

1. Who has primary responsibility for managing student behaviour?
2. What is the goal of classroom management?
3. How do you view time spent on management issues and problems?
4. How would you like students to relate to each other within your management system?
5. How much choice will you give students within your management system?
6. What is your primary goal in handling misbehaviour?
7. What interventions will you use to deal with misbehaviour?

8. How important to you are individual differences among students?
9. Which teacher authority bases are most compatible with your beliefs?

Articulating one's beliefs is the initial step toward developing a systematic plan for managing student behaviour. These nine basic questions are used to analyze three theories of classroom management: student-directed, collaborative, and teacher-directed.

Teachers may use the information and questions provided in this chapter to develop a plan for preventing classroom-management problems and for dealing with disruptive student behaviour that is congruent with their basic beliefs about teaching and learning.

Key Terms

collaborative management: the belief that the control of student behaviour in the classroom is the joint responsibility of the student and the teacher.

expert authority: where students view the teacher as a good, knowledgeable teacher who can help them to learn; the authority of professional competence.

legitimate authority: where students behave because the teacher is the teacher; inherent in that role are a certain authority and power.

referent authority: where students behave as the teacher wishes because they like the teacher as a person and they feel the teacher cares about them.

reward and coercive authority: where students behave to avoid some form of punishment or to gain a predetermined reward.

student-directed management: where the primary goal of schooling is to prepare for life in a democracy; students are allowed to make many decisions in the classroom.

person-centered classroom management: the belief that person-centered practices are necessary but to be successful must be embedded in an environment where all participants know that they are respected and valued.

teacher-directed management: the belief that students become good decision-makers by internalizing rules and guidelines for behaviour that are provided by a responsible and caring teacher.

Exercises

1. If one of the long-term goals of classroom management is for students to gain control over their own behaviour, what are some advantages and disadvantages of using each of the four teacher authority bases to help students achieve that goal?
2. Given your knowledge of cognitive and moral development, what factors facilitate or limit the use of each of the four teacher authority bases at (a) the primary elementary grades, (b) the intermediate elementary grades, (c) the junior high level, and (d) the senior high level?
3. Do you think there is any relationship between teacher job satisfaction and the authority base the teacher uses most frequently to influence student behaviour?
4. Which specific teacher behaviours would indicate to you that a teacher was trying to use (a) referent authority and (b) expert authority?
5. Using referent authority successfully requires the teacher to convey her caring nature to students. (a) How can a teacher communicate caring without initiating personal friendships? (b) As you see it, is there a danger in initiating personal friendships with students?
6. How would teachers operating at each of the four authority bases respond to the following situations?

Behaviour	Referent	Expert	Legitimate	Reward and Coercive
a. A student throws a paper airplane across the room.				
b. A student publicly shows disrespect for the teacher.				
c. A student makes funny noises while another student is giving an oral report.				

7. If one of the long-range goals of classroom management is to help students gain control over their own behaviour, what are the advantages and disadvantages of each of the three theories of classroom management in helping students meet that goal?

8. Given your knowledge of cognitive and moral development, what factors facilitate or limit the use of each of the three theories of classroom management at (a) the primary elementary level, (b) the intermediate elementary level, (c) the junior high level, and (d) the senior high level?

9. How would teachers using each of the theories of classroom management respond to the following situations?

Behaviour	Student-Directed	Collaborative	Teacher-Directed
a. A student uses power equipment in a dangerous way.			
b. A student chews gum loudly and blows bubbles.			
c. A student draws moustaches and beards on all the pictures in a textbook.			

10. Is there any danger in using techniques to manage student behaviour that are not consistent with your basic beliefs about student learning and behaviour?

11. Think of the best teacher that you have ever had when you were a student. Which authority base and classroom-management theory was this teacher using the majority of the time?

12. Think of the worst teacher you have ever had. Which authority base and classroom-management theory was this teacher using the majority of the time?

Weblinks

Bright Hub - The Hub for Bright Minds
www.brighthub.com/education/k-12/ articles/39644.aspx
The site helps with designing a philosophy of classroom management.

Positive Discipline
www.endcorporalpunishment.org/pages/ resources/further.html
This site provides links to "Web resources for parents and teachers on discipline without corporal punishment."

Managing Today's Classroom: Finding Alternatives to Control and Compliance
http://www.ascd.org/publications/newsletters/ education-update/sept96/vol38/num06/ Managing-Today%27s-Classroom.aspx
This site has links to many educational resources and articles that may help teachers with classroom-management challenges and other classroom issues.

Iterative Case Study Analysis

Second Analysis

Considering the concepts discussed in Part I's Foundations section, Chapters 1 through 5, reanalyze your first analysis. What has changed and what has stayed the same since your last analysis? Once again, consider why the students may be choosing to behave inappropriately and how you might intervene to influence the students to stop the disruptive behaviour and resume appropriate on-task behaviour.

Elementary School Case Study

During silent reading time in my grade 4 class, I have built in opportunities to work individually with students. During this time, the students read to me and practice word work with flash cards. One student has refused to read to me but instead wants only to work with the flash cards. After a few sessions, I suggested we work with word cards this time and begin reading the next time. He agreed. The next time we met, I reminded him of our plan, and he screamed, "I don't remember! I want to do word cards!" At this point, I tried to find out why he didn't like reading, and he said, "There's a reason, I just can't tell you," and he threw the word cards across the room, some of them hitting other students. What should I do?

Middle School Case Study

I can't stop thinking about a problem I'm having in class with a group of 12-year-old boys. They consistently use profanities toward one another and some of the shyer kids in the class, especially the girls. In addition, they are always pushing and shoving each other. I've tried talking to them about why they keep using bad language when they know it's inappropriate. The response I get is "'cause my buddies do it." I have implored them to use more appropriate language in the classroom but that has not worked. I haven't even started to address the pushing and shoving. What should I do?

High School Case Study

This past week, I had a student approach me about a problem he was experiencing in our class. The grade 11 student had recently "come out" as being gay. He said he was tired and upset with the three boys who sit near him. These boys frequently call him a "homo" and a "fag" every time they see him, both in and out of class. What should I do?

6

The Professional Teacher

FOCUS ON THE PRINCIPLES OF CLASSROOM MANAGEMENT

1. How can a teacher maximize student learning and on-task behaviour?
2. What is the importance of the research on **effective teaching** for classroom teachers?

INTRODUCTION

Frequently, classroom management is conceptualized as a matter of control rather than as a dimension of curriculum, instruction, and overall school climate (Martin, Sugarman, and Hichinbottom, 2009; Mastropieri and Scruggs, 2005). In reality, classroom management is closely intertwined with effective instruction. It is widely accepted that teachers who approach classroom management by establishing a positive learning environment are more likely to be successful in promoting student learning than those who rely solely on their roles as authority figures (Hansen, 2006; Pace and Hemmings, 2006). This is not always easy for beginning teachers. As research suggests, when they are beginning their careers, they tend to try and teach through establishing their authority as "teacher" (Huntly, 2008; Pelegrino, 2010; Putman, 2009). In the hierarchical decision-making model of classroom management presented in this text, teachers must ensure that they have done all that they can to prevent problems from occurring before using coping techniques (Edwards and Watts, 2010). The teacher's classroom instructional behaviours, therefore, must match the behaviours defined as best professional practices; that is, those that most likely maximize student learning and enhance appropriate student behaviour. If there is a mismatch, employing techniques to remediate misbehaviour is likely to prove fruitless because the behavioural problems will inevitably recur (Jones and Jones, 2006).

Unfortunately, one of the problems that have long plagued classroom teachers has been identifying the yardstick that should be used to measure their teaching behaviour against best professional practices. Fortunately, there is now a reliable knowledge base that, when used appropriately, can help teachers to ensure that their behaviour will enhance student learning and encourage appropriate behaviour. In this chapter, divided into two parts, we present a synopsis of that knowledge base. In the first section, "The Basics of

Effective Teaching," we describe and explain research that endorses teacher behaviours promoting student achievement as measured by most standardized paper-and-pencil tests. In the second section, "Beyond the Basics," we examine more recent conceptualizations of teaching that focus primarily on student cognition and student performance on higher-level cognitive tasks.

As you'll see, a major difference between the first and second sections of this chapter concerns the drastic shift in emphasis over the decades on teacher behaviour vis-à-vis student behaviour. Early research on effective teaching was based primarily on the premise that the teacher is the most important person in the classroom and the one who possessed the knowledge; thus, this research focused on the overt behaviour of the teacher during instruction. In the mid-1980s, however, researchers began to see the student as the most important person, and the student's thought processes as the key elements during instruction. As a result, the focus of the research switched from the overt behaviour of the teacher to the covert behaviour of the learner during instruction. This shift in mindset is most obvious in the research on student motivation. Indeed, it has led to the inclusion of two sections on student motivation in this chapter. In the first section, "The Basics of Effective Teaching," we focus on student motivation as influenced by teacher behaviour; in the second section, "Beyond the Basics," we examine student motivation as influenced by student cognition.

THE BASICS OF EFFECTIVE TEACHING

Most of the research findings discussed here were derived from studies of teacher behaviours that were effective in promoting student achievement as defined by lower-level cognitive objectives, which are efficiently measured by paper-and-pencil tests (Akey, 2006; Fullan, Hill and Crevola 2006; Marsh and Seaton 2013). It appears that general principles for teaching behaviour derived from these studies apply to the acquisition of knowledge and skills that have been organized and systemized so that learning is assessed through performance activities that are accompanied by feedback (Baker and Linn (2004). The research findings that general principles have been drawn from are the result of various long-term research projects that usually followed a three-step process.

> *Step 1:* Teams of researchers observed classroom teachers who were considered to be either very effective or very ineffective. Effectiveness was most often defined as enhanced student achievement on paper-and-pencil tests and higher results on standardized tests. From the observations, it was possible to develop a list of teaching behaviours that were used frequently by the **effective teachers** but not by the ineffective teachers. Researchers hypothesized that at least some of these teaching behaviours were responsible for the success of the effective teachers.

> *Step 2:* Correlational studies were conducted to find positive relationships between the use of these "effective" teaching behaviours and student behaviour or student learning as measured by paper-and-pencil achievement test scores. The correlational studies indicated that some of the effective teaching behaviours were positively related to student behaviour and achievement, whereas others were not; thus, the result of step 2 was to narrow the list of effective teaching behaviours to those that were used by effective teachers *and* had a positive relationship with student behaviour or student achievement test scores.

Step 3: Experimental studies were conducted; the researchers trained an experimental group of teachers to use the narrowed-down list of effective teaching behaviours consistently in their teaching. The achievement scores and classroom behaviour of their students were then compared with that of students taught by a control group of teachers who had not been trained to use the effective teaching behaviours. This body of research has concluded that teachers' classroom behaviours and teaching skills have a much stronger positive impact on student achievement than any school policies related to curriculum, assessment, staff collegiality, or community involvement (Darling-Hammond and Bransford, 2005; Hawley and Rollie, 2007). The current emphasis on performance-based measures of the attainment of standards makes understanding this research extremely important because students who have a teacher who has developed strong teaching skills are likely to outperform those whose teacher possesses weaker skills (Nye, Konstantopoloulos, and Hedges, 2004). Additionally, in early elementary grades particularly, teachers who are good at enhancing social and behavioural skills provide an additional indirect boost to academic skills (Jennings and DiPrete, 2010; Palardy and Rumberger, 2008).

Lesson Design

During the 1970s and 1980s, Madeline Hunter (1982), Barak Rosenshine, Robert Stevens (1986), and other researchers spent a great deal of time trying to identify the type of **lesson** structure that was most effective for student learning. Robert Marzano (2007) has continued that tradition by providing excellent summaries of research in the last few years. Although the various researchers tend to use their own specialized language, they agree that lessons that include the following components are the most effective in helping students learn new material: a lesson introduction, clear explanations of the content, checks for student understanding, a period of coached practice, a lesson summary or closure, a period of solitary practice, and periodic reviews. As you read the discussion of these components that follow, remember that a lesson does not equal a class period. A lesson is defined as the amount of instructional time required for students to achieve a specific learning objective. As lessons are often extended over two or more class periods, it is not essential to have all of these components in each class period. Conversely, if two lessons are taught in the same class period the essential lesson components should be repeated.

1. *Lesson introduction.* A good introduction makes students aware of what they are supposed to learn, activates their prior knowledge of the topic, focuses their attention on the main elements of the lesson to come, motivates them to be interested in the lesson, and engages them in introductory activities. It is critical to establish clear goals at this stage in terms of knowledge to be gained and skills to be developed (Marzano, 2007).
2. *Clarity.* Clear explanations of the content of the lesson proceed in a step-by-step fashion, illustrate the content by using concrete examples familiar to the students, and are interspersed with questions that check student understanding (Morgan and Saxton, 2006). "Lessons in which learners perceive links among the main ideas are more likely to contribute to content learning than are lessons in which links among the main ideas are less easily perceived by learners"

(Anderson, 1989, 102). Techniques for ensuring that lesson presentations are well organized include (a) using structured overviews, advance organizers, and statements of objectives near the beginning of the presentation; (b) outlining the content, signalling transitions between ideas, calling attention to main ideas, and summarizing subsections of the lesson during the presentation; and (c) summarizing main ideas near the end of the presentation. Using visual aids such as pictures, diagrams, concept maps, and other graphic organizers clarifies new content. The use of metaphors, similes, and analogies helps students connect new information with their prior knowledge. Instructional strategies that also enhance clarity of learning include previewing content, presenting information in small chunks, and setting up group activities where students must collaborate while processing new information (Marzano, Frontier, and Livingston, 2011). Also, student learning is more assured if teachers develop summarization skills, note-taking skills, and the ability to make nonlinguistic representations of the content. Finally, a teacher can ask inferential questions to help students elaborate on the content; this also helps identify any confusion. This last activity can be accomplished effectively through collaborative group activities (Marzano, 2007).

3. ***Checking for understanding.*** Effective teachers do not assume that students understand the lesson. They frequently stop and ask specific critical questions or engage students in a focused activity (possibly a writing task) to assess comprehension. These activities should engage all students so the teacher can ensure the appropriate degree of comprehension; for instance, when asking a question, it is more effective to take several responses before commenting on the accuracy of the responses. Students can also be encouraged to comment on the responses of their peers. If a large number of students appear to be having difficulty, the teacher needs to re-teach the material in a different manner. If only a few students are having problems, those students can be taught again individually or in a small group.

4. ***Coached practice.*** Effective lessons include a period of coached or guided practice during which students practise using the new skill or knowledge, through written exercises, oral questions and answers, or some type of group work. The teacher closely monitors this initial practice so that students receive frequent feedback and correction. Students should experience high amounts of success (over 75 percent) with the coached practice exercises before moving on to solitary practice. Otherwise, they may spend a large portion of the solitary practice period practising and learning the wrong information or skill. *Scaffolding*, as an additional important aspect of the coached practice portion of lessons, is designed to help students acquire cognitive strategies, such as study skills, problem-solving skills, and critical thinking skills (Marin and Halpern, 2011; Vygotsky, 1978). It is a process that underlies all of the elements of lesson design; in other words, the teacher plans instruction to move from modelling and instruction to feedback and coaching, and increasingly transfers control to students.

5. ***Closure.*** A good lesson summary, or closure, asks students to become actively involved in summarizing the key ideas that have been learned in the lesson and gives students some ideas about where future lessons will take them.

6. ***Solitary practice.*** Effective lessons also include a period of solitary or independent practice during which students practise the skill on their own and experience significant amounts of success (over 75 percent). This practice often takes the

form of independent seatwork or homework. The effectiveness of homework as a tool for promoting learning is directly related to whether it is checked and whether feedback is provided to students.

7. ***Review.*** Finally, periodic reviews conducted on a weekly and monthly basis help students consolidate their learning and provide additional reinforcement.

These seven research-based components, which are especially effective in lessons designed to impart basic information or specific skills and procedures, should not be viewed as constraints on the teacher's creativity and individuality. Each component may be embellished and tailored to fit the unique teaching situations that confront every teacher. Together, however, the components provide a basic framework that lessens student confusion about what is to be learned and ensures that learning proceeds in an orderly sequence of steps. When students try to learn specific content before they have mastered prerequisites and when they are not given sufficient practice to master skills, they become confused and uninterested, and thus are much more likely to cause behavioural problems in the classroom.

Another approach to lesson planning is **backward design or design-down planning**, where planning begins with the end in mind; that is, teachers plan by asking themselves what they want their students to know or be able to do as a result of the instruction. This approach to planning is based on the research that shows that both the students and teacher will understand lesson objectives more clearly if summative assessment is explicitly outlined from the beginning (Jones, Vermette, and Jones, 2009). Beginning with an emphasis on the enduring understandings or concepts that students will learn and be able to apply followed by developing the summative assessment or culminating task will inform the teacher when the students have achieved the objectives. In this approach, teachers plan backwards by designing the culminating task first, followed by the essential subtasks, which are themselves developed in the reverse order from the actual instructional delivery. Student learning and overall concept/skill development is assessed at each stage as earlier.

For more information on backward design/design-down planning, please refer to the following texts:

Isecke, H. (2010). *Backwards Planning: Building Enduring Understanding Through Instructional Design.* Huntington Beach, CA: Shell Educational Publishing.

Wiggins, G. and McTighe, J. (2011). *The Understanding by Design Guide to Creating High Quality Units.* Baltimore, ND: Association for Supervision and Curriculum Development.

Student Motivation: Teacher Variables

Motivation refers to an inner drive that focuses behaviour on a particular goal or task and causes the individual to be persistent in trying to achieve the goal or complete the task successfully. Fostering motivation in students is undoubtedly one of the most powerful tools the teacher has in preventing classroom behavioural problems. When students are motivated to learn, they usually pay attention to the lesson, become actively involved in learning, and direct their energies to the task. Else, they lose interest in lessons quickly, look for sources of entertainment, and may direct their energies at amusing themselves and disrupting the learning process of others. There are many variables that a professional teacher can employ to increase student motivation to learn. According to a review of research on student motivation (Brophy, 1987), some of the most powerful variables are the following:

1. *Student interest.* Teachers can increase student motivation by relating subject content to life outside of school; for example, an English teacher can relate poetry to the lyrics of popular music, and a chemistry teacher can allow students to analyze the chemical composition of products they like to use. There is no subject in which every topic can be related to the real world, but teachers can often use games, simulations, videos, or group work, and allow students to plan or select activities to increase their interest. Although these strategies can't be used effectively every day, all teachers can employ them at intervals.

2. *Student needs.* Motivation to learn is increased when students perceive that learning activities provide an opportunity to meet some of their basic human needs as identified by Maslow (1968); for example, simply providing students with the opportunity to talk while the whole group listens can be an easy way to help meet students' needs for self-esteem. Also, allowing students to work together with peers on learning activities helps to meet students' needs for a sense of belonging and acceptance by others. At the most basic level, providing a pleasant, task-oriented climate in which expectations are clear helps meet students' needs for psychological safety and security.

3. *Novelty and variety.* When the teacher has designed learning activities that include novel events, situations, and multimedia and concrete materials, students are likely to be motivated to learn. The popcorn lesson in Case 6.1 is an excellent example of using novelty to gain student attention. Once student attention has been captured, a variety of short learning activities will help to keep it focused on the lesson. Human attention spans can be remarkably long when people are involved in an activity that they find fascinating. Most students, however, do not always find typical school activities fascinating—their attention spans can, thus, tend to be rather short. For this reason, the professional teacher plans activities that last no longer than 15 to 20 minutes. A teacher who gives a lecture in two 15-minute halves interspersed with a 5-minute oral exercise is much more likely to maintain student interest than a teacher who gives a 30-minute lecture followed by the 5-minute oral exercise. Music videos and TV shows are good examples of how frequently changing the focus of activity can hold an audience's attention.

CASE 6.1

The Popcorn Popper

As Mr. Armour's students walk into his grade 10 creative writing classroom in their usual desultory manner, they hear an unusual noise. As they look around for the source of the noise, they see that on the teacher's desk an electric popcorn popper is running. As the room fills with the aroma of fresh popcorn, students smile in anticipation. Someone says aloud, "This smells like a movie theatre." Another responds, "Yeah, let's sit back and enjoy. I love the movies."

When the popping is finished, Mr. Armour passes three large bowls around and students help themselves to fistfuls of the popcorn. He admonishes his students that eight people need to get popcorn from each bowl and that they must stay in their seats and take turns. The students comply, appearing to be pleased with the unusual beginning to their lesson.

After giving an appropriate amount of time for students to finish their snack, and after eating some popcorn himself, Mr. Armour starts an oral lesson by asking students to describe the sights, sounds, taste, smell, and feel of the popcorn. Mr. Armour puts each response on the board under the categories of the five senses. The participation is enthusiastic and the descriptive words become increasingly clever and sophisticated. Students laugh over some of the descriptions. This is the introduction to a writing exercise on the five senses.

Questions to Consider

1. What variables for motivating did Mr. Armour achieve with this activity?
2. What other strategies might he have used to introduce this lesson in a motivational manner?

4. *Success.* When students are successful at tasks they perceive to be somewhat challenging, their motivation for future learning is greatly enhanced. It is unreasonable to expect students who fail constantly to have any motivation to participate positively in future learning activities; thus, it is especially important for teachers to create success for students who are not normally successful. Teachers help to ensure that all students experience some success by making goals and objectives clear, teaching content clearly in small steps, and checking to see that students understand each step. Teachers can also encourage success by helping students to acquire the study skills they need when they must work on their own—outlining, note-taking, summarization, and using textbooks correctly. The most powerful technique for helping students to succeed is to ensure that the material being covered is at the appropriate level of difficulty and that their prior knowledge on the subject is reviewed.

5. *Tension.* In teaching, tension refers to a feeling of concern or anxiety on the part of students because they know that they will be required to demonstrate their learning. A moderate amount of tension increases student learning. When there is no tension in the learning situation, students may be so relaxed that no learning occurs. On the other hand, if there is an overwhelming amount of tension, students may expend more energy in dealing with the tension than they do in learning. Creating a moderate amount of tension motivates without tension overload. When a learning task is inherently interesting and challenging for students, there is little need for the teacher to add tension to the situation. When the learning task is routine and uninteresting for students, a moderate amount of tension created by the teacher enhances motivation and learning. Teacher behaviours that raise the level of tension include moving around the room, calling on volunteers and nonvolunteers to answer questions in a random pattern, giving quizzes on class material, checking homework and seatwork, and reminding students that they will be tested on the material they are learning.

6. ***Feeling tone.*** Feeling tone refers to the emotional atmosphere or climate in the classroom. The most effective feeling tone is a moderately positive one in which the atmosphere is pleasant and friendly but clearly focused on the learning task at hand. The teacher can help to create such a feeling tone by making a room comfortable and pleasantly decorated, treating students in a courteous and friendly manner, expressing sincere interest in students as individuals, and communicating positively with students both verbally and nonverbally (Matsumura, Slater and Crosson, 2008). See how one teacher expresses his interest in students in Case 6.2. Although a moderately positive-feeling tone is the most motivating one, it is sometimes necessary to create, temporarily, a moderately negative-feeling tone. If students are not doing their work and not living up to their responsibilities, it is necessary to shake them out of their complacency with some well-chosen, corrective comments. The wise teacher understands that undesirable consequences may result from a classroom feeling tone that is continuously negative and, therefore, works to create a moderately positive classroom climate.

7. ***Assessment and feedback.*** Because it provides both information that can be used to improve performance and a yardstick or criterion by which progress can be measured, formative assessment and timely feedback also increases motivation (Marzano, 2007). Formative assessment, successfully implemented, can do a great deal more to improve student achievement than any of the most powerful instructional innovations or one-on-one tutoring (Volante, 2010). Well-designed formative assessment begins with pre-instructional diagnostic testing designed to identify both what students know and what misconceptions they may possess. Tools for formative assessment include KWL (Know, Want to Know, Learned) charts paper-and-pencil quizzes, small and large group discussions, homework assignments, and teacher observation and conferences with individuals. None of these needs to be threatening in any way; rather, the teacher should convey that what the students know now indicates

CASE 6.2

Talking Between Classes

Mr. Dailey, the grade 8 English teacher, does not spend the time in between classes standing out in the hallway or visiting with friends. Instead, he uses the three minutes to chat with individual students. During these chats, he talks with students about their out-of-school activities, hobbies, feelings about school and his class in particular, plans and aspirations, and everyday school activities. He feels that these three-minute chats really promote a more positive-feeling tone in his classroom and allow him to relate to his students as individuals.

Questions to Consider

1. Try to imagine a typical student's feelings about Mr. Dailey and his class.
2. Describe a teacher in your background who was like Mr. Dailey.

what learning needs to come next (Shepard, Hammerness, Darling-Hammond, and Rust, 2005).

Making as transparent as possible the assessment process and the criteria by which students' learning will be evaluated facilitates helping students understand the process more fully. Marzano (2007) suggests making a rubric for each important learning goal. A well-designed rubrics, exemplars of previous students' work, and encouraging student participation in developing the criteria for assessing the work are useful strategies for making goals of learning and criteria for assessment clear. One additional way to use feedback as a motivator is to have students keep track of their own progress over time and to provide periodic opportunities for them to reflect on their progress.

Feedback is most effective when it is specific and is delivered soon after or at the time of performance. Teachers usually provide feedback in the form of oral and written comments on tests and assignments or through individual conferences. The feedback process is enhanced when teachers provide the emotional support and encouragement that the student needs to persist in achieving the stated and understood outcomes.

8. ***Encouragement.*** Encouragement is a great motivator. It emphasizes the positive aspects of behaviour; recognizes and validates real effort; communicates positive expectations for future behaviour; and conveys that the teacher trusts, respects, and believes in the student. Pointing out shortcomings and focusing on past transgressions erodes student's self-esteem, whereas encouraging communication enhances self-esteem (Purkey, Schmidt, and Novak, 2010). Encouragement emphasizes present and future behaviour, rather than past transgressions, and focuses on what is being learned and done correctly rather than on what has not been learned; for example, consider the way the teacher in Case 6.3 emphasized the negative and the impact it had on the student.

CASE 6.3

Nonconstructive Feedback

While Ms. Lapierre was handing back the grade 7 students' reports on their library books, Heidi waited anxiously to receive her corrected work from the teacher. She had read a book on archaeology and had really gotten into it. Heidi spent quite a bit of time explaining in her report how neat it must be to relive the past by examining the artifacts people left behind. When she received her book report, Heidi was dejected. The word *artifact*—Heidi had spelled it *artafact*—was circled twice on her paper with *sp* written above it. At the bottom of the paper, Ms. Lapierre had written, "Spelling errors are careless and are not acceptable." The only other mark Ms. Lapierre had made on the paper was a grade of C.

Questions to Consider

1. What has happened to Heidi's motivation for this topic and this assignment?
2. If Heidi's report was going to receive a C, what should the teacher have done to motivate her to continue learning?

Ms. Lapierre in Case 6.3 would have had a far more positive impact on Heidi's motivation if she had pointed out the positive aspects of Heidi's work in addition to the error in spelling. After all, a child who gets a mark of 68 percent on an exam has learned twice as much as she has failed to learn. For more on encouragement, see Dreikurs's *Discipline Without Tears: How to Reduce Conflict and Establish Cooperation in the Classroom* (2004). How can you use these research findings to improve student motivation in your own classroom? Ask yourself the following questions as you plan classroom activities for your students:

1. How can I make use of natural student interests in this learning activity?
2. How can I help students meet their basic human needs in this activity?
3. How can I use novel events and/or materials in this activity?
4. How can I provide for variety in these learning activities?
5. How can I ensure that my students will be successful?
6. How can I create an appropriate level of tension for this learning task?
7. How can I create a moderately pleasant feeling tone for this activity?
8. How can I provide feedback to students and help them to recognize their progress in learning?
9. How can I encourage my students?

This list of nine questions is also an important resource when behavioural problems occur. By answering the questions, the teacher may find ways to increase students' motivation to learn and decrease their motivation to misbehave.

Teacher Expectations

Teacher expectations influence both student learning and motivation. In a famous study entitled *Pygmalion in the Classroom: Teacher Expectations and Pupils' Intellectual Development*, Rosenthal and Jacobson (1968) began a line of inquiry that still continues and has yielded powerful insights into the effects of teacher behaviour and expectations on student achievement. For their study, Rosenthal and Jacobson told teachers in an inner-city elementary school that they had developed an intelligence test designed to identify "intellectual bloomers"; that is, students who were on the verge of taking a tremendous leap in their ability to learn. They also told these teachers that certain students in their classes had been so identified. This was a total fabrication. There was no such test; however, when Rosenthal and Jacobson checked student achievement test scores at the end of the year, the students identified as intellectual bloomers had actually bloomed. Compared to a matched group of their peers, the researcher-identified bloomers had made much greater gains in achievement. As a result, Rosenthal and Jacobson (1968) assumed that the teachers must have treated the bloomers differently in some way in the classroom, but they had no observational data to support this assumption. Although still considered controversial, the study provided the impetus for further research (Wineburg, 1987).

Beginning in the 1970s, researchers such as Thomas Good and Jere Brophy conducted observational studies of teacher behaviour toward students whom the teachers perceived as high achievers and toward students they perceived as low achievers (Brophy and Good, 1974). Multiple research studies (e.g., Erwin and Worrell, 2012; Good and Brophy, 2008; Jussim and Harber, 2005) found that teachers often unintentionally communicate low expectations toward students whom they perceive as low achievers. These lower expectations are communicated by behaviours such as the following:

1. Calling on perceived low achievers less often to answer questions
2. Giving perceived low achievers less think time when they are called on
3. Providing fewer clues and hints to perceived low achievers when they have initial difficulty in answering questions
4. Praising correct answers from perceived low achievers less often
5. Criticizing wrong answers from perceived low achievers more often
6. Praising marginal answers from perceived low achievers but demanding more precise answers from high achievers
7. Staying farther away physically and psychologically from perceived low achievers
8. Rarely expressing personal interest in perceived low achievers
9. Smiling less frequently at perceived low achievers
10. Making eye contact less frequently with perceived low achievers
11. Complimenting perceived low achievers less often

Some of these behaviours may be motivated by good intentions on the part of the teacher, who, for example, may give perceived low achievers less think time to avoid embarrassing them if they don't know an answer; however, the cumulative effect is the communication of a powerful message: "I don't expect you to be able to do much." This message triggers a vicious circle, wherein students begin to expect less of themselves, produce less, and confirm the teacher's original perception of them. While in many cases, the teacher may have a legitimate reason to expect less from some students, communicating low expectations produces only negative effects. Researchers have demonstrated that when teachers equalize response opportunities, feedback, and personal involvement, student learning can improve. The message is clear: Communicating high expectations to all learners appears to influence low achievers to learn more, whereas communicating low expectations, no matter how justified, has a debilitating effect (Good and Brophy, 2008). The "self-fulfilling prophecy effect" leads to behaviour that becomes true even though it is originally based on unfounded expectations. The "sustaining expectation effect" is better founded because teachers tend to expect students to maintain the same level of achievement; however, always projecting the same expectation can also have serious limitations because it can limit a teacher from seeing changes in potential (Good and Brophy, 2008).

Good and Brophy (2008) provide an excellent and comprehensive overview of the research on teacher expectation effects and suggest that teachers take three specific steps to ensure that they are communicating high levels of expectations for all students. First, when establishing expectations for students, they should consider the full range of the students' abilities including multiple intelligences; second, they should keep expectations flexible and current, not based on past performance; and third, they should always emphasize the positive while staying realistically honest with the student.

Although empirical research in this area has been limited to the effects of teacher expectations on achievement, we believe that the generalizations hold true for student behaviour as well. Communicating high expectations for student behaviour is likely to bring about increased positive behaviours; communicating low expectations for student behaviour is likely to bring about increased negative behaviour. A teacher who says, "I am sure that all of you will complete all of your homework assignments carefully because you realize that doing homework is an important way of practising what you are learning" is more likely to have students complete homework assignments than a teacher who says, "I know you probably don't like to do homework, but if you fail to complete homework assignments, it will definitely lower your grades." Projecting consistent positive expectations helps create an environment that is conducive to fostering positive self-concepts as well as one that is more likely to be accompanied by pro-social behaviour (Denham and Brown, 2010; Zins, Bloodworth, Weissberg and Walberg, 2007).

Given the powerful research results in this area, all teachers should step back and reflect on the expectations they communicate to students through their verbal and nonverbal classroom behaviour; for instance, when a teacher has a challenging and continually disruptive student in his class, the other students may receive a low-frequency message that it is acceptable behaviour to ostracize that child. The teacher sends such messages by modelling anger, making cutting remarks, and showing dismissive behaviour toward the problem student.

CANADIAN ABORIGINAL EDUCATION

Another serious example of low-frequency communication to the class pertains to Aboriginal education in non-Aboriginal settings. Even though research points to variations in the way that Aboriginal and non-Aboriginal people learn (St. Denis, 2007), many Aboriginal students are taught in traditional provincial schools with methods that are not meaningful to them. The Aboriginal students attending mainstream schools are likely to be challenged by a curriculum and associated expectations that have little cultural relevance and thus do not resonate with their past experiences. Equally concerning is the fact that across Canada, many Aboriginal students attending residential schools rather than mainstream schools will not complete high school. While multiple factors have been identified as significant, one glaring factor is that funding is substantially lower for these schools than for corresponding mainstream schools; thus, both in mainstream schools and on the reserves, Aboriginal schooling is plagued by unequal funding, irrelevant curriculum, and low expectations from teachers, which all contribute to a poor rate of success in provincial and national standardized tests. There is currently great concern that Aboriginal students do not achieve academic success to the same level as non-Aboriginal students, and the predictable result is a high number of high school dropouts (Hallett, Want, Chandler, Koopman, Flores, and Gehrke, 2008). This chronic problem has prompted many First Nations leaders to assert that First Nations need to control their own education (Henderson and Wakeham, 2009; Laboucane, 2010).

It must be acknowledged that Canada has a painful past regarding the education of its First Nations children. The creation of residential schools was a misguided attempt to assimilate First Nations people into the Canadian mainstream by removing children from their home environments and sending them to boarding schools. This punitive policy, which lasted for over one hundred years, was debilitating and cruel. This policy has been condemned, and the Canadian government officially apologized to our Aboriginal peoples in 2008. Not surprisingly, the pain associated with this policy reverberates in the lives of Aboriginal people today.

This issue can be discouraging, but there are specific steps that can be taken to help Aboriginal children achieve today, and negative statistics related to success do not have to be a foregone conclusion. Research indicates that significant correlations are found between achievement, appropriate behaviour, and close friendships. A school that provides opportunities for Aboriginal children to develop social and behavioural skills in a culturally sensitive manner and encourages the development of friendships combined with an emphasis on explicit study skills can help them achieve academically (Rasmussen, et al., 2009). Research has also identified a number of key factors that have contributed to the academic success of Aboriginal students, including good teachers who establish high expectations, who care about their students, and who show explicit respect for them. Also, classrooms that honour Aboriginal students' culture, language, and knowledge and that establish strong partnerships with the Aboriginal community experience a better academic performance (Toulouse, 2008). Success is also more likely if schools build strong partnerships with the students' community;

Portrait of children with raised hands in the classroam.
© racorn/Shutterstock

for example, a small school in British Columbia in Bella Coola has an enviable record in terms of keeping students in school and demonstrating superior performance on provincial examinations compared to other Aboriginal students. These results have been accomplished by incorporating a number of changes in the education system. First, the schools have taken advantage of distance-learning programs and provincial programs that have enabled them to choose Aboriginal-influenced credits in high school. Second, they have prioritized literacy support programs that reflect differentiated learning needs. At the same time, they have provided places for students to complete their homework and receive additional academic help. Most significantly, however, Aboriginal experiences and culture provide the centre learning point of the curriculum. Similar successes have been experienced at an Aboriginal school in Fort Nelson, British Columbia. The graduation rate from high school has dramatically increased over the last ten years moving from 40.1 percent to 87.1 percent (Fisher 2013). These successes are being replicated in other Aboriginal educational settings and provide hope for the future as more students complete high school and pursue postsecondary education (Preston, 2008; Wilson, 2007).

Classroom Questioning

Whatever the desired instructional outcome, "effective teaching depends primarily upon the teacher's skill in being able to ask questions which generate different kinds of learning" (Morgan and Saxton, 2006, 3). Of all the instructional tools and techniques classroom teachers possess, the art of effective questioning is perhaps the most versatile and important for learning (Parker and Hurry, 2007; Ritchart, Church, and Morrison, 2011). In addition, the use of good questioning skills is a powerful means of keeping students actively involved in lessons and thus minimizing disruptive behaviour. In order to develop this skill, teachers need to be thoughtful about the kinds of questions they ask, be patient as they wait for answers to be formulated, and listen in order to continue the discussion with another effective question. All questions are not equal, and the skill of asking good questions does not develop without conscious effort and careful personal reflection and evaluation.

Good questioning skills depend upon teachers asking themselves what kind of thinking their questions are producing as well as whether their questions are helping students engage with new learning. Morgan and Saxton (2006) have created what they call a "Taxonomy of Personal Engagement" that identifies a variety of questions:

Interest: questions that promote curiosity about what is being presented.

e.g., "What can I ask to gain their attention and interest?"

Engaging: questions that promote a desire to be involved in the task.

e.g., "What questions can I ask that will draw them into active involvement and encourage them to willingly share their ideas?"

Committing: questions that cause a sense of responsibility toward the task.

e.g., "What questions shall I ask that will invite them to accept some responsibility for this inquiry?"

Internalizing: questions that enable students to grasp concepts or new ideas for long-term understanding.

e.g., "What questions can I ask that will create an atmosphere where they will reflect upon their personal thoughts, feelings, points of view, experiences, and values in relation to this lesson?"

Interpreting: questions that encourage students to express the new understanding in their own words or in order to communicate with others.

e.g., "What questions shall I ask to encourage them to express their understanding of their world, their peers' world, and the world of the lesson?"

Evaluating: questions that enable students to put their new understandings to the test in a personal application.

e.g., "What questions shall I ask that will give them an opportunity to test their new thinking or knowledge in a different context?" (Morgan and Saxton, 2006)

Other findings on classroom management indicate that the following behaviours help promote student learning through questioning:

1. Ask a variety of questions that promote student thinking.
2. Ask good questions that challenge existing thinking and encourage reflection.
3. Ask the kind of question that enables many students to respond before another question is asked; for example, ask for an occasional response from the entire group, ask students to indicate their agreement or disagreement with answers, or redirect the question to obtain several individual answers.
4. After asking a question, allow students three to five seconds of "wait time" before accepting an answer. This time is particularly important when asking higher-level questions that require students to make inferences, connections, and judgments.
5. Vary the type of positive reinforcement you give for a correct or thoughtful response. Save very high praise for exceptional answers. The teacher's intention is not to give praise but to encourage students to share and discuss their ideas.
6. Ask follow-up or probing questions to expand student thinking after both correct and incorrect responses. Some sample types of follow-up questions include (a) asking for clarification, (b) asking a student to recreate the thought process he used to arrive at an answer, (c) asking for specific examples to support a statement, (d) asking for elaboration or expansion of an answer, and (e) asking a student to relate his answer to previous answers or questions.

Teachers who use these techniques, which may be adapted to fit their own classroom context, are likely to improve student learning and to increase their involvement in the learning activities, thereby minimizing disruptive student behaviour.

Maximizing Learning Time

One of the variables that affect how much students learn is the amount of time they spend learning. As Lieberman and Denham (1980) have found, there is a statistically positive relationship between time devoted to learning and scores on achievement tests. This is not, however, a simple relationship. Other factors, such as the quality of instruction and the kinds of learning tasks, must be considered in assessing the potential impact of increased time spent on learning. In other words, spending more instructional time with a weak teacher or on poorly devised learning tasks will not increase student learning. Results from a similar foundational Canadian study conducted in Alberta suggest that veteran teachers were more effective in fostering improvements in students' skills than less experienced teachers (Lytton and Pyryt, 1998). Subsequent research has supported the fundamental importance of effective, experienced teachers to the learning of students (Fleming and Raptis, 2004; Hattie, 2009).

Assuming that the teacher is competent and the learning tasks are appropriate, students who spend more time learning will probably learn more and create fewer management problems because they are occupied by the learning activities. Two areas that teachers can control to increase the amount of time students spend learning are the time allocated for instruction and the rate of student engagement in the learning tasks.

ALLOCATED TIME.   Allocated time refers to the amount of time that the teacher makes available for students to learn a subject. Although elementary school curriculum expectations are clearly defined in each province of Canada, it is at the discretion of the teacher to determine the amount of time that's needed to achieve those expectations. Educators would agree that the time varies from class to class and student to student.

In secondary schools, the amounts of time actually allocated to instruction also vary widely among teachers. The need to deal with routine attendance and housekeeping chores (e.g., "Who still owes lab reports?" and "Who needs to write a makeup for Friday's test?"), as well as the need to deal with disruptions that can range from behavioural problems to PA announcements, can steal large chunks of time from learning activities (see Chapter 2, "The Nature of Behavioural Problems"). Usually, both elementary and secondary school teachers need to examine how much time they make available for students to learn the various subjects they teach. Elementary teachers should investigate how they allocate time to their various subjects. Secondary teachers should investigate how to handle routine duties more efficiently and how to minimize disruptions.

TIME ON TASK.   In addition to increasing allocated time, teachers need to maximize student time on task (Earl, 2013; Nelson, Martella, and Marchand-Martella, 2002). For instance, one key to successful management is the ability of the teacher to maximize classroom time on task by minimizing classroom transitions such as forming learning groups, waiting for lessons to start, and passing out materials. Undue time accomplishing any such tasks can lead to more lost time as some students may take the opportunity to misbehave.

Here are some guidelines to increase student time on task:

1. The use of substantive interaction—a teaching mode in which the teacher presents information, asks questions to assess comprehension, provides feedback, and monitors student work—usually leads to higher student engagement than independent or small group work that is not led by the teacher.
2. Teacher monitoring of the entire class during the beginning and ending portions of a seatwork activity as well as at regular intervals during the activity leads to higher engagement rates.
3. Making sure that students understand what the activity directs them to do, that they have the skills necessary to complete the task successfully, that each student

has access to all needed materials, and that each student is protected from disruption by others leads to greater student time on task during seatwork.

4. Giving students oral and written directions concerning how to do a seatwork activity and what to do when they have finished the activity also leads to greater time on task during seatwork.

5. Communicating teacher awareness of student behaviour seems to lead to greater student involvement during seatwork activities.

6. "Providing a variety of seatwork activities with concern for students' attention spans helps keep students on task and allows the teacher more uninterrupted small group instruction" (Brophy, 2010).

7. Taking breaks with physical movement such as stretching or chatting for a few minutes with a partner enhances energy and engagement (Marzano, 2007).

8. Using games that focus on academic content but that have low-level stakes and a measure of fun leads to greater engagement.

9. Teacher modelling of enthusiasm and high energy that is focused on academic content is likely to increase engagement in learning (Marzano, 2007).

When students are on task, they are engaged in learning and are less apt to disrupt the learning of others. The effective teacher uses these guidelines to increase student learning and to minimize disruptive student behaviour—in other words, keep them busy, engaged, and productive!

BEYOND THE BASICS

Canadian Response to Educational Change

Since the early 1990s, ministries and departments of education in each province across Canada have been implementing standardized tests and more rigorous curricula in response to concerns that students must be educated to compete in a global economy (Drake, 2007). These changes occurred because of overall dissatisfaction with the current system at the time, as curricula focused almost exclusively on low-level outcomes and teaching and learning strategies, paying little attention to contextual variables and the subject matter being taught. In response, the Canadian Council of Ministers of Education (1997) established an agreement called the Pan-Canadian Protocol for Collaboration on School Curriculum. This agreement set out issues that are of common interest for each of the provinces, such as English and French curriculum, student assessment, technology, electronic exchange of information, and curriculum outcomes and standards and has affected the development of curriculum across the country. More recently, the media focus on global warming and concerns about environmental issues have prompted a mandate to increase curricular attention to the human impact on our planet (Nazir, Pedretti, Wallace, Montemurro and Inwood, 2009).

Each province developed its own response to this environment of challenge and change. Most provincial and territorial governments allocated large budgets for funding research and public surveys that were used and endorsed when campaigns were launched by ministries and departments of education to implement new and, in most cases, more stringent curriculum and testing standards. In some cases, educators and the public did not always agree with the latest changes that were recommended by those in charge of policy. In fact, full-scale disputes and unrest in some provinces have resulted in disruptions to education through teachers' work-to-rule actions and strikes because of proposed changes to education. Many teachers were resistant to change and were threatened by suggestions that they were not teaching effectively.

In addition, in 2009 the Council of Atlantic Ministers of Education and Training announced a regional action plan to improve literacy skills across the Maritimes. Within this plan in 2011, Newfoundland and Labrador focused on birth to three years by developing a focused early childhood learning curriculum framework. A similar program called StrongStart BC was established in British Columbia. In 2013, British Columbia started a consultative process to transform the curriculum to meet the needs of all learners with special focus on immigrant and aboriginal populations (Mamele'awt Aboriginal Education, 2013). Newfoundland and Labrador Ministry of Education introduced programs and funding through the province's Stepping into the Future early-childhood-development initiative aimed at increasing childhood and family literacy.

In Nova Scotia, through its Department of Education's Learning for Life plan, has been endeavouring to add teachers to the school system in order to reduce class sizes. This included resource teachers, speech language pathologists, Reading Recovery experts and other special needs professionals. Technological initiatives in reading and writing programs aimed at increasing the number of women in science, trades, technical and technology-related occupations have also been established in Nova Scotia. Nova Scotia will spend $6.7 million over the next five years to review course curriculum and teacher certification in schools in an effort to better prepare students for the workforce. Prince Edward Island created a document called the Strategic Plan, 1999–2004, to communicate the strategy and educational guidelines for the coming years. This manuscript outlines the goals for the province's schools and administration and sets out key performance measures for the strategies that have been designed to implement those goals. The Ministry of Education for PEI has also been working on other issues, including approaches to encourage graduates to return to or remain in the province. In 2010, the Government of Prince Edward Island launched the Preschool Excellence Initiative—a five-year plan to phase in important changes to the early childhood education. The Initiative included the largest one-time increase in funding for early childhood education in the history of the province.

In 2003, the premier of New Brunswick announced new spending in an initiative called the Quality Learning Agenda, which was brought in as a ten-year plan to strengthen New Brunswick's education system. The Quality Learning Agenda continues to concentrate on improving academic achievement, enhancing teaching practices, and guaranteeing increased accountability of the education system to students and parents. The plan calls for New Brunswick students to place in the top three provinces in Canada for academic achievement, high school graduation rates, and advancement to post-secondary institutions.

The province of Quebec has publically funded French and English schools. All students, however, must attend a French school. The only exceptions are the children who have parents who have done most of their elementary studies in English anywhere in Canada and the parents are Canadian citizens. In addition, if children have already done all or most of their elementary or secondary studies in English anywhere in Canada, or have a sibling who has received most of his education in English anywhere in Canada and again provided that the parents are Canadian citizens, they can be educated in English schools. Since 2006, English is taught as a second language in

French schools from Grade 1 onwards, and a few schools also offer English immersion programs for advanced students. English schools offer a large range of programs that include French as a second language, French immersion, and fully bilingual programs that teach both English and French as first languages. Quebec has also developed a long-term document, called the Strategic Plan of the Ministère de l'Éducation. The summary for the document lists guidelines for measuring the components of the education system and defines actions to accomplish the objectives. Other programs that are currently offered in Quebec involve special-needs students and technology.

In keeping with other provincial initiatives, Ontario's educational landscape has undergone a great number of changes over the past few years; for instance, in 2013, the ministry of education established a new initiative, *Achieving Excellence*. The goals of this program include the achievement of excellence in academic performance and the demonstration of good citizenship, the ensuring of equality, enhanced mental and physical health, and finally enhancing public confidence in the education system (Ontario Ministry of Education, 2014). In 2003, Ontario faced a major challenge in reducing secondary education by one year. In 2009, Ontario started to phase in full day Kindergarten for four- and five-year-olds with the plan to have the full day program available for all by 2015–16. Ontario's basic belief is that strong literacy and numeracy skills are the critical foundation for all other academic achievement and for a lifetime of success. The government's goal is to have 75 percent of students achieving the provincial standard (equivalent to a B grade) in reading, writing and mathematics. According to the Ontario Ministry of Education, by 2013 up to 71% of grade 3 and 6 students had achieved high provincial standards.

Manitoba began its focus on upgrading curriculum with an early years Numeracy Grant. This grant assisted school divisions/districts to implement early-intervention strategies aimed at improving mathematical skills, knowledge, and attitudes of students from kindergarten to grade 4. In 2014, James Allum, the Minister of Education and Advanced Learning in Manitoba, made a commitment with the initiative "Smaller Classes" saying, "our government's commitment to limit class sizes in kindergarten to grade three classes. Smaller Classes will enhance the quality of education in our schools by providing students with more one-on-one time with their teachers. The early years are critical to student success: we want to ensure that teachers are able to provide students with the support they need to get a strong start in reading, writing and math." (Allum, 2014)

Listening and speaking: First steps into literacy—a support document for kindergarten teachers, speech-language pathologists and educators, begun in 2008—has been implemented. It includes a parent video promoting oral language skills of children in the early years. The Safe and Caring Schools initiative promotes a positive approach to safety and belonging with a focus on preventing violence and bullying (Manitoba Education. Safe and Caring Schools, 2014).

The main issues for Saskatchewan were examining technological methods to further enhance their distance-learning programs. The Evergreen Curriculum is an example of how computer technology provides users who have online access with Saskatchewan's core curriculum guides, bibliographies, links to online resources, discussion areas, and a search function. In addition in 2014, the Ministry of Education committed to establishing electronic information services that will provide teachers and students access to more than 18,000 online journals, newspapers, reference books and more. "Quality online resources are key to successful learning experiences for students" (Morgan, 2014). The province is also examining and revising many areas of the curriculum. Overall, Saskatchewan's education sector plays a significant role in the province's present and future by establishing a foundation for lifelong learning and developing citizens who are highly literate with excellent workplace skills.

Alberta's Commission on Learning was established in 2002. The commission members visited communities across Alberta and talked with education stakeholders—parents, teachers, and support staff—to determine which educational issues were most important to these groups and to determine the commission's next steps. Alberta had not completed a comprehensive review of education in 30 years, so this process was deemed well overdue. While the *New Ministerial Order on Student Learning* intends to further strengthen Kindergarten to Grade 12 education in Alberta by outlining the goals and standards for student learning—with the primary focus on a learner-centred system to support students in developing competencies needed to be engaged thinkers and ethical citizens with an entrepreneurial spirit, *Curriculum Redesign* seeks to ensure Alberta's curriculum remains responsive and relevant for students. This project reflects the province's commitment to continually improve its work in providing a world-class, student-centred curriculum for students now and in the future. Another initiative is an inclusive education system where all students belong and receive a quality education regardless of their ability, disability, language, cultural background, gender, or age.

In 2002, British Columbia also initiated an educational task force to gather perceptions on student achievement, human and social development, and safety. The British Columbia education ministry surveyed students in grades 4, 7, 10, and 12, as well as parents and school staff members in 1582 schools. British Columbia used these results and those from its 2002 administration of the foundation skills assessment (FSA) to set out implications for instruction in reading comprehension, writing, and numeracy in grades 4, 7, and 10. In 2010, British Columbia also started a full day Kindergarten program with a focus on the StrongStart BC program (StrongStart BC, 2009). A new web-based service will dramatically improve the ability of British Columbia parents and teachers to follow and support students' educational progress—from kindergarten through to graduation. British Columbia's web-based initiative, the Education Plan, prioritizes students, with teachers collaborating with students and their families. The initiative aims at providing student-centred learning so that every student achieves full potential.

Canada's territories also participated in educational change with their own initiatives based on perceived needs; for example, the Yukon Ministry of Education is committed to channelling significant resources to projects that use the internet. Several monetary awards were allocated to projects from Canada's SchoolNet grassroots program (Kitagawa, 2001). In addition to new projects that have received funding, the ministry has a full webpage devoted to projects that have already been completed. The mandate of the Yukon Department of Education is to deliver accessible and quality education to all Yukon students. Its primary responsibilities are to provide a public education system for Kindergarten to Grade 12 (K-12), to support adult education, and to encourage lifelong learning.

The Northwest Territories (NWT) in 2001 launched a literacy initiative. The purpose of the NWT strategy was to enhance existing literacy programs and to ensure every

NWT community has access to literacy training. The government budgeted $2.4 million yearly to encourage partnerships and programs that assist NWT residents to raise their literacy skills and education level. This program, called Towards Literacy: A Strategy Framework, offers literacy programs to all NWT residents through many community-based programs and partnerships with non-governmental organizations (NGOs), individuals, families, communities, and government agencies and is an ongoing initiative. Teacher education in the NWT is committed to preparing aboriginal teachers by increasing accessibility to a program that provides personal, professional, cultural, and academic learning. It is anticipated that the success of this program will support more fully a culture-based educational system (Auditor General of Canada, 2010).

Canada's newest territory, Nunavut, also participates in grassroots programs through SchoolNet. The development of a state-of-the-art technological infrastructure is receiving high priority, along with an emphasis on cultural, literacy, and numeracy skills. An on-going initiative is through the Department of Environment, which is committed to supporting teachers in bringing environmental and wildlife education into the classroom, and in bringing students into the environment to experience nature's classroom.

Researchers' Responses to Change

The major impetus for the current models of teaching and learning is the rise in popularity of **constructivism** as a philosophical set of beliefs about learning. Until relatively recently, education and its research have been dominated by behaviourist and information-processing views of learning, which, although different in many respects, share a conception of the learner basically as a passive receptor of information received from the outside environment. In contrast, constructivism emphasizes active construction of knowledge by the learner; thus, constructivism places the learner squarely in the centre of the learning paradigm and sees the role of the teacher as one of coaching, guiding and supporting the learner as needed. The tenets of constructivism are the following five points: (1) knowledge is actively constructed, (2) knowledge should be structured around a few powerful ideas, (3) prior knowledge exerts a powerful influence on new learning, (4) restructuring prior knowledge and conceptual change are key elements of new learning, and (5) knowledge is socially constructed (Good and Brophy, 2008). Using the constructivist paradigm, teachers must provide opportunities for students to make new knowledge their own through questions, discussion, debate, and other interactive activities (MaaB and Artigue, 2013).

The research on student cognition, constructivism, conceptual-change teaching, and subject-specific teaching has led to several changes in our thinking about instructional practice. Indeed, such research has led to a *new paradigm for learning* that rests on the following: (1) teaching for understanding as the major goal for teaching; (2) using authentic instructional tasks as the basis for classroom learning; (3) emphasizing teaching frameworks that highlight the importance of thinking skills, problem-solving, and student self-regulation; (4) moving from individual learning to the creation of learning communities; (5) teaching for multiple types of intelligence; and (6) emphasizing student cognitive variables rather than overt teacher behaviour as the key aspect of student motivation in the classroom. In this section of the chapter, these concepts will be described individually, even though they are interwoven and closely related to each other.

Another shift in understanding has come as a result of changing views of the meaning of literacy as it relates to existing communication patterns. The term *multiliteracies* has emerged to describe the increasingly complex world of communication (Cope and Kalantzis, 2000; Elliott, Woloshyn, Bajovic, and Ratkovic, 2007; Roswell and Lapp, 2011). Multiliteracies comprise both the multitude of communication methods through media and the burgeoning cultural and linguistic diversity through globalization (Bajovic and Elliott, 2011; Cope and Kalantzis, 2000); for instance, written communication is changing with social-networking websites, such as Facebook, LinkedIn, Twitter, Instagram, and blogs and text messaging having their own languages and set of ethical behaviours. Thus, educators are starting to respond to this reality by broadening their views of literacy instruction to include critical literacy in order to help children become discerning consumers who are properly prepared to participate in rapidly changing global communication patterns (Bajovic and Elliott, 2011). This particular imperative to change and the overwhelming research support for viewing literacy differently is colliding with the immediacy of standardized testing related to traditional literacy and numeracy skills. Teachers feel they have little time to devote to newer forms of literacy no matter how much they dominate children's lives (Elliott, Woloshyn, Bajovic, and Ratkovic, 2007).

Teaching for Understanding

For much of the history of education in Canada, the goals for classroom learning have focused on the acquisition of factual information, learning routine skills, and following procedures. Although still important, these goals have become increasingly less sufficient for enabling students to function competently in today's technologically sophisticated, information-rich society. In order to function effectively in a global, interactive society, students need to go beyond memorization of content and routine skills to much deeper levels of understanding and interdisciplinary skills. Howard Gardner (2006a) has asserted that our schools have never really taught for deep understanding. Instead, they have settled for what Gardner calls the "correct answer compromise"; that is, students give agreed-upon answers that are counted as correct, but their real-world behaviour indicates that they have failed to truly understand the material. Gardner believes that we need to enable students to achieve a deep understanding of the material that they encounter in school. **Deep understanding** means being able to do a variety of thought-demanding tasks, such as explaining a topic in one's own words, making predictions, finding exemplars in new contexts, and applying concepts to explain new situations. Gardner's work has gone on to identify naturalistic intelligence, which focuses on the synthesis of information through its relationship with the natural world. This ability to identify the big picture and make connections between concepts is seen to be an important component of deep understanding and thus, has been included as an existential intelligence (McCoog, 2010). Educators must remember, however, that the recognition and identification of strengths within the multiple intelligences should be used to empower learning rather than to label students (Gardner, 2006b).

The first step in making deep understanding one of our goals for student learning involves the teacher coming to grips with the content-coverage dilemma. Teaching for understanding involves time. Learners' deep understandings of content or skills that transfer across disciplines do not develop overnight. Learners need opportunities to become engaged with the content in different contexts. They need the opportunity to see many examples, ask many questions, discuss ideas with peers and with the teacher, and practise demonstrating their personal understanding in a variety of situations. If the transfer of skills is to occur, students need explicit prompts by the teacher to remind them to employ a strategy learned in one context to a new situation (Almesi and Fullerton, 2012; Goeke, 2008). As a result, it is simply not possible to cover the same amount of material that can be covered in a classroom in which student memorization is the goal. The teacher who wants to teach for understanding must be willing to take the time to allow students to become deeply involved with the material.

For those teachers who are willing to cover less material at deeper levels of student understanding, Wiske (1998) offers a four-part framework that can be used to focus classroom learning on creating deeper understanding. The first part of the framework calls for the teacher to use "generative topics" as the focus for classroom learning. In order for a topic to qualify as generative, it must meet three criteria: (1) it must be an important topic in the discipline; (2) it must be easily conveyed by teachers to learners at various developmental levels; and (3) it must be relatable to learners' lives and interests outside of school. The second part of Wiske's framework asks the teacher to set learning goals that require students to demonstrate their understanding; for example, students might identify examples of Newton's laws of motion in everyday sports events. The third part of the framework requires students to demonstrate their understanding through classroom activities and performances, such as discussions, debates, experiments, problem-solving, and so forth. The final part of the framework calls for ongoing assessment of student progress using publicly shared criteria for success, frequent feedback by the teacher, and periodic opportunities for students to reflect on their own progress toward demonstrating a deep understanding of the particular topic.

Authentic Instruction

While the concept of teaching for understanding focuses on three separate but related elements (the content selected for instruction, the selected learning goals, and general strategies for assessing student learning), the concept of authentic instruction emphasizes actual classroom activities. When these two concepts are melded together in the classroom, the teacher has a powerful set of ideas for enhancing both student understanding and student interest in the teaching–learning process (Marks, 2000).

According to foundational and influential work by Newmann and Wehlage (1993), there are five key elements to authentic instruction. They have developed a continuum for each element that can be used by a teacher or an observer to determine the degree to which authentic instruction is happening in a classroom. The first continuum looks at the emphasis on higher-order thinking versus the emphasis on lower-order thinking. When authentic instruction is in progress, students are asked to manipulate, transform, and use information in new and unpracticed ways rather than to receive information and use it in repetitive and routine ways.

The second continuum—depth of coverage—is closely related to the concept of teaching for understanding. When authentic instruction is taking place, students encounter a small number of ideas but are expected to develop a deep level of understanding of the ideas as opposed to encountering many ideas that are dealt with only at surface level.

The third continuum focuses on the connection of school activities to the world outside the classroom. Teachers using authentic instruction present real-world problems as topics of study, and students are expected to apply their knowledge to settings outside the classroom. Information is not seen as useful *only* for continued success in school.

The fourth continuum—substantive conversation—focuses on the nature of the verbal interaction that occurs in the classroom and the relationships between teachers and students (Roorda, Koomen, Split, and Oort, 2011). When authentic instruction takes place, both the learners and the teacher are engaged in dialogue and argumentation that is unscripted and uncontrolled and that builds on participants' understandings, as opposed to verbal interactions that are characterized primarily by short, pre-planned, predictable conversations and interactions.

The final continuum focuses on the push for achievement in the classroom. When authentic instruction is in place, the classroom environment is marked by mutual respect, intellectual risk taking, and a widely accepted belief that all learners can learn, as opposed to a classroom environment that discourages effort and participation and in which only some students are viewed as capable learners (Wang and Holcombe, 2010).

Classrooms that use authentic instruction differ from traditional classrooms not only in terms of the problems students are asked to solve but also in terms of the teacher's role in structuring student learning. Because authentic instruction forces students to solve real-world types of problems rather than to simply apply previously learned formulas or concepts to solve textbook problems, the problems are not well-defined and are not usually confined to one specific discipline (Drake, 2007). In order to solve such problems, students must first define the problems, then gather additional information or acquire additional skills.

Consequently, teachers usually introduce these complex, ill-structured problems early in the learning sequence and then allow the instructional sequence to emerge from the way in which the problems are defined. In other words, lower-level knowledge and skills are not introduced as separate topics. The need to develop lower-level skills and acquire lower-level knowledge arises directly from the students' attempt to define and solve the problem that serves as the focus for learning. The old paradigm, which held that students must first acquire a host of prerequisite knowledge before being introduced to problem-solving activities, has been replaced by a new paradigm: It asserts that lower-level knowledge and skills should be acquired as a result of students needing specific information or specific skills in order to solve real-world problems (Drake, 2007). In authentic instruction, the teacher is active early in the learning process, modelling appropriate problem-solving behaviour, providing cues and information to the learner, and structuring the learning process; however, as time goes on and students acquire a better understanding of the real-world problem and the information and skills needed to solve it, the students become more self-regulated and take an active role in structuring their own learning (Kessler and Bikowski, 2010;

Reeve, 2009). As we noted earlier in the section on lesson design, this type of structuring is sometimes referred to as *scaffolding*.

Emphasis on Thinking and Problem-Solving Skills

Clearly, the concepts of teaching for understanding and authentic instruction emphasize student thinking and problem-solving skills; however, because thinking and problem-solving skills are seen as tools for acquiring a deep understanding of content, they play a secondary rather than primary role in the conceptualization of the teaching and learning process. Thinking and problem-solving skills, however, play an important role in the conceptualization of teaching developed by Marzano (2007). This conceptualization, entitled *dimensions of learning*, provides a comprehensive framework for focusing teaching and learning on the development of higher-order thinking, problem-solving, and understanding. Marzano assumes that the process of learning involves the interaction of five types of thinking, which he has called dimensions of learning.

Dimension 1, which comprises "positive attitudes and perceptions about learning," states that all learning activities are filtered through the students' attitudes and perceptions; therefore, effective teachers shape their lessons to foster positive attitudes and perceptions. They help to create these positive attitudes by making students feel accepted, providing physical and psychological comfort (see Chapter 3, "Understanding Why Children Misbehave"), creating a sense of order and routine in the classroom, helping students to understand what they are required to do in performing classroom tasks, and helping students believe that they can be successful in completing those tasks.

Dimension 2 concerns the acquisition of new knowledge and skills. According to this dimension, early in the learning process, effective teachers help students to acquire new knowledge by encouraging them to relate the new knowledge to what they already know and by providing them with opportunities to organize the information in ways that will help them to store it in their long-term memory. These teachers aid the acquisition of new skills by structuring the learning sequence: They first help students to build a cognitive model of the new skill, and then gradually shape skill performance to make it more refined, automatic, and internalized. This dimension corresponds nicely to the research on effective teaching described in the first section of this chapter.

Dimension 3 concerns the extension and refinement of knowledge by learners. Effective teachers help learners to refine and extend their knowledge by providing opportunities for them to use such thinking skills as comparing and contrasting information, classifying information and observations, analyzing arguments, constructing support for ideas and arguments, abstracting information, and analyzing diverse perspectives on issues and questions.

The final two dimensions concern using knowledge meaningfully and developing productive habits of mind. These two dimensions remind us that teachers should involve students in long-term, self-directed projects that require investigation, decision-making, research, problem-solving, and invention. Effective teachers should also help their students to develop sensitivity to feedback, a desire for accuracy, persistence in the face of difficulty, an unconventional view of situations, and an ability to avoid impulsive actions. These traits help learners solve the complex problems and issues that they face both in the classroom and throughout their lives. When used as a framework for planning, implementing, and analyzing instruction, these five dimensions of learning serve as valuable tools for enhancing student thinking, problem-solving, and self-regulated learning.

Creating Communities of Learners

One of the most dramatic changes that have taken place in our thinking about teaching during the last 15 years has been the emphasis we now place on the importance of building learning communities in the classroom. In the past, we emphasized individual student learning and interaction between individual students and the teacher. Note that the research on effective teaching described in the first section of this chapter focuses almost exclusively on interaction between individual students and their teacher. Early research on effective teaching viewed peers as superfluous to the learning process; however, because of the foundational work on cooperative learning conducted by Johnson, Johnson, and Holubec (1993), Slavin (1989–90), Kagan (1994), and others, we now believe that peers can play a tremendously important role in enhancing student learning and in developing positive classroom environments. For this reason, we now believe that the creation of a classroom learning community in which students engage in dialogue with each other and with the teacher is a critical step toward making classrooms productive learning environments (Young and Talanquer 2013).

Creating communities of learners often begins with designing lessons to involve students in cooperative learning activities. Cooperative learning should not be equated with simply putting students into groups. Cooperative learning activities share a set of common characteristics. Although the number of specific elements in cooperative learning differs among theorists—Johnson, Johnson, and Holubec (1993), for example, favour five elements, while Slavin (1989–90) favours three—there seem to be at least three elements that are critical to its success. These are (1) face-to-face interaction, (2) a feeling of positive interdependence, and (3) a feeling of individual accountability.

Face-to-face interaction requires placing students in close physical proximity to each other and ensuring that they are required to talk to each other in order to complete the assigned tasks. If students can complete the task without interacting with each other, they have been engaged in an individual learning activity rather than a cooperative learning activity.

Establishing a feeling of *positive interdependence* means that students believe each individual can achieve the particular learning goal only if all the learners in the group achieve the learning goal. Johnson, Johnson, and Holubec (1993) and Gilles and Boyle, 2010, who refer to this as "sinking or swimming together," have identified several types of interdependence that the teacher can work to create. *Positive reward interdependence* occurs when everyone is rewarded or no one is rewarded, and everyone gets the same reward. *Positive resource interdependence* occurs when each member of the group has only a portion of the information or materials needed to complete the task. A teacher is using positive resource interdependence when each student has only one piece of a puzzle or one section of required reading. *Positive task interdependence* occurs when a task is broken into a series of steps and is then completed in assembly-line fashion, with each group member completing only one section of the total task. *Positive role interdependence* is the practice of assigning roles to individual group members; for example, consensus checker, writer, reader, timekeeper, and so on. Obviously, each role must be important to the completion of the task. Finally, *positive identity interdependence* is established by allowing the group to form its own identity—for example, by creating a group name, decorating a group folder or flag, or developing a group motto or some other symbol that describes the group. The researchers suggest that the teacher build as many of these types of positive interdependence into cooperative learning lessons as possible in order to increase the likelihood of creating feelings of positive interdependence.

Individual accountability refers to each group member's feeling that he is responsible for completing the task and cannot rest on the laurels of the group or allow other members to do the work for him. Feelings of individual accountability can be established in a variety of ways, including assigning individual grades; giving individual tests, worksheets, and quizzes; or structuring tasks so that they must be completed by the group while making it clear that individual members will be called on at random to answer questions about the task.

In addition to face-to-face interaction, positive interdependence, and individual accountability, the researchers believe two more elements—teaching social skills and processing group functioning—are crucial for the creation of cooperative learning activities. These two elements are described at length in Chapter 7, "Structuring the Environment." As Case 6.4 illustrates, cooperative learning activities can have a positive impact on student motivation and behaviour.

CASE 6.4
Cooperative Learning in Biology

Because of my position as department head, I am often in and out of teachers' classrooms for quick conversations about curriculum and/or students. One day, as I walked into Mr. Higgins's grade 12 biology class, which was filled primarily with vocational technical students, I was surprised to see a variety of specimen samples lying on the lab tables. Mr. Higgins began class by informing his students that they would be having a lab quiz— he referred to it as a "practical"—the next day, which would constitute a major grade for the marking period. The students, who were busily engaged in their own private conversations, met this news with shrugs of indifference. Mr. Higgins continued speaking: "The practical will also be a cooperative learning team activity. Each of your individual scores on the quiz will be added together and averaged to form a team score. Your team score will be counted as part of the scores for our team competition. Just to review team standings so far, we have the Plumbers in first place with 93 points, followed by the Body Fixers with 88 points, the Hair Choppers with 87, and the Electricians in last place with 86 points. Don't forget that we have all agreed that the winning team will be treated to a pizza party by the rest of the class. Now, you may go ahead and get started studying in teams for tomorrow's practical."

For a brief moment, the room fell completely silent. This was followed by the scrape of chairs and scuffling of feet as students moved into cooperative learning teams. Within minutes, the students were busy looking at the specimens and relating them to the diagrams in their textbook. Students were clearly engaged in helping each other to memorize the various

(Continued)

(*Continued*)

specimen parts that they would need to know for the quiz. Suddenly, one of the students from the Electricians sat down and began to read a comic book. Within a few minutes, however, the other members of the team informed him that he was not going to sit there and do nothing. They assured him that they would help him to obtain a passing grade on the quiz whether he liked it or not. The student got to his feet with a look of resignation and resumed looking at the specimens.

Questions to Consider

1. What beliefs about learning are influencing Mr. Higgins's decisions about administering tests to this class?
2. How could Mr. Higgins also encourage individual accountability in this class?

Teaching Toward Multiple Intelligences

Through the work of Howard Gardner and his colleagues many educators have come to realize that success in school has been unnecessarily restricted to those individuals who have talents in the areas of mathematical and verbal intelligence (2006a,b). Many of the tasks and learning activities performed in schools require learners to use verbal and mathematical reasoning while ignoring other ways of expressing talent. One need only look at standardized achievement tests, traditional IQ tests, and the scholastic aptitude tests (SATs) and standardized testing in Canada across the provinces to recognize our overdependence on verbal and mathematical ability. Fortunately, Gardner's theory of multiple intelligences and its application have helped us recognize how other types of talent can be tapped.

Gardner's theory asserts that there are many types of human intelligence and that it is possible to group the various types into seven comprehensive categories: linguistic, logical/mathematical, spatial, bodily/kinaesthetic, musical, interpersonal, intrapersonal and naturalistic intelligences. Each one of us, according to Gardner, possesses these types of intelligence to some degree. Those who exhibit high degrees of linguistic intelligence are able to use oral and written language effectively. They are often individuals who succeed in areas such as politics, sales, advertising, and writing. Individuals with strengths in the area of logical/mathematical ability work with numbers effectively and tend to use reason and logical arguments well. Such individuals are accountants, lawyers, scientists, and so on. Some individuals—for example, artists, architects, and interior designers—excel at tasks that require them to perceive and transform graphic and visual representations of reality. Athletes, dancers, and craftspeople, such as mechanics, fall into the category of bodily/kinaesthetic intelligence. They are able to use their bodies to express feelings and ideas and are able to use their hands to produce things. Musicians, conductors, music critics, and composers have a special capacity to perceive and express musical form. Thus, they have a high degree of musical intelligence. Individuals who are very sensitive to the feelings, moods, and intentions of others display interpersonal intelligence. They are often quite successful in people-oriented occupations, such as teaching, counselling, and psychology. There are certain individuals who seem to possess a high degree of self-knowledge and awareness. They understand themselves well and are able to act on that knowledge. Finally, those who possess naturalist intelligence are able to draw on materials and features of the natural environment to solve problems and fashion products. Farmers, national park rangers, environmentalists and wilderness guides draw heavily on this type of intelligence.

Although good teachers have always been aware of the variety of ways in which students demonstrate high ability, standard classroom practices and assessment devices have not allowed students to demonstrate their knowledge in ways compatible with their strengths. More recently, Drake (2007), Huber and McKinney (2013), and others have begun to help teachers figure out how to structure classroom activities and assessments to take full advantage of the range of intelligences that learners possess. According to research, learners who are linguistically talented benefit from activities such as storytelling, listening to and giving lectures, journal writing, and participating in classroom discussions. Students who have high aptitudes in mathematical/logical ability usually enjoy activities such as problem-solving, observing and classifying, Socratic questioning, and experiments. Students who have strengths in spatial reasoning often profit from visual displays, colour coding and colour cues, and graphic representations, such as semantic maps and webs. Students who are talented in the bodily/kinaesthetic area profit from learning activities that include body movement. Such activities might include acting out stories and concepts, and using manipulatives. Learners who exhibit high degrees of musical ability usually learn more effectively when learning activities include songs, raps, chants, and the use of music as either a teaching tool or a background environment. Learners who are strong in interpersonal intelligence perform best when they are engaged in collegial interactions, such as peer tutoring, cooperative learning, simulations, and board games. Finally, students who possess a high degree of intrapersonal intelligence learn best when provided with opportunities for personal goal setting, for connecting school work to their personal lives, for making choices about learning activities, and for individual reflection on their own learning. These students often are exceptionally good at self-assessment.

Armstrong (1994) suggests that teachers ask themselves the following questions when planning a unit of instruction:

1. How will I use the spoken or written word in this unit?
2. How can I bring numbers, calculations, and logic into the unit?
3. How can I use visual aids, colour, and symbolism in the unit?
4. How can I involve movement and create hands-on activities?
5. How can I use music or environmental sounds?
6. How can I involve students in peer tutoring, cooperative learning, and sharing?
7. How can I evoke personal feelings and connections and provide students with the opportunity to make individual choices about the unit?

Differentiating Instruction

Gardner's theory of multiple intelligences represents only one dimension of difference among the learners in any classroom. Anyone who has spent time in a kindergarten classroom understands that children are not the same when they begin school, and anyone who has spent time working with high school seniors recognizes that the students are not all the same when they graduate. Even students who are grouped for instruction homogeneously differ from each other in significant ways; for instance, students differ on the basis of readiness to learn, prior knowledge, motivation, thinking ability, metacognitive understanding, subject interest, self-regulation ability, cultural background, and learning style. It is not realistic to assume that we can teach all students in exactly the same way. Research reveals that effective differentiation of instruction:

1. Uses small, flexible instructional groups to meet learner needs.
2. Employs a wide variety of materials to address learner needs.
3. Allows learners to proceed at different paces.
4. Demands a knowledgeable teacher who understands what the essential learnings of each unit of instruction are.
5. Is learner-centred, which means the teacher observes individual students to identify specific needs (Tomlinson, 2005).

Teachers who want to differentiate instruction to better meet their students' needs should be cognizant of several principles that underlie the differentiation process:

1. Good curriculum comes first. If the curriculum is poorly designed and not engaging, differentiation will make little difference.
2. When in doubt, teach up. Ask students to stretch rather than teach at a lower level.
3. Ongoing assessment is crucial. Both informal and formal assessment tools should be employed to assess student learning as well as to adjust the differentiation strategies.
4. Flexible groups are a critical factor. Students must have the opportunity to move easily from one group to another to better meet their academic needs.
5. The emphasis should always be on student strengths. Make sure that students have multiple opportunities to learn in preferred ways and to demonstrate their understanding in ways that are comfortable for them.
6. Make your expectations for student learning clear. Students should have a clear picture of what they are supposed to learn as well as an understanding of the criteria that will guide assessment (Tomlinson, 2005).

Student Motivation: Student Cognition

In the first section of this chapter, "The Basics of Effective Teaching," we discussed theories and models of motivation that emphasized factors external to the student. Indeed, the focus of that section was on overt teacher behaviours that have an impact on student motivation. In this section, we will look at motivation from a different perspective—that of student cognition and its impact on motivation to learn. There are at present at least three theories of student motivation—student cognition, attribution, and expectancy H (Hope) value theory—that have interesting implications for teaching.

The primary developer of the social cognition theory of student motivation was Albert Bandura (1997). Bandura took issue with the behavioural notions of motivation that emphasized external reinforcers. He asserted that the individual's thoughts play a central role not only in determining the individual's motivational levels but also in determining how the individual will perceive variables that are intended to be reinforcers. Bandura's research demonstrated that personal evaluation and self-satisfaction are potent reinforcers of behaviour—in fact, probably more potent than reinforcers provided by others. Bandura's research findings showed that involving students in personal goal setting and providing frequent opportunities for students to monitor and reflect on their progress toward these goals can increase student learning efforts. In fact, according to Bandura, external praise can diminish self-evaluation and create dependency on others, thereby reducing an individual's intrinsic motivation to succeed.

Bandura's work on personal evaluation and self-satisfaction led to a related concept that he called **self-efficacy**. Self-efficacy refers to an individual's expectation of success at a particular task. When feelings of self-efficacy are high, individuals are much more likely to exert effort toward task completion than they are when feelings are low, because they believe they have the potential to be successful. When feelings of self-efficacy are low, efforts are diminished. Feelings of self-efficacy develop from judgments about past performance as well as from vicarious observations of others in similar situations. The greater the perceived similarity between the person we are observing (the model) and ourselves, the greater the impact that person's fate will have on our own feelings of self-efficacy.

When social cognition theory is in action in the classroom, the teacher's task is to focus encouragement on the improvement of individual effort and achievement over time. Teachers who wish to use this theory in the classroom should begin by engaging students in setting personal goals that are concrete, specific, and realistic. Teachers should then involve students in monitoring their own performance toward the achievement of these goals. When students are successful, teachers must encourage them to engage in self-reinforcement so that they will build positive feelings of self-efficacy toward the accomplishment of future tasks. Attribution theory deals with student-perceived causes of success and failure in school tasks. Clearly, students' perceptions of why they succeed or fail at school tasks have a direct impact on their motivation to perform (Stipek, 2002; Tollefson, 2000). Research has identified five factors to which students are likely to attribute success or failure. These factors are ability, effort, task difficulty, luck, and other people, such as the teacher or parents (Gonzalez-DeHass, Willems, and Holbein, 2005). The only factor that can be controlled directly by the student is effort. When students attribute success to effort, and failure to lack of effort or inappropriate types of effort, they are likely to exert additional effort in the future. Those students who are most likely to learn believe that their learning is a result of their own efforts while those who believe learning is dependent upon the quality of the teaching, the difficulty of the task or even just luck are less likely to be successful (Wang and Palinscar, 1989).

When students attribute failure to lack of ability, the impact on future performance is devastating. Negative feelings of self-efficacy develop, and students see little value in making any effort since they believe that they are not likely to be successful. As negative judgments of ability become more internalized and self-worth more damaged, students stop making any effort as a defence mechanism. Not making the effort allows them to protect their self-concept from further damage. They can simply shrug their shoulders and claim, "I could have done it if I wanted to, but I really didn't think it was worth it." This face-saving device prevents further ego damage that would result from additional negative ability attributions. To avoid setting up the vicious circle of failure and lack of future effort, teachers need to recognize the danger of placing students in competitive situations in which they do not have the ability to compete, or of asking students to complete tasks that are too difficult for them.

The implications of attribution theory for classroom teaching are clear. Students need to be assigned tasks that are moderately challenging but within their capability. This may mean that the teacher has to break complex tasks into subtasks that the student can handle and provide a great deal of scaffolding for the student, especially early in the learning process. The teacher should encourage students to make the right kind of effort in completing classroom tasks. When students are successful, the teacher can attribute their success to this effort. When students are not successful, the teacher may want to focus attention on the lack of effort or on the use of inappropriate strategies. Research has demonstrated that teacher statements concerning attributions for success or failure are the key variables in influencing students to attribute success or failure to one variable rather than another. Case 6.5 illustrates the impact of changing attributions.

The expectancy H value theory proposes that the effort an individual is willing to put forth in any task is directly related to the product of two factors: the belief that he will be successful and the value of the outcomes that will be gained through successful completion of the task (Schwartz, 2012). A multiplication sign is used to indicate the interaction between the two factors. Note that if either of the two factors is 0, no effort will be put forth; thus, if a student believes that he has the potential to be successful in academic work and values good grades and the other outcomes that accompany academic success, he will be highly motivated to put forth a strong effort. On the other hand, if the student doubts his ability to perform the academic tasks successfully or does not value good grades and the other outcomes attached to academic success, he is likely to put forth a limited, feeble effort. Teachers can increase a student's effort at success either by encouraging the learner to believe that he can be successful or by increasing the value of the outcomes. Good and Brophy (2008) have suggested that teachers take the following steps to implement and to ensure the success of the expectancy H value theory in the classroom:

1. Establish a supportive classroom climate.
2. Structure activities so that they are at the appropriate level of difficulty.
3. Develop learning objectives that have personal meaning and relevance for the students.
4. Engage students in personal goal setting and self-appraisal.
5. Help students recognize the link between effort and outcome suggested by attribution theory.

CASE 6.5

Three Years of History Rolled into One

Mark was a senior who had failed both grade 10 and grade 11 history and was now taking grade 10, grade 11, and grade 12 history in order to graduate on time. The school guidance counsellor, who was working with him to improve his study skills, began by helping Mark to prepare for a test on Canadian Confederation. When the counsellor asked which material seemed important for the test, Mark replied, "Well, I know that one thing she is going to ask is, 'What is the significance to Confederation of building the railroad across Canada?'" With this response, it became clear to the counsellor that Mark was not good at distinguishing important from unimportant material. Over the next couple of weeks, they spent a great deal of time looking at Mark's notes and his textbook, separating important from unimportant material.

Two days before the test, Mark had a list of important material to study and did a reasonably good job learning that material. Immediately after taking the test, Mark went to the guidance counsellor's office and announced, "You know what? I noticed something on the test." "What did you notice?" asked the counsellor. "I noticed that the stuff I studied for, I knew, and the stuff I didn't study, I didn't know." At first, the counsellor thought that Mark was putting him on; however, as the conversation continued, it became clear that Mark was serious. Until this point in his life,

Mark had felt that success on tests was simply a matter of luck. If you happened to be paying attention to the right things in class, you did well on tests. If you were unfortunate enough to be daydreaming during key information, you did poorly. It was all a matter of luck in terms of when you were paying attention.

Armed with this information, the guidance counsellor now had a two-pronged approach to working with Mark. Not only did they work on identifying important information but also on attributing both success and failure to personal effort rather than to chance. As a result of this work, Mark managed to pass (albeit barely) all three histories and graduate on time.

Questions to Consider

1. Why had Mark developed such a dysfunctional belief about tests?
1. The skill of *learning how to learn* is more important than the content being learned. Discuss.

Summary

In the first section of this chapter, we presented an overview of the research on teaching that, as we see it, constitutes the basics of effective teaching. In the second section, we described several conceptualizations of teaching that have influenced our current understanding of best teaching practices. These conceptualizations focus on student cognition and higher-order thinking and understanding. Taken together, the two major sections of the chapter provide the reader with a comprehensive understanding of current thinking concerning best teaching practices. All teachers have a professional obligation to examine their teaching behaviour to ensure that it

reflects best practices. This is a critical step toward making sure that the teacher has done all that can be done to prevent classroom-management problems. Among the questions teachers should ask in assessing the congruence between their own teaching and best practices are the following:

1. Do the lessons I design include an introduction, a clear presentation of content, checks for student understanding, guided practice, independent practice, closure or summary, and periodic reviews?
2. Have I considered each of the following factors in trying to increase my students'

motivation to learn: student interests, student needs, novelty and variety, success, student attributions, tension, feeling tone, feedback, and encouragement?

3. Have I communicated high expectations for learning and behaviour to all students by equalizing response opportunities, providing prompt and constructive feedback on performance, and treating all students with personal regard?

4. Have I used classroom questioning to involve students actively in the learning process by asking questions at a variety of cognitive levels, using questions to increase student participation and to probe for and extend student thinking?

5. Have I maximized student learning by allocating as much time as possible to this objective and increasing the percentage of student engagement in learning activities?

6. Am I teaching to enable students to develop a deep understanding of content rather than a surface-level knowledge?

7. Am I using authentic instruction in terms of the learning activities I plan and carry out?

8. Am I using a comprehensive framework to help students develop thinking skills, problem-solving skills, and the capacity to regulate their own learning?

9. Am I building communities of learners?

10. Am I teaching so that students can demonstrate their learning by using a variety of intelligences?

11. Am I using student cognition to increase student motivation to learn?

The teacher who can answer *yes* honestly to each of these questions has made giant strides toward ensuring that his classroom will be a learning place for students in which behavioural problems are kept to a minimum.

Key Terms

backward design or design-down planning: begins with the end in mind, the enduring understanding, then moves further up the planning continuum (please examine other documentation for more complete explanation).

constructivism: learning that is initiated and directed by the learner.

deep understanding: being able to do a variety of thought-demanding tasks.

effective teacher/teaching: most often defined as enhanced student achievement on paper-and-pencil tests.

lesson: the amount of instructional time required for students to achieve a specific learning objective.

self-efficacy: an individual's expectation of success at a particular task.

Exercises

1. Select a concept from any discipline with which you are familiar.
   a. Write a series of questions on the concept at each of the following levels: knowledge, comprehension, application, analysis, synthesis, and evaluation.
   b. Would there be any difference in the use of wait time in asking the six questions you wrote? Why?
   c. Why is a hierarchical ordering of questions important in classroom management?
2. Why is it better to ask the question first and then call on someone to answer it? Would there be any justification for doing it the other way around?
3. What specifically can teachers do to communicate high expectations for learning and behaviour to students?

4. What would be the effect on student learning if the following were omitted from the teaching act?
   a. the introduction
   b. a check for understanding
   c. closure or summary
5. What are some things teachers can do to ensure that their explanation of content is clear?
6. Using your knowledge of students' cognitive and moral development, give some important techniques for motivating students at each of the following grade levels:
   a. primary/elementary
   b. junior/elementary
   c. intermediate/elementary
   d. grades 9 and 10
   e. grades 11 and 12
7. If you were observing a teacher, what specific behaviours would you look for to indicate that the teacher was attempting to maximize student time on task during
   a. a lecture?
   b. a discussion?
   c. a seatwork activity?
8. How might secondary teachers handle routine chores, such as taking attendance and receiving slips for excuses or early dismissals, to maximize the time allocated for learning? What might elementary teachers do to ensure that all subjects receive the appropriate amount of allocated time?
9. Make a list of the topics taught in a given unit of instruction and identify those topics that can be considered generative topics to be taught at a deeper level of understanding.
10. Observe a class taught by a colleague or record on video a class that you teach and, using the five key elements for authentic instruction identified by Newmann and Wehlage, assess the class.
11. List three or four habits of mind that you hope to cultivate in your students, and briefly describe what you would do to help students develop them.
12. Take a lesson you have taught using an individual lesson structure and redesign it as a cooperative learning lesson with all three critical elements of cooperative learning. Include as many types of positive interdependence as possible in the lesson.
13. Choose an assignment that you or a colleague has used in the past to assess student learning of a concept or topic. Identify how many types of intelligence were tapped by this assessment. Now, redesign the assignment to include all seven types of intelligence.
14. Carefully review the two bodies of knowledge on teaching presented in the two major sections of this chapter ("The Basics of Effective Teaching" and "Beyond the Basics") and answer the following questions:
   a. In what ways are the two knowledge sets similar?
   b. In what ways are they different?
   c. Can the two approaches be used compatibly in the same classroom?

Weblinks

Council of Ministers of Education, Canada
www.cmec.ca
Canadian Council of Ministers of Education—issues of common interest for each of the Canadian provinces.

Ontario Ministry of Education
www.edu.gov.on.ca/eng/teacher/develop.html
A site that promotes Teacher Professional Development

Canadian Teachers' Federation/Fédération canadienne des enseignantes et des enseignants
www.ctf-fce.ca
This site contains many good resources for educators. For curriculum documents, please refer to websites for each province or territory. For example (from west to east): British Columbia – www.gov.bc.ca/bced; Alberta – www.education.gov.ab.ca; Ontario – www.edu.gov.on.ca; Quebec – http://www.mels.gouv.qc.ca/; and Newfoundland and Labrador – www.ed.gov.nl.ca/edu.

Structuring the Environment

FOCUS ON THE PRINCIPLES OF CLASSROOM MANAGEMENT

1. What are the environmental conditions that emphasize learning and minimize disruptive behaviour?

2. What are the teacher behaviours that encourage students to follow classroom guidelines?

3. What can a teacher do to help students learn that they are responsible for the consequences of their behaviour and thus are responsible for controlling their own behaviour?

4. What is the relationship between the culture of the students' home and community and the classroom guidelines?

INTRODUCTION

(Mis)behaviour does not occur by chance. Psychologists believe that behaviour is controlled or influenced by the events and conditions—**antecedents**—that precede it as well as by the events, conditions, and consequences that follow it. Antecedents may increase the likelihood that appropriate behaviour will take place, or they may set the stage for the occurrence of misbehaviour; therefore, when teachers act to prevent or modify inappropriate behaviour, they must examine antecedents carefully before resorting to the delivery of consequences (i.e. The **Calm Model**). The start of the school year and the introduction of novel learning activities are two critical times when antecedent variables must be carefully considered. Unfortunately, teachers may give only cursory attention to antecedent variables. It must be stressed that well-designed learning activities are more successful when teachers have pre-planned seating arrangements, supplies, and rules and routines (Stoughton, 2007; Alvarez, 2007; Wolfgang, 2009).

Because of the impact of antecedent variables on student behaviour, teachers should take time to examine the two most crucial variables—the *physical environment* and *classroom guidelines*. Teachers must realize that classrooms are not culturally neutral; it is important to consider how well the culture of the classroom is congruent with the diverse needs of the students. In this chapter, teachers will discover multiple ideas for creating group expectations that are supportive of engagement in learning activities and achievement by students.

Whenever student behaviour is discussed, and because reactions to student (mis)behaviour can vary dramatically, the issue of students' rights and responsibilities must be considered. Most schools and institutions now refer to the Canadian Charter of Rights and Freedoms along with the applicable provincial statutes, as each province designs a charter of students' rights and responsibilities; for example, in Ontario, Brock University (2010) has a well-defined charter that outlines students' rights and responsibilities.

The Manitoba Human Rights Commission (2007) has prepared a charter entitled Human Rights in the School, which also refers directly to the Canadian Charter of Rights and Freedoms and the United Nations' Universal Declaration of Human Rights. Human Rights in the School details the argument that "human rights education is simply good education."

Although each charter has been individually developed, there are similarities in the content across the provinces because they all develop their approach from the Charter of Rights and Freedoms. The implications of all these documents for educators act as reminders that it is imperative to examine both attitudes and conduct that might threaten the dignity and rights of students. It is, therefore, necessary for teachers to make a conscious effort to be aware and monitor their own behaviour and reactions to student (mis)behaviour.

DESIGNING THE PHYSICAL CLASSROOM ENVIRONMENT

Environmental Conditions

The importance of doing as much as possible to create environmental conditions conducive to learning cannot be stressed enough, as students must be physically comfortable before their attention is voluntarily given to learning (Kern and Clemens, 2007).

Although there are clear limitations to the physical characteristics of our classroom environments, teachers should ensure that the physical environment of the classroom is the most appropriate one for learning. For instance, teachers can control lighting intensity. Dim lights, a flickering ceiling light, or inadequate darkening of the room for movies or other media presentations cause frustration, a growing lack of interest, and off-task behaviour among students. Given Canada's significant temperature variations, there are usually days in every season when rooms may be uncomfortably hot or cold. While a teacher may not be able to adjust the thermostat, she can open windows to let in fresh air, turn off unnecessary lights to cool the room, and remind students to dress appropriately.

Depending on the school's location, outside noise may be uncontrollable, but inside noise is manageable. When possible, teachers should insist that noisy repairs be completed either before or after in-school hours. They should also request that announcements be given at predetermined times. Finally, school policy should enforce quiet hallway use when classes are in session.

Use of Space

Although Canadian teachers have no control over the size of their classrooms and little control over student numbers, they usually can decide how best to utilize space within the classroom. Careful use of physical space makes a considerable difference in classroom behaviour (Jankowska and Atlay, 2008; Vinciarelli, Pantic, and Bourland, 2009).

SEATING ARRANGEMENTS. A teacher's first concern should be the arrangement of seating. No matter what basic seating arrangement is used, it should be flexible enough to accommodate and facilitate the various learning activities that occur in the classroom. If a teacher's primary instructional strategy involves a lot of group work, the teacher may put three or four desks together to facilitate these activities. On the other hand, if a teacher emphasizes teacher-directed lectures and discussion followed by individual seatwork, the traditional rows of desks separated by aisles may be the appropriate seating arrangement. It is quite acceptable, and often warranted, for the teacher to alter the primary seating arrangement to accommodate changing instructional activities. Seating arrangements in which high- and lower-achieving students are interspersed throughout the room can increase involvement and participation. Also, when lower-ability students are seated closer to the front of the room, their achievement may improve (Jones and Jones, 2006).

An effective seating arrangement should allow the teacher to gain close proximity to all students, so that she can reach any student in the class without disturbing others. Such a set-up also enables all students to see instructional presentations. An effort should be made to avoid having students face distractions, such as windows or hallways. Finally, seating should not interfere with high-usage areas—those areas where there are pencil sharpeners, sinks, closets, or wastepaper cans. For relevant classroom-layout designs, please use your favourite internet search engine and type the following keywords: *classroom layout design*, *seating*, and *physical arrangements* (NCEF, 2010; Technology and Instruction, 2006).

Besides planning the location of seats and desks, which occupy most of the classroom space, the teacher must decide where learning centres, computers, storage cabinets, and large work tables are to be placed. Appropriate placement of these things helps the classroom reflect the excitement and variety of the learning that is occurring (Andrews and Lupart, 2000). Because many people find a cluttered area an uncomfortable environment in which to work and learn, classrooms should be neat and tidy. A messy classroom with items strewn about suggests to students that disorganization and sloppiness are acceptable, which may lead to behaviour problems.

BULLETIN BOARDS AND DISPLAY AREAS. The bulletin boards in Mr. Jaffee's room in Case 7.1 serve two purposes: they publicly recognize students' efforts and provide an opportunity for students to enrich their mathematics learning through their own

CASE 7.1
Fourteen to Ten, iPods Win

Each of Mr. Jaffee's grade 9 math classes has a bulletin board committee, which is responsible for the design of one classroom bulletin board during the year. To be board-worthy, a piece need meet only one of two criteria: the topic has to be related to mathematics or its design must use some mathematical skill.

The period five bulletin board committee is ready to present three ideas to the class. Before the presentation, Mr. Jaffee reminds his students that they can vote for only one idea. Dana presents the first idea: "We would like to make a graph showing iPod sales in 2011." Tina presents the second idea: "I propose that we make bar graphs comparing the 2010 Vancouver Olympic hockey results for each team." Jamie presents the third idea: "It would be interesting to have a display showing the many careers there are in mathematics."

After the class asks the presenting students questions about each idea, Mr. Jaffee calls for a vote. The iPod sales graph receives 14 votes, the Olympics gets 10, and, not surprisingly, mathematics careers garners a mere 4. Although Mr. Jaffee is inwardly disappointed with the vote, he supports the outcome because he recognizes the importance of modelling the democratic process. So, he begins a dialogue with the class about the process of developing the bulletin board. As a first step, the committee immediately begins its research on iPod sales so that the bulletin board will be completed before parents' back-to-school night.

Questions to Consider

1. Do you think Mr. Jaffee should have tried to influence the vote? Discuss your reasons.
2. What are the risks of giving complete control for decision-making to students?

efforts and ideas. This is in striking contrast to bulletin boards that are packed away unchanged at the end of each school year (only to reappear again in September), or those that have only a few yellowed and outdated notices pinned to them.

The more bulletin boards are used to recognize students effectively, as Ms. White attempts to do in Case 7.2, or to provide students with opportunities to actively participate, the more likely they are to facilitate and enhance appropriate student behaviour. Bulletin boards and display areas may also be used to post local or school newspaper articles mentioning students' names and displaying their work. A part of a bulletin board or other wall space may be set aside for a list of classroom guidelines. Remember that decisions about the use of classroom space and decorations may be shared with students to create a more student-directed learning environment.

CONCENTRIC CASE STUDY KALEIDOSCOPE

CASE 7.2

Having Your Name Placed on the Board Isn't Always Bad

The Story

One by one, the grade 7 students enter Ms. White's room and cluster around the bulletin board. They are jostling each other and looking at a list to attempt to locate their names. It is evident that students are interested and even anxious about the display. Today is the day after the test and the new Commendable Improvements list has gone up. The list notes those students who have made improvements from one test to another regardless of test grade. Names appear on it

(Continued)

(Continued)

in alphabetical order and do not reflect a grade ranking. Cathy hollers, "Great! I made it!" Rahul says, "Me, too, thank goodness!" Ardra mutters, "My name isn't there." Jimmy pushes and elbows his way to the front of the group and argues, "I think my name should be there, too. I can't understand it." He returns to his desk and slumps in his seat. The enthusiasm and, in a few cases, negative reaction with which students greet this bulletin surprises even Ms. White, and she now realizes that she must carefully consider her comments to the class about the test and the corresponding list.

The Students' Perspectives

Cathy: Cathy enters Ms. White's classroom and notices everyone clustering around the bulletin board. She becomes aware that the Commendable Improvements list is posted and feels her apprehension as well as her excitement rise. As she jostles for a spot near of the list, several thoughts are spinning in her head. "Uh oh, the results are up. I hope I made the list. I think I worked hard enough this term and studied for my tests carefully enough to be on the list. I'll feel really embarrassed in front of my friends if I didn't make it. After all, I decided not to go to a movie on Sunday night just before the big test. I hope my sacrifice was worth it."

Finally, Cathy manages to find her name and in relief she hollers, "Great—I made it!" She takes her seat in the classroom feeling validated, happy, and proud. She thinks, "I can't wait to tell my parents tonight."

Suddenly, Cathy hears Jimmy angrily say that his name is not on the list and that it should be. She also notices that her friend Ardra's name is missing. She looks around the room, noting that Jimmy is slumped in his seat looking very discouraged. "Oh, no," Cathy thinks, "Jimmy looks really unhappy.

I feel sorry for him because he must feel stupid. Glancing at Ardra, she notes that eye contact with her friend is impossible because Ardra is busily focused on getting her books out. Cathy reflects, "Too bad everyone can't make the list—but I am glad that I did."

Ardra: Ardra feels apprehension when she enters the classroom and notes the excitement over at the bulletin board. She knows that the much-anticipated Commendable Improvements list is out. Ardra has been worrying about this all week because she feels fairly certain that she will not be on the list. She also feels fairly certain that her best friend Cathy will be on the list. Ardra wonders why learning poses such a challenge for her and yet seems to come so easily for Cathy. She wonders if she had made a bad choice going to the movies the night before the last big test. She also worries that her parents might be angry that she has not done better as Ardra had assured them she knew the material before heading out to the movies. Ardra sighs to herself and wishes that the list had not been posted today.

Jimmy: Jimmy comes to Ms. White's class feeling a mixture of anticipation and dread, although he covers these emotions with a nonchalant air. He knows that the list might be up and, while he believes that he will finally see his name on it, he still feels the usual apprehension. Jimmy knows that he worked hard during the term, partly in response to a contract he had with his parents about doing his homework and studying for tests. He is acutely aware that if he does not achieve at a higher level this term, his parents will suggest that he give up some of his after-school activities in order to take tutoring. He believes, however, that he showed substantial improvement on the recent test, although he is also aware that there were certain sections that gave him problems.

Along with the rest of the students, Jimmy pushes and elbows his way to the front of the group. Finally he gets a look at the list and quickly scans it for his name. Then he reads the list more slowly, feeling a sinking feeling as he realizes that his name is not there. Jimmy feels a surge of anger and blurts out, "I think my name should be there, too. I can't understand it." Now, he realizes that he has drawn attention to the fact that his name, yet again, is not on the list. In discouragement, he returns to his desk and slumps in his seat. When Ms. White moves to the front of the room and begins speaking to the class, Jimmy does not even look up.

Ms. White's Perspective

As Ms. White tacks the new Commendable Improvements list to her bulletin board, she reflects with pride on her students' improvements. "What a good idea the Commendable Improvements list is. It gives everyone a chance to achieve but at his or her own level, by focusing on the improvement rather than on the actual mark. Also, my students seem to really value getting their names on the list."

As the students enter, Ms. White watches with amusement as they jostle each other to see if their names are posted. She notices the enthusiasm among her successful students and thinks about how she can channel their energy into today's class. Suddenly, Jimmy's angry comment about being left off the list shifts Ms. White's focus to his behaviour specifically. She feels disconcerted while observing his negative and frustrated body language as he slumps in his desk. Ms. White then notices that some of the other students appear deflated as well. As all the students take their seats and wait for her to begin the class, Ms. White realizes that she must be very careful about what she says to the class about the results of the test and the posting of the new Commendable Improvements list. For a long moment, Ms. White stands silently in front of her students as she now focuses her thoughts on those who are experiencing a feeling of lack of success.

Questions to Consider

1. What do you think Ms. White should say at this point to the whole class?
2. What do you think she should say to Jimmy, Ardra, and the others who are not on the Commendable Improvements list?
3. How does such a list affect the class positively? Negatively?
4. Is there a better way to handle this list?
5. How can Ms. White help Jimmy and Ardra?
6. What kind of correspondence should Ms. White send home to the parents or guardians?

New Technologies in the Classroom

The communications media that exist today are simply a glimpse of the power of imminent devices and the implications these technologies hold for future generations. Educators quickly become aware of the advances in technology as their students arrive in classrooms with smaller and more powerful communications devices. Of course, many educators are also very curious about the effectiveness of these devices and purchase them for personal and professional use.

However, a paucity of research exists addressing the efficacy of high-tech devices in the classroom. Some educators express concern about the use of personal electronic devices such as cell phones, MP3 players, gaming systems, and other similar "hi-tech" media (Scornavacca, Huff, and Marshall, 2009). At the same time, others advocate the use or investigation of their usefulness in classroom environments; for example, the premier of Ontario, Dalton McGuinty, suggested that educators should consider the use of cell phones in the classrooms. In September 2010, he said, "Telephones and BlackBerrys and the like are conduits for information today, and one of the things we want our students to do is to be well-informed. And it's something that we should be looking at in our schools" (The Canadian Press, 2010). Further research will undoubtedly lead to both positive and negative arguments for introducing these technologies into our classrooms.

ESTABLISHING CLASSROOM GUIDELINES

There is at least one antecedent variable over which the teacher has much control: the development of classroom guidelines, which are necessary for the efficient and effective running of a classroom. The classroom experience is a complex interaction of students, teachers, and materials. Guidelines help increase the likelihood that these interactions are orderly and that the environment is conducive to learning. Properly designed guidelines should support teaching and learning and provide students with clear expectations and well-defined standards, which in turn will give them the feeling of safety, security, and direction. A safe, secure environment often provides students with the motivation and rationale to countermand those peer pressures that oppose behaviours conducive to learning (Jones and Jones, 2006).

Classroom Routines

There are two types of classroom guidelines: routines and rules. They are not meant for managing disruptive behaviour.

Routines are taught to students through examples and demonstrations. Properly designed and learned, routines maximize on-task student behaviour by minimizing the need for students to ask for directions and the need for teachers to give instructions for everyday classroom events. Examples of routines include methods of handing out and turning in materials, entering and leaving the classroom, and taking attendance. Certain important routines—for instance, steps to be followed during fire drills and required heading information that students need to fill in for tests and assignments—may be prominently displayed for all to reference.

Because students often do not learn and use a teacher's routines immediately, feedback and practice must be provided at the beginning of the term; however, the time spent on teaching the routines is well invested and eventually leads to a successful management system (Elementary Teachers' Federation of Ontario, 2010; Myers, 2010). Often in art, science, industrial arts, and physical education classes (which require distinct routines), teachers may have students practise the required routines initially until they become a consistent and integral part of the classroom/gymnasium dynamic.

The use of natural and **logical consequences** is appropriate for students who fail to follow classroom routines. **Natural consequences** are outcomes of behaviour that occur without teacher intervention. Examples of natural consequences are a poor grade if a student hands in an assignment with no name or if an assignment is not handed in at all.

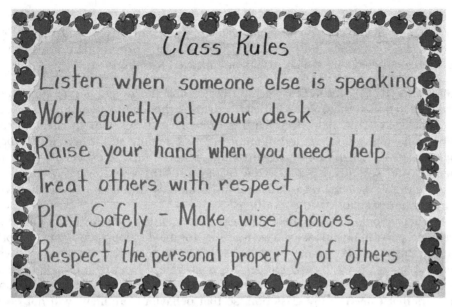

Primary classroom rules handwritten by the teacher.
© Hannamariah/Shutterstock

Logical consequences are outcomes that are directly related to behaviour but require teacher intervention to occur. Examples of logical consequences are students having less time for recess because they did not line up correctly to leave the room and students having to pay for the damage to their textbooks because of careless use.

Natural and logical consequences are powerful management concepts because the consequences that students experience are directly related to their behaviour. In addition, because it is only the student who is responsible for the consequences, the teacher is removed from the role of punisher.

Classroom Rules

In contrast to routines, rules focus on appropriate behaviour. They provide the guidelines for those behaviours that are required if teaching and learning are to take place in the classroom. Because they cover a wider spectrum of behaviour than routines, the development of rules is usually a more complex and time-consuming task.

THE NEED FOR RULES. Schools in general, and classrooms in particular, are dynamic places. Within almost any given classroom, learning activities vary widely and may range from individual seatwork to large group projects that necessitate co-operative working arrangements among students. While this dynamism helps to motivate student learning, human behaviour is highly sensitive to differing conditions across situations as well as to changing conditions within situations (Walker, 1979). Evidence indicates that children in general, and disruptive children in particular, are highly sensitive to changing situations and conditions (Andrews and Lupart, 2000; Rotheram-Borus, Swendeman, and Becker, 2014.). Given this, the need for rules is apparent.

Rules should be directed at organizing the learning environment to ensure the continuity and quality of teaching and learning and not at exerting control over students (Belfiore, Basile, and Lee, 2008; Uusiautti, 2013). Appropriate rules increase on-task student behaviour, which results in improved learning.

DETERMINING NECESSARY RULES.   A long list of dos and don'ts is one sure way to reduce the likelihood that rules will be effective. Teachers who attempt to cover every conceivable classroom behaviour with a rule place themselves in the untenable position of having to observe and monitor the most minute and insignificant student behaviours. This can interfere with teaching time. Students, especially in upper-elementary and secondary grades, view a long list of dos and don'ts as picky and impossible to follow. They regard teachers who monitor and correct every behaviour as nagging, unreasonable, and controlling.

Teachers should develop their own list of rules and/or a list with students that is fair, realistic, and can be rationalized as necessary for the development of an appropriate classroom environment (Emmer and Everston, 2008; Simonsen, Fairbanks, Briesch, Myers, and Sugai, 2008). To accomplish this goal, before meeting a class for the first time, the teacher must seriously consider the question, "What are the necessary student behaviours that I need in my classroom so that behaviour problems will not occur?" To assist in answering this question, teachers must keep in mind that the definition of a behavioural problem is *any behaviour that interferes with the teaching act, interferes with the rights of others to learn, is psychologically or physically unsafe, or destroys property.* Thus, any rule that is developed by the teacher or jointly by the students and the teacher must be vetted as necessary to ensure that (1) the teacher's right to teach is protected, (2) the student's right to learn is protected, (3) the student's psychological and physical safety is protected, and (4) school property is protected (see the section "Defining a Behavioural Problem" in Chapter 2, "The Nature of Behavioural Problems"). Rules that are so developed and rationalized make sense to students because they are not arbitrary. Such rules also lend themselves to the use of natural and logical consequences when students do not follow them.

Teachers who develop a more student-directed approach to creating a classroom learning environment (see Chapter 4, "Bullying and Cyberbullying: Implications for the Classroom") may prefer to provide students with the opportunity to develop rules in collaboration with the teacher. Brady, Forton, Porter, and Wood (2003, p. 22) suggested the following four-part process for carrying out this task:

1. Begin by having the teacher and students discuss their hopes, dreams, and goals for the year.
2. Generate an initial list of rules by discussing what types of classroom conditions and behaviours will be necessary to help everyone achieve their goals.
3. Reframe the list of rules in positive terms, that is, what to do instead of what not to do.
4. Trim the list down to a small number (four or five) of global rules.

DEVELOPING CONSEQUENCES.   When students choose not to follow classroom rules, they should experience consequences (Andrews and Lupart, 2000; Simonsen, Fairbanks, Briesch, Myers, and Sugai, 2008). The types of consequences and how they are applied may determine whether or not students follow rules and whether or not they respect the teacher; therefore, the development of appropriate consequences is as important as the development of the rules themselves.

Unfortunately, teachers usually give considerably more thought to the design of rules than they do to consequences. When a rule is not followed, teachers often simply determine the consequence on the spot. Such an approach may lead to inconsistent, irrational consequences that are interpreted by students as unfair and unrelated to their behaviour. This view of the teacher's behaviour eventually undermines the teacher's effectiveness as a classroom manager and leads to more disruptive student behaviour.

Although the teacher should plan consequences in advance, there is some debate about whether or not students should know ahead what the consequences will be. Some teachers feel that sharing potential consequences helps students to live up to teacher expectations and avoids later complaints about the fairness of the consequences. Other teachers believe that announcing consequences in advance gives students the impression that the teacher expects students not to live up to expectations. They prefer to act as if they have no need to think about consequences since they know that all the students will be successful in meeting both behavioural and academic expectations. There is no empirical answer to this debate. It is a matter of teacher beliefs and preferences.

As we have already noted in the discussion of routines, there are two types of consequences: natural and logical. Natural consequences, which occur without anyone's intervention and are the result of a behaviour, are powerful modifiers of the way students act. After all, have you ever

- had an accident because you drove through a red light or a stop sign?
- injured your foot while walking barefoot?
- locked yourself out of your house because you forgot your key?
- lost or broken something because of carelessness?
- missed a bus or train because of lateness?

These events usually lead to a change in behaviour, and they all have certain characteristics. Each is an undesirable consequence, is experienced by all persons equally (regardless of who they are), and transpires without external intervention. Dreikurs (1964; Dreikurs, Cassel, and Ferguson, 2004) has emphasized that children are provided with an honest and real learning situation when they are allowed to experience the natural consequences of their behaviour.

Allowing students to experience the natural consequences of their behaviour in classroom situations is a very effective learning technique. It clearly communicates a cause-and-effect relationship between a student's chosen behaviour and the experienced consequence, and it removes the teacher from negative involvement with the students. Some examples of natural consequences in schools are

- obtaining a low test grade because of failure to study.
- losing assignments or books because of carelessness.
- ruining a shop project as a result of the inappropriate use of tools.
- losing a ball on a roof because of playing with it inappropriately.

Of course, inherent ethical, moral, and legal restraints prohibit a teacher from allowing some natural consequences to happen; for instance, the natural consequences of failing to follow safety precautions in science laboratories, physical education classes, or industrial arts classes can be serious.

When natural consequences are not appropriate or do not closely follow a given behaviour, the teacher needs to intervene and apply a logical consequence. Have you ever

- been subjected to a finance charge because you were late paying a bill?
- delayed installing the snow tires and skidded into another car during the first snowfall?
- had a cheque returned for insufficient funds because you didn't balance your chequebook?

These are logical consequences because they are directly and rationally related to the behaviour. In school, the teacher ideally administers logical consequences in a calm, matter-of-fact manner. If logical consequences are imposed in anger, they cease to be consequences and tend to become punishments. Children are likely to respond favourably or positively to logical consequences because they do not consider such consequences mean or unfair, whereas they often argue, fight back, or retaliate when punished (Dreikurs, 1964; Dreikurs et al., 2004). Logical consequences may be applied in two different ways. In the first way, the teacher prescribes the logical consequence without giving the student a choice:

"Joe, you spilled the paint; please clean it up."

"Darjeet, you continue to call out. When you raise your hand, you will be called on."

"Antonia, you wrote on your desk. You will have to clean it up during recess."

In the second way, the teacher offers the student a choice of changing her behaviour or experiencing the logical consequence. The use of this technique places the responsibility for appropriate behaviour where it belongs: on the student. If the student chooses to continue the disruptive behaviour, the logical consequence is forthcoming. If the student chooses to cease the disruptive behaviour, there is no negative consequence:

"Phong, you have a choice to walk down the hall without pushing or to hold my hand."

"Heidi, you have a choice to stop disturbing Jeff or to change your seat."

"Mike, you have a choice to raise your hand or not to be chosen to answer."

Notice that in all instances the phrasing clearly identifies the student being addressed and the desired behaviour as well as the logical consequence if the behaviour does not change. Using the words "*you* have a choice" communicates to the student that the teacher is in a neutral position and thus serves to remove the teacher from arguments and power struggles with the student. This is crucial, especially in highly explosive situations. Natural or logical consequences often are not readily apparent to an extremely angry and upset student who has spewed vulgarities at her teacher during class. If, in response to this behaviour, the teacher says, "Your behaviour is unacceptable. If this occurs again, your parents will be contacted immediately," the student is made aware of exactly what will happen if he chooses to continue her behaviour; furthermore, the teacher remains neutral in the eyes of not only the student but also the rest of the class.

A third form of consequence is *contrived consequence*, more commonly known as punishment. The strict definition of punishment is any adverse consequence of a targeted behaviour that suppresses the behaviour; however in day-to-day school practice, punishment takes on three forms: removal of privileges, which may be applied by the teacher; suspension, which is a decision made by the principal; and expulsion, which is a decision made by the board of education. In days gone by, punishment included painful physical experiences such as giving the strap to students; however, such physical punishments have become increasingly rare since Section 43 of the Criminal Code of Canada (the "Spanking" Law) was passed by the federal government. Section 43 provides a defense to assault only if the force used is considered "reasonable under the circumstances." It is worded in the following way:

Correction of a Child by Force

Every schoolteacher, parent or person standing in the place of a parent is justified in using force by way of correction toward a pupil or child, as the case may be, who is under his care, if the force does not exceed what is reasonable under the circumstances. (R.S.C., 1985, c. C-4)

This section of the Canadian Criminal Code was upheld by the Supreme Court in 2004 when the Canadian Foundation for Children and the Law challenged the ruling. In the following years, there have been many dissentions from this ruling by educators; for example, Mark Carter (2005) has argued that this position denies children their rights under *The Canadian Charter of Rights and Freedoms* and instead it designates the perpetrators of violence against children as the most deserving recipients of concern in the disagreement over the retention of corporal punishment. Others have contended that this ruling removes the protection from assault less for one group of citizens on the basis of their age (Durrant, 2007; McGillivary and Durrant, 2006). The result of this ongoing debate currently in Canada is that the punishment that causes physical pain is not supported by many professional and parental groups including the Canadian Teachers' Federation (O'Brien and Pietersma, 2000). In addition, critics have expressed concern that "the force does not exceed what is reasonable under the circumstances" is extremely vague and open to a variety of interpretations (Durrant, Trocme, Fallon, Milne, and Black, 2009; McGillivary, 2011; Watkinson, 2011). This interpretive quagmire is shown again in this editorial quotation from a national newspaper:

Legal precedents have interpreted the meaning of reasonable force in Section 43. In actual child abuse trials, courts have decided it is generally impermissible to strike a child under age two, or one older than 12. Blows to the head, even slaps, are typically not allowed. Striking with a closed fist usually constitutes abuse, and using "objects" such as belts, rulers and canes is to be discouraged. Alternatives to spanking, such as "withdrawal of privileges" are to be attempted first. And no form of corporal punishment should be "administered in anger." What is permitted are mild to moderate "smacks" using an open hand to the buttocks or "extremities"—usually a child's hands. (National Post, 2003)

In the past several years, there have been varied and on-going reactions to Section 43. Interestingly, The Toronto Board of Education formally abolished the use of corporal punishment in its schools in 1971 although it continued to be practiced in some other Ontario school boards (Axelrod, 2010). More recently many groups (e.g., World Corporal Punishment Research, www.corpun.com; the Repeal 43 Committee, www.repeal43.org/schools.html; the Canadian Teachers' Federation, www.ctf-fce.ca/documents/Priorities/EN/advocacy/section43/index.asp) have expressed either concern over or support for Section 43 and have engaged in legal actions to repeal or maintain this component of the Criminal Code. In 1996, Canada received negative feedback from the United Nations Committee on the Rights of the Child based on Section 43. The UN committee argued that Section 43 is contrary to Articles 19, 28, and 37 of the Convention on the Rights of the Child. These three articles are written in a way that is meant to protect children from all forms of violence, punishment, abuse, or cruelty from any person who cares for the child. These articles also require the state to guard the child's human dignity. Even though the Canadian Teachers' Federation disagrees with the use of corporal punishment in public schools, it supports the retention of Section 43 in the Criminal Code. One example that this organization uses for retaining Section 43 is that if teachers are called on to use force to break up a fight between students, assault charges are possible, and without Section 43 teachers would have no legal defense. On balance, it seems that since force is such a contentious issue, teachers should make every effort to select alternative actions whatever the position of their school board.

If appropriately planned by the teacher, and if it is clearly linked to student misbehaviour, the removal of privileges becomes a logical consequence. For example, it is a logical consequence to take away a student's recess time because she has to complete classwork that she missed while she was daydreaming; however, if the teacher cancels a student's participation in next week's trip to the zoo, it is a punishment and not a logical consequence because it is not directly linked to helping the student complete her work.

As we've discussed, punishment should not be physically painful. Psychological punishment, such as yelling, sarcasm, or threats, is also questionable professionally. Other types of punishment often take the form of added assignments (extra homework or writing lines a set number of times). Such punishments are often poorly designed, pedagogically unsound, and are meant only to hurt and get even. The use of painful punishment has been and remains a highly controversial issue on the grounds of morality, ethics, law, and proven ineffectiveness (Bear, 2010; Jones and Jones, 2012).

Research has indicated consistently that painful punishment suppresses undesirable behaviour for short periods of time without effecting lasting behavioural change (Ateah, Secco, and Woodgate, 2003). Because avoidance or escape behaviour is often a side effect of painful experiences, frequent punishment may only teach a child how to be "better at misbehaving." In other words, the child will likely continue to misbehave and find ways to avoid detection and, thus, punishment. Because it seldom is logically related to the behaviour and does not point to alternative acceptable behaviour, punishment deprives the student of the opportunity to learn acceptable behaviour. In addition, punishment reinforces a low level of moral development because it models undesirable behaviours. Students come to believe that it is appropriate to act in punishing ways toward others when one is in a position of authority (Jones and Jones, 2012; Osher, Bear, Sprague, and Doyle, 2010).

As punishment focuses the child's concerns on the immediate effect rather than on the misbehaviour itself, it does not prompt the child to examine the motivation behind the behaviour and the consequences of the behaviour for herself and others, which is important for her to do as she learns to control her disruptive behaviour (Jones and Jones, 2006). Punishment also limits the teacher's ability to help the child in this examination process because the child frequently does not associate the punishment with her actions but with the punisher. This often leads to rage, resentment, hostility, and an urge to get even (Dreikurs, Grundwald, and Pepper, 1998; Jones and Jones, 2012).

As we mentioned earlier, there has been an ever-increasing opposition to the use of physical or corporal punishment in schools. Most educators believe that there is no justification for teachers to inflict pain on their students as such actions can cause physiological as well as physical harm. At the very least, children may develop a dislike and distrust of the teacher that can have negative effects on a child's motivation to learn. These negative effects can also manifest themselves in escape and avoidance behaviours that may take the form of lying, skipping class, or daydreaming when the teacher is speaking.

Those who advocate the use of physical punishment usually cite one of two myths (Smith, Gollop, Taylor, and Marshall, 2003). The first myth advocates punishment

TABLE 7.1 Comparison of Consequences versus Punishment

Natural/Logical Consequence	Punishment
Expresses the reality of a situation	Expresses the power of authority
Logically related to misbehaviour	Contrived and arbitrary connection with misbehaviour
Illustrates cause and effect	Does not illustrate cause and effect
Involves no moral judgment about person—you are okay; your behaviour isn't	Often involves moral judgments
Concerned with the present	Concerned with the past
Administered without anger	Anger is often present
Helps develop self-discipline	Depends on extrinsic control
Choices often given	Alternatives are not given
Thoughtful, deliberate	Often impulsive
Does not develop escape and avoidance behaviours	Develops escape and avoidance behaviours
Does not produce resentment	Produces resentment
Teacher is removed from negative involvement with student	Teacher involvement is negative
Based on the concept of equality	Based on superior–inferior relationship
Communicates the expectation that the student is capable of controlling her own behavior	Communicates that the teacher must control the student's behaviour

Sources: Dreikurs, R., Grunwald, B. B., and Pepper, F. C. (1998). Maintaining sanity in the classroom, Classroom management techniques, 2nd ed. New York: Taylor and Francis. Sweeney, T. J. (1981). Adlerian counseling, proven concepts and strategies, 2nd ed. Muncie, IN: Accelerated Development.

as a tried-and-true method that aids students in developing a sense of personal responsibility, self-discipline, and moral character. In reality, however, studies have consistently shown that physical punishment correlates with delinquency and a low development of conscience. The second myth is that it is the only form of discipline some children understand. This has never been shown to be true. Perhaps it is a case of projection on the part of the teacher. In the past, teachers who relied heavily on physical punishment appeared not to know other means of solving classroom-management problems. Teachers must understand that if a technique has not worked in the past, more of the same technique will not produce desirable results.

COMMUNICATING RULES.   If the teacher decides to develop classroom rules by herself, she must communicate them clearly to the students (Jones and Jones, 2012; Schwartz and Pollishuke, 2002). Clear communication entails a discussion of what the rules are and a rationale for each and every one of them (Good and Brophy, 1997). When students understand the purpose for rules or participate in the making of the rules, they are likely to view them as reasonable and fair, which increases the likelihood of appropriate behaviour (Schwartz and Pollishuke, 2002). When students understand the purpose of rules, they are likely to view them as reasonable and fair, which increases the likelihood of appropriate behaviour (Schwartz and Pollishuke, 2002).

The manner in which rules are worded is important. Certain rules need to be stated so it is clear that they apply to both the teacher and the students. This is accomplished by using the phrase, "We all need to" followed by the behavioural expectation and the rationale; for example, the teacher might write the rules on a poster with the students and post the result for a few weeks. At various times the teacher can reiterate the rules that everyone has participated in making and agreed to practise. In this way, they can be reinforced in a positive manner.

Although it is essential for the teacher to communicate behavioural expectations and the rationales behind them, in some cases, this does not ensure student understanding and acceptance of the rules. A final critical strategy, then, is to obtain from each student a strong indication that she understands the rules as well as a commitment to attempt to abide by them (Jones and Jones, 2012). The stated rules or acceptable behaviours can serve as a focus for individual private discussion when a student is being disruptive.

OBTAINING COMMITMENTS.   When two or more people reach an agreement, they often finalize it with a handshake or a signed contract. Although agreements are often violated, a handshake, verbal promise, or written contract increases the probability that the agreement will be kept. With this idea in mind, it is a wise teacher who has her students express their understanding of the rules and their intent to abide by them. In Case 7.3, the teacher uses an interactive approach to develop rules for the classroom.

Both Mr. Merit and Ms. Lu in Cases 7.3 and 7.4 are attempting to get their students to understand and agree to follow the classroom rules; however, notice that they use different methods because the maturity level of their students is different. Unlike Mr. Merit, Ms. Lu only asks her students to confirm that they understand the rules, not that they will abide by them. This is an important distinction that should be made when working with older students because taking this more respectful approach reduces the potential of a student confrontation during a time when the development of teacher–student rapport is critical.

CASE 7.3

"I'm Not Sure If I'll Always Remember"

At the beginning of the school year, Mr. Merit presents a list of six class rules to his grade 5 students. He explains each rule and gives examples. Mr. Merit then asks if the students have any suggestions for changes to the list— he indicates they could be additions or deletions. After consideration, it is evident that the students are satisfied with the list. He then has a more detailed discussion of the class rules with his students. Members of the class are asked to give the reason for each rule. The class as a whole is encouraged to ask questions about the rules, and Mr. Merit in turn asks questions to assess their understanding of the rules.

After the discussion, Mr. Merit says, "All those who understand our rules please raise your hand." Next, he says, "All those who will attempt to follow our rules please raise your hands." He notices that Helen and Gary do not raise their hands and asks them why. Helen says, "I'm not sure if I'll always remember the rules and if I can't remember I can't

promise to follow the rules." Mr. Merit replies, "Helen, I understand your concern, but I have written our rules on a poster, which I am going to place on the front bulletin board. Do you think that this will help you?" Helen answers yes and both she and Gary then raise their hands.

Mr. Merit shows the class the poster of rules, which is entitled, "I Will Try to Follow Our Classroom Rules." One by one, each student comes up and signs his or her name at the bottom of the poster. When all the students have signed it, Mr. Merit asks Helen to staple the poster to the front bulletin board.

Questions to Consider

1. What message does Mr. Merit's approach send to his students?
2. Do you think that signing the rules sheet was important? Give reasons.
3. What rules would you develop for your own class?

CASE 7.4

"I'm Not Promising Anything"

On the first day of class, Ms. Lu explains the classroom rules to her grade 10 mathematics classes. She discusses with each class why these rules are necessary for the teaching and learning of mathematics.

Ms. Lu then says to the class, "I am going to pass out two copies of the rules that we just discussed. You'll notice that at the bottom is the statement, 'I am aware of these rules and understand them' followed by a place for your signature. Please sign

one copy and pass it up front so I can collect them. Place the other copy in your notebook."

In Ms. Lu's second-period class, Alex raises his hand and says, "I can't make any promises about my future behaviour in this class. I'm not sure what the class is even going to be like." Ms. Lu replies, "Although I can understand your concern, please read what you are signing." Alex reads, "I am aware of these rules and understand them"

(Continued)

(Continued)

and says out loud, "Oh, I see. I'm not promising anything." Alex then signs the sheet and passes it to the front of the room.

Questions to Consider

1. Compare Ms. Lu's and Mr. Merit's respective approaches and consider the appropriateness of each to its grade level.

2. To what extent do you think that students should participate in establishing classroom rules?

3. How would Ms. Lu's process change if she had required students to sign a promise?

4. Should Ms. Lu follow up with Alex's comment at any time during the term? If so, what should the nature of the follow-up be?

In Case 7.5, He models consistency as he works with students to reinforce the classroom rules. Mr. Martinez understands that students often need help learning rules, and he indicates he is willing to remind and prompt without showing frustration.

Although many experts recommend having classroom rules on display or available for quick reference (Jones and Jones, 2012), it should be noted that merely displaying them has little effect on maintaining appropriate student behaviour. Teachers must refer to and use the displayed rules to assist individual students in learning the rules and developing self-control. Mr. Martinez in Case 7.5 not only displays and teaches the rule to Lowyn but also reinforces the behaviour when she finally does raise her hand. He understands that noting appropriate behaviour and positively encouraging it enhances the likelihood of appropriate behaviour in the future (Cihak, Kirk, and Boon, 2009; Ritchie, Rinholm, Flewelling, Kelly, and Sammon, 1999).

CASE 7.5

Calling Out Correct Answers

Mr. Martinez, a grade 4 teacher, posts his classroom rules on the front bulletin board. One by one, each student signs the poster, thus agreeing to follow the rules.

Mr. Martinez soon notices that Lowyn is having a difficult time remembering to raise her hand before answering questions. Instead, Lowyn just calls out the answers. At first Mr. Martinez ignores her answer. The next time she calls out, he makes eye contact with her and shakes his head in a disapproving fashion. Finally, he moves close to Lowyn and quietly says, "Lowyn, you have great answers, but you must raise your hand so that everyone has an equal chance to answer."

The next lesson begins, and Mr. Martinez asks the class, "Who can summarize what we learned about magnets yesterday?" Enthusiastically, Lowyn calls out, "Every magnet has a north and south pole."

Because Mr. Martinez has half expected that Lowyn will continue to call out answers, he is prepared for the situation and says, "Class, please, put down your hands. Lowyn, please look at the rules on the bulletin board and find the one that you are not obeying." Lowyn answers, "Number four. It says we need to raise our hands to answer a question." Mr. Martinez responds, "Yes it does, and why do we need such a rule?" "So that everyone in the class has a chance to answer questions," she replies. Mr. Martinez then asks, "Lowyn, did you agree to follow these rules when you signed the poster?" "Yes," Lowyn says.

Mr. Martinez asks her to try harder in the future and tells her that he will help her by pointing to the rules if she calls out again. The first time Lowyn raises her hand Mr. Martinez calls on her, and afterwards says, "Lowyn, that was a great answer and thank you for raising your hand."

Questions to Consider

1. How do rules simplify teacher expectations for behaviour?
2. How would this scenario have changed if the rules had not been clearly established?

Teachers also may employ student self-analyses to remind them of appropriate behaviour and to help enhance their self-control. Indeed, self-analysis of one's behaviour can be used by any student, although the actual manner of employment of the technique varies. Whereas Mr. Boudreau's smiley faces in Case 7.6 are appropriate for younger elementary students (see Figure 7.1), older students evaluate their behaviour better by using rating continua. As with younger students, self-analysis is requested of all students or individual students as the need arises. Figure 7.2 is an example of a continuum rating scale that was successfully used to manage a grade 7 art class. Similar scales can be developed for self-analysis or group analysis after collaborative learning activities.

CASE 7.6

The Smiley Face Self-Analysis

Mr. Boudreau teaches grade 1. After analyzing the types of behaviours he feels are necessary for the proper running of his class, he shares the rules with the children and explains what he calls the Smiley Face Procedure. "We all know what smiley faces are, and we are going to use smiley faces to help us learn and obey the classroom rules." Holding up a sheet of paper (see Figure 7.1), he continues, "As you can see, this sheet has faces next to each rule for every day of the week. At the end of class each day, you will receive one of these sheets and you will circle the faces that are most like your behaviour for the day."

Each day, Mr. Boudreau collects the sheets and reviews them. When a pattern of frowns is observed or when he disagrees with a student's rating, he is quick to work with the student in a positive, supportive manner.

After a few weeks, Mr. Boudreau discontinues the self-analysis sheets on a regular basis. They are, however, brought back into use whenever the class's behaviour warrants it. Mr. Boudreau also uses the sheets for individual students who need assistance in self-control. When outdoor or new activities such as field trips occur throughout the year, Mr. Boudreau develops new sheets for the students using the same smiley-face format.

Questions to Consider

1. Identify the positive and negative aspects of the smiley-face system.
2. Are there any benefits to the students if they use this procedure?
3. How would you modify Figure 7.1?

CIRCLE THE APPLE THAT IS MOST LIKE YOUR BEHAVIOUR TODAY

	MONDAY	TUESDAY	WEDNESDAY	THURSDAY	FRIDAY
Shared with Others					
Listened to the Teacher					
Listened While Others Talked					
Was Friendly to Others					
Worked Quietly					
Joined in Activities					
Stayed in My Seat					
Followed Directions					
Cleaned My Area					
Helped Put Away Materials					

FIGURE 7.1 Smiley Face Self-Analysis

Name _____ Date _____

Class _____

Teacher–Student Evaluation
Class Behaviour

1. Have you worked successfully with minimum supervision during the class period?

0% of the time		50% of the time		All the time
1	2	3	4	5

2. Have you been respectful and considerate to other students and their property?

0% of the time		50% of the time		All the time
1	2	3	4	5

3. Have you been co-operative with your teacher?

0% of the time		50% of the time		All the time
1	2	3	4	5

4. Have you used art materials properly?

0% of the time		50% of the time		All the time
1	2	3	4	5

5. Have you shown a high degree of maturity and responsibility through proper class behaviour?

0% of the time		50% of the time		All the time
1	2	3	4	5

6. Have you been considerate of your classmates and teacher by talking softly, remaining in your seat, and helping classmates if help is needed?

0% of the time		50% of the time		All the time
1	2	3	4	5

7. Have you cleaned your area and put your materials away?

0% of the time		50% of the time		All the time
1	2	3	4	5

FIGURE 7.2   **Behaviour Self-Analysis for Art Class**

TEACHING AND EVALUATING. Teachers do not expect all students to learn a mathematical skill on its first presentation because they know students need practice and feedback. Frequently, however, teachers forget this when it comes to rules. (They expect students to follow classroom rules immediately). But rules, like academic skills, must be taught (Jones and Jones, 2012; Schwartz and Pollishuke, 2002). This entails practice and feedback. The amount of practice and feedback depends on the grade level and the novelty of the routines and rules.

New activities often require new routines and rules. It is customary for teachers to spend up to an entire lesson on how to conduct a debate, co-operatively work on a group project, safely operate machinery, set up and care for science apparatus, or behave on field trips or outdoor activities. In such cases, specific objectives directed toward the routines and rules are formulated and incorporated into the lesson plans. In these situations, they become an integral part of the course content, and, therefore, their evaluation and consideration in grading decisions are warranted.

Some teachers evaluate their students' understanding of rules through the use of written exams or student demonstrations (Erford, 2012; Gregson, 2013). Science and industrial arts teachers often insist that students pass safety exams and demonstrate the appropriate use of equipment before progressing to the learning activities.

To summarize, teachers must communicate to students the importance of the rules for learning and teaching (McIntosh, 2009). This is best accomplished through a no-nonsense approach that involves the following:

1. Analyzing the classroom environment to determine the necessary rules and routines needed to protect teaching, learning, overall safety, and property
2. Clearly communicating the rules and their rationales to students
3. Obtaining students' commitments to abide by the rules
4. Teaching and evaluating students' understanding of the rules
5. Enforcing each rule consistently with natural or logical consequences

THE CULTURAL EMBEDDEDNESS OF RULES AND ROUTINES

When teachers are establishing and teaching classroom rules and routines, they need to remember that their students come from a variety of cultural backgrounds. *Culture* refers to the knowledge, customs, rituals, emotions, traditions, values, and standards shared by members of a population and embodied in a set of behaviours designed for survival in a particular environment. Because Canadian students come to the classroom from many different cultural backgrounds, they bring with them different values, standards, and behavioural expectations; therefore, it is not wise to behave as if everyone shares the same cultural expectations. Schools and classrooms are not culturally neutral or culture-free. Some schools may still follow the values, standards, and behavioural patterns of middle-class, white, European cultures. As Blades, Johnston, and Simmt (2000) have pointed out, however, these values and standards differ in significant ways from the values, standards, and behavioural expectations found in cultural groups from diverse backgrounds. This is particularly prominent in large urban centres where the Canadian population has become increasingly cosmopolitan. As a result of differences in values and standards, some behaviour patterns displayed by children who come from a nondominant culture, while acceptable at home and in the community, often are not as acceptable in schools. Indeed, cultural differences occur in many areas, including language patterns, nonverbal behaviour, amount and freedom of movement, use of personal space, expression of emotions, and dress.

As a result of these cultural differences, many children from under-represented groups experience cultural dissonance or lack of cultural synchronization in school; that is, some teachers and students may be out of step with each other when it comes to their expectations for appropriate behaviour. Cultural synchronization is an extremely important factor in the establishment of positive relationships between teachers and students. According to Jeanette Abi-Nader (1993), one of the most solidly substantiated principles in communication theory is the principle of *homophily*, which holds that the more two people are alike in background, attitudes, perceptions, and values, the more effectively they will communicate with each other and the more similar they will become. A lack of cultural synchronization leads to misunderstandings between teachers and students that can, and often do, result in conflict, distrust, hostility, and possibly school failure (Modood, 2013; Windahl, Signitzer, and Olson, 2009).

To illustrate their discussion of the importance of cultural synchronization, Blades, Johnston, and Simmt (2000) have pointed out some of the ways that teachers are modifying courses in an attempt to remove cultural bias; for example, foods and textiles teachers examined food and clothing from many cultures. Those who taught issues related to health and health care discussed various strategies that different cultural groups use to heal or maintain health. Some teachers select multicultural novels for class members to read and direct the discussions to help students develop tolerance and an understanding of the universality of the human condition.

Part of the terrible fallout of the September 11, 2001, attacks in the United States is the rise of Islamophobia in North America. Overgeneralization and paranoia have led to public discourse and antiterrorist policies that disproportionately and unfairly target Canadians of Arab descent and other Muslims as visible threats to public safety (Arora, 2013; Collet, 2007). For instance, in Vancouver where a sizable number of Sikhs reside, a number of hate crimes against this visible minority have been perpetrated largely because Sikhs seem reminiscent of the terrorists of 9/11. In response, the Muslim community in Canada is currently undertaking new initiatives to educate the public about Islam through the Muslim Educational Network Training and Outreach Service (MENTORS). This group has developed resource kits for schools (Zine, 2003). In 2012, Statistics Canada reported that Punjabis is the third most common language in Canada and in response, several school boards in British Columbia are offering Punjabi classes at both the elementary and High school levels as an option (Sanghera, 2013).

Differences in values, standards, and expectations resulting from cultural differences have several implications for teachers. First, teachers must understand that schools are culturally situated institutions. It is extremely difficult to promote values, standards, and behaviours in schools that are culturally neutral. They are always influenced by some particular cultural mindset; therefore, school and classroom rules and guidelines must be seen as culturally derived. Second, teachers should strive to learn more about the cultural backgrounds of the students they teach. This can be accomplished by talking to students about their behaviour and allowing them to teach about cultural differences. Parents and community members should be encouraged to be involved in the classroom and to discuss the institutions in their home community. "Students are less likely to fail in school settings where they feel positive about both their own culture and the majority culture and are not alienated from their own cultural values" (Cummins, 1986). In addition, when bilingual instruction is compared to English only instruction, students who receive both are more successful on measures of English reading proficiency (August and Shanahan, 2006). Third, teachers should acknowledge and intentionally incorporate students' cultural backgrounds and expectations into their classrooms. When classroom rules and expectations conflict with student cultural expectations, it may be appropriate to re-examine and renegotiate rules and routines. In a variety of studies in different settings and contexts—and with students from different cultural groups—the findings are remarkably similar. When teachers incorporate language and participation patterns from the home and community into the classroom, relationships and academic learning improve significantly (Elliott and Woloshyn 2013; Hollins, 2008). At the very least, students need to be provided with a clear rationale for why the rules and routines are important. It goes without saying that the rationale for the rules should be in keeping with the four guidelines that we articulated earlier in this chapter. Finally, when a student behaves inappropriately, the teacher should step back and examine the misbehaviour in terms of the student's cultural background. Using a different set of cultural lenses to view behaviour may shed a very different light on the teacher's perceptions of individual students. Obviously, misbehaviour that results from differences in cultural background and expectations should be handled quite differently from misbehaviour that signifies intentional disruption on the part of the student. When teachers hear offensive cultural, racial, or prejudicial comments in the classroom, it is incumbent upon them to make it clear that such comments are unacceptable.

CREATING GROUP STANDARDS TO STRUCTURE APPROPRIATE BEHAVIOUR

Although students and teachers bring their own cultural backgrounds with them to school, each classroom tends to develop a culture unique unto itself; that is, certain standards that develop over time can exert a great influence on student behaviour. During the early years of schooling, it is the teacher's wishes and behaviour that create the standards for student behaviour. However, as students grow older, they become the dominant influence in establishing the cultural standards within a given classroom. According to Johnson, Johnson, and Holubec (1993), the relationships that develop among peers in the classroom exert a tremendous influence on social and cognitive development and student socialization. In their interactions with peers, children and adolescents learn attitudes, values, skills, and information that may be different from those learned from adults. Interaction with peers provides support, opportunities, and models for personal behaviour. Through peer relationships, a frame of reference for perceiving oneself is developed (Harris, 1998). In both educational and work settings, peers influence productivity. Students' educational aspirations are influenced more by peers than by any other social influence (Flint, T. K. 2010; Johnson, Johnson, and Holubec, 1993).

Teachers sometimes have focused their attention on individual learners and have viewed influencing students to behave appropriately as an issue between the teacher and the individual student. As a result, the development of peer culture and group standards among students has been left to chance; however, there is growing evidence that teachers can intervene to create group standards that will promote prosocial behaviour as well as lead to peer relationships that will enhance the four components of self-esteem identified earlier: significance, power, competence, and virtue. Co-operative learning lessons that include face-to-face interaction, positive interdependence, and individual accountability can help to establish positive group standards. When teachers make a concentrated effort to help students develop the social skills necessary to function effectively as group members during co-operative learning activities, they enhance the power of co-operative learning activities to create positive group standards.

Johnson, Johnson, and Holubec (1993) as well as Elliott and Woloshyn (2013) have identified four sets of skills—*forming skills*, *functioning skills*, *formulating skills*, and *fermenting skills*—that students need to develop over time in order to function most effectively as a group. When these skills are in place and groups function successfully, group standards develop that lead students to (1) be engaged in learning activities, (2) strive toward learning and achievement, and (3) interact with each other in ways that will facilitate the development of positive self-esteem.

Forming skills are an initial set of management skills that are helpful in getting groups up and running smoothly and effectively. These skills include moving into groups quietly without bothering others, staying with the group rather than moving around the room, using quiet voices that can be heard by members of the group but not by others, and encouraging all group members to participate.

Functioning skills are group-management skills aimed at controlling the types of interactions that occur among group members. These skills include staying focused on the task, expressing support and acceptance of others, asking for help or clarification, offering to explain or clarify, and paraphrasing or summarizing what others have said.

Formulating skills refer to a set of behaviours that help students to process material mentally. These skills include summarizing key points, connecting ideas to each other, seeking elaboration of ideas, finding ways to remember information more effectively, and checking explanations and ideas through articulation.

Fermenting skills are a set of skills needed to resolve cognitive conflicts that arise within the group. These skills include criticizing ideas without deriding people, synthesizing diverse ideas, asking for justification, extending other people's ideas, and probing for more information.

Johnson, Johnson, and Holubec (1993) suggest that educators teach these social skills just as they teach academic content; therefore, when teachers plan a co-operative learning activity, they must plan social-skill objectives as well as the academic objectives. Making the social skills explicit as lesson objectives helps to focus both student and teacher attention on them. To do this, the teacher should explain the skill before the activity begins and make sure students know what the skill looks like and sounds like as it is expressed in behaviour. Once the teacher is convinced that students understand the meaning of the skill, students may practise the skill during the co-operative learning activity. While the students are practising, the teacher moves from group to group monitoring the use of the skill. When the activity has been completed, the teacher engages each group in reflecting on how successfully the skill was used and in setting goals for improving their use of the skill in the future. Although teaching social skills in addition to academic content takes time, the time is well spent for two reasons. First, many of these skills are exactly the kinds of skills students will need to help them succeed as adults. Second, when students are skilled at interacting with each other in positive ways, group standards develop in the classrooms that are supportive of prosocial behaviour and of engagement in appropriate learning activities.

Educators would like to acquire a list of proven and effective strategies for addressing various disruptive classroom behaviours. Although such a list would be helpful ideally, the reality is that most classroom mishaps have enough uniqueness that they would render a specific one-size-fits-all solution relatively useless; therefore, we have decided that a defined method for analyzing and managing behavioural concerns would be a superior approach to trying to anticipate all classroom challenges and providing methods for coping with each challenge separately. After carefully considering the types of questions that educators—from teacher candidates to experienced classroom teachers—raise about classroom management, we have developed a flexible, hierarchical model for examining and managing challenges that may affect the classroom environment.

THE CALM MODEL

The CALM model/strategy provides the following steps as a general guide for handling classroom-management issues. The model can become automatic and be applied as needed. When these levels become an instinctive part of the teacher's repertoire of strategies along with other components of the effective classroom—including the development of a positive rapport—the effective teacher should be able to determine quickly the suitable level in order to avoid serious disruptions to the learning environment.

Level I

When a student's behaviour becomes disruptive, in order to initiate a response process the teacher should **consider** whether the behaviour changes, affects, or disrupts the classroom learning environment, teacher, or students.

When an inappropriate behaviour occurs, the most important and critical question to answer is, "Does this disruption affect the ability of the teacher to continue teaching and/or the ability of the students to continue learning?" If the answer to the question is no, then the teacher may choose to totally disregard the situation rather than alter the positive focus from the lesson; for example, two students may have a small disagreement in which a few angry gestures are exchanged. If the students resolve the issue and get back to work, there may be no reason for the teacher to disrupt the flow of the lesson and divert the other students' attention. If the learning can continue seamlessly, then there is no need to move to the next level. However, not all situations can be ignored and the teacher may feel that it is best to proceed to the next level. (A general rule: If the situation affects a small group of students, and is temporary, then it is usually best to let the students resolve a small dispute themselves.)

Level II

At times it becomes necessary to **act**.

There are situations where it is essential that the teacher respond quickly to avoid jeopardizing the learning environment. If it becomes necessary to respond to a disruption, the teacher decides whether an immediate action is required or if it would be best for her to respond to the situation later. The only question the teacher needs to ask at this level is, "Do I need to act now or can I postpone any action?" For example, if the arguing students described in Level I of CALM escalate their altercation, it may be necessary to direct some attention to the students to be sure that they get back to the task at hand. If the teacher determines that acting is necessary, then she moves to the next level.

Level III

Wherever possible, **lessen** the invasive response in dealing with the situation.

If the teacher determines that the situation will not resolve itself, then she needs to make a decision on the degree of intervention necessary. It is very important that whenever an intervention must occur, there should be no doubt in the students' minds that there will be a consequence.

If the teacher decides that a response is needed, then it is critical that any action she implements be the least invasive action possible; for example, if the arguing students from Level I continue to react to each other, "the look" may be enough to refocus their attention. The teacher may choose to use proximity as the management strategy. Maybe a simple tally on the board or just asking the student(s) to come to a conference later will suffice. Possibly, some other unobtrusive technique will be enough to bring the students back to the lesson. On the other hand, if it appears that a more direct response may be essential or that a lack of sufficient response may lead to loss of respect, then the teacher needs to react with a greater presence.

Three broad stages of action and intervention can be identified.

Action Stage A: At this stage, the teacher uses an action that will not affect the flow of the learning environment and will affect only the student(s) involved in the misbehaviour. Usually, a very minimal action is appropriate and other students do not even notice. At this stage, the teacher can proceed without 'missing a beat.'

Action Stage B: Here, the teacher determines that she must make a brief interruption of the learning environment and that a greater degree of intervention is needed. The teacher determines that the disruptive student(s) need attention. At this stage, the misbehaviour requires a more direct approach and the teacher may call the student(s) by name to refocus attention to the task. Other possible actions at this stage include moving the offending student(s) to a different area of the room, giving them a *timeout*, establishing a conference at a time that is convenient for the teacher, using a token economy strategy that has been predefined with the class, or implementing other consequences that the teacher concludes are fitting in this case. Again, this action should be administered quickly, and the teacher resumes where she left off without delay. It is important to reiterate: When the students understand that consequences *will* definitely follow misbehaviours, the lesson or task can continue with minimal disruption. The students will quickly understand the teacher's modus operandi.

Action Stage C: Hopefully, this stage is needed only in rare cases. To move to this stage, the student(s) has/have misbehaved to the point where the teacher has no option but to interrupt the process to address the misbehaviour. The teacher may again try using the strategies outlined in Action Stage B, but once it is apparent that these relatively moderate techniques are not going to be sufficient, it may be necessary to remove the student(s) from the room using the procedures that are defined within the school and board of education.

Level IV

Manage the milieu to quickly return to an effective learning environment.

Throughout this process, the teacher should remain composed, and she should refocus as quickly as possible on the effective learning environment that was interrupted. It is imperative that she display a positive demeanour to the rest of the class at this time and avoid commenting on the disruptive situation. Remember, the teacher is the adult and should remain fair but firm.

Summary

In this chapter, we first examined two of the critical variables that influence behaviour in the classroom: the physical environment and classroom rules and routines. This discussion was followed by a consideration of the role of culture in the establishment of classroom routines and rules. In the final section of the chapter, we discussed the creation of group standards that are supportive of appropriate behaviour.

Although teachers have no control over the size of their classrooms, they can control the seating arrangement within the classroom and the use of bulletin boards. The seating arrangement should accommodate the learning activity. It must also permit all students to see instructional presentations and allow the teacher to be close to all students. Bulletin boards should reflect and add to the motivation for learning. Properly used, they can provide students with the opportunity to enrich and actively participate in their learning and allow the teacher to recognize and display students' work and achievements.

When they are well designed, rules and routines provide students with clear expectations. The teacher can increase the effectiveness of rules and routines by (1) analyzing the classroom environment to determine what is needed to protect teaching, learning, overall safety, and property; (2) communicating the

rules and routines and their rationales to students; (3) obtaining student commitments to abide by the rules; (4) teaching and evaluating student understanding of the rules; and (5) enforcing each rule and routine with natural or logical consequences.

Classrooms and schools are never culturally neutral or value free; they are always situated within a particular cultural context. When the culture of the school and the culture of the students are synchronized, positive behaviour increases and positive relationships are established between teachers and students; however, when teachers and students hold differing values, standards, and behavioural expectations, the potential for misunderstanding, conflict, and mistrust is greatly enhanced.

Each classroom also develops its own culture with its own set of group standards and values. Traditionally, some teachers have ignored the communal aspects of classroom life, focusing instead on individual relationships. Evidence now indicates that the use of co-operative learning activities that contain all essential elements combined with the teaching of prosocial skills will lead to the establishment of group standards that are supportive of appropriate student behaviour. The CALM model is used as a guide to help teachers attain such goals in a logical manner.

Key Terms

antecedents: preliminary courses of action that may increase the likelihood that appropriate behaviour will take place, or they may set the stage for the occurrence of misbehaviour.

logical consequences: outcomes that are directly related to the behaviour that require teacher intervention to occur.

natural consequences: outcomes of behaviour that occur without teacher intervention.

forming skills: an initial set of management skills that are helpful in getting groups up and running smoothly and effectively.

functioning skills: group-management skills aimed at controlling the types of interactions that occur among group members.

formulating skills: a set of behaviours that help students to process material mentally.

fermenting skills: a set of skills needed to resolve cognitive conflicts that arise within the group.

CALM Model: Consider, Act, Lessen, Manage

Exercises

1. For each of the following activities, design a seating arrangement for 24 students that maximizes on-task behaviour and minimizes disruptions.
   a. teacher lecture
   b. Small group work (four students per group)
   c. open discussion
   d. individual seatwork
   e. class project to design a bulletin board
   f. teacher-led group work and simultaneous individual seatwork
   g. group debate
   h. teacher demonstration

2. Give examples of how a teacher can use the classroom environment (bulletin boards, shelves, walls, chalkboard, and so on) to create a pleasant atmosphere that increases the likelihood of appropriate student behaviour.

3. With your present or future classroom in mind, determine the common activities that do or will regularly occur. Design appropriate routines to accomplish those activities. How would you teach these routines to the class?

4. a. With your present or future classroom in mind, determine what general student behaviours are necessary to ensure that learning and teaching take place and that students and property are safe.
   b. State a positive rule for each of the behaviours you previously listed.

   c. For each behaviour, give a rationale you can explain to students that is consistent with the definition of a behaviour problem and appropriate for the age of the students you teach or will teach.
   d. For each behaviour, determine a natural or logical consequence that will occur when the rule is broken.
   e. How will you communicate these rules to students?
   f. How will you obtain student commitment to these rules?

5. Determine a natural, logical, and contrived consequence for each of the following misbehaviours:
   a. grade 4 student who interrupts small group work
   b. grade 11 student who continually gets out of her seat
   c. grade 7 student who makes noises during class
   d. grade 10 student who makes noises during class
   e. grade 12 student who refuses to change her seat when requested to do so by the teacher
   f. grade 1 student who interrupts reading group to tattle on a student who is not doing his seatwork
   g. a group of grade 6 students who drop their pencils in unison at a given time

h. grade 9 student who threatens to beat up another student after class

i. grade 8 student who continually pushes the chair of the student in front of her

j. grade 10 student who does not wear goggles while operating power equipment

6. The following are examples of some rules developed for a grade 8 science class. Identify and correct any problems in the rule, rationale, or consequences.

Rule	Rationale	Consequences
a. Don't be late to class	Because we have a lot of material to cover and we need the whole class period	a. Reminder by teacher b. Student required to get a note c. Student writes 100 times, "I will not be late"
b. We all need to work without disrupting others	Because everyone has a right to learn and no one has a right to interfere with the learning of others	a. Reminder by teacher b. Student moved where she cannot disrupt others c. Student removed from class d. Student fails
c. We all have to raise our hands to answer questions or contribute to a discussion	Because I do not like to be interrupted	a. Student ignored b. Reminder by teacher c. Parents notified
d. We must use lab equipment properly and safely	Because it is expensive to replace	a. Pay for broken equipment b. Pay for equipment and additional fine

7. For each of the following scenarios, explain why the student behaved as he or she did:

a. Juanita, a recently arrived student from Mexico, is being reprimanded by her teacher for not doing her homework. Despite repeated attempts by her teacher to get Juanita to look her in the eye, Juanita refuses to do so.

b. Eunsook, a student from Korea, is obviously upset about something. When Mr. Barber bends close to her and tries to find out what is happening, Eunsook simply clams up and does not say a word.

c. Justin, a Jamaican-born grade 1 student, continually sings along and talks along with his teacher, Ms. Gray, when she is telling stories to the class. Ms. Gray finds Justin's behaviour rude.

8. How do differences in cultural values, standards, and behavioural expectations influence the development of teacher expectations for student achievement?

9. For each of the following social skills, develop an explanation of what the social skill means for students at the grade 3 level, at the grade 7 level, and at the grade 11 level.

a. encouraging everyone to participate

b. paraphrasing what others have said

c. seeking elaboration

d. asking for justification for ideas

Weblinks

British Columbia Department of Education

www.bced.gov.bc.ca/specialed

This website is designed to address a wide range of issues related to special education.

Ontario Ministry of Education's Violence-Free Schools Policy

http://www.edu.gov.on.ca/extra/eng/ppm/120.html

This memorandum "is to provide direction to school boards on the development of procedures for reporting violent incidents to the Ministry of Education." Other documents are available from this site by searching terms like *violence and violence in schools.*

Department of Education for Newfoundland and Labrador's Programming for Individual

Needs: Policy, Guidelines, and Resource Guide on Discipline, School Violence and Safe Schools Teams

www.ed.gov.nl.ca/edu
This site describes in general and specific terms how teachers can develop programming that will minimize violence.

The League of Peaceful Schools

http://olc.spsd.sk.ca/DE/resources/betterworld
This site states that it "provides support and recognition to schools that have declared a commitment to creating a safe and peaceful environment for their students."

The Muslim Educational Network, Training and Outreach Service (MENTORS)

www.mentorscanada.com/index.php
MENTORS is a website that provides resources for schools that include information and curriculum packages that impart Islamic knowledge, culture, and practice.

Iterative Case Study Analysis

Third Analysis

Considering the concepts discussed in Part II, Prevention, reanalyze your second analysis. What has changed and what has stayed the same since your last analysis? Once again consider why the students may be choosing to behave inappropriately and how you might intervene to influence the students to stop the disruptive behaviour and resume appropriate on-task behaviour.

Elementary School Case Study

During silent reading time in my grade 4 class, I have built-in opportunities to work individually with students. During this time, the students read to me and practice word work with flash cards. One student has refused to read to me but instead wants only to work with the flash cards. After a few sessions, I suggested we work with word cards this time and begin reading the next time. He agreed. The next time we met, I reminded him of our plan, and he screamed, "I don't remember! I want to do word cards!" At this point, I tried to find out why he didn't like reading, and he said, "There's a reason, I just can't tell you," and he threw the word cards across the room, some of them hitting other students. What should I do?

Middle School Case Study

I can't stop thinking about a problem I'm having in class with a group of 12-year-old boys. They consistently use profanities toward one another and some of the shyer kids in the class, especially the girls. In addition, they are always pushing and shoving each other. I've tried talking to them about why they keep using bad language when they know it's inappropriate. The response I get is that "it makes me look cool and funny in front of my friends." I have implored them to use more appropriate language in the classroom, but that has not worked. I haven't even started to address the pushing and shoving. What should I do?

High School Case Study

This past week, I had a student approach me about a problem he was experiencing in our class. The grade 11 student had recently "come out" as being gay. He said he was tired and upset with the three boys who sit near him. These boys frequently call him a "homo" and a "fag" every time they see him, both in and out of class. What should I do?

8

Managing Common Misbehaviour Problems: Nonverbal Interventions

FOCUS ON THE PRINCIPLES OF CLASSROOM MANAGEMENT

1. What is the ultimate goal of a teacher's classroom-management techniques for individual students?

2. What preplanning is absolutely essential if teachers are to manage misbehaviour?

3. What are the teacher behaviours that are most effective in maximizing management alternatives?

INTRODUCTION

Most student misbehaviours tend to be verbal interruptions, off-task behaviour, and disruptive physical movements. These behaviours—sometimes called **surface behaviours**—are present in every classroom in every school almost every day. With proper planning, instructional strategies, and environmental structuring, the frequency of surface behaviours can be reduced greatly; however, no matter how much time and energy the teacher directs toward prevention, surface behaviours do not disappear and to some extent are an ever-present fact of life for all teachers.

There are many intervention skills that the successful teacher may use to deal with surface behaviours in a manner that is effective, expedient, and least disruptive to the teaching and learning process. These skills may be divided into three sequenced categories: (1) nonverbal intervention, (2) verbal intervention, and (3) use of logical consequences (see also Figure 9.2). Each tier of the sequence consists of a variety of intervention skills, which are themselves sequenced. The degree of intrusiveness and the potential for disruption to the teaching/learning environment determine which skills the teacher employs. When these intervention skills are applied in a pre-planned, systematic manner, they have been shown to be quite effective.

In this chapter, we discuss nonverbal skills, the first tier in the decision-making hierarchy. This group of skills is the least intrusive and has the least potential for disrupting the teaching/learning process while leaving the teacher with the maximum number of management alternatives for future use.

PREREQUISITES TO MANAGEMENT

All too often, teachers are quick to place total responsibility for inappropriate behaviour on their students without carefully analyzing their own behaviour. It is quite common to hear teachers say, "There's nothing I can do. All they want to do is fool around" or "These kids are impossible! Why even try?" Such comments clearly indicate that teachers have assigned all blame for student misbehaviour to the students themselves; however, effective teaching and maximum learning occur in classrooms when teachers and students understand that teaching and learning are the responsibility of both the student and the teacher.

The responsibilities of the students are obvious. Students must prepare for class, study, ask questions to enhance their understanding, and remain on task. Many of the preventive techniques that we have discussed in previous chapters, as well as the management techniques to be discussed in this chapter, assist students in accepting responsibility for their learning; however, students more readily accept their responsibilities when it is clear to them that the teacher is fulfilling his responsibilities. These professional responsibilities, which we have already examined, are the basic minimum competencies that all teachers must possess. They are the prerequisites to appropriate classroom management:

1. The teacher is well prepared to teach. Prior to class, he has designed specific learning objectives and effective teaching strategies based on accepted principles of learning.
2. The teacher provides clear directions and explanations of the learning material.
3. The teacher ensures that students understand evaluation criteria.
4. The teacher clearly communicates, rationalizes, and consistently enforces behavioural expectations.
5. The teacher demonstrates enthusiasm and encouragement and models the behaviours expected from students.
6. The teacher builds positive, caring relationships with students.

When teachers reinforce the concept of shared responsibility for teaching and learning through their behaviour, management techniques, if needed, are more likely to be effective in encouraging appropriate student behaviour.

SURFACE BEHAVIOURS

The most common day-to-day disruptive behaviours are verbal interruptions (talking, humming, laughing, calling out, whispering), off-task behaviours (daydreaming, sleeping, combing hair, playing with something, doodling), physical movement intended to disrupt (visiting, passing notes, sitting on the desk or on two legs of the chair, throwing paper), and disrespect (arguing, teasing/heckling, vulgarity, talking back) (Leflot, Lier, Onghena, and Colpin, 2010; Sayeski and Brown, 2011). These disruptive behaviours, which are usually readily observable to an experienced teacher, are called surface behaviours because they usually are not a result of any deep-seated personal problem but are normal developmental behaviours of children (Sayeski and Brown, 2011).

Some teachers are able to manage surface behaviours appropriately, almost intuitively. They have a near instinctive grasp of the necessary classroom skills of "overlapping," or attending to two matters at the same time, and "with-it-ness," a subtle nonverbal communication to students that they are aware of all activities within the classroom (Hester, Hendrickson, and Gable, 2009; Kounin, 1970; Schwartz and Pollishuke, 2002). Other teachers acquire these skills through hard work and experience. Teachers who do not have or do not develop these skills have to cope with high frequencies of surface behaviours, and in some instances, as in Case 8.1, the absence of these skills actually causes disruptive behaviour.

PROACTIVE INTERVENTION SKILLS

Effective classroom managers are experts in the matter-of-fact use of not only *overlapping* and *with-it-ness* skills but also other more specific and narrower **proactive intervention skills**. Their expertise can be seen in the way they employ these skills with little if any disruption in the teaching/learning process. Developing expertise in the following proactive skills should lessen the need for more intrusive management techniques:

CASE 8.1

. . . 3, 2, 1, Blast Off!

The students in Mr. Berk's grade 7 English class have science before English. Today, their science teacher illustrated the concept of propulsion by folding a piece of tin foil around the tip of a match. When he heated the tin foil, the match was ignited and accelerated forward. The students were intrigued and asked him to repeat the experiment.

During English class, Mickey, seated in the back row, decides to try the propulsion experiment for the entertainment of those around him. It is not long before many students are aware of Mickey's activity and are sneaking glances at him. Mickey is enjoying the attention and continues to propel matches across his desk.

It does not take Mr. Berk long to become aware that many of his students are not paying attention. Instead of attempting to determine what the distraction is, he reacts impulsively. He sees Terri turn around to look at Mickey and says sharply, "Terri, turn around and pay attention!" Terri immediately fires back defiantly, "I'm not doing anything." The class begins to laugh, because Mr. Berk is the only person in the room who is unaware of the aerospace activity in the back of the room.

Questions to Consider

1. Why is Mr. Berk unaware of Mickey's activities?
2. When he became aware of the lack of attention, what should Mr. Berk have done?
3. Why was his impulsive discipline of Terri destructive to his classroom management?
4. Consider the levels of the CALM model and discuss how they could be applied in this case. Start with the applicability of Level I to begin the discussion and proceed through all four levels.

1. ***Change the pace of classroom activities.*** Rubbing eyes, yawning, stretching, and staring out the window are clear signs that a change of pace is needed. This is the time for the teacher to restructure the situation and involve students in games, stories, or other favourite activities that require active student participation and help to refocus student interests. To reduce the need for on-the-spot, change-of-pace activities, lesson plans should provide for a variety of learning experiences that accommodate the attention spans and interests of the students both in time and in type.

2. ***Remove distracting objects.*** This skill may be used with little, if any, pause in the teaching act; however, there should be an agreement that the objects will be returned after class. Teachers who find themselves competing with extraneous objects may simply walk over to the student, collect the object, and quietly inform the student that it will be available after class.

3. ***Boost the interest of a student who shows signs of off-task behaviour.*** Rather than using other, less positive techniques, the teacher shows interest in the student's work, thereby bringing the student back on task. Interest boosting is often called for when students are required to do individual or small-group classwork. It is during these times that the potential for chatter, daydreaming, or other off-task behaviours is high. If the teacher observes a student engaging in activities other than the assigned math problems, for example, he can boost the interest of the student by walking over to the student and asking how his work is going or checking the answers of his completed problems. Asking the student to place correct problems on the board is also effective. Whatever technique is decided on, it must be employed in a matter-of-fact supportive manner to boost the student's interest in the learning activity.

4. ***Redirect the behaviour of off-task students.*** This skill helps to refocus the student's attention. Students who are passing notes, talking, or daydreaming may be asked to read, do a problem, or answer a question. When this technique is used, it is important to treat the student as if he were paying attention; for instance, if you call on the off-task student to answer a question and the student answers correctly, give positive feedback. If he doesn't answer or answers incorrectly, reformulate the question or call on someone else. A teacher who causes the student embarrassment or ridicule invites further misbehaviour.

5. ***Provide a "nonpunitive" time out.*** This skill should be used for students who show signs of encountering a provoking, painful, frustrating, or fatiguing situation. The teacher quietly asks the student if he would like to get a drink or invites him to run an errand or do a chore. The change in activity gives the student time to regain his control before re-entering the learning environment. Teachers must be alert to the signs of frustration so they can act in a timely fashion to help students cope.

6. ***Encourage the appropriate behaviour of other students.*** A statement such as, "I'm glad to see that Andrea and Carl have their books open" reminds off-task students of the behaviour that is expected of them.

7. ***Provide cues for expected behaviours.*** Cues can be quite effective in obtaining the desired behaviour, but the teacher must be sure the cue is understood by all; for example, a teacher who expects students to be in their seats and prepared for class when the bell rings must make sure that everyone understands that the bell

Group of students with an advisor at the university.
© Andresr/Shutterstock

signals the start of class. In schools without bells or other indicators, closing the door is an appropriate cue. Some teachers flick the lights or clap hands in a pattern to cue a class that the noise has reached unacceptable levels. Using the same cues consistently usually results in an appropriate student response.

REMEDIAL INTERVENTION SKILLS

In order to describe and clarify the CALM model further, in the following section we provide an in-depth discussion of the rationale for each level of CALM.

The masterful use of proactive skills diffuses many surface behaviours and causes minimal disruptions of the teaching act; however, there will always be classroom situations that induce misbehaviour or students who continue to display disruptive behaviours.

These behaviours may range from mildly off-task to very disruptive. Mastering the delivery of the intervention skills discussed here and in Chapter 9, "Managing Common Misbehaviour Problems: Verbal Interventions and Use of Logical Consequences," and Chapter 10, "Classroom Interventions for Chronic Problems," should help to produce an exceptional classroom in which misbehaviour is minimized and teachers are free to teach and children are free to learn.

Before any intervention may be used, the teacher must have a basis on which to make decisions concerning common inappropriate behaviours in the classroom. To avoid inconsistency, teachers must also have a systematic intervention plan of predetermined behaviours that clearly communicate disapproval to the student who calls out, throws paper, walks around, passes notes, or in any way interferes with the teaching or learning act (Canter and Canter, 2001; Tsouloupas, Carson, Matthews, Grawitch, and Barber, 2010). This follows our definition of teaching presented in Chapter 1, "The Foundations,": the conscious use of predetermined behaviours that increase the likelihood of changing student behaviours. Such a systematic intervention plan also follows the levels of the CALM model for examining and managing classroom challenges that are described in Chapter 1.

As outlined in the CALM model, the intervention decision-making approach is a sequence of teacher behaviours. Because we believe that students must learn to control their own behaviour, the initial interventions are subtle, nonintrusive, and very student-centred. Although these behaviours communicate disapproval, they are designed to provide students with the opportunity to control their own behaviour. If the misbehaviours are not curbed, the interventions become increasingly more intrusive and teacher-centred; that is, the teacher takes more responsibility for managing the students' behaviour (Emmer and Evertson, 2009).

Because we also believe that management techniques should not in themselves disrupt the teaching and learning act (Dhaem, 2012; Kerr and Nelson, 2002), early intervention behaviours are almost a private communication between the teacher and the off-task student. They alert the student to his inappropriate behaviour but cause little, if any, noticeable disruption to either teaching or learning. If these nonverbal interventions, which make up the first level of the CALM decision-making model, are not successful, they are followed by the second, third, and fourth levels. These levels are increasingly more teacher-centred, more intrusive, and may cause some interruption to the teaching/learning act. (These techniques are discussed in Chapters 9 and 10.) Please refer to Levels I through IV of the CALM model.

CALM is intended to be a dynamic model, not one that binds a teacher into a lockstep, sequential, cookbook intervention approach. Instead, the model requires the teacher to make a decision as to which intervention in the hierarchy to use first. The decision should depend on the type and frequency of the disruptive behaviour and should be congruent with the five implementation guidelines that follow. These guidelines should help to ensure that any beginning intervention, as well as those that may follow, meets the two foundational precepts of the model: increasing student self-control and decreasing disruptions to the teaching and learning environment.

1. The intervention provides the student with opportunities for self-control of the disruptive behaviours. Self-control is not developed to its fullest in classrooms where teachers immediately intervene with teacher-centred techniques to manage student behaviour. Because we believe that individuals make conscious choices to behave in certain ways and that individuals cannot be forced to learn or exhibit appropriate behaviour, early interventions should not force students but rather *influence* them to manage themselves. Students must be given responsibility in order to learn responsibility.

2. Our CALM model does not cause more disruption to the teaching and learning environment than the disruptive behaviour itself. We have all witnessed teacher interventions that were more disruptive to the class than the off-task student behaviour. This usually occurs when the teacher uses an intervention too far up the decision-making hierarchy. Use of CALM should reduce the likelihood of such occurrences; for example, a teacher unacquainted with the CALM approach

might choose to use a public verbal technique when a private nonverbal intervention would be more effective and less disruptive. When this happens, the teacher becomes a more disruptive factor than the student.

3. The model lessens the probability that the student will become more disruptive or confrontational. Interventions should lessen and defuse confrontational situations. When teachers choose to employ public, aggressive, or humiliating techniques, they increase the likelihood of escalating confrontations and power struggles. Again, deciding where in the decision-making hierarchy to begin has a significant effect on whether a disruptive student will be brought back on task or will become confrontational.

4. CALM can protect students from physical and psychological harm. When a teacher observes behaviours that could be harmful to any student, intervention should be swift and teacher-centred. In such situations, nonverbal techniques are usually bypassed for the assertive delivery of verbal interventions. In all cases, care must be taken that the interventions are not in themselves a source of harm to students or the teacher.

5. Every teacher knows that it often takes more than one type of intervention to manage student behaviour. It is rare that when a disruptive behaviour is noted, a teacher simply intervenes and the student is back on task forever. It is the unwise teacher who sends a student out of the classroom for the first occurrence of a disruptive behaviour. Such an intervention leaves few options available to the teacher if the student continues to misbehave when he returns. By using the CALM model, the savvy teacher reserves many alternative interventions.

It is important to remember that the teacher's goal in employing any remedial intervention skill is to redirect the student to appropriate behaviour. Stopping the misbehaviour may be the initial step in the process, but it is not sufficient in itself. The teacher's goal is not reached until the student becomes re-engaged in learning activities; thus, whenever the teacher is faced with a disruptive behaviour, one of the questions he should ask is, "What level of the CALM model is likely to be the most effective?"

In Chapter 1, the four levels of the CALM model are outlined. Briefly, those levels are as follows:

LEVEL I—CONSIDER. When a student's behaviour becomes disruptive, the teacher should *consider* the following question to initiate a response process: "Does the behaviour change, affect, or disrupt the classroom learning environment, teacher, or students?"

LEVEL II—ACT. Once the behaviour has become a "distracting" force for the teacher, the next level of intervention is introduced because it becomes necessary to *act*.

LEVEL III—LESSEN. Because it is important to minimize distraction and not give undue attention to inappropriate behaviour, it is best to *lessen* the use of invasive responses in dealing with a situation that requires action.

LEVEL IV—MANAGE. *Manage* the milieu to quickly return to an effective learning environment.

As is evident, the initial levels of CALM consist of moderate techniques, which should be considered before more invasive action. These preliminary techniques could be described as planned ignoring, signal interference, and proximity interference, which are body-language interventions first identified by Redl and Wineman (1952). When they are used randomly, a teacher is unlikely to manage minor disruptions effectively; however, when they are consciously used in a predetermined logical sequence, they serve to curb milder forms of off-task behaviour (Dhaem, 2012; Tsouloupas et al., 2010).

Planned Ignoring

Planned ignoring is based on the reinforcement theory that if you ignore a behaviour, it will lessen and eventually disappear. Although this sounds simple, it is difficult to ignore a behaviour completely. That is why *planned* is stressed. When a student whistles, interrupts the teacher, or calls out, the teacher instinctively looks in the direction of the student, thereby giving the student attention and reinforcing the behaviour. In contrast, planned ignoring intentionally and completely ignores the behaviour. This takes practice.

And, there are limitations to this intervention. First, according to reinforcement theory, when a behaviour has been reinforced previously, removal of the reinforcement causes a short-term increase in the behaviour in the hope of again receiving reinforcement; thus, when planned ignoring is first used, there probably will be an increase in the off-task behaviour. This technique, therefore, should be used to manage only those behaviours that cause little interference to the teaching/learning act (Brophy, 2010; Reinke, Herman, and Sprick, 2011). Second, other classmates who pay attention to the misbehaving student often are reinforcing the disruptive behaviour. If so, planned ignoring by the teacher has little effect.

The behaviours that usually are managed by planned ignoring include not having materials ready for the start of class, calling out answers rather than raising a hand, mild or infrequent whispering, interrupting the teacher, and daydreaming. Obviously, the type of learning activity has much to do with the behaviours that can or cannot be ignored. If, after a reasonable period of time of ignoring the off-task behaviour, the behaviour does not decrease or the point is reached at which others are distracted by it, the teacher has to move quickly and confidently to the next step in the hierarchy: signal interference.

Signal Interference

Signal interference is any type of nonverbal behaviour that communicates to the student, without disturbing others, that the behaviour is inappropriate. Signal interventions must be clearly directed at the off-task student. There should be no doubt in the student's mind that the teacher is aware of what is going on and that the student is responsible for the behaviour (Sayeski and Brown, 2011). The teacher's expression should be businesslike. It is ineffective for the teacher to make eye contact with a student and smile. Smiling sends a double message, which confuses students, who may interpret it as a lack of seriousness on the teacher's part.

Examples of signal-interference behaviours are making eye contact with the student who is talking to a neighbour, pointing to a seat when a student is wandering around, head shaking to indicate "no" to a student who is about to throw a paper airplane, and holding up an open hand to stop a student's calling out. Like all coping skills, signal-interference behaviours may be hierarchically ordered, depending on the type, duration, and frequency of off-task behaviour. A simple hand motion might be sufficient for calling out the first time, whereas direct eye contact with a disapproving look may be needed the next time the student calls out.

For disruptive behaviours that continue or for disturbances that more seriously affect others' learning, the teacher moves to the next intervention skill in the hierarchy: proximity interference.

Proximity Interference

Proximity interference is any movement toward the disruptive student. When signal interference doesn't work or when the teacher is unable to gain a student's attention long enough to send a signal because the student is so engrossed in the off-task behaviour, proximity interference is warranted.

Often, just walking toward the student while conducting the lesson is enough to bring the student back on task. If the student continues to be off task, the teacher may want to conduct the lesson in close proximity to the student's desk, which is usually quite effective. This technique works well during question-and-answer sessions.

Proximity interference combined with signal interference results in a very effective nonverbal management technique. It's the rare student who is not brought back on task by a teacher who makes eye contact and begins walking toward his desk. Like signal interference, proximity-interference techniques may be hierarchically ordered from nonchalant movement in the direction of the student to an obvious standing behind or next to the student during class.

EFFECTIVENESS OF NONVERBAL INTERVENTION SKILLS

The use of these three remedial nonverbal intervention skills is considered successful if any one or any combination in the hierarchy leads the student to resume appropriate classroom behaviour.

Notice how Mr. Rothman in Case 8.2 skilfully uses the three nonverbal remedial-intervention techniques in combination with the proactive skills of removing seductive objects, interest boosting, and redirecting the behaviour to manage the note passing between Leo and Ben without noticeably disrupting the teaching/learning act. He is able to do this because the intervention skills are not randomly and applied.

Mr. Rothman has a mental flow chart of the intervention sequence so that movement from one behaviour to the next is accomplished quickly, calmly, and confidently. This does not happen overnight. Teachers must pre-plan and practise proactive and remedial-intervention techniques before they need to implement them.

Shrigley (1985) studied the efficiency of nonverbal proactive- and remedial-intervention skills when used in a hierarchical sequence. He found that after a few hours of in-service training, 53 teachers were able to curb 40 percent of 523 off-task surface behaviours without having to utter a word or cause any interruption to either teaching or learning. Five percent of the behaviours were corrected by the use of

CASE 8.2

Notes Versus Math

Mr. Rothman asks each student in his grade 6 class to write one math problem from an assignment on the board. As two students write their problems, he notices, out of the corner of his eye, Leo passing a note to Ben. Mr. Rothman decides to ignore the behaviour, waiting to see if it is a matter of a single occurrence. When all the problems are on the board, Mr. Rothman asks questions about the solutions. During this questioning period, he notices Ben returning a note to Leo. After a few attempts, Mr. Rothman makes eye contact with Leo while at the same time questioning Ben about one of the problems. This technique stops the note passing for the remainder of the questioning activity.

The next activity calls for the use of calculators, and Mr. Rothman asks Leo to please pass one calculator to each predetermined pair of students. Leo and Ben are partners, and Mr. Rothman monitors their behaviour from a distance. As he circulates around the room helping students with the classwork, Mr. Rothman makes sure that he stops to look over Leo and Ben's work, encouraging them on its accuracy. Throughout the activity, both boys are on task.

Following the group work, the students separate their desks, and Mr. Rothman begins to review the answers to the problems. He immediately notices that the two boys have begun to pass notes again. He quickly takes a position next to the boys, taps Leo on the shoulder, and holds out his hand for the note. Leo hands Mr. Rothman the note and he puts it in his pocket. Mr. Rothman stands near the boys for the rest of the period, asking questions of the class and reviewing the problems. Both Ben and Leo volunteer and participate for the remainder of the class.

Questions to Consider

1. What are Mr. Rothman's options related to the note he has confiscated? Examine each option and select the one most congruent with the CALM method. Provide a rationale for your choice.
2. Find three ways in which Mr. Rothman adhered to the CALM model.
3. Discuss the appropriateness of each of Mr. Rothman's interventions.

planned ignoring. Signal interference was the most effective technique, rectifying 14 percent of the behaviours. Twelve percent of the behaviours were stopped by proximity. To manage the remaining 60 percent of unresolved behavioural problems, the teachers needed to use verbal intervention (Shrigley, 1985). We discuss verbal-intervention skills in Chapter 9.

Remember, however, that the hierarchy is a decision-making model. Depending on the type, frequency, and distracting potential of the behaviour, the teacher may decide to bypass the initial intervention skills in favour of a later technique. There are certain behaviours that need immediate attention—they can neither be ignored nor allowed to continue. This is demonstrated in Case 8.3, in which Ms. Niaz decides to bypass planned ignoring and signal interference in favour of proximity interference to manage a disruption during a test.

No matter which technique eventually brings the student back on task, efforts need to be directed toward maintaining the appropriate behaviour. This is most easily accomplished by the teacher, who encourages and attends to the student's new behaviour. The student must realize that he can obtain the same or even more attention and recognition for appropriate behaviour than he did for disruptive behaviour. The student who is ignored when calling out answers should be called on immediately when he raises his hand. The student who ceases walking around the room should be told at the end of the period that it was a pleasure having him in the class. These simple efforts of recognizing appropriate behaviour are often overlooked by teachers, but they are necessary for the teacher who wants to maximize the effectiveness of proactive- and remedial-intervention skills. Frequently, these strategies are referred to as **behaviour modification**.

CONCENTRIC CASE STUDY KALEIDOSCOPE

CASE 8.3

Let Your Fingers Do the Walking

The Story

Ms. Niaz explains the test-taking procedures to her large grade 10 math class. She emphasizes the need for each student to do his own work, and in order to expedite this necessity, she asks the students to separate their desks into rows. Ms. Niaz hands out the tests face down. When everyone has a copy, she announces, "Okay, you may begin." All the students turn their tests over and begin to read. For the next 15 minutes, she walks around the room, answers a few questions, and makes sure that her students are aware of her presence.

When Ms. Niaz is at one side of the room, she glances across the class and notices that Danny, a good student, is walking his fingers up Tonya's back in front of him. In a few seconds, Tonya, who is also a good student but has to work harder at it than Danny, turns around and whispers, "Stop it." As soon as she turns back to her test, Danny starts running his fingers up her back again with a slight smile on his lips. Ms. Diaz walks toward Danny and spends the next 10 minutes standing in close proximity to him.

The Students' Perspectives

Danny: "Okay, I get the routine for writing the test. It's the same every time. Let's get started." As he turns the test over, Danny quickly scans the questions and then relaxes, as he knows that he can answer all the questions quite easily. He starts writing and works for about 15 minutes steadily. Looking up, he glances at the time and realizes that he has a lot of time left to do the last couple of questions. He stares at Tonya's back and notes that she is concentrating hard on her work. "I like Tonya," he muses and remembers dancing with her at the Friday night school dance last week. His mind begins to wander and he feels as though he wants to tease Tonya and get her attention. After all, the test is half over. He slowly and lightly begins to walk his fingers up her back while glancing over to see where the teacher is standing. It's okay because Ms. Niaz is on the other side of the room.

At first, Tonya ignores Danny's touch, so he increases the pressure. He's hoping she'll turn around and smile at him. Instead, she rotates and whispers gently (but firmly),

(Continued)

(Continued)

"Stop it!" "I think she's flattered that I'm teasing her," Danny thinks. Again, he starts running his fingers up her back. Glancing up, he notices that Ms. Niaz is now moving purposefully toward him. He quickly returns to focusing on his test and is busily solving the next question when she moves next to him. As Ms. Niaz stays positioned near him for the next few minutes, Danny thinks, "Oh, she obviously saw me touching Tonya and thought I was bothering her or trying to cheat." He keeps his head down and focuses on his test until the end of the allotted time. When Danny hands in the test, he fails to meet Ms. Niaz's eyes and leaves feeling a bit sheepish and anxious to make certain that Tonya is not annoyed with him.

Tonya: "I'm glad Ms. Niaz reminds us about the procedures for writing a test every time. I know tests are important—I really like to study hard beforehand and I need to concentrate hard during the test if I am going to get a good mark. I really like getting good marks and I'm extra prepared for this test. Last night, I didn't even watch *Survivor* and I really wanted to see the next episode. My parents told me what happened but I spent my time in my room with the door closed doing practice questions. I feel much better about myself when I get good marks and my parents are so proud of me."

As Tonya turns her paper over, she feels apprehension, hoping that she has studied well enough to allow her to answer the questions. At first glance, Tonya feels confident, but she knows that she works slowly and methodically and will have to use her time well. No time for daydreaming or distractions. She gets down to work.

"What is that feeling? . . . Oh, no! Danny is running his fingers up my back. I don't have time for this now, although I do like him." She really wishes that he would stop, as

he is interfering with her concentration. Finally, she turns around and says gently in a whisper so as not to draw attention to the incident, "Stop it!" For a moment, Danny stops. But then he begins to run his fingers up her back again. Just as Tonya is preparing to speak more sharply to him, she notices the teacher moving toward them. "Thank goodness," she thinks. "Now I don't have to hurt his feelings or deal with the disruption anymore." As Tonya refocuses on her paper, she feels confident and grateful that Ms. Niaz is standing beside them ensuring that Danny leaves her alone. At the end of the test, Tonya hands in her paper feeling confident that she has done well. As they leave the room, she smiles at Danny to let him know that she holds no hard feelings about his disruptive attentions.

Ms. Niaz's Perspective

When Ms. Niaz gives her students a test, she always stresses procedures because she thinks that it helps her students take the work seriously. She also encourages them to study by reminding them of the test in advance and by giving them guidelines about what material to expect on the test. When handing out papers, she further emphasizes the seriousness of the test process by relocating desks and reminding them of the rules. As a result, she prides herself on the serious way her students treat her tests and by the level of preparation many of them engage in. She also believes that her students are young and that she needs to monitor their behaviour carefully. "I am really helping to prepare them for higher education and the way they administer tests in university."

As Ms. Niaz watches the students focus on their test, she feels a sense of pride in the seriousness with which they approach it. "My

(Continued)

(Continued)

attention to details is conveyed to them and is part of the reason that my classes always have a slightly higher average mark than the other grade 10 math class." She watches Danny begin to touch Tonya and reflects that Danny is a very capable student who really does not have to spend much time in order to achieve high results on his tests. But Ms. Niaz also knows that Tonya appears to be a very good student but that her efforts are much greater. She often comes in early to ask questions about the previous night's homework if she has difficulty. She also asks questions and volunteers answers readily in class in order to enhance her own learning. Now, Danny is breaking Tonya's focus.

"Oh, no you don't!" Ms. Niaz thinks as she moves over toward Danny. As she moves, she notes that he immediately begins to focus on his work again. In order to make sure that Tonya has uninterrupted time, Ms. Niaz stays beside Danny until the end of the test nears. "They really are good kids," she thought. "But I bet they'll talk after class!"

Questions to Consider

1. Describe the steps of CALM employed by Ms. Niaz and discuss the effectiveness of her decisions.
2. What should Ms. Niaz have done if Danny bothered Tonya for a third time?
3. Do you think that Ms. Niaz was conducting her tests appropriately? Why or why not?

Summary

In this chapter, we stressed that teaching/learning is the joint responsibility of the teacher and the students. Students are more willing to accept their responsibilities when it is clear to them that teachers are fulfilling their responsibilities. These responsibilities include being well-prepared to teach by developing learning objectives and using effective teaching strategies; providing clear directions and explanations; ensuring that students understand evaluation criteria; communicating and consistently enforcing behavioural expectations; demonstrating enthusiasm and encouragement; and modelling expected behaviour. These behaviours are minimum competencies that all teachers must possess and are considered prerequisites to effective classroom management.

Teachers proficient in classroom management are experts in the use of a variety of proactive intervention skills. Techniques such as changing the pace, removing seductive objects, boosting interest, redirecting behaviour, giving nonpunitive time out, encouraging appropriate behaviour, and providing cues are used to bring students back on task while causing little if any disruption to the teaching/learning process.

The CALM model of remedial-intervention skills provides a means to manage the inappropriate surface behaviours that are not brought on task through proactive-intervention skills. The structure of the hierarchy ranges from nonintrusive techniques that cause little disruption and provide students with the opportunity to control their own behaviour to intrusive techniques that potentially disrupt teaching and learning. The first tier of nonverbal remedial intervention consists of three nonverbal behaviours: planned ignoring, signal interference, and proximity interference. When used systematically, these techniques are effective in managing many surface behaviours.

Key Terms

behaviour modification: a method that involves the use of stimuli through positive and negative reinforcement to change behaviours and reactions. B. F. Skinner(1938) is credited with much of the theoretical work that he referred to as *operant conditioning*.

proactive intervention skills: when an instructor observes the start of, or even anticipates, inattentive behaviour, she usually gives a non-intrusive action or verbal cue to indicate to a student or students that they are required to return quickly to the "task at hand."

surface behaviours: the most common day-to-day disruptions, such as verbal interruptions, off-task behaviours, physical movement intended to disrupt, and disrespect.

Exercises

1. Near the beginning of this chapter, we listed six teacher behaviours that are prerequisites for achieving appropriate student behaviour. Should these teacher behaviours be considered prerequisites? Why or why not?

2. Predict what type of student behaviour may result if the teacher does not meet each of the six prerequisite teacher behaviours.

3. What, if any, deletions or additions would you make to the six prerequisite teacher behaviours? Explain any modification you suggest.

4. Suggest specific techniques a teacher could use that demonstrate each of the following proactive-intervention skills:
   a. changing the pace
   b. interest boosting
   c. redirecting behaviour
   d. encouraging appropriate behaviour
   e. providing cues

5. The hierarchy of remedial-intervention skills is presented as a decision-making model, not as an action model. Explain why.

6. Two effective remedial-intervention skills are signal interference and proximity interference. Suggest specific techniques that would demonstrate their use.

7. What types of student behaviours would cause you to decide to bypass initial remedial nonverbal intervention skills and enter the hierarchy at the proximity interference level?

8. Explain why you agree or disagree with the premise that classroom-management techniques should be used in a manner that provides students with the greatest opportunity to control their own behaviour.

9. Some teachers consider the use of remedial-intervention skills a waste of time. They say, "Why spend all this time and effort when you can just tell the student to stop messing around and get back to work?" Explain why you agree or disagree with this point of view.

Weblinks

CanTeach

www.canteach.ca/elementary/classman.html
A good classroom resource; it provides links to resources that may help with behavioural problems and classroom management.

Classroom Management Tips and Beginning of the Year Ideas

http://www.fvsd.ab.ca/school/STM/Pages/default.aspx

This site is applicable to primary teachers.

Saskatchewan's Department of Education—Caring and Respectful Schools Bullying Prevention

www.publications.gov.sk.ca/details.cfm?p=11449
Examines how to deal with misbehaviours and bullying and also outlines how to build "caring and respectful schools."

Managing Common Misbehaviour Problems: Verbal Interventions and Use of Logical Consequences

FOCUS ON THE PRINCIPLES OF CLASSROOM MANAGEMENT

1. What should a teacher do if nonverbal intervention is ineffective?
2. What are the risks associated with verbal intervention?
3. If verbal intervention is ineffective, what strategies can the teacher use?

INTRODUCTION

In this chapter, we present 12 verbal intervention techniques in a systematic, hierarchical format. As in the nonverbal intervention skills subhierarchy presented in Chapter 8, "Managing Common Misbehaviour Problems: Nonverbal Interventions," the verbal intervention subhierarchy begins with techniques designed to foster students' control over their own behaviour and proceeds to those that foster greater teacher management over student behaviour. Because, as we noted in Chapter 8, this is a decision-making hierarchy, the teacher must decide which particular verbal intervention technique to use with a student who is misbehaving after determining that nonverbal interventions have not worked. The last section of the chapter discusses the final tier of the management hierarchy and the use of logical consequences to manage student behaviour.

Case 9.1 is an example of a teacher tirade and its effect upon student behaviour. Although it is true that John has caused many problems for Mr. Hensen and the other students in his class, what does Mr. Hensen accomplish by yelling at him? Although he does get his long-suppressed feelings off his chest, Mr. Hensen does more harm than good. He disrupts any learning that is taking place. He forces the other students to concentrate on John's behaviour rather than on the content of the lesson, and he extends the off-task time by prolonging the

CASE 9.1

Blowing His Stack

"John, you are one of the most obnoxious students I have ever had the misfortune to deal with. How many times have I asked you not to call out answers? If you want to answer a question, raise your hand. It shouldn't tax your tiny brain too much to remember that. I'm sick and tired of your mistaken idea that the rules of this classroom apply to everyone but you. It's because of students like you that we need rules in the first place. They apply especially to you. I will not allow you to deprive other students of the chance to answer questions. Anyway, half of your answers are totally off the wall. I'm in charge here, not you. If you don't like it, you can tell your troubles to the principal. Now get back to your work and be quiet."

When Mr. Hensen finished his rant and turned to walk to the front of the room, John discreetly "flipped him the bird" and laughed with his friends. John spent the rest of the period drawing pictures on the corner of his desk. The other students spent the remainder of the period in either uncomfortable silence or invisible laughter. Mr. Hensen spent the rest of the class trying to calm down and get his mind back on the lesson.

Questions to Consider

1. How and why did John effectively undermine Mr. Hensen's relationship with the rest of the class?
2. Assuming Mr. Hensen's level of frustration, what could he have said to John to ensure a more effective outcome?
3. Try to imagine and describe the previous relationship between Mr. Hensen and John.
4. Describe John's classroom behaviour over the past year.
5. What can be done to avoid future clashes?

reprimand. He reacts negatively and sarcastically to John, who already dislikes him and now is probably more determined than ever to "get Hensen's goat." Finally, by overreacting to a minor incident, Mr. Hensen has probably created some sympathy for John among the other students.

Although we know Mr. Hensen has overreacted, we also know that he is not alone. Many teachers find themselves in Mr. Hensen's position at one time or another. They allow many incidents of relatively minor misbehaviour to build up until one day they just can't take it anymore, and they explode. Often this makes the situation worse rather than better. Teachers can avoid this by using the CALM intervention skills model (presented in detail in Chapter 7, "Structuring the Environment," and outlined in Chapters 1, "The Foundations," as well as 7) to contend with classroom behavioural problems.

Teachers should proceed through the stages from the least to most invasive, as follows: (1) nonverbal intervention skills, (2) verbal intervention, and (3) use of logical consequences. When teachers use this hierarchy to guide their thinking about classroom behavioural problems, they are able to cope with misbehaviour more effectively. In this chapter, we present the second and third tiers of the hierarchy. **Verbal intervention** is one of the most powerful and versatile tools the teacher has for classroom management. When used effectively, verbal intervention makes classroom management relatively easy and less stressful. When used poorly and thoughtlessly, however, it may create new management problems, make existing problems worse, or turn temporary problems into chronic ones.

CLASSROOM VERBAL INTERVENTION

There are, as explained in Chapter 8, four advantages to using nonverbal intervention whenever possible: (1) disruption to the learning process is less likely to occur; (2) hostile confrontation with the student is less apt to happen; (3) the student is provided the opportunity to correct her behaviour before more teacher-centred, public interventions are used; and (4) a maximum number of remaining alternative interventions is preserved. Nonverbal intervention, however, is not always possible. When misbehaviour is potentially harmful to any student or potentially disruptive for a large number of students, it should be stopped quickly, and, often, verbal intervention is the quickest way to do so. Before discussing specific techniques, there are some guidelines teachers should keep in mind when using verbal intervention:

1. Whenever possible, use nonverbal interventions first.
2. Keep verbal intervention as private as possible. This minimizes the risk of having the student become defensive and hostile to avoid losing face. Experts suggest that this is one of the most important general principles for disciplinary intervention (Hue and Li, 2008; Sheffield and Waller, 2010).
3. Make the verbal intervention as brief as possible. Your goal is to stop the misbehaviour *and* redirect the student to appropriate behaviour. Prolonging the verbal interaction extends the disruption of learning and enhances the likelihood of a hostile confrontation.
4. As Ginott (2009) suggests, speak to the situation, not the person. In other words, label the *behaviour* as bad or inappropriate, not the person. If, for example, a student interrupts a teacher, "Interrupting others is rude" is a more appropriate response than "You interrupted me. You are rude." Labelling the behaviour helps the student to see the distinction between herself and her behaviour, which in turn helps her to understand that it is possible for the teacher to like her but not her behaviour. If the student is labelled, she may feel compelled to defend herself. Furthermore, the student may accept the label as part of her self-concept and match the label with inappropriate behaviour in the future. This is exactly what Jimmy Dolan decides to do in Case 9.2.

CONCENTRIC CASE STUDY KALEIDOSCOPE

CASE 9.2

Jimmy, the Little Sneak

The Story

Jimmy Dolan is in a grade 11 math class at Princess Elizabeth High School. He is a fine student who rarely misbehaves and certainly has given none of his teachers any difficulty. His math teacher, Mr. Gamble, has had a long history of difficulty in dealing with classroom misbehaviour. The students are well aware of this reputation and each new class tend to come to Mr. Gamble with a predetermined sense of disrespect based on hearsay gleaned from previous students. This poor reputation makes Mr. Gamble's job very difficult. At times,

(Continued)

(Continued)

he feels helpless to break the pattern of mis-behaviour that always emerges in his classes.

On the second day of class, as his back is partially turned to the students, Mr. Gamble notices Jimmy talking to a neighbour. In a flash of self-determination, he turns and pounces on Jimmy, who was only asking Craig Rutler for an easier way to correct a mistake in his homework. "So, you are the one who has been causing all the noise," Mr. Gamble snaps. "You are a little sneak. Since the beginning of class, I thought you were one of the few students I could count on not to cause trouble in here. Well, I've got my eye on you. You'll not get away with any more sneaky behaviour in my class."

For a week or so, Jimmy goes back to his typical good behaviour, but every time something goes wrong or anyone misbe-haves, he feels as though Mr. Gamble blames him. After a week or so of unjust blame, Jimmy decides that he may as well start caus-ing some trouble—after all, he's going to get blamed for classrooms mishaps anyway.

In a very short time, Jimmy becomes a great troublemaker who causes all sorts of havoc. Because he is subversive and sneaky about it, he rarely gets caught in the act.

Mr. Gamble's Perspective

Mr. Gamble knows that he has a reputation for suffering through misbehaviour in his classes. He finds teaching very frustrating and difficult and, because of this, often goes home very discouraged. He is aware of stu-dents' disrespect for him and that he has been viewed as ineffectual over the years.

Mr. Gamble wonders how he can break the cycle, stop struggling with his students for their attention, and establishing himself as a strict disciplinarian.

This year, he has determined to change his behaviour and nip every off-task behaviour

in the bud right from the start. He says to himself, "I will have a good class this time and I will do what I have to do to maintain very strict discipline." He determines to watch for every slight deviation from perfect behav-iour and make an example of the perpetrator.

In the second class of the semester, Mr. Gamble partially turns his back on the class and then immediately notices Jimmy Dolan talking to his friend. "Aha," he thinks, "now is my opportunity to set this class straight about what I expect from students." He challenges Jimmy very harshly, feeling as though he is addressing all the past disrespectful behav-iour that he has endured. It actually feels good to vent.

Jimmy seems surprised, but he does little to rebut the attack by his teacher. Mr. Gamble feels vindicated and believes that he has sent an important message to the class. "Things will be different this year," he thinks.

Over the next couple of weeks, though, Mr. Gamble notices very little change in the class. He constantly tries to recapture the moment of success he felt with Jimmy and blames him for much of the noise in the classroom. Jimmy's behaviour appears to be deteriorating rather than improving, and Mr. Gamble has more and more difficulty actually catching Jimmy in acts of misbehaviour. He begins to dislike Jimmy intensely.

The Students' Perspectives

Jimmy: Jimmy likes school and seldom causes any trouble in his classes. He is a good student who generally listens carefully in class and does his classwork and homework with con-scientious diligence. He enters Mr. Gamble's class knowing that this teacher has a reputa-tion for having poor classroom-management skills. This fact does not hold much signifi-cance for Jimmy, as it is not his pattern to take advantage of such situations. He does expect some of his friends and fellow classmates to make things difficult for Mr. Gamble, though.

Early in the first week of class, Jimmy is doing an assignment and notices that the homework he has done is not correct. He wonders if he has used the wrong page in his text or if he has actually done the questions incorrectly. To solve this dilemma, he asks his friend Craig Rutler what page the homework is on. Before Craig has an opportunity to answer, Mr. Gamble turns around and starts to attack him verbally. Jimmy is stunned and embarrassed at the same time. He feels unnerved by the threat Mr. Gamble utters to him. He leaves class feeling annoyed, although he notices that his friends are angrily talking about the teacher's unfair behaviour.

The next few classes are very difficult for Jimmy and he becomes increasingly upset at the way he is being made the scapegoat by his teacher. Soon, Jimmy actively begins to dislike and disrespect Mr. Gamble. He feels as though he's getting blamed for all excessive noise in the classroom. "I wonder if I should go and talk to the teacher alone," he thinks. He rejects this idea, as he genuinely feels that the teacher would not be approachable on the subject.

Finally, Jimmy feels angry when he enters the class and becomes determined to get back at Mr. Gamble for his unfairness by causing noise and encouraging other students to misbehave. He does so subtly and successfully. He thinks, "Now you can blame me if you want because I really am doing some things to get under your skin. I don't care because you have been unfair to me and now I will be unfair to you." Jimmy talks to his friends and to other students outside of class about his disrespect for Mr. Gamble and how easy it is to disrupt his classes. He begins to take satisfaction in causing trouble. He doesn't learn much math in the class and soon stops paying attention and neglects his homework.

Craig: Craig has heard about Mr. Gamble's lack of classroom-management skills and he

expects this class will be no different. Early in the first week, he answers a question that Jimmy asks about the homework page. He is surprised that Mr. Gamble makes such a big deal about Jimmy's supposed misbehaviour. He feels sorry for the way Mr. Gamble speaks to Jimmy and thinks, "This teacher is really unfair to Jimmy. He did nothing wrong and Gamble is not giving him a chance to explain."

As the days go by, Craig notices that Jimmy starts to get blamed for everything that goes wrong. He talks to Jimmy about the unfairness of the accusations and commiserates with him about the way Mr. Gamble is "picking on" him. In this conversation, Jimmy confides that he is getting really angry and Craig suggests, "Well, you might as well act any way you like because it is clear that you're going to get into trouble whether you do something or not." Jimmy agrees.

Craig watches with some amusement as the weeks pass and Jimmy starts misbehaving for real and encouraging others to do so as well. Craig feels free to talk with his neighbours and ignore the teacher during class and he gets up and walks around the room whenever he feels like it. He reasons that Jimmy will get blamed for everything anyway.

Craig sympathizes with Jimmy and actually feels that his friend is a bit of a hero.

Questions to Consider

1. What do you believe is the overall cause of Mr. Gamble's reputation as a poor manager of his classroom?
2. Why do you think Mr. Gamble targeted Jimmy?
3. What will Jimmy's fellow classmates responses be to his new-found "troublemaker" identity?
4. What could Mr. Gamble do to help restore Jimmy as a good student?
5. How can Mr. Gamble's ineffective classroom-management skills be remedied? (Consider the roles of administration, department head, parents, and other colleagues.)
6. How would implementing the CALM model have helped the situation?

5. As Ginott has urged, set limits on behaviour, not on feelings; for instance, a teacher should tell the student, "It's okay to be angry, but it's not okay to show your anger by hitting" or "It's okay to feel disappointed, but it's not okay to show that disappointment by ripping your test paper up in front of the class and throwing it in the basket." Students need to recognize, trust, and understand their feelings. When teachers and parents tell students not to be angry or disappointed, they are telling them to distrust and deny their genuine and often justified feelings. The appropriate message for teachers and parents to communicate and understand is that there are appropriate and inappropriate ways to express feelings (Ginott, 2009).

6. Avoid sarcasm and other verbal behaviours that belittle or demean the student. Using verbal reprimands to belittle students lowers self-esteem and creates sympathy for the "troublemaker" among classmates (Gatongi, 2007).

7. Begin by using a technique that fits the student and the problem and is as close as possible to the student-control end of the decision-making hierarchy.

8. If the first verbal intervention does not result in a return to appropriate behaviour, use a second technique that is closer to the teacher-control end of the hierarchy.

9. If more than one verbal intervention technique has been used unsuccessfully, it is time to move to the next step of the management hierarchy—the use of logical consequences.

Equally as important as these guidelines on how to use verbal interventions is the need for the teacher to be aware of commonly used ineffective verbal interventions. Many of these are instantaneous teacher reactions to disruptive students rather than systematic, planned, professional decisions enhanced by the use and understanding of the hierarchy of remedial-intervention skills. There are many ineffective verbal interventions, and they all share the common characteristics of not speaking directly to the disruptive behaviour and not directing the students toward controlling their own behaviour (Dhaem, 2012; Emmer and Evertson, 2009; Gatongi, 2007). Some ineffective verbal interventions encourage inappropriate behaviour. They may increase the possibility of further confrontation when the student attempts to "save face."

With the guidelines in mind and a cognizance of ineffective verbal reactions, let's turn our attention to the hierarchy of effective verbal intervention. Remember that this is a hierarchy of decision-making that begins with verbal interventions that foster student control over their own behaviour and gradually progresses to interventions that call for greater teacher management over student behaviour. The teacher uses the hierarchy as a range of options to consider, not as a series of techniques to be tried in rapid succession. The teacher should begin the intervention at the point on the hierarchy that is likely to correct the misbehaviour and still allow the student as much control and responsibility as possible. It is entirely appropriate to begin with a teacher-centred technique if the teacher believes that it is important to stop the misbehaviour quickly and only a teacher-centred intervention will do so (e.g., CALM, Level III, Action Stage B; please refer to Chapter 7). It is also important to remember that not all of these interventions are appropriate for all types of misbehaviour or for all students. Dhaem (2012) suggests that teacher-centred interventions are more appropriate for younger, developmentally immature children and student-centred interventions are more appropriate for older, developmentally mature learners; therefore, the effective

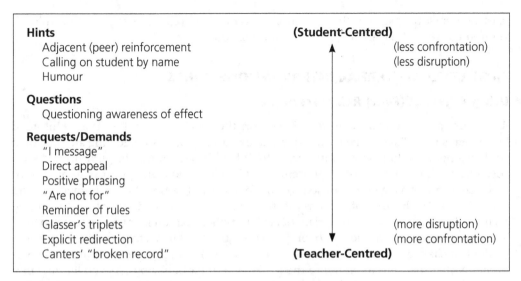

FIGURE 9.1   Hierarchy of Classroom Verbal Intervention Techniques

use of this verbal intervention hierarchy requires the teacher to decide which particular intervention techniques are appropriate for both the students and the particular types of misbehaviour that are occurring.

As Figure 9.1 indicates, the verbal intervention hierarchy has been broken into three major categories: *hints*, *questions*, and *requests/demands*. Hints are indirect means of letting the student know that her behaviour is inappropriate. They do not directly address the behaviour itself; thus, of all the verbal interventions, hints provide the greatest student control over behaviour and are the least likely to result in further disruption or confrontation. The first level of verbal interventions is classified as hints and includes adjacent or peer reinforcement, calling on students by saying their names, and humour.

The second level of verbal interventions is classified as questions and includes questioning awareness of effect. The teacher uses questions to ask if the student is aware of how she is behaving and how that behaviour is affecting other people around her. The questions are more direct than hints but provide greater student control, and there is less likelihood of confrontation when the teacher questions rather than demands; however, almost any request or demand can be reworded as a question. For example, "Pencils are not for drumming" can be rephrased as "What are pencils for?"

The third level of verbal interventions is identified as requests/demands and comprises teacher statements making clear that the teacher wants an inappropriate behaviour stopped. Requests and demands exert greater teacher management over student behaviour and have the potential to be disruptive and confrontational. Despite their disadvantages, it is sometimes necessary for teachers to use these interventions when lower-level interventions have proved unsuccessful. The potential for confrontation can be minimized if the demands are delivered calmly, privately, and assertively rather than aggressively. This level of verbal interventions includes: "I message," direct appeal, positive phrasing, "are not for," reminder of rules, Glasser's triplets, explicit redirection, and Canters' "broken record." No matter which interventions a teacher uses, she must be aware of the limitations and of the implicit message that each intervention conveys about managing student behaviour.

FIRST LEVEL OF VERBAL INTERVENTIONS: HINTS

Using Adjacent (Peer) Reinforcement

Adjacent (peer) reinforcement is based on the learning principle that reinforced behaviour is more likely to be repeated. While this usually means reinforcing an individual student's personal behaviour, Bandura (1977) has demonstrated through his work on social learning theory that other students are likely to imitate an appropriate behaviour when their peers have been praised for that behaviour (Moore, 2011; Zimmerman and Schunk, 2013) The use of peer reinforcement as a verbal intervention technique focuses class attention on appropriate behaviour rather than on inappropriate behaviour. This intervention technique has been placed first in the hierarchy because it gives the students a chance to control their own behaviour without any intervention on the part of the teacher that calls attention to the students or their behaviour. As you'll remember from Chapter 8, positive reinforcement can not only stop misbehaviour but also prevent other students from misbehaving.

To use this technique effectively, a teacher who notes a disruptive behaviour finds another student who is behaving appropriately and commends that student publicly for the appropriate behaviour. Recall from Case 9.1 Mr. Hensen's anger at John. Mr. Hensen could have handled the problem by saying, "Fred and Bob, I really appreciate that you raise your hands to answer questions" or "I am really glad that most of us remember the rule that we must raise our hands before speaking."

This particular verbal intervention technique is more useful at the elementary level than at the secondary level. Younger students are usually more interested in pleasing the teacher than are older students and often vie for the teacher's attention; thus, public praise by the teacher is a powerful reinforcer of appropriate behaviour. At the secondary level, peer approval is more highly valued than teacher approval; thus, public praise by the teacher is not a powerful reinforcer and indeed may not be a reinforcer at all. For these reasons, it is best to only sparingly use public praise of individuals. Public reinforcement of the group as a whole, however, may be an appropriate intervention at the secondary level (Emmer and Evertson, 2009).

Calling on the Student by Name

Using this technique, the teacher redirects the student to appropriate behaviour by calling on the student to answer a question or by inserting the student's name when the teacher observes "off-task" behaviour. Hearing her name is a good reminder to a student that her attention should be focused on the lesson. This technique may be used to redirect students who are off task but are not disrupting the learning of others (e.g., daydreaming, see Chapter 8) as well as those students who are overtly disrupting the learning process.

There are two possible formats for calling on disruptive students. Some teachers state the student's name first and then ask a question; others ask the question and then call on the student. The latter technique, however, invariably results in the student being unable to answer the question because she most likely did not hear it.

It is generally preferable to call on the student first and then ask the question. Using the name first achieves the goal of redirecting the student's attention without embarrassing her.

In Case 9.1, calling on John to answer or saying John's name are not appropriate techniques for Mr. Hensen to use in dealing with the situation because they encourage John's calling out by giving him recognition. Although inappropriate in that particular case, calling on the student by name is appropriate in a wide range of situations with learners of all ages.

Using Humour

Humour can be a powerful tool in establishing relationships and defusing confrontations. Humour that is directed at the teacher or at the situation rather than at the student can defuse tension in the classroom and redirect students to appropriate behaviour. The use of humour tends to depersonalize situations and can help to establish positive relationships with students (Booth-Butterfield and Wanzer, 2010; Levin and Nolan, 2007).

If Mr. Hensen wished to use humour to handle John's calling out, he might say something like this: "I must be hallucinating or something. I'd swear I heard somebody say something even though I haven't called on anyone yet." There is a fine line between humour and sarcasm. Used as a verbal intervention, humour is directed at or makes fun of the teacher or the situation, whereas sarcasm is directed at or makes fun of the student. It is important to keep this distinction in mind to ensure that what is intended as humour does not turn into sarcasm (Booth-Butterfield and Wanzer, 2010).

SECOND LEVEL OF VERBAL INTERVENTIONS: QUESTIONS

Questioning Awareness of Effect

Our research indicates that even students who have chronic behavioural problems learn to control their behaviour when they are forced to acknowledge both its positive and negative effects (Levin and Nolan, 2007). Given this, making disruptive students aware of how their behaviour affects other people can be a powerful technique for getting them to control their own behaviour. Usually, a teacher can make a student aware of the impact of her behaviour by asking a rhetorical question, which requires no response from the disruptive student. The teacher who wants to handle Mr. Hensen's problem by questioning the student's awareness of his behaviour's effect might say something like this: "John, are you aware that your calling out answers without raising your hand robs other students of the chance to answer the question?" As soon as the question was asked, the teacher would continue with the lesson without giving John an opportunity to respond.

The informal questioning not only makes the student aware of the impact of his behaviour but also communicates to other students the teacher's desire to protect their right to learn and may build peer support for appropriate behaviour. In using this intervention, however, especially with adolescent students, the teacher must be prepared for the possibility that the student will respond to the question. If the student responds and does so in a negative way, the teacher may choose to ignore the answer, thereby sending the message that she will not use class time to discuss the issue; or the teacher may respond, "John, your behaviour is having a negative impact on other people, and so I will not permit you to continue calling out answers." This option sends the message that the teacher is in charge of the classroom and will not tolerate the misbehaviour. In dealing with a possible negative response from the student, it is important to remember that the teacher's goal is to stop the misbehaviour and redirect the student to appropriate behaviour as quickly as possible. Prolonged confrontations may further aggravate that goal.

THIRD LEVEL OF VERBAL INTERVENTIONS: REQUESTS/DEMANDS

Sending an "I Message"

Thomas Gordon (1989), the author of *Teaching Children Self-Discipline at Home and in School*, has developed a useful technique for dealing with misbehaviour verbally. He terms the intervention an *I message*. The I message is a three-part message that is intended to help the disruptive student recognize the negative impact of her behaviour on the teacher. The underlying assumption of the technique is the same as that for the questioning awareness of effect that we discussed in the previous section: Once a student recognizes the negative impact of her behaviour on others, she will be motivated to stop the misbehaviour. The three parts of an I message are (1) a simple description of the disruptive behaviour, (2) a description of its tangible effect on the teacher and/or other students, and (3) a description of the teacher's feelings about the effects of the misbehaviour. Using I messages models for students the important behaviour of taking responsibility for and owning one's behaviour and feelings. There is one important caveat, however, in the use of this technique. Just as the teacher expects students to respect the feelings that are expressed in an I message, the teacher must respect feelings expressed by students.

To use an I message to stop John from calling out, Mr. Hensen might say, "John, when you call out answers without raising your hand (part 1), I can't call on any other student to answer the question (part 2). This disturbs me because I would like to give everyone a chance to answer questions (part 3)." Teachers who enjoy a positive relationship with students, which gives them referent power (see Chapter 5, "Philosophical Approaches to Classroom Management"), are usually successful in using I messages. When students genuinely like the teacher, they are motivated to stop the behaviour that has a negative impact on the teacher. On the other hand, if the teacher has a poor relationship with students, she should avoid the use of I messages. Allowing students who dislike you to know that a particular behaviour is annoying or disturbing may result in an increase in that particular behaviour.

Using Direct Appeal

Another technique that is useful for instances when a teacher enjoys a referent or expert power base is **direct appeal**. Direct appeal means courteously requesting that a student stop the disruptive behaviour; for example, Mr. Hensen could say, "John, please stop calling out answers so that everyone will have a chance to answer." The direct appeal is not made in any sort of pleading or begging way.

Teachers must not use direct appeal in a classroom in which students seem to doubt the teacher's ability to be in charge. In this situation, the appeal may be perceived as a plea rather than as a straightforward request.

Using Positive Phrasing

Many times, parents and teachers fall into the trap of emphasizing the negative outcomes of misbehaviour more than the positive outcomes of appropriate behaviour (Mackenzie and Stanzione, 2010; Moore, 2011). We tell children and students far more frequently what will happen if they don't finish their homework than tell them the good things that will occur if they do finish. Of course, it is often easier to identify the short-range negative outcomes of misbehaviour than it is to predict the short- and long-range positive impact of appropriate behaviour. Still, when the positive outcomes of appropriate behaviour are easily identifiable, simply stating what the positive outcomes are can redirect students from disruptive to proper behaviour. Shrigley (1985) has called this technique **positive phrasing**. It usually takes a form such as this: "As soon as you do X (behave appropriately), we can do Y (a positive outcome)."

In using positive phrasing to correct John's calling out, Mr. Hensen might say, "John, you will be called on as soon as you raise your hand." The long-term advantage of using positive phrasing whenever possible is that students begin to believe that appropriate behaviour leads to positive outcomes (Mackenzie and Stanzione, 2010). As a result, they are more likely to develop internalized control over their behaviour.

Using "Are Not For"

Of all the verbal interventions discussed in this chapter, the phrase "are not for" (Shrigley, 1985) is the most limited in use. It is implemented primarily when elementary or preschool children misuse property or materials; for example, if a student is drumming on a desk with a pencil, the teacher may say, "Pencils *are not for* drumming on desks; pencils *are for* writing." Although it is usually effective in redirecting behaviour positively at the elementary or preschool level; most secondary students perceive this intervention as insulting. Using "are not for" is not an appropriate technique for Mr. Hensen since John is a secondary student and is not misusing property or material.

Reminding Students of the Rules

When a teacher has established clear guidelines or rules early in the year (see Chapter 7) and students have committed to them, merely reminding disruptive students of the rules may curb misbehaviour (Mackenzie and Stanzione, 2010). Notice that at this point in the hierarchy, the teacher is no longer relying on the students' ability to control their own behaviour but instead is using external rules to manage behaviour.

In using this technique, Mr. Hensen might say, "John, the classroom rules state that students must raise their hands before speaking" or "John, calling out answers without raising your hand is against our classroom rules." The technique is particularly effective for elementary and younger high school students. Although it may be used in senior high, many students at this level resent the feeling that they are being governed by too many rules. It is important to note that when a reminder of the rules does not redirect the misbehaviour, applying consequences must follow. If this does not occur, the effectiveness of rule reminders will be diminished because students will not see the link between breaking classroom rules and negative consequences.

In William Glasser's (2010) system for establishing suitable student behaviour, which is outlined in *Choice Theory in the Classroom*, he proposed that teachers direct

Group of elementary pupils in classroom listening to teacher.
© Monkey Business Images/Shutterstock

students to appropriate behaviour through the use of three questions: (1) What are you doing? (2) Is it against the rules? (3) What should you be doing? The use of these questions, which are known as Glasser's triplets, obviously requires a classroom in which the rules have been firmly established in students' minds. To stop John from calling out answers, Mr. Hensen would simply ask Glasser's triplets. The expectation underlying Glasser's triplets is that the student will answer the questions honestly and will then return to the appropriate behaviour. Unfortunately, not all students answer the triplets honestly, and therein lies the intervention's inherent weakness. Asking open-ended questions may result in student responses that are dishonest, improper, or unexpected.

If a student chooses to answer the questions dishonestly or not to reply at all, the teacher responds by saying (in John's case), "No, John, you were calling out answers. That is against our classroom rules. You must raise your hand to answer questions." To minimize the likelihood of an extended, negative confrontation ensuing from the use of Glasser's triplets, it is suggested that teachers use three statements instead of questions: "John, you are calling out. It is against the rules. You should raise your hand if you want to answer."

Using Explicit Redirection

Explicit redirection consists of an order to stop the misbehaviour *and* return to acceptable behaviour. The redirection is a teacher command and leaves no room for student rebuttal. If Mr. Hensen used explicit redirection with John, he might say, "John, stop calling out answers and raise your hand if you want to answer a question." Notice the contrast between this technique and those discussed in the earlier stages of the hierarchy in terms of the amount of responsibility the teacher assumes for managing student behaviour.

The advantages of this technique are its simplicity, clarity, and closed format, which do not allow for student rebuttal. Its disadvantage is that the teacher publicly confronts the student, who either behaves or defies the teacher in front of peers. Obviously, if the student chooses to defy the teacher's command, the teacher must be prepared to proceed to the next step in the hierarchy and enforce the command with appropriate consequences.

Canter and Canter's Broken Record Strategy

Canter and Canter (2001) have developed a strategy for clearly communicating to students that the teacher will not engage in verbal bantering and intends to make sure that the student resumes appropriate behaviour. The Canters have labelled their strategy **broken record** because the teacher's constant nagging sounds like a broken record. The teacher begins by giving the student an explicit redirection statement. If the student doesn't comply or if the student tries to defend or explain her behaviour, the teacher repeats the redirection. The teacher may repeat it two or three times if the student continues to argue or fails to comply. If the student tries to excuse or defend her behaviour, some teachers add the phrase, "that's not the point" at the beginning of the first and second repetitions. The following is an example of this technique as applied by Mr. Hensen:

HENSEN: "John, stop calling out answers and raise your hand if you want to answer questions."

JOHN: "But I really do know the answer."

HENSEN: "That's not the point. Stop calling out answers and raise your hand if you want to answer questions."

JOHN: "You let Mabel call out answers yesterday."

HENSEN: "That's not the point. Stop calling out answers and raise your hand if you want to answer questions."

We have found the broken record technique to be very good for avoiding verbal battles with students. If, however, the statement has been repeated three times without any result, it is probably time to move to a stronger measure, such as logical consequences.

COMPLY OR FACE THE LOGICAL CONSEQUENCES: "YOU HAVE A CHOICE"

Although nonverbal and verbal interventions often stop misbehaviour, sometimes the misbehaviour remains unchecked. When this occurs, the teacher needs to use more overt techniques. The final tier on the decision-making hierarchy is the use of logical consequences to manage student behaviour.

As the reader will recall from Chapter 7, there are three types of consequences: *natural*, *logical*, and *contrived* (Pagliaro, 2011). Natural consequences result directly from student misbehaviour without any intervention by the teacher, although the teacher may point out the link between the behaviour and the consequence. Using natural consequences is a management strategy because the teacher decides to let the natural consequences occur; that is, the teacher decides not to take any action to stop the consequence. Unlike natural consequences, logical consequences require teacher intervention and are related as closely as possible to the behaviour; for example, a student who comes to class five minutes late is required to remain five minutes after school to make up the work. Contrived consequences are imposed on the student by the teacher and are either unrelated to student behaviour or involve a penalty beyond what is fitting for the misbehaviour. Requiring a student who scribbles on her desk to write 1000 times, "I will not write on my desk" or sentencing a student who comes once to class five minutes late to two weeks of detention are contrived consequences. Since contrived consequences fail to help students see the connection between a behaviour and its consequence and place the teacher in the role of punisher, we do not advocate their use. For this reason, contrived consequences are not part of our decision-making hierarchy. When nonverbal and verbal interventions have not led to appropriate behaviour, the teacher must take control of the situation and use logical consequences to manage student behaviour. To do so, the teacher applies logical consequences calmly and thoughtfully in a forceful but not punitive manner.

Brophy (2010) suggests that the teacher who uses logical consequences should emphasize the student changing her behaviour rather than the teacher seeking retribution. When this is done, the teacher makes sure that the student understands that the misbehaviour must stop immediately or negative consequences will result. Often, it is effective to give the student a choice of either complying with the request or facing the consequence. This technique is called "you have a choice." For example, if John continued to call out answers after Mr. Hensen had tried several nonverbal and verbal interventions, Mr. Hensen would say, "John, you have a choice. Stop calling out answers immediately and begin raising your hand to answer or move your seat to the back of the room and you and I will have a private discussion later. You decide." Phrasing the intervention in this way helps the students to realize that they are responsible for the positive as well as the negative consequences of their behaviour and that the choice is theirs. It also places the teacher in a neutral rather than punitive role. Remember, students do, in fact, choose how to behave. Teachers can't control student behaviour; they can only influence it.

Once the teacher moves to this final level of the hierarchy, the dialogue is over. Either the student returns to appropriate behaviour or the teacher takes action. The manner in which the consequences are delivered is important and provides the teacher with another opportunity to reinforce the idea that the student is in control of her behaviour, that the choice to behave or misbehave is hers to make, and that her choice has consequences. In Mr. Hensen's case, if John chose to continue to call out, Mr. Hensen would say, "John, you have chosen to move to the back of the room; please move." There are no excuses, no postponements. The teacher has stated his intentions clearly. Because consistency is crucial, it is imperative that the teacher not move to this final tier on the hierarchy unless ready to enforce the consequences that have been specified.

The exact consequence varies with the student misbehaviour; however, one principle is always involved in the formulation of consequences: It should be as directly related to the offence as possible. Consistent application of this principle helps students to recognize that their behaviour has consequences and helps them learn to control their own behaviour in the future by predicting its consequences beforehand.

Because it can be difficult to come up with directly related logical consequences on the spur of the moment (Brophy, 2010), teachers should consider logical consequences for common types of misbehaviour before the misbehaviours occur. Developing one or two logical consequences for each of the classroom rules that we discussed in Chapter 7 is a good way to begin. When misbehaviour occurs for which there is no planned logical consequence, a teacher should ask the following questions to help formulate a consequence directly related to the misbehaviour:

1. What would be the logical result if this misbehaviour went unchecked?
2. What are the direct effects of this behaviour on the teacher, other students, and the misbehaving student?
3. What can be done to minimize these effects?

CASE 9.3

"I Don't Want to Do Nothin'"

Doug is a grade 7, learning-disabled student who has serious reading difficulties and poses behavioural problems for many teachers. At the beginning of the year, he is assigned to Ms. Ramonda's remedial reading class. Since Doug hates reading, he is determined to get out of the class and causes all sorts of problems for Ms. Ramonda and the other students. Ms. Ramonda's first reaction is to have Doug removed from her class to protect the other students; however, after talking to Doug's counsellor and his resource room teacher, she comes to believe that it is important for Doug not to get his way and that he desperately needs to develop the reading skills that she can teach him.

Ms. Ramonda decides to try to use Doug's personal interests to motivate him.

The next day, she asks, "Doug, what would you like to do?" Doug answers, "Nothin', I don't want to do nothin' in here. Just leave me alone." For the next two days Doug sits in the back of the room and doodles as Ms. Ramonda tries to determine what the next step should be. Finally, Ms. Ramonda asks herself what the logical result is of doing nothing. She decides that the logical result is boredom and resolves to use that to motivate Doug.

On the following day, she announces to Doug that he will get his wish. From then on, he can do nothing as long as he wants to. She explains that he will no longer need books or papers or pencils since books are for reading, and papers and pencils are for writing, and doing nothing means doing none of those things. He will not be allowed to talk to her

(Continued)

(Continued)

or to his friends, she explains, since that too would be doing something and he wants to do nothing. "From now on, Doug, you will be allowed to sit in the back corner of the room and do nothing, just as you wish."

For one full week, Doug sits in the back corner and does nothing. Finally, he asks Ms. Ramonda if he can do something. She replies that he can do some reading but nothing else. Doug agrees to try some reading. That breaks the ice. Ms. Ramonda carefully selects some low-difficulty, high-interest material for Doug and gradually pulls him into the regular classroom situation.

Questions to Consider

1. What does Ms. Ramonda's decision to keep Doug in her class tell you about her teaching beliefs?
2. How did Ms. Ramonda approach Doug's problem?
3. Why was her approach relatively successful?

The answers to these three questions usually will help a teacher to identify a logical consequence. In Case 9.3, note how Ms. Ramonda uses the first of the three questions to formulate the logical consequences for Doug's behaviour.

WHEN "YOU HAVE A CHOICE" DOESN'T WORK

At this point, almost all readers are probably thinking, what if the approach of "you have a choice" doesn't work? Some teachers believe that providing a choice is "not working" when a student chooses the negative consequences rather than choosing to change her behaviour. Remember, teachers cannot force students to behave appropriately, but they can deliver the logical consequences when students choose them. Beyond this point, teachers can only hope that if they are consistent and follow the guidelines for verbal interventions, students will internalize the relationship between behaviour and its consequences and choose to behave appropriately the next time.

Teachers can increase the likelihood of a student choosing appropriate behaviour by responding assertively when using "you have a choice." Assertiveness is communicated to others by the congruent use of certain verbal and nonverbal behaviours. Do not confuse assertiveness with aggressiveness, which leads to unwanted student outcomes. An aggressive response is one in which a teacher communicates what is expected but in a manner that abuses the rights and feelings of the student. When this happens, students perceive the stated consequences as threats. An aggressive delivery of "you have a choice" would probably be viewed by students as "fighting words" and escalate both hostility and confrontation, leading to further disruptive behaviours. When a teacher uses an assertive response style, the teacher clearly communicates what is expected in a manner that respects a student's rights and feelings. An assertive style tells the student that the teacher is prepared to back up the request for behavioural change with appropriately stated consequences, but is never threatening. Table 9.1 compares the verbal and nonverbal behaviours that differentiate assertive response styles from aggressive ones.

TABLE 9.1   Comparison of Assertive and Aggressive Response Styles

	Assertive	Aggressive
Audience	Private only to student	Public to entire class
How student is addressed	Student's name	"You, hey you"
Voice	Firm, neutral, soft, slow	Tense, loud, fast
Eyes	Eye contact only	Narrowed, frowning eyes
Stance	Close to student without violating personal space	Hands on hips, violating personal space
Hands	Quietly approach student or student's desk	Sharp, abrupt gestures

Of course, there will always be some students who do not choose to behave. When the teacher assertively delivers the consequence, these students argue or openly refuse to accept and comply with the consequence. If this happens, the teacher must not be sidetracked by the student and enter into a public power struggle with the student. Instead, the teacher should integrate the use of Canter and Canter's (2001) broken record and a final "you have a choice" in a calm, firm, assertive manner. The following example between Mr. Hensen and John illustrates the integration of these verbal interventions:

1. Mr. Hensen gives John a choice of raising his hand or moving to the back of the room. John calls out again. Mr. Hensen says, "John, you called out; therefore, you have decided to move to the back of the class. Please move."
2. John begins to argue. At this point Mr. Hensen uses the broken record and, if necessary, a final "you have a choice."

JOHN: "You know Tom calls out all the time and you never do anything to him."

HENSEN: "That's not the point. Please move to the back of the room."

JOHN: "I get the right answers."

HENSEN: "That's not the point. Please move to the back of the room."

JOHN: "This is really unfair."

HENSEN: "That's not the point. Move to the back of the room."

JOHN: "'I'm not moving and don't try to make me."

HENSEN: "John, you have a choice. Move to the back of the room now, or I will be in touch with your parents. You decide."

As this interaction illustrates, after two or three broken records, the teacher issues a final "you have a choice" and then disengages from the student. Some teachers will have the student removed from the classroom by an administrator as the consequence for the final "you have a choice." Whatever the consequence, the teacher must be willing and be able to follow through (e.g., CALM, Level III, Action Stage C; please refer to Chapters 1 and 7). Thus, teachers must be sure the consequence can be carried out. Since interaction between a student and teacher at this level is likely to be of great interest to the other students in the class, it is imperative for the teacher to remain calm, firm, and assertive. This is a time for the teacher to show the rest of the class that she is in control of her behaviour and that she means what she says. A teacher who remains in control, even if the student refuses to comply, will garner more respect from students than the teacher who tries to humiliate, is harsh, or lacks control.

Summary

In this chapter, we have presented the final two tiers of the hierarchy introduced in Chapter 8: verbal intervention and the use of logical consequences. We developed the following guidelines for verbal intervention: (1) use verbal intervention when nonverbal is inappropriate or ineffective; (2) keep verbal intervention private if possible; (3) make it as brief as possible; (4) speak to the situation, not the person; (5) set limits on behaviour, not feelings; (6) avoid sarcasm; (7) begin with a verbal intervention close to the student-centred end of the hierarchy; (8) if necessary, move to a second verbal intervention technique closer to the teacher-centred end of the hierarchy; and (9) if two verbal interventions have been used unsuccessfully, move to the application of consequences.

In addition to the nine guidelines, three types of ineffective verbal communication patterns were reviewed: (1) encouraging inappropriate behaviour, (2) focusing on irrelevant behaviours, and (3) providing abstract, meaningless directions and predictions.

Twelve specific intervention techniques were presented in a hierarchical format, ranging from techniques that foster greater student control over behaviour to those that bring about greater teacher management over student behaviour. The verbal interventions were divided into three categories: hints, questions, and requests/demands. Hints include the following: (1) adjacent or peer reinforcement, (2) calling on the student or name dropping,

and (3) humour. The sole questioning intervention that was presented was (4) questioning awareness of effect. We noted that many interventions could be used in a question format. The interventions classified as requests/demands include (5) I messages, (6) direct appeal, (7) positive phrasing, (8) "are not for," (9) reminder of rules, (10) Glasser's triplets, (11) explicit redirection, and (12) Canter and Canter's broken record.

In the last section of the chapter, we discussed the final tier of the hierarchy: the use of logical consequences. We suggested that this intervention should be phrased in terms of student choice and the consequences should be related as directly as possible to the misbehaviour. Three questions were proposed to help teachers formulate logical consequences for those misbehaviours for which the teacher has not developed a consequence hierarchy. The use of an assertive response style and the integration of "you have a choice" with Canter and Canter's broken record were presented as a means to increase the likelihood that a student chooses to behave appropriately.

When taken together with the information presented in Chapter 8, the ideas presented in this chapter constitute a complete hierarchy that teachers can use to guide their thinking and decision-making concerning interventions to cope with classroom misbehaviour. The hierarchy is presented in its complete format in Figure 9.2.

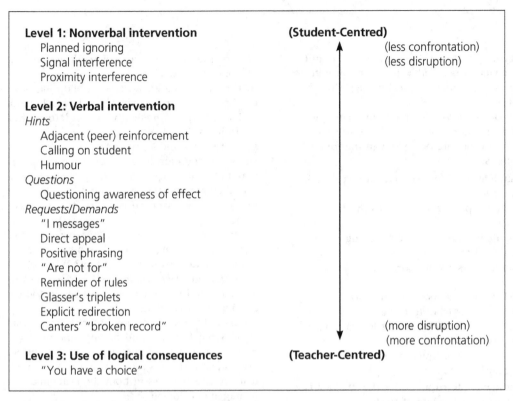

Level 1: Nonverbal intervention   **(Student-Centred)**
    Planned ignoring   (less confrontation)
    Signal interference   (less disruption)
    Proximity interference

Level 2: Verbal intervention
Hints
    Adjacent (peer) reinforcement
    Calling on student
    Humour
Questions
    Questioning awareness of effect
Requests/Demands
    "I messages"
    Direct appeal
    Positive phrasing
    "Are not for"
    Reminder of rules
    Glasser's triplets
    Explicit redirection
    Canters' "broken record"   (more disruption)
        (more confrontation)
Level 3: Use of logical consequences   **(Teacher-Centred)**
    "You have a choice"

FIGURE 9.2   Hierarchy for Management Intervention

Key Terms

adjacent (peer) reinforcement: based on the learning principle that reinforced behaviour is more likely to be repeated. The use of peer reinforcement as a verbal intervention technique focuses class attention on appropriate behaviour rather than on inappropriate behaviour.

broken record: the use of repetition by a teacher to reinforce a direction to a student.

direct appeal: means courteously requesting that a student stop the disruptive behaviour.

explicit redirection: consists of an order to stop the misbehaviour *and* to return to acceptable behaviour.

positive phrasing: this is done in instances where the teacher states what the potential positive outcomes are for a student who exhibits appropriate behaviour in the classroom; the teacher, thus, aims to redirect a student from disruptive to proper behaviour.

verbal intervention: a systematic hierarchy of spoken techniques that first is designed to foster students' control over their own behaviour and moves to greater teacher management over student behaviour.

Exercises

1. Which types of student misbehaviour might lead a teacher to use verbal intervention without first trying nonverbal techniques? Justify your answer.

2. Use each of the verbal intervention techniques presented in this chapter to help redirect the student to appropriate behaviour in the following situations:

   a. The student won't get started on a seatwork assignment.

   b. The student pushes her way to the front of the line.

   c. The student talks to a friend sitting on the other side of the room.

   d. The student lies about a forgotten homework assignment.

3. Under what circumstances, if any, would it be appropriate for a teacher to move directly to the third tier of the hierarchy, use of logical consequences? Justify your answer.

4. Develop logical consequences for each of the following misbehaviours:

   a. The student interrupts while the teacher is talking to a small group of students.

   b. The student steals money from another student's desk.

   c. The student copies a homework assignment from someone else.

   d. The student squirts a water pistol during class.

   e. The student throws spitballs at the blackboard.

   f. The student physically intimidates other students.

   g. Graffiti is found on the restroom wall.

5. List some common teacher verbal interventions that fall under the three types of ineffective verbal communication patterns.

6. Role-play the assertive delivery of "you have a choice."

7. When a teacher uses an aggressive response style, what feelings and behaviours are commonly elicited from the student? What effect does an aggressive response style have on overall teacher effectiveness in both the academic and management domains?

8. When a teacher uses an assertive response style, what feelings and behaviours are commonly elicited from the student? What effect does an assertive response style have on overall teacher effectiveness in both the academic and management domains?

Weblinks

Bridges4Kids
www.bridges4kids.org/news /GRPress8-20-02.html
This website gives suggestions for classroom-management techniques and "positive behavior support."

Cherryville Elementary School
www.sd22.bc.ca/district_policy/ nine/PO_9-14-0.pdf
Illustrates a very detailed code of conduct where philosophy, responsibilities, and consequences are clearly spelled out.

Vancouver School Board—Code of Conduct
http://www.vsb.bc.ca/district-policy/j-students
This section of the website provides a repository for statements concerning students—admissions, attendance, rights and responsibilities, conduct, discipline, health and welfare services.

Nova Scotia Provincial School Code of Conduct Guidelines can be found by searching "code of conduct" from the website.
www.ednet.ns.ca/

William King Elementary Code of Conduct and Shine Initiative (example)

http://wkes.ednet.ns.ca/wp-content/
uploads/2012/01/Code-of-Conduct-2010-20111.doc
More examples are found by searching the website:
http://gsa1.gov.ns.ca/search?q=code+of+conduct&bt
nG=Search&site=GOVNS_EDNET&client=GOVNS_
EDNET&proxystylesheet=GOVNS_
EDNET&proxyreload=1&output=xml_no_dtd

Ontario Code of Conduct

http://www.etfo.ca/IssuesinEducation/SafeSchools/
Documents/Code%20Of%20Conduct.pdf
The Ontario Code of Conduct outlines clear provincial standards of behaviour and specifies the mandatory consequences for student actions that do not comply with these standards.

10

Classroom Interventions for Chronic Problems

FOCUS ON THE PRINCIPLES OF CLASSROOM MANAGEMENT

1. When dealing with students who pose chronic behavioural problems, which strategies should teachers use first?

2. What can teachers do to increase the possibility that chronic behavioural problems can be resolved within the classroom?

3. What are the benefits of breaking the cycle of discouragement in which most students with chronic behavioural problems are trapped?

4. Why are private conferences and the use of effective communication skills with students so important for teachers?

5. Why is it important for teachers to use interventions that require students to recognize their inappropriate behaviour and its impact on others?

6. What interventions can be used to promote daily accountability for students with chronic behavioural problems?

7. What interventions can be used to promote gradual but consistent improvement in classroom behaviour?

INTRODUCTION

Research, as well as our own experience, indicates that the overwhelming majority of behavioural problems (somewhere in the neighbourhood of 97 percent) can be either prevented or redirected to positive behaviour by the use of a preplanned hierarchy of nonverbal and verbal interventions (Charney, 2002; Rathvon, 2008; Shrigley, 1980), but there are some students who pose more chronic classroom behavioural problems. These students misbehave even after all preventive and intervention techniques, both verbal and nonverbal, have been appropriately employed. They disrupt learning, interfere with the work of others, interfere with teaching, challenge teacher authority, and often try to entice others to misbehave on a fairly consistent basis. These are the students who prompt teachers to say, "If only I could get rid of that Sammy, period 3

CASE 10.1

"I Just Dropped My Book"

Jodi, a grade 9 student, entered Mr. Voman's guidance office hesitatingly, sat down, and looked blankly at Mr. Voman.

MR. VOMAN: "Well, Jodi, What are you doing here?"

JODI: "Ms. Kozin sent me out of class and told me not to ever come back. She told me to come see you."

MR. VOMAN: "Why did she send you out of class?"

JODI: "I don't know. I just dropped my book on the floor accidentally!"

MR. VOMAN: "Now, come on, Jodi. Ms. Kozin wouldn't put you out of class just for that. Come on now. What did you do?"

JODI: "Honest, Mr. Voman, you can ask the other kids. All I did was drop my book."

MR. VOMAN: "Jodi, I'm going to talk to Ms. Kozin about this. Wait here until I get back."

JODI: "Okay, Mr. Voman, I'll wait here and you'll see that I'm not lying."

Questions to Consider

1. After Mr. Voman talks to Ms. Kozin, what should he say to Jodi?
2. Recently, Jodi has been chronically misbehaving. What are some of the possible underlying causes that may trigger a normally well-behaving student to act out?
3. What else might Ms. Kozin do to help Jodi behave appropriately?

would be a pleasure to teach"; or "If that Jodi weren't in this class, I would certainly have a lot more time to spend on helping the other students learn." Jodi, the student described in Case 10.1, is a good example.

As Mr. Voman discovered when he talked to Ms. Kozin, Jodi had been a constant nuisance for the past month. The book-dropping incident was simply the last straw. Jodi continually talked during the lesson; forgot to bring pencils, books, and paper to class; refused to complete homework; didn't even attempt quizzes or tests; and reacted rudely whenever Ms. Kozin approached her. Ms. Kozin had tried nonverbal and verbal interventions, time outs, detentions, and notes to parents. By the time Jodi accidentally dropped her book, Ms. Kozin was completely fed up with her.

Many, though not all, students like Jodi have problems that extend beyond school. Some have poor home lives with few, if any, positive adult role models. Others have no supporters who really care about them or express real interest in what they are doing in their lives (Bailey et al., 2013). Still others simply view themselves as losers who couldn't succeed in school even if they tried. As a result, they act out their frustrations in class and make life miserable for both their teachers and their peers.

Although teachers are always concerned for the future of the disruptive student, they are also responsible for ensuring that misbehaviour does not deprive the other students of their right to learn; thus, chronic misbehaviour must not be allowed to continue.

In attempting to deal with chronically disruptive students, classroom teachers often fall into a trap. They may give in to that natural, fully understandable, human

Stressed out primary girl child thinking hard to recollect the answer.
© Iakov Filimonov/Shutterstock

urge to "get even." They may turn to punishment and retaliation. When retaliation fails (and it is apt to fail), and because the chronically disruptive student often loves to see the teacher explode, the teacher may feel helpless and seeks outside assistance by sending the student to somebody else. Usually, chronically disruptive students are sent to an administrator or counsellor and sentenced to some form of in-school or out-of-school suspension (Charney, 2002; Emmer and Evertson, 2009; Tillson, 2010). It is often the case for schools to handle disruptive behaviours by focusing on the external indicators of the behaviours without considering the underlying issues and assigning immediate consequences to students' misbehaviours.

Because outside referral removes the disruptive student from the class, the disruptive behaviour does cease until the student returns to the classroom. Unfortunately, the severity and frequency of the misbehaviour after a return to the classroom often increase. It has been hypothesized that misbehaviour increases because the student views the referral either as a further punishment or as a victory over the teacher (Schaubman, Stetson, and Plog, 2011). When they view referrals as punishments, many disruptive students retaliate as soon as they return to the classroom. When they view referrals as victories, disruptive students often feel compelled to demonstrate even more forcefully their perceived power over the teacher. As a result, in Canada, school administrators are beginning to examine the fundamental causes of problem behaviour and are attempting to incorporate this knowledge into their management strategy (Tillson, 2010).

Contrary to popular belief, chronic behavioural problems often can be managed successfully within the confines of the regular classroom and with a minimum of additional effort by the teacher. When such problems are resolved within the conventional classroom setting, the disruptive student, the other students, and the teacher all benefit. The disruptive student learns to control his behaviour without loss of instructional time and without developing the negative attitudes that are often evident in students who have been excluded from the classroom. The teacher gains a more tranquil classroom and additional confidence in his ability to handle all types of behavioural problems successfully. Finally, the other students in the class are again able to concentrate their attention on the learning tasks before them.

In this chapter, we will present two long-term strategies for solving chronic behavioural problems and three specific management techniques in addition to the CALM model that teachers can use. The problem-solving strategies and management techniques are used simultaneously in the classroom; that is, as the teacher is managing the chronic misbehaviour using the management techniques, he is also seeking ways to solve the long-term problems. The two long-term problem-solving strategies—**relationship building** and breaking the **cycle of discouragement**—are described first. This discussion is followed by a section on how to conduct effective private conferences with students. Effective private conferences are an important component of both the long-term problem-solving strategies and the management techniques. In the final section of this chapter, we introduce three specific management techniques: student self-monitoring, which is a student-directed management strategy; anecdotal record keeping, a collaborative management strategy; and behaviour contracting, a teacher-directed management strategy.

RELATIONSHIP BUILDING

The development of a positive relationship between the teacher and the student with a chronic behavioural problem is one of the most effective strategies for helping such students (Leitao and Waugh, 2012). Usually, these students do not have positive relationships with their teachers or perhaps other adults. Indeed, teachers often tend to avoid interaction with such students. Students who have chronic behavioural problems are often challenging and cause the teacher to doubt his own competence.

These doubts about competence arise from the misconception that the teacher can *control* a student's behaviour. As we have noted continually in this text, the teacher can only influence a student's behaviour and react to that behaviour. He cannot control anyone's behaviour except his own. If a teacher has the mistaken notion that his job is to control a student's behaviour, he will feel that he is not as competent as he should be every time the student acts inappropriately; thus, one of the first steps a teacher should take in working with students who have chronic behavioural problems is to recognize that his role is to help these students learn to control their own behaviour. The teacher can only be held accountable for controlling his own behaviour in such a way that it increases the likelihood that the students will learn and want to behave appropriately. The CALM model expedites this approach to influencing student behaviour.

The teacher should try to disregard any negative feelings he has toward the chronically disruptive student and work at building a positive relationship with that student. We are not suggesting that the teacher must be fond of the student. No teacher honestly likes every student whom he has ever encountered; however, a truly professional teacher does not act on or reveal negative feelings. Our experience has given us two important insights into working with students who have chronic behavioural problems. First, teachers who look for and are able to find some positive qualities—no matter how small or how hidden—in chronically disruptive students are much more successful in helping those students learn to behave appropriately than those who do not. Second, the primary factor that motivated the vast majority of students who were at one time chronically disruptive to rectify their behaviour was the development of a close, positive relationship with a caring adult. Teacher–student relationships are the basis for classroom management and are the key for increasing student positive behaviour (Marzano, Frontier, and Livingston, 2011). Case 10.2 illustrates the impact that a caring relationship can have on such an individual.

CASE 10.2

Jordan

Jordan, who was born to a single mother in a rundown, crime-ridden neighbourhood in a large Canadian city, was raised by his grandmother, who was the one kind, protective figure in his early life. Despite her efforts to shield him, Jordan was exposed to the availability of drugs, street gangs, and a variety of illegal and often violent activities while he was still in elementary school. Many of the young men in his neighbourhood had a very bad reputation because of the proliferation of guns and shootings.

In high school, Jordan described himself as full of anger and energy, and he became involved in a gang that conducted petty and often violent attacks on other adolescents and adults. As a result, he was eventually sent to a juvenile detention facility and, after he had served the required time, was released. Upon his release, Jordan was assigned to Barbara, a juvenile probation officer.

Barbara was a streetwise veteran in her fifties who had worked with many troubled adolescents. Jordan said to his friends, "She doesn't take any crap." Barbara insisted that Jordan stop his aggressive behaviour and made it clear to him that she thought he was an intelligent young man with the potential to be successful in life if he consciously changed his behaviour. For six years Jordan and Barbara worked together and built a strong interpersonal relationship based on mutual respect and caring. Over this period, Jordan changed dramatically. According to Jordan, "Barbara taught me how to take my anger and aggression and turn them into positive forces in my life. My first successes were on the basketball court and then I began to be successful in the classroom, too." As a result of the close relationship Barbara painstakingly built, Jordan earned passing grades in school, stayed out of trouble, and became a good enough point guard that he earned a scholarship to a small college in the United States. Throughout these years, Barbara's efforts were recognized and supported by Jordan's increasingly proud grandmother. Jordan studied hard, was successful and became a special education teacher. He returned to his hometown expressly hoping to make a difference in the lives of kids like him.

After returning with his strong personal motivation, he saw the need to change the education system itself but felt powerless in his capacity as a teacher to do so. After a few frustrating years, he left teaching and devoted

himself to earning a master's degree in counselling, followed by a Ph.D. in curriculum
and a principal's certificate. Today, Jordan is
a high school principal in the inner city
where he was raised. He lives with his wife
and young son and spends his time helping
inner-city children turn their energy and
anger to useful purposes in much the same
way Barbara helped him. In fact, he often
tells his personal story to kids who are getting into trouble. Jordan and Barbara remain
close friends.

Questions to Consider

1. Describe the positive approach that Barbara
   took with Jordan. Why does such an
   approach sometimes fail to be effective?
2. What do you think is the most important element of Barbara's relationship with Jordan?
3. Describe Barbara's approach as it might
   relate to the CALM model.
4. Given what you know, what other solutions
   might have been helpful for Jordan and
   other children in his situation if someone
   like Barbara were not available?

Of course, building positive relationships with students who have chronic behavioural problems is not always an easy task. Many students with chronic behavioural problems have a long history of unsuccessful relationships with adults. Because the adults in
these relationships may have ended up being nonsupportive or negative in one way or
another, many of the students actively resist attempts to build positive relationships
(Bailey et al., 2013). For some students, it becomes safer not to build any relationships at
all than to risk another relationship that will result in hurt and disappointment. Teachers
who dedicate their time to building positive relationships with such students may
". . . compensate for other challenges [in the students'] lives, and they can provide them
with a safe haven during uncertain times" (Schaubman, Stetson, and Plog, 2011, p.74).

Thus, teachers who want to build relationships with such students must be persistent, consistent, and predictable in their own behaviour toward the student
(Brendtro, Brokenleg, and Van Bockern, 2002; Leitao and Waugh, 2007). They must
search for positive qualities in the students and work at building the relationship without much initial encouragement or response from the student. As Brendtro, Brokenleg,
and Van Bockern note, the desire to build a relationship does not have to spring from
a feeling of liking or attraction. The teacher simply has to choose to act toward the
student in caring and giving ways. Over time, positive feelings of liking and attraction
develop. Notice how Carol, the student teacher in Case 10.3, slowly builds a relationship with Cindy. Although such dramatic results do not always or even typically occur,
the efforts can be rewarding.

Bob Strachota (1996) calls attempts to build positive relationships with students
who have chronic behavioural problems "getting on their side." He notes that teachers
need to view themselves as allies rather than opponents of these students and has
suggested several steps to help teachers do so. The first step is "wondering why."
Strachota points out that many teachers become so preoccupied with techniques for
stopping the misbehaviour that they forget to ask such fundamental questions as,
(1) Why is the student behaving in this way? and (2) What purpose does it serve or
what need does it fulfill? Strachota's underlying assumption is that behaviour is pur-
poseful rather than random. It is directed at meeting some need even if the goal of the
behaviour is faulty or mistaken (see Chapter 3, "Understanding Why Children

CASE 10.3

Relating to Cindy

Carol, a student teacher in chemistry, decided to make Cindy "her project." Cindy was an overweight, physically unattractive grade 12 student who did not seem to have any friends at all. She spoke to no one, did not participate in class activities, and had failed every test and quiz from September to late January when Carol took over the class.

Every day in the four minutes before class began, Carol walked back to Cindy's desk and tried to chat with her. For two full weeks, Carol got absolutely no response, not even eye contact. Cindy completely ignored her. Although upset and disappointed, Carol decided to persist. One day during the third week without a response, Carol noticed Cindy reading the college newspaper during class. Instead of viewing this as a behavioural problem, Carol decided to use it as the foundation for a relationship. She had Cindy stay after class and told her that she had seen the newspaper. She asked if Cindy was interested in newspapers. Cindy replied that she wanted to be a journalist. Carol told Cindy she would be happy to bring her a copy of the college newspaper every day as long as Cindy would

read it after class. For the first time, Cindy replied: "That would be great."

Every day for the next 10 weeks, Carol drove 15 minutes out of her way to pick up a newspaper for Cindy. The impact on Cindy was remarkable. She began coming to class early and staying after class each day to speak with Carol. She attended class activities and even participated verbally about once a week or so. Remarkably, she passed every test and quiz from that point until Carol's student teaching experience ended. Given the cumulative nature of the content of chemistry, this academic turnaround astounded Carol, her supervisor (one of the authors), and her cooperating teacher.

Questions to Consider

1. Based on this incident, describe Carol's belief about the role of a teacher.
2. Prior to Carol's presence, describe Cindy's beliefs about herself and her teachers.
3. What was the turning point in Carol's relationship with Cindy and how was this related to the CALM model?
4. What else might Carol have done to gain Cindy's confidence?

Misbehave"). If the teacher can identify the need, it is often possible to promote a positive behaviour that will result in fulfillment of the need.

The second step is to develop a sense of empathy and intimacy with the student. Teachers who show greater empathy are more likely to understand their students better and act accordingly (Byers, Nerina Caltabiano, and Caltabiano, 2011). Have you ever found yourself in a situation in which you wanted to stop one of your own irritating behaviours but couldn't? If so, you were presented with a great opportunity to develop a sense of empathy with these students. If you can view yourself and the student in similar terms—wanting to stop a behaviour but not being able to—you are much more likely to be able to work successfully with the student.

The third step is to stay alert for cues and behaviours that reveal other aspects of the student's personality. Sometimes, teachers become so obsessed with the misbehaviour that they do not look at other aspects of the student's behaviour and personality. When a teacher is controlled and focused enough to see the student's personality and behaviour in its entirety, he is often able to find positive and attractive aspects that can be used as a foundation for building a positive relationship.

Strachota's fourth and final step is for the teacher to monitor carefully his own behaviour in interacting with the student. He points out, "What's going on for me leaks out in the way I talk. I know what I sound like when I am happy, relaxed, curious, flexible, enthusiastic, etc. I know the difference when I feel tense, short, angry, controlling, hurried, sarcastic, or harsh" (Strachota, 1996, 75). Sometimes, teachers unintentionally communicate negative feelings toward disruptive and low-achieving students (see Chapter 6, "The Professional Teacher"). If a teacher listens closely to what he is saying and observes how he is behaving, he can avoid negative messages and instead offer positive, caring ones.

The teacher's mindset is critical. In most chronic behaviour situations, the teacher sees the student as an opponent in the conflict. Teachers who are successful in resolving chronic behavioural problems see themselves on the student's side, working together to overcome the problem (Malti, Perren, and Buchmann, 2010; Tsouloupas, Carson, Matthews, Grawitch, and Barber, 2010).

Breaking the Cycle of Discouragement

Many students with chronic behavioural problems suffer from low self-esteem and have a low success-to-failure ratio (see Chapters 3, "Understanding Why Children Misbehave" and 11, "Seeking Outside Assistance"). Their need for a sense of significance or belonging, competence or mastery, power or independence, and virtue or generosity has not been fulfilled. As we explained in Chapter 3, when these needs are not met, individuals take action to fulfill them. Unfortunately, the student with chronic behavioural problems often takes actions that are inappropriate and negative. These negative behaviours are met with negative teacher responses, punishments, and consequences that further reduce the student's self-esteem and lead to more misbehaviour, negative responses, punishments, and consequences. This cycle of discouragement, which is depicted in Figure 10.1, will continue until a teacher takes action to break it (Cummins, 1998).

Although it is entirely appropriate for these students to receive negative messages about their inappropriate behaviour and to experience the negative consequences of such actions, if that is all that occurs, the cycle of discouragement is simply

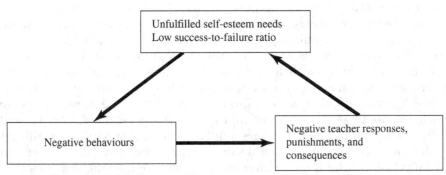

FIGURE 10.1 The Cycle of Discouragement

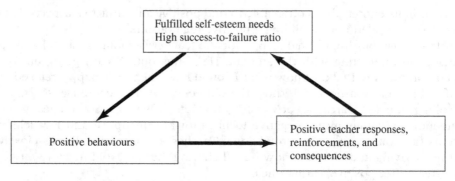

FIGURE 10.2 The Cycle of Encouragement

reinforced. Since it is necessary to stop the misbehaviour, the teacher must also find ways to meet unfulfilled needs and break the cycle of discouragement.

Just as there are students who are caught in the cycle of discouragement, there are those who flourish in a cycle of encouragement. These students have a high success-to-failure ratio. As a result, they behave in positive and caring ways toward teachers and peers. These positive behaviours are reciprocated, and students are given the message that they are attractive, competent, and virtuous, resulting in the cycle of encouragement depicted in Figure 10.2. We believe that the appropriate way to solve chronic behavioural problems is to break the cycle of discouragement by stopping the inappropriate behaviour through management techniques *and* at the same time engaging in behaviours that will help to meet the student's needs for feelings of significance, competence, power, and virtue. Together, these two actions result in the disruption of the cycle of discouragement as shown in Figure 10.3.

To accomplish this, teachers who are dealing with students with chronic behavioural problems should ask themselves four questions:

1. What can I do to help meet this student's need for significance or belonging?
2. What can I do to help meet this student's need for competence or mastery?
3. What can I do to help meet this student's need for power or independence?
4. What can I do to help meet this student's need for virtue or generosity?

Clearly, behaviour on the part of the teacher that aims to build a positive student–teacher relationship is one powerful tool for meeting a student's need for significance. In the previous section of this chapter, we provided a variety of guidelines and suggestions for building such relationships. Cooperative learning strategies (see Chapters 6 and 7) and other forms of group work help to meet the student's need for feelings of belonging. Student teams that work together productively can, over time, also help the student to develop a sense of group identity and belonging. The likelihood of positive group interaction can be increased greatly by the teacher's careful selection of the appropriate group for the disruptive student. Typically, the optimum group includes students who are good at controlling their own behaviour, are sensitive to the needs of others, and can tolerate some initial conflict. It is also helpful if the teacher uses cooperative learning activities to teach students productive social skills (Leitao and Waugh, 2007).

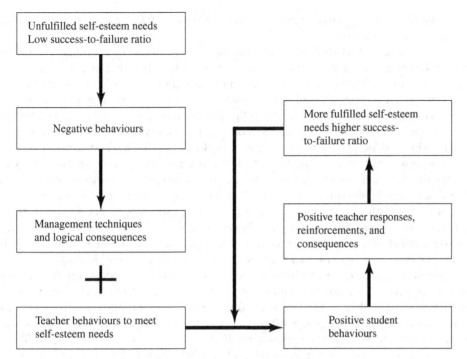

FIGURE 10.3 **Disrupting the Cycle of Discouragement**

At the elementary level, it is sometimes effective to place those students with chronic behavioural problems in a responsible role; for example, message carrier. This often enhances the student's sense of belonging. In middle school and high school, helping the student find clubs, intramurals, or other extracurricular activities or out-of-school activities (sometimes a job) in which he has some interest and talent and then supporting his participation in this activity helps enhance his sense of belonging (Emmer and Evertson, 2009). At all levels, the teacher should make it a point to give the student attention and positive feedback when he engages in appropriate behaviour. Often, students with chronic behavioural problems and their parents receive only negative messages. Showing an interest in those things that the student values and making sure that you, as the teacher, recognize those strengths will help increase his sense of competence. Sometimes, setting short-term goals with the student and then helping him keep track of his progress in meeting the goals helps him feel more competent.

At all times, feedback to the student with chronic behavioural problems should emphasize what he can do as opposed to what he cannot do. Suppose a student with chronic behavioural problems takes a test, makes a concerted effort to do well, and receives a mark of 57. In some classrooms, he may receive the message that this was not a good mark, which would reinforce his own feelings of incompetence; therefore, rather than communicating that the student is not successful, the teacher can point out that he has indeed learned and then use that limited success to encourage him to continue to make the effort to learn. Using encouraging communication, engaging the student in short-term goal setting, stressing effort and improvement, and focusing on the positive aspects of his behaviour and performance can increase his sense of competence.

We all need to feel that we have control over the important aspects of our lives. When students are deprived of the opportunity to be self-directing and to make responsible choices, they often become bullies or totally dependent on others, unable to control their own lives. A teacher can enhance the student's sense of power by providing opportunities to make choices and by allowing the student to experience the consequences of those choices (Jennings and Greenberg, 2009). There is a wide range of classroom decisions in which, depending on the teacher's philosophy, the student can have a voice. When the teacher chooses to involve students in classroom decisions, he conveys the message that he cares about the students and tries to accommodate their personal interests and abilities. When students are deprived of the opportunity to make choices, especially students with chronic behavioural problems, they often become resentful and challenging of the teacher's authority. It is very important for the teacher not to engage in power contests with these students; thus, the best course of action for the teacher is to find appropriate opportunities for these students to make responsible choices.

The need for a sense of virtue or generosity revolves around our desire to feel that we are givers and not just takers. When we have a fulfilled sense of virtue, we realize that we are able to give to and nurture others. Elementary teachers often use "book buddies" and cross-grade tutoring opportunities to develop a sense of virtue among their students. Many secondary students have their sense of virtue fulfilled by participating in food drives, marathons, and walkathons for charities, and other types of community service projects. Some of the most successful rehabilitation programs for juvenile offenders engage these adolescents in activities that are beneficial to others in the community (Brendtro, Brokenleg, and Van Bockern, 2002; Jennings and Greenberg, 2009). Although it is sometimes difficult to arrange classroom activities that tap into the need for a sense of virtue, peer tutoring and other opportunities to share talents can enhance a student's sense of virtue or generosity. Before turning to techniques for managing chronic behavioural problems, it should be emphasized that relationship building and breaking the cycle of discouragement require commitment, persistence, patience, and self-control on the part of the teacher. It is extremely hard to do, but it is often the only thing that makes a real difference in the long run to students with chronic behavioural problems.

PRIVATE CONFERENCES

Holding private conferences with students who have chronic behavioural problems is the *sine qua non* of the strategies that are intended to manage or solve these behavioural problems. Until the teacher takes the time to sit down with the student to discuss his behaviour and to attempt to find ways to help him behave in more productive ways, the teacher has not begun to try to manage or solve the problem (Koshik, 2010). A private conference or a series of conferences with the student accomplishes a couple of important tasks. First, it makes sure that the student is aware that his behaviour is a problem that must be dealt with. Second, sometimes it is one of the basic steps toward building a positive relationship with the student; thus, it can be an important step toward helping the student take ownership of the behaviour and find ways to bring it under control.

Receiving Skills

During private conferences, the teacher needs to be aware of the student's perception of the problem and also his point of view in order to be sure that the intervention focuses on the actual problem. Suppose, for example, the student's chronic misbehaviour is motivated by the student's belief that he doesn't have the ability to do the assigned work. Solutions that ignore the student's underlying feeling of incompetence are not likely to be successful in the long run; therefore, it is important to be sure you receive the message that the student is sending. The following receiving skills will help to ensure that you receive the student's message:

1. *Use silence and nonverbal attending cues:* Allow the student sufficient time to express his ideas and feelings, and use nonverbal cues such as eye contact, facial expressions, head nodding, and body posture (for example, leaning toward the student) to show that you are interested in and listening to what he is saying. Most important, make sure these cues are sincere; that is, that you really are listening carefully to him.

2. *Probe:* Ask relevant and pertinent questions to elicit extended information about the current topic, to clarify ideas, and to justify a given idea. Questions such as, "Can you tell me more about the problem with Jerry?" or "What makes you say that I don't like you?" or "I'm not sure I understand what you mean by 'picking on you'; can you explain what that means?" show that you are listening and want more information.

3. *Check perceptions:* Paraphrase or summarize what the student has said using slightly different words. This acts as a check on whether you have understood him correctly. This is not a simple verbatim repetition of what the student has said. It is your attempt to capture the student's message as accurately as possible in your words. Usually a perception check ends by giving the student an opportunity to affirm or negate your perception; for example, "So, as I understand it, you think that I'm picking on you when I give you a detention for not completing your homework, is that right?" or "You're saying that you never really wanted to be in the gifted program anyway, and so you don't care whether you are removed from the program. Do I have that right?"

4. *Check feelings:* Feeling checks refer to attempts to reach student emotions through questions and statements. In formulating the questions and statements, use nonverbal cues (for example, facial expression) and paralingual cues (voice volume, rate, and pitch) to go beyond the student's statements and understand the emotions behind the words. For instance, "It sounds as if you are really proud of what you're doing in basketball, aren't you?" or "You look really angry when you talk about being placed in the lower section. Are you angry?" (Koshik, 2010; Poole and Vertson, 2012).

Sending Skills

Individual conferences not only allow the teacher to be sure he understands the problem from the student's vantage point, but also allow him to be sure the student understands the problem from the teacher's point of view. As a teacher, using your sending skills to clearly communicate your thoughts and ideas is a first step toward helping the student gain that insight. Ginott (1972) and Jones (1980) offer the follow-ing guidelines for sending accurate messages:

1. ***Deal in the here and now:*** Don't dwell on past problems and situations. Com-municate your thoughts about the present situation and the immediate future. Although it is appropriate to talk about the past behaviour that has created the need for the private conference, there is nothing to be gained by reciting a litany of past transgressions.

2. ***Make eye contact and use congruent nonverbal behaviours:*** Avoiding eye contact when confronting a student about misbehaviour gives the student the impression that you are uncomfortable about the confrontation. In contrast, maintaining eye contact helps to let the student know that you are confident and comfortable in dealing with problems. Because research indicates that students believe the nonverbal message when verbal and nonverbal behaviour are not congruent (Poole and Vertson, 2012), be sure nonverbal cues match the verbal messages.

3. ***Make statements rather than asking questions:*** Asking questions is appropri-ate for eliciting information from the student; however, when you have specific information or behaviours to discuss, you should lay the specific facts out on the table rather than try to elicit them from the student by playing "guess what's on my mind."

4. ***Use "I"—take responsibility for your feelings:*** You have a right to your feel-ings. It can be appropriate to be annoyed at students, and it can be appropriate to be proud of students. Students must know that teachers are people who have legitimate feelings and that their feelings must be considered in determining the effects of the student's behaviour on others.

5. ***Be brief:*** Get to the point quickly. Let the student know what the problem is as you see it and what you propose to do about it. Once you have done this, stop. Don't belabour the issue with unnecessary lectures and harangues.

6. ***Talk directly to the student, not about him:*** Even if other people are present, talk to the student rather than to parents or counsellors. Use "you" and specifi-cally describe the problem to the student. This behaviour sends the student the powerful message that he, not his parents or anyone else, is directly responsible for his own behaviour.

7. ***Give directions to help the student correct the problem:*** Don't stop at identify-ing the problem behaviour. Be specific in setting forth exactly which behaviours must be replaced and in identifying appropriate behaviours to replace them.

8. ***Check student understanding of your message:*** Once you have communi-cated clearly what the specific problem is and what steps you suggest for solving it, ask a question to be sure the student has received the message correctly. Often, it is a good idea to ask the student to summarize the discussion. If the student's summary indicates that he has missed the message, you have an oppor-tunity to restate or rephrase the main idea in a way that he can understand.

With these guidelines for effective communication in mind, we can now consider three specific techniques (*self-monitoring, anecdotal record keeping,* and *behaviour contracting*) for managing students with chronic behavioural problems. There are five assumptions underlying these techniques:

1. The number of students in any one class who should be classified as having chronic behavioural problems is small, usually fewer than five. If there are more than five, the teacher should look inward.
2. The teacher is well prepared for each class, engages the students in interesting learning activities, and uses a variety of effective teaching strategies.
3. The expectations for behaviour are clearly understood by students and enforced on a consistent basis (see Chapter 7).
4. The teacher manages commonplace disruptions with a pre-planned hierarchy of nonverbal and verbal interventions and logical consequences and by using the CALM model.
5. The teacher attempts to build positive relationships with students who have chronic behavioural problems and attempts to break the cycle of discouragement by helping them to meet their self-esteem needs.

When there are several students who exhibit chronic behavioural problems, they usually fall into one of two categories—those who have the greatest potential for improving their behaviour quickly and those whose behaviour causes the greatest disruption. Usually those with the greatest odds for quick improvement are the students with the least severe behavioural problems; thus, even if the teacher succeeds in helping them, the general level of disruption in the classroom may remain quite high. On the other hand, those students who have the most severe and most disruptive behaviour usually require the longest period of time to improve, but their improvement tends to have a more dramatic impact on the classroom.

There are no clear guidelines as to which category of students teachers should choose. If the teacher is the type of individual who needs to see results quickly in order to persist, he is probably better off choosing those students with the greatest likelihood for quick improvement. If, however, the more serious behaviour is threatening to any individuals, the teacher must begin intervention with those students.

It must be noted that self-monitoring, anecdotal record keeping, or behaviour contracting probably will not be effective in managing chronic behavioural problems if the five assumptions underlying these techniques have not been met. If these assumptions have been met, then the teacher has done all that he can do to prevent behavioural problems from occurring, and the following three management techniques have a reasonable chance of success.

MANAGEMENT TECHNIQUES

Self-Monitoring

Some students who exhibit chronic disruptive behaviours perceive a well-managed private conference as a sign of a teacher's caring and support. Some students leave the conference with a new understanding that their behaviours are interfering with the rights of others and will no longer be tolerated in the classroom. Given the nature and background of chronic behavioural problems, however, most students will need more intensive and frequent intervention techniques. The challenge is to design techniques that are congruent with the belief that students must be given opportunities to learn how to control their own behaviour.

Self-monitoring of behaviour is a student-directed approach that is often effective with students who are really trying to behave appropriately but seem to need assistance to do so. The technique is usually more appropriate for elementary students who have extremely short attention spans or who are easily distracted by the everyday events of a busy classroom (Glaser, Palm, and Brunstein, 2012). While self-monitoring can be effective with some older students, the teacher must consider the age appropriateness of the self-monitoring instrument that the student will use.

For self-monitoring to be effective, the instrument must clearly delineate the behaviours to be monitored and must be easy for a student to use. The student must also clearly understand the duration of the self-monitoring and the frequency of behavioural checks. Unfortunately, teachers occasionally design an instrument that is too cumbersome to use or is too time consuming. Thus, using the instrument actually interferes with on-task behaviour.

In the beginning, the student may require teacher cues to indicate when it is time to check behaviour and record it on the self-monitoring instrument. These cues may be private, nonverbal signals agreed upon by the teacher and the student. In the beginning, it is a good idea for the teacher to co-monitor the student's behaviour using the same instrument. When this is done, the teacher and the student can compare their monitoring consistency and discuss the proper use of the instrument as well as the progress that is being made.

The effectiveness of self-monitoring relies heavily on how the use of the instrument is explained to the student. If self-monitoring is presented as a technique that students can use to help themselves with the teacher's assistance, support, and encouragement, the likelihood of improved behaviour is high. When teachers have successfully communicated the purpose of the technique and stressed the possible positive outcomes, students have actually thanked them for the opportunity and means to demonstrate on-task behaviour (Glaser, Palm, and Brunstein, 2012). On the other hand, if the intervention is introduced as a form of punishment, the likelihood of positive behavioural change is diminished.

While other examples of more comprehensive self-monitoring instruments may be found in Chapter 6, Figure 10.4 is an example of a simple self-monitoring instrument for a wide range of behaviours. When a teacher uses this instrument, it is imperative that he and the student clearly understand which behaviours are defined as on task, and therefore coded "1," and which behaviours are off task and coded "0." In addition, a workable coding period needs to be established so that each block represents a predetermined period of time.

As with any intervention that focuses on the improvement of chronic misbehaviour, progress may be slow. Two steps forward and one step backward may be the

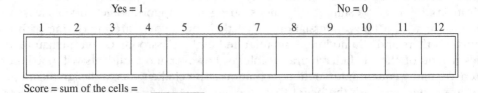

FIGURE 10.4   Am I on Task?

best a student can do in the beginning. We must remember that chronic misbehaviour does not develop in a day, and it will not be replaced with more appropriate behaviour in a day. It is difficult to learn new behaviours to replace behaviours that have become ingrained and habitual; therefore, the teacher must be patient and focus on improvements. It is usually best to work on one behaviour at a time. For example, if a student continually talks to neighbours and calls out, the teacher and student should decide which behaviour to work on first. If the student is successful in managing the selected behaviour, experience has shown that subsequent behaviours are more readily corrected.

As behaviour improves, the teacher should begin to wean the student from self-monitoring. As a first step, once the teacher is convinced that the student is reliably monitoring his own behaviour, the teacher stops co-monitoring and relies solely on the student's report and self-monitoring (Moore, Anderson, Glassenbury, Lang, and Didden, 2013). Next, as behaviours begin to improve, the teacher lengthens the period of time between self-checks. Finally, the teacher removes the student completely from self-monitoring. When this happens, the teacher uses the event to build self-esteem and self-control by making the student aware that he has changed his behaviour on his own and should be quite proud of his accomplishments. Any corresponding improvements in academics or peer interactions should also be noted and tied to the student's improved behaviour.

Figure 10.5 shows a checklist that teachers can use to evaluate the self-monitoring procedures and instruments that they design.

Anecdotal Record Keeping

If the teacher either has tried self-monitoring or has decided not to try this technique because of philosophical objections or the student's refusal to make the required commitments, there is a second option, called **anecdotal record keeping**, for remediating chronic behavioural problems. This method, which is a collaborative approach to managing classroom behaviours (see Chapter 5, "Philosophical Approaches to Classroom Management"), has been used successfully by student teachers and veteran

1. Do the teacher and student clearly understand and agree on the behaviours to be monitored?	_____ Yes	_____ No
2. Is the time period for self-checks clearly specified?	_____ Yes	_____ No
3. Does the student understand how to use the instrument?	_____ Yes	_____ No
4. Have the teacher and student agreed on a meeting time to discuss the self-monitoring?	_____ Yes	_____ No
5. Is the instrument designed so that small increments of improved behaviour will be noted?	_____ Yes	_____ No
6. Is the instrument designed to focus on one behaviour?	_____ Yes	_____ No

FIGURE 10.5   Self-Monitoring Checklist

teachers alike to handle a variety of chronic behavioural problems at a number of different grade levels (Emmer and Evertson, 2009; Poole and Vertson, 2012). It is based on the principles of *Adlerian psychology* which state that changes in behaviour can be facilitated by making people aware of their behaviour and its consequences for themselves and others (Sweeney, 1981).

Anecdotal record keeping is usually most appropriate for middle and secondary students because students at these levels have better-developed self-regulation. To use the technique, the teacher merely records the classroom behaviour, both positive and negative, of a chronically disruptive student over a period of a few weeks. Although it is preferable to have the student's cooperation, anecdotal record keeping can be employed without it.

The record the teacher has made of the student's behaviour and the measures that have been taken to improve that behaviour form the basis for a private conference with the student. There are nine guidelines that should be followed in conducting this initial conference:

1. The teacher should begin on a positive note.
2. The teacher should help the student to recognize the past behaviour and its negative impact, showing the student the record of past behaviours and discussing it if necessary.
3. The teacher should explain that this behaviour is unacceptable and must change.
4. The teacher should tell the student that he will keep a record of the student's positive and negative behaviour on a daily basis and that the student will be required to sign the record at the end of class each day.
5. The teacher should record the student's home phone number on the top of the record and indicate that he will contact the parents/caregivers to inform them of continued unacceptable behaviour. (This option may not be useful for senior high students because parents/caregivers are often not as influential at this age.)
6. The teacher should be positive and emphasize expectations of improvement.
7. The conference should be recorded on the anecdotal record.
8. A verbal commitment for improved behaviour from the student should be sought. This commitment, or the refusal to give it, should be noted on the anecdotal record.
9. The student should sign the anecdotal record at the end of the conference. If the student refuses to sign, the refusal should be recorded.

After the initial conference, the teacher continues the anecdotal record, each day highlighting positive behaviours, documenting negative behaviours, and noting any corrective measures taken. The teacher reinforces the student's improved behaviours and, if possible, clarifies the connection between improved behaviours and academic achievement (Marzano, Frontier, and Livingston, 2011). Thus, the teacher "catches the student being good" (Canter and Canter, 2001.) and demonstrates the concept of encouragement (Moore et al., 2013). To illustrate the concept of student accountability, the teacher must be consistent in recording behaviours, sharing the record with the student, and obtaining the student's signature on a daily basis (Moore et al., 2013). If the student refuses to sign the record on any day, the teacher simply makes note of this fact on the record. Figure 10.6 is the anecdotal record used with one grade 10 student over a three-week period. The technique succeeded after the management hierarchy had been used with little improvement in the student's behaviour. Note that the teacher highlighted positive behaviours to "catch the student being good."

Student's Name _____

Home Phone _____

Date	Student Behaviour	Teacher Action	Student Signature
4/14	Talking with Van Out of seat three times Refused to answer question	Verbal reprimand Told him to get back Went on	
4/16	Had private conference Rhonda agreed to improve	Explained anecdotal record Was supportive	
4/17	Stayed on task in lab	Positive feedback	
4/20	Late for class Worked quietly	Verbal reminder Positive feedback	
4/21	Worked quietly Wrestling with Jill	Positive feedback Verbal reprimand	
4/22	No disruptions Volunteered to answer	Positive feedback Called on him three times	
4/23	Late for class Left without signing	Detention after school Recorded it on record	
4/24	Missed detention	Two days' detention	
4/27	Stayed on task all class	Positive feedback	
4/28	Listened attentively to film	Positive feedback	
4/29	Worked at assignment well	Positive feedback	
4/30	Participated in class No disruptions Left without signing	Called on him twice Positive feedback Recorded it	
5/1	Conference to discontinue anecdotal records		

FIGURE 10.6   An Anecdotal Record

While teachers may think that this technique will consume a lot of instructional time, it does not. If the documentation occurs in the last few minutes of class, perhaps when students are doing homework or getting ready for the next class, the two or three minutes required for it compare favourably to the enormous amount of time wasted by unresolved chronic behavioural problems. Thus, this technique actually helps to conserve time by making more efficient use of classroom time.

In studying the use of anecdotal record keeping, Levin and Nolan (2007) requested teachers to log their views on the effectiveness of the procedure. Here are two representative logs by secondary teachers.

TEACHER'S LOG—GRADE 11 ENGLISH

About a week and a half ago, I implemented the anecdotal record in one of my classes. Two male students were the subjects. The improvement shown by one of these students is very impressive.

On the first day that I held a conference with the student, I explained the procedure, showed him my records for the day, and asked for his signature. He scribbled his name and looked at me as if to say, "What a joke." On the second day, his behaviour in class was negative again. This time, when I spoke to him and told him that one more day of disruptive behaviour would result in a phone call to his parents, he looked at me as if to say, "This joke isn't so funny anymore." From that moment on, there was a marked improvement in his behaviour. He was quiet and attentive in class. After class, he would come up to me and ask me where he was supposed to sign his name for the day. And he "beamed" from my remarks about how well-behaved he was that day. Only one time after that did I have to speak to him for negative behaviour. I caught him throwing a piece of paper. As soon as he saw me looking at him, he said, "Are you going to write that down in your report?" Then, after class, he came up to me with a worried expression on his face and asked, "Are you going to call my parents?" I didn't, because of model behaviour in the previous days.

I must say that I was skeptical about beginning this type of record on the students. It seemed like such a lengthy and time-consuming process. But I'll say what I'm feeling now. If the anecdotal record can give positive results more times than not, I'll keep on using it. If you can get one student under control, who is to say you can't get five or ten students under control? It truly is a worthwhile procedure to consider.

TEACHER'S LOG—GRADE 8 SCIENCE

Day 1

I discovered a method with which to deal with some major behavioural problems in one of my classes. It uses an anecdotal record, which is a record of student actions and student behaviours. I think it will probably work because it holds the student accountable for her behaviours. If something must be done, the student has nobody to blame but herself.

Day 2

Today, I set up private conferences with anecdotal record students. I wonder if they'll show up—and if they do, how they will respond.

Day 3

Two students (of three) showed up for their anecdotal record conferences. The third is absent. Both students were very cooperative and made a commitment to better behaviour. One student even made the comment that she thought this idea was a good one for her. The way things look, this will work out fairly well. We'll see. . . .

Day 4

One of the students on anecdotal record has improved in behaviour so much that I informed her that if her good behaviour kept improving, I'd take her off the record next Wednesday. I think it will be interesting to see how her behaviour will be; will it keep improving or will it backtrack again?

Implementing any new strategy may be difficult, and anecdotal record keeping is no exception. The teacher must expect that a handful of students will be quite hostile when the procedure is introduced. Some may even refuse to sign the record. The teacher must remain calm and positive and simply record these behaviours. This action communicates to the student that he is solely responsible for his behaviour and that the teacher is only an impartial recorder of the behaviour. Student behaviour will usually improve, given time. Since improved behaviour becomes a part of the record, the anecdotal record reinforces the improvement and becomes the basis for a cycle of improvement.

When the student's behaviour has improved to an acceptable level, the teacher informs him that it will no longer be necessary to keep the anecdotal record because of the improvement in his behaviour. It is important, as suggested earlier, to connect the improved behaviour to academic success and improved grades, if possible. The teacher must also make clear to the student that his fine behaviour is expected to continue. Because continued attention is a key link in the chain of behaviours that turn disruptive class members into students who behave appropriately, the teacher must continue to give the student attention when he behaves appropriately. If the student's behaviour shows no improvement, it may be time to discontinue the process.

It can be quite difficult to decide when to stop recording behaviour. There are no hard and fast rules, but there are some helpful guidelines. If the student has displayed acceptable behaviour for a few days to a week, the record may be discontinued. If the student's behaviour remains disruptive continuously for a week, the anecdotal record keeping should be discontinued and the student should be informed why. If the misbehaviour is somewhat reduced, it may be advisable to have a second conference with the student to determine whether to continue record keeping.

Functional Behaviour Assessment

The third short-term strategy for working with students who exhibit chronic behaviour problems is **functional behaviour assessment**, also known as FBA. Functional behaviour assessment is a teacher-directed strategy (Chapter 5) based on behavioural learning theory. "A functional behaviour assessment simply means that someone skilled at observing behaviour tries to determine the function (i.e., the motive) for the student's behaviour" (Hall and Hall, 2003, p. 149). The intent of functional behaviour assessment is to identify the purpose that the behaviour serves either consciously or unconsciously, for the student; the antecedents that provoke the behaviour; and the consequences that maintain the behaviour. Once the function, antecedent, and consequences have been identified, a positive behaviour support plan can be developed for extinguishing the unproductive or disruptive behaviour and replacing it with appropriate behaviour. The behavioural support plan might take many forms, including but not limited to altering the instructional environment and/or context in which the behaviour occurs, teaching the student new social and academic skills, or modifying the consequences that follow the behaviour (Dunlap, Iovannone, Wilson, Kincaid, and Strain, 2010) Modifying consequences could involve the use of behaviour contracting (see section "Behaviour Contracting").

Several assumptions underlie functional behaviour assessment: "(1) behaviour is learned not innate, (2) behaviour serves a specific purpose, and (3) behaviour is related to the context in which it occurs" (PaTTAN, 2008). The most common functions of behaviour, according to Hall and Hall (2003), are to get or avoid attention, to become engaged in or avoid particular activities, to obtain or avoid certain objects or items, or to obtain or avoid sensory stimulation. The following questions should be addressed:

1. How often does the target behaviour occur and how long does it last?
2. Where does the behaviour typically occur or never occur?
3. Who is present for the occurrence/nonoccurrence of the behaviour?
4. What is going on during the occurrence/nonoccurrence of the behaviour?
5. When is the behaviour most likely/least likely to occur?
6. How does the student react to the usual consequences that follow the behaviour? (PaTTAN, 2008)

Functional behaviour assessment (FBA) has been used most often with special needs students. Most often, a team of professionals that includes the special education teacher, regular education teacher, behaviour specialist and/or school psychologist, and other therapists collaborates in carrying out the FBA. We would suggest that you, as a classroom teacher, engage colleagues who have expertise in FBA to assist you in carrying out the process.

Behaviour Contracting

Behaviour contracting is a teacher-directed strategy (see Chapter 5). This technique is grounded on the principles of operant conditioning, which state that a behaviour that is reinforced is likely to be repeated and that a behaviour that is not reinforced will disappear.

This technique involves the use of a written agreement, known as a *behaviour contract*, between the teacher and student. This contract commits the student to behave appropriately and offers a specified reward when the commitment is met. The contract details the expected behaviour, a time period during which this behaviour must be exhibited, and the reward that will be provided. The purposes of the contract are to manage behaviour that is not managed by normal classroom procedures, to encourage self-discipline, and to foster the student's sense of commitment to appropriate classroom behaviour. Although behaviour contracting can be used with students at any grade level, it often is more appropriate and effective with elementary and middle school students since older students often resent what they are likely to see as an obvious attempt to manipulate their behaviour. This technique is frequently and effectively used in special education classes (Miltenberger, 2011).

Because an integral part of behaviour contracting is the use of rewards—often extrinsic, concrete rewards—some teachers may be philosophically opposed to the technique. These teachers often overcome their philosophical objections by replacing concrete, extrinsic rewards with those more focused on learning activities, such as special assignments of classroom duties and responsibilities. Teachers who feel that students should not be rewarded for behaviour that is normally expected should keep in mind the fact that this technique has been shown to be effective and is one of the last possible strategies that can be used within the classroom; however, if there are strong philosophical objections to the technique, the teacher should not use it because the likelihood of its successful use is diminished if its philosophical underpinnings are in contradiction to the teacher's (see Chapter 5).

Teachers who decide to use behaviour contracting should remember that it is unlikely that one contract will turn a chronically disruptive student into the epitome of model behaviour. Usually, the teacher must use a series of short-term behaviour contracts that result in steady, gradual improvement in the student's behaviour. A series of short-term behaviour contracts allow the student to see the behaviour changes as manageable and receive small rewards after short intervals of improvement. In other words, a series of contracts provides the student with the opportunity to be successful. Manageable changes in behaviour, shorter time intervals, and frequent opportunities for success make it more likely that the student will remain motivated (Miltenberger, 2011).

In designing the series of contracts, the teacher should keep three principles in mind. First, design the contracts to require specific, gradual improvements in behaviour. For example, if a student normally disrupts learning six times a period, set the initial goal at four disruptions or fewer per day. Over time, increase the goal until it is set at zero disruptions per day. Second, gradually lengthen the time period during which the contract must be observed in order to gain the reward. For instance, the set time is one day for the first contract, a few days for the second contract, a week for the third contract, and so on. Third, move little by little from more tangible, extrinsic rewards to less tangible, more intrinsic rewards; thus, a pencil or other supplies are the rewards under the first few contracts, and free time for pleasure reading is the reward under a later contract. Using these three principles takes advantage of a behaviour-modification technique called *behaviour shaping* and gradually shifts management of the student's behaviour from the teacher to the student, where it rightfully belongs.

Before writing the contract, the teacher should make a record of the student's past misbehaviours and the techniques that were used to try to ameliorate these transgressions. The teacher should use all available evidence, including documents and personal recollections, and try to be as accurate and neutral as possible. This record will help the teacher to decide which specific behaviours must be changed and how much change seems manageable for the student at one time.

It also ensures that all appropriate management techniques have been used before the implementation of the behaviour contract process. Once the record is compiled, the teacher holds a private conference with the student. It is best to begin the conference on a positive note. The teacher should communicate to the student that he has the potential to do well and to succeed if he can learn to behave appropriately. In doing this, the teacher is using the concept of encouragement (Emmer and Evertson, 2009; Poole and Vertson, 2012).

The teacher should then attempt to get the student to acknowledge that his behaviour has been inappropriate and to recognize its negative impact on everyone in the classroom. Stressing the effect of the student's behaviour on others promotes the development of higher moral reasoning (Narvaez, 2010). To help the student recognize that his behaviour has been unacceptable, the teacher may want to use questions similar to these: "What have you been doing in class?"; or "How is that affecting your chances of success?"; or "How would you like it if other students treated you like that?"; or "How would you like it if you were in a class you really liked but never got a chance to learn because other students were always causing trouble?" Thereafter, the teacher should tell the student that his behaviour, no matter what the explanation for it, is unacceptable and must change. This is followed by a statement such as, "I'd like to work out a plan with you that will help you to behave more appropriately in class."

The teacher must clearly state how the plan works. Because a contract is an agreement between two people, if the student refuses to make a commitment to the contract, the technique cannot be used. If, however, the student commits herself to improvements in classroom behaviour for a specified period of time, some positive consequences or rewards result. The reward may be free time for activities of special interest; a letter, note, or phone call to parents/caregivers describing the improvements in behaviour; or supplies, such as posters, pencils, and stickers. The most important consideration in deciding which particular reward to use is whether the student perceives it as motivating. For that reason, it is often a good idea to allow the student to suggest possible rewards or to discuss rewards with the student. If the student's parents/caregivers are cooperative, it is sometimes possible to ask them to provide a reward at home that is meaningful to the student. At this point, the teacher should draw up the contract, setting forth the specific improvements in behaviour, the time period, and the reward. Both the teacher and student should then sign the contract and each should receive a copy. In the case of young students, it is often a good idea to send a copy of the contract home to parents/caregivers as well. It might also be deemed appropriate for parents/caregivers to sign the contract, particularly with younger students. The conference should end as it began, on a positive note. The teacher, for example, might tell the student that he is looking forward to positive changes in the student's behaviour.

Figure 10.7 is an example of a behaviour contract and a behaviour contract checklist that may be used by teachers to evaluate the quality of contracts that they draw up. The sample contract was the third in a series between Jessica and her grade 5 teacher, Ms. Jones. Before the behaviour contract intervention, Jessica spent the vast majority of each day's 40-minute social studies period wandering around the room. The first two contracts resulted in her being able to remain seated for roughly half the period.

1. *Expected behaviour*
Jessica remains in her seat for the first 30 minutes of each social studies period.

2. *Time period*
Monday, February 27 to Friday, March 3.

3. *Reward*
If Jessica remains in her seat for the first 30 minutes of each social studies period,

    a. She can choose the class's outdoor game on Friday afternoon, March 3, or

    b. Ms. Jones will telephone her parents to tell them of the improvement in Jessica's behaviour on Friday afternoon, March 3.

4. *Evaluation*

    a. After each social studies period, Ms. Jones records whether Jessica did or did not get out of her seat during the first 30 minutes.

    b. Jessica and Ms. Jones will meet on Friday, March 3 at 12:30 p.m. to determine whether the contract has been performed and to write next week's fourth contract.

Student _____

Teacher _____

Date _____

Behaviour Contract Checklist

1 Is the expected behaviour described specifically?	_____ Yes	_____ No
2 Is the time period specified clearly?	_____ Yes	_____ No
3 Has the reward been specified clearly?	_____ Yes	_____ No
4 Is the reward motivating to the student?	_____ Yes	_____ No
5 Is the evaluation procedure specified?	_____ Yes	_____ No
6 Has a date been set to meet to review the contract?	_____ Yes	_____ No
7 Has the student understood, agreed to, and signed the contract?	_____ Yes	_____ No
8 Has the teacher signed the contract?	_____ Yes	_____ No
9 Do both the teacher and student have copies?	_____ Yes	_____ No
10 Did the student's parents get a copy of the contract?	_____ Yes	_____ No

FIGURE 10.7 Third Contract Between Jessica and Ms. Jones

Once the contract is drawn up, the teacher should record the behaviour of the student each day regarding the terms specified in the contract. At the end of the contract period, the teacher can use this record to conduct a conference with the student. If the student has kept his commitment, the teacher should provide the reward. If the student's behaviour needs further improvement, the teacher can draw up a new contract that specifies increased improvement over a longer time period. If at the end of the contract the student's behaviour has improved sufficiently to conform to final expectations, the teacher can inform the student that a behaviour contract is no longer needed. If possible, the teacher should point out to the student the direct relationship between the improved behaviour and the student's academic success in the classroom (Marzano, Frontier, and Livingston, 2011). The teacher also should make clear that he expects acceptable behaviour and success to continue. Of course, the teacher must continue to give the student attention after the contract has ended. This consistent attention helps the student to recognize that positive behaviour results in positive consequences and usually helps to maintain appropriate behaviour over a long period of time.

If at the end of the contract period the student has not kept the commitment, the teacher should accept no excuses. During the conference, the teacher should assume a neutral role, explaining that the reward cannot be given because the student's behaviour did not live up to the behaviour specified in the contract. The teacher should point out to the student that the lack of reward is simply a logical consequence of the behaviour. This helps the student to see the cause-and-effect relationship between behaviour and its consequences. If the student learns only this, he has learned an extremely valuable lesson.

At this point, the teacher must decide whether or not it is worth trying a new contract with the student. If the teacher believes that the student tried to live up to the contract, a new contract that calls for a little less drastic improvement or calls for improvement over a slightly shorter time frame may be worthwhile.

If the student has not made a sincere effort to improve, obviously the contracting is not working. It is time to try another option. Nothing has been lost in the attempt except a little bit of time, and the teacher has accumulated additional documentation, which will be helpful if it is necessary to seek outside-the-classroom assistance.

There is one final technique for the teacher to try when these classroom management techniques do not work: the exclusion of the student from the classroom until he makes a written commitment to improve his behaviour.

Prior to exclusion, the teacher tells the student that he is no longer allowed in the class because of his disruptive behaviour, which is interfering with the teacher's right to teach and the students' right to learn. The teacher then tells the student to report to a specified location in the school where appropriate classroom assignments involving reading and writing will be given. The student is also told that he will be held accountable for the completion of all assignments in an acceptable and timely manner, the same as required in the regular classroom. The teacher stresses that the student may return to the classroom at any time by giving a written commitment to improve his behaviour. This written commitment must be in the student's own words and must specify the changed behaviour that will be evident when the student returns to the classroom. Of course, exclusion presupposes that the administration is supportive of such a technique and has made appropriate arrangements for the setting.

Our experience has shown that those few students who have been excluded from the classroom and have then made the written commitment and returned have remained in the classroom with acceptable behaviour. Exclusion finally demonstrates to the student that his behaviour will no longer be tolerated and that the entire responsibility for the student's behaviour is on the student and only the student.

If a student does not make the written commitment within a reasonable period of time, usually no more than a few days, outside assistance (in the form of parents, the counsellor, principal, or outside agency) must be sought (see Chapter 11, "Seeking Outside Assistance"). If it is necessary to seek outside assistance, the teacher's use of self-monitoring, anecdotal record keeping, or behaviour contracting will provide the documented evidence needed to make an appropriate referral.

Summary

In this chapter, we have discussed the strategies that can be used in working with students who have chronic behavioural problems. We discussed two long-term strategies for resolving chronic problems: building positive relationships and breaking the cycle of discouragement. In addition, four techniques for managing students with chronic behaviour problems were introduced: self-monitoring, anecdotal record keeping, functional behaviour assessment, and behaviour contracting. Of these techniques, self-monitoring is most compatible with the student-directed philosophy; anecdotal record keeping is most compatible with the collaborative philosophy; and functional behaviour assessment and behavioural contracting are most compatible with the teacher-directed philosophy. We also discussed *when*, *how*, and *with which* students to use these strategies and techniques. We divided the communication skills needed for a private conference, an essential component of any strategy for working with students who have chronic behavioural problems, into receiving skills and sending skills. Finally, we presented the technique of exclusion from the classroom—the final step between in-class teacher management and outside referral.

Key Terms

anecdotal record keeping: the teacher records positive and negative classroom behaviour of a chronically disruptive student over a period of a few weeks.

behaviour contracting: involves the use of a written agreement, known as a *behaviour contract*, between the teacher and student.

cycle of discouragement: often occurs when students suffer from low self-esteem and a low success-to-failure ratio.

functional behaviour assessment: identifies the purpose that the behaviour serves, either consciously or unconsciously, for the student; the antecedents that provoke the behaviour; and the consequences that maintain the behaviour.

relationship building: the conscious attempt by a teacher to build a positive relationship with students.

self-monitoring: student-directed approach; often effective with students who are trying to behave appropriately but need assistance to do so.

Exercises

1. Think of the teachers you had in school who were most successful in building positive relationships with students. What qualities did these teachers possess? How was their behaviour toward students different from the behaviour of teachers who were not good at building relationships? What implications do these differences have for building positive relationships with students who have chronic behavioural problems?

2. In this chapter, we suggest that teachers should attempt to empathize with students who have chronic behavioural problems. Does this mean that disruptive behaviour should be excused or condoned?

3. In this chapter, we present several ideas for breaking the cycle of discouragement by helping to meet students' self-esteem needs. In each of the following four categories of self-esteem needs, suggest additional behaviours that a teacher might use to enhance student self-esteem: (a) the need for significance, (b) the need for competence, (c) the need for power, (d) the need for virtue.

4. Form a triad with two other classmates. Designate a letter (A, B, or C) for each of you. Role-play three conferences between a teacher and a chronically disruptive student. In each instance, the individual playing the teacher will create the scenario that has led to the conference. During each conference, the person who plays the role of teacher should practise using effective receiving and sending skills. The process observer will give feedback to the teacher on his use of effective communication. Divide the roles for the three conferences according to the following format:

If not, how should it be classified? If not, is it possible to have a student-directed technique to manage chronic behavioural problems?

7. Should chronically disruptive students receive special rewards for behaviours that are typically expected of other students? Justify your answer.

8. Make a list of rewards under the regular classroom teacher's control that could be used in behaviour contracts for students at each of the following levels: (a) elementary, (b) middle or junior high, (c) senior high.

9. Develop a list of learning-focused positive consequences that could be substituted for the use of concrete, extrinsic rewards in behaviour contracts.

10. Design an initial behaviour contract for the following situation: Jonathan, a grade 6 middle school student who loves sports, has during the past three weeks refused to do homework, started fights on three different occasions, and disrupted class two or three times each day.

11. We classify anecdotal record keeping as a collaborative approach to classroom management. Do you agree? If so, what makes it a collaborative approach? If not, how should it be classified?

12. Examine the sample anecdotal record in Figure 10.6. Explain whether you concur with

	Person A	Person B	Person C
Conference 1	Teacher	Student	Process observer
Conference 2	Process observer	Teacher	Student
Conference 3	Student	Process observer	Teacher

5. Design a self-monitoring instrument that is appropriate for elementary children and that monitors (a) calling out, (b) talking to neighbours, and (c) staying focused on seat work.

6. This chapter classified self-monitoring as a student-directed approach to the management of chronic behavioural problems. Do you agree? If so, what makes it a student-directed approach?

the following decisions made by the teacher: (a) to continue the intervention after 4/23 and 4/24; (b) to stop the record after 4/30. Justify your answers.

13. Which types of misbehaviour constitute sufficient grounds for exclusion from the classroom? Justify your answers.

Weblinks

Centre for Addiction and Mental Health

www.camh.net

This site provides useful resources related to students who are disruptive in the classroom

and the possible underlying causes. Links are provided for the *Journal of Addiction and Mental Health*.

Facts About Corporal Punishment Worldwide (NCACPS)

http://www.stophitting.com/
Offers facts and links to information about corporal punishment in Canada and around the world.

The National Crime Prevention Strategy

http://www.publicsafety.gc.ca/
The NCPS provides a policy framework for the implementation of crime prevention interventions in Canada. It is administered by the National Crime Prevention Centre (NCPC) in the Community Safety and Partnerships Branch of Public Safety Canada, and managed in collaboration with the provinces and territories.

Intervention Central

www.interventioncentral.org
"Intervention Central offers free tools and resources to help school staff and parents to promote positive classroom behaviours and foster effective learning for all children and youth."

Canadian Prevention Science Cluster

http://www.preventionsciencecluster.org/#!about-cpsc
The Canadian Prevention Science Cluster (CPSC) brings together leading researchers and practitioners from across Canada who are dedicated to reducing violence and abuse and promoting healthy relationships among youth.

11

Seeking Outside Assistance

FOCUS ON THE PRINCIPLES OF CLASSROOM MANAGEMENT

1. What actions should professional teachers initiate when they recognize that some chronic misbehaviour problems are beyond their expertise?

2. When is using a multidisciplinary team approach the most effective approach to manage chronic misbehaviour problems?

3. What techniques are essential to ensure parental support and cooperation with the school when attempting to manage a student who chronically misbehaves?

INTRODUCTION

Even when teachers use all of the strategies suggested in this text to prevent, cope with, and solve behavioural problems, there are some students who simply cannot behave appropriately without some type of specialized **outside assistance** or intervention. In these cases, the most extreme step of the CALM model must be applied. Indeed, students who exhibit unmanageable behavioural problems are capable of overshadowing the positive educational climate of the classroom to such an extent, that teachers can begin to question their own professional competence; thus, it is very important for teachers to acknowledge that there are certain circumstances under which they are forced to seek outside support and expertise. In fact, the mark of skilled professionals is to recognize the limits of their expertise and to make the necessary and appropriate consultations and referrals without any sense of professional inadequacy. In Canada, each board/school has a set of procedures that describe the appropriate steps for teachers to take when confronted by patterns of extreme student behaviours. Teachers are expected to be familiar with the board/school policies.

Sometimes, the first referral teachers make is to the student's parents or caregivers. They may do this through written correspondence or a phone conversation. Teachers should make this contact when (1) the misbehaviour is a minor surface behaviour that continues after the teacher has used the strategies discussed in this text and (2) the teacher is confident that parental input is all that is needed to assist in managing the misbehaviour. The contact should be made only after the student has been given a choice between improving her behaviour and having her parents/caregivers informed of it. The teacher should point out to the student that the primary responsibility for controlling her behaviour rests her, not her parents or caregivers. Often, this, in itself, will bring the desired change. If not, parental contact is made—and this often results in consequences at home that are enough to motivate a change in school behaviour.

At other times, the behaviour is such that the teacher decides parental contact will not be sufficient to remedy the problem and that she needs outside expertise to understand and cope with the student. In these cases, parental contact comes after consultation with other professional staff members. Consultation ensures that the student's parents will have an adequate description of the problem, an explanation of the intervention strategies attempted, and a comprehensive proposed plan of action.

Whether parental contact is the first step or a later step in seeking outside assistance, it is critical that the contact sets the stage for a cooperative home–school relationship. For this to occur, it is often necessary to overcome negative, defensive parental perceptions and attitudes toward the school and/or the teacher; thus, any parental contact must be preceded by careful planning and preparation. In addition to the student's parents/caregivers, the teacher should consult with the school's administrators, psychologists, learning resource teachers, and social workers. By doing this, specialized expertise is brought to bear on understanding and working with both the student who is displaying unremitting misbehaviour and her family. In some cases, referrals outside the school may be necessary.

In this chapter, we discuss the nature of persisting misbehaviour, the point at which a teacher needs to seek outside assistance, preparing for and conducting parent conferences, and the roles of other school staff members. In the section "Symptoms of Serious Problems," later in this chapter, we detail behaviours that may not be disruptive but which teachers must be aware of. These behaviours may be symptomatic of other serious problems that require outside referrals.

THE NATURE OF PERSISTING MISBEHAVIOUR

In Chapter 3, "Understanding Why Children Misbehave," which dealt exclusively with why children misbehave, we noted that much of the daily disruptive behaviour observed in children is characteristic of the developmental stages that all children go through and is a normal reaction to their developmental changes and the changes in society; however, there are some students who display deviant behaviours that resist all attempts at modification.

These students often are reacting to negative influences within their environment. These influences may be quite obvious and identifiable, or they may be rather subtle. When a teacher is trying to understand a long-term pattern of misbehaviour, environmental influences must be viewed in a summative manner. Long-term behaviour is not understood by examining one or two snapshots of specific environmental influences. A history of influences must be considered.

One concept that is especially helpful in understanding historical influences is the success–failure ratio. This is a ratio of the amount of success a student experiences in her daily life to the amount of failure she experiences. Most students exhibit adaptive, productive behaviour and feel good about themselves when they are successful.

Students who do not meet with a reasonable degree of success become frustrated and discouraged, and their behaviour becomes maladaptive and destructive (Glaser, Palm, and Brunstein, (2012). Although students with chronic behaviour difficulties may appear hard and defiant, they are often very damaged and vulnerable. Frequently, negative experiences have left them unresponsive to the normal classroom reinforcements intended to increase the success–failure ratio. What are the influences that cause students to have a low success–failure ratio?

Failure in the Classroom Environment

Some students simply are not—or cannot find a way to be—successful at school in academic, social, and/or extracurricular activities. For these students, school is a daily source of failure that significantly reduces their overall success–failure ratio. Success in school and behaviour are so interrelated that it has been concluded that many misbehaving students do not feel successful in school (Wolfgang, 2008). In some cases, social failure can cause the child to resort to bullying or, conversely, could result in the child being bullied. In either case, the child is experiencing social failure that, in turn, can interfere with successful learning (Durlak, Weissberg, Dymnicki, Taylor, and Schellinger, 2011; Marini, Fairbain, and Zuber, 2001; Zentall and Beike, 2012). In some cases, careful observation and evaluation will uncover a learning or behavioural disability. The disability may have gone undiagnosed because it did not become apparent until the child moved toward higher grade levels, where behavioural expectations and the conceptual demands of the curriculum increased. These students are not involved or interested in what they learn. Their misbehaviour serves as a protection from further hurt and feelings of inadequacy (Wolfgang, 2008). In other cases, students may possess personality traits that cause classmates to either torment or ignore them. The behavioural difficulties that these students display may be understood as an expression of their frustration and discouragement, which many times escalate into the observable behaviours of anger and retaliation. For these students, reward and gratification stem more from their success at focusing attention on themselves than from meeting appropriate behavioural and instructional expectations.

Failure Outside the Classroom Environment

Some students exhibit extreme behaviours that seem to have little to do with the day-to-day realities of the class environment. Extreme apprehension, distrust, disappointment, hurt, anger, or outrage can be triggered in them under the most benign circumstances or with the slightest provocation. A teacher may find such a student reacting to her as if she were abusive or rejecting. These distorted emotional responses are reactions that often have been shaped outside the classroom and reflect challenges that exist within the home and family or long-standing problems with peers. Some studies have concluded that 50 percent of children who experience behavioural problems at school also experience them at home (Bailey et al., 2013; Whannell and Allen, 2011). Some students with long-standing interpersonal relationship difficulties find the normal social pressures of the classroom too much to tolerate. Just as failure within the classroom lowers a student's perceived success–failure ratio, so too does failure outside the classroom.

Failure as a Result of Primary Mode of Conduct

For some students, misbehaviour seems to be the natural state of affairs. Their behaviour seems to be an expression of their own internal tension, restlessness, and discomfort rather than a reaction to any apparent environmental influence. These students' difficulties emerge during the preschool and kindergarten years. Their teachers view them as immature, emotionally volatile, inattentive, demanding, overly aggressive, and self-centred. They are usually quick to react with anger to any sort of stress or frustration. Unfortunately, their behaviour is too often explained simplistically as the natural expression of the "difficult child" temperament (Turecki and Tonner, 2012). For some, there is a significant improvement with age, for others, the problems intensify as negative reactions to home and school further reduce the success–failure ratio. Many of these children are eventually diagnosed with attention deficit hyperactivity disorder (ADHD) or oppositional defiant disorder (ODD).

WHEN OUTSIDE ASSISTANCE IS NEEDED

Symptoms of social difficulty, illness, anxiety, depression, learning difficulty, abuse, substance abuse, suicide, and family discord become apparent to the knowledgeable and sensitive teacher. How do teachers decide when to seek outside consultation or referral? Although there are no rules, two general guidelines can assist with the decision. First, referral is warranted when teachers recognize that a developing problem is beyond their professional expertise. When true professionals recognize this, they act to identify and contact specialized professional assistance. Second, the more deviant, disruptive, or frequent the behaviour, the more imperative it is to make referrals. In other words, referral is necessary when either of the following occurs:

1. A misbehaving student does not improve after the hierarchical interventions described in this text have been exhausted.
2. The hierarchical approach has resulted in a small improvement, but the student continues to manifest problems that disrupt either teaching or learning. This is the kind of case where the CALM model is an important approach for the teacher to take. Clearly, some action is necessary as learning/teaching are being affected negatively.

THE REFERRAL PROCESS

When outside assistance is warranted, the teacher must have access to a network of school support personnel who are trained to cope with children with unremitting problematic classroom behaviour. Most often, the first referral is to a specially trained teacher such as a learning resource teacher or an administrator. Contact with the appropriate personnel helps to ensure that parents are not called in before the school has explored all the possible interventions at its disposal. Except for serious problems, parents/caregivers should be contacted only when it is apparent that the school has no other alternatives (Jones and Jones, 2010). Parents are apt to be responsive and cooperative if they can see a history of teacher and school interventions. Working closely with the parents of students who exhibit chronic behavioural problems is so critical that it will be discussed in depth later in this chapter (see section "Working with Parents"). First, let us look at the roles the learning resource teacher, the administrator, and the school psychologist play in school interventions.

The Role of the Learning Resource Teacher

In schools where there is a learning resource teacher on staff, teachers should contact her as soon as the decision has been made to seek outside assistance. Teachers should be prepared to present documented data on the student's misbehaviour and all approaches used in the attempt to manage the disruptive behaviour (Miltenberger, 2011). Anecdotal records and behaviour contracts (see Chapter 10, "Classroom Interventions for Chronic Problems") are excellent sources for this information.

In difficult situations, a teacher may repetitively apply strategies that do not work. As an outside observer, the learning resource teacher is quite useful. She is a neutral onlooker with a fresh view from outside the classroom who may be able to suggest modifications in the strategies or techniques the teacher has tried. The learning resource teacher may want to explore further the student's behaviour, the teacher's style, the nature of the teacher–student interaction, and the learning environment by visiting the classroom or by scheduling further conferences with the student and/or teacher, either alone or together. Once this has been done, the learning resource teacher may be able to provide more objective feedback and offer suggestions for new approaches. She may also work closely with the student to help develop more acceptable in-class behaviours.

The learning resource teacher also can help to improve the strained teacher–student relationship by acting as an intermediary, thus assisting the teacher and the student simultaneously. She can offer support to the teacher, who must cope with the stress of managing a child who exhibits chronically disruptive behaviour, and she can discuss with the student classroom problems that arise from behaviour, academics, or social interactions. Often, problems are adequately handled at this level; however, in those cases where this is not sufficient, additional consultants are called on. Typically, they include an administrator, parents, or representatives from appropriate outside agencies.

The Role of the Administrator

In many cases of chronic misbehaviour, certain in-school strategies or decisions require the authoritative and administrative power of the principal or vice-principal; for example, decisions to remove a student from a classroom for an extended period of time, to change a student's teacher, and to implement in-school or out-of-school suspensions must be approved and supported by an administrator (Smith and Hains, 2012).

Very deviant behaviour may require action at the school board level. In cases of expulsion or recommendations for placement in specialized educational settings outside the school, the administrator will be expected to provide testimony at any hearings that may be held and, thus, must be thoroughly familiar with the student's history.

The Role of the School Board Psychologist

If there are indications that a student's problems are rooted in deeper and more pervasive personality disturbances or family problems, the clinical resources of the school board psychologist should be sought. The initial role of the school board psychologist, who, in some cases, has a psychometrist to assist her, is one of evaluation and diagnostic study. Although this team will apply independent observational, interview, and testing techniques, these are really an extension of the day-to-day data that may have already been accumulated by the classroom teacher(s), other in-school learning resource teachers, and the administrator(s). The results of these evaluative studies may lead to recommendations for further study, specialized programming, or referral to outside resources.

The Role of the Consultative Team

Once the administrator(s) and possibly a learning resource teacher or psychologist are involved, a **consultative team** has been created. Although a team approach is not formalized in many schools, it can be quite effective in delineating responsibilities and keeping the lines of communication open and clearly defined. The team approach facilitates group problem solving, offers a multidisciplinary perspective, and reduces the possibility that any one individual will become overburdened with a sense of responsibility for "the problem." As with any team, a leader is needed to coordinate the team's efforts. The learning resource teacher may be a good coordinator because she is thoroughly familiar with the student and has quick access to all members of the team (Miltenberger, 2011).

Most school boards have come to realize that teachers cannot be expected to possess the expertise necessary to manage effectively all the learning and behavioural problems found in today's classrooms. To provide support in addressing these problems, school-based consultation teams that follow systematic models of assistance and/or intervention have been implemented. These teams, made up of classroom teachers, instructional support specialists, principals, parents/caregivers, and others, work together to modify the regular classroom environment to increase student achievement and improve behaviour before a student can be referred for testing for possible placement in special education. In Ontario, such a team is called the Identification, Placement, and Review Committee (IPRC); New Brunswick has Collaborative Educational Planning for Students with Exceptionalities; and British Columbia has Individual Educational Plans. At the secondary level, these teams are often made up of teachers, guidance counsellors, principals, and others who provide assistance to students who have serious personal, behavioural, and/or academic difficulties.

WORKING WITH PARENTS

When it is apparent that the teacher and the school administration have explored all the interventions at their disposal, the student's parents should be contacted. It is essential to have the support and cooperation of parents in working effectively with a chronically misbehaving student (Rogers, Wiener, Marton, and Tannock, 2009). It is imperative to minimize negativity and maximize positive support and cooperation. This takes careful planning and a great deal of skill in interpersonal interaction and conferencing techniques on the part of the consultative team members (Canter and Canter, 2001; Koshik, 2010). If the teacher has started to build a positive relationship with parents before the problem really begins, parental contacts concerning problems are likely to result in much greater parental cooperation. Many teachers send a beginning-of-the-year letter home to parents. This letter explains a little bit about the teacher and her academic and behavioural goals and hopes for the coming year. In addition to providing information about how to contact the teacher, the letter also spells out opportunities for parental involvement in the classroom and suggestions for how parents can help their child to be successful. Many effective teachers follow up on this beginning-of-the-year letter with positive messages to parents in the form of emails, telephone calls, and "good news notes."

When Parents Should Be Contacted

Parents should be contacted concerning behavioural problems under the following conditions:

1. When the student displays unremitting misbehaviour after the teacher and the school have employed all available interventions.
2. When the consultative team decides that the student needs a change in teacher or schedule.
3. When the consultative team decides that the student should be removed from a class for an extended period of time or from school for even one day.
4. When the consultative team decides that the student needs to be tested for learning, emotional, or physical difficulties.
5. When the consultative team decides that outside specialists such as psychiatrists, physicians, and social workers are required.

Son and father answer questions of a social worker in home.
© Iakov Filimonov/Shutterstock

The Importance of Working with Parents

When the school has exhausted its alternatives in attempting to manage a chronically misbehaving student, it is essential for the student's parents to be contacted and made members of the consulting team. After all, whether a student exhibits disruptive behaviour or not, all parents have the right to be informed of their child's behavioural and academic progress. Furthermore, parental support of the school has a major impact on a child's positive attitude toward school (El Nokali, Bachman, and Votruba-Drzal, 2010; Rogers, Wiener, Marton, and Tannock, 2009). When a student's parents feel good about the teacher and school, the student usually receives encouragement and reinforcement for appropriate school behaviour (Jones and Jones, 2010). Parents can, in fact, be one of the teacher's strongest allies, which is particularly helpful when the student exhibits chronic behavioural problems (El Nokali, Bachman, and Votruba-Drzal, 2010). Thus, parental support and cooperation must be cultivated by the teacher and other school staff members. To this end, programs such as parent visitation; meet-the-teacher nights; parent–teacher organizations; parent advisory boards, such as school councils; and volunteer programs have been widely instituted. As we have noted, individual teachers complement such schoolwide efforts by communicating positive aspects of children's education to their parents by sending notes and phone calls, inviting parents to call when they have any questions, and requiring students to take home graded assignments and tests.

Frequently, these children, especially when they are adolescents, are not motivated or are unresponsive to the encouragements a school can provide. Their parents, on the other hand, can provide a wider variety of more attractive encouragements. Indeed, a system of home consequences contingent on school behaviour can be an effective means for modifying classroom behaviour (Kearney, Turner, and Gauger, 2010). Such a system is illustrated in Case 11.1. Because parents usually care greatly about their children, they represent an interested party that can provide an inexpensive, continuous treatment resource to augment school efforts. The school's positive working relationship with parents often is the most critical component for effectively influencing a disruptive student.

Understanding Parents

Even though parents or caregivers may be able to offer help, teachers and other school personnel often feel uncomfortable contacting them. Some parents may harbour negative feelings toward their child's teachers and school. Teachers may feel intimidated by parents who think that teachers should be able to maintain control of their child without parental help; however, as professionals, teachers and other school staff must not allow these feelings to jeopardize the opportunity to gain the support and cooperation of parents.

If parental contacts result in distrust, apprehension, and dissatisfaction for both parents and teachers, efforts to assist the disruptive student probably will fail. In time, the parents' sense of alienation from the school will be passed onto the child, further lessening the possibility of the school working with the parents to find a means to redirect the student toward acceptable behaviour; therefore, the members of the consultative team must create an atmosphere that facilitates positive perceptions and communications. This is more easily accomplished when team members understand the parents' perspectives (Kearney, Turner, and Gauger, 2010).

CASE 11.1

In Order to Drive, You Must Speak French

Dawn is 16 years old. Her grades have gone from Bs to Ds in French and history. The decline in her academic performance is a result of inattentiveness and poor study habits. After the teacher and guidance counsellor speak to Dawn without any noticeable improvement, her parents are called.

During a conference, Dawn explains that she doesn't like French or history and doesn't see why she needs these subjects anyway. Her teachers try to explain why these subjects are important, especially in today's world, but have little success. Finally, her parents intervene and point out to Dawn that she has scheduled driver's education for the spring semester. If she expects to be able to drive, they say, she must demonstrate responsibility and discipline and one way to do so is to do well in all school subjects. They finally give Dawn a choice: either her grades improve or she will not be allowed to take driver's education and obtain her learner's permit.

Her teachers and parents keep in contact; by the end of the fall semester, Dawn's grades are again Bs.

Questions to Consider

1. What lesson(s) did Dawn learn from this experience?
2. What other methods might have been used to motivate Dawn? Discuss the likelihood of success.
3. How could/should the parents and teachers have reacted if Dawn had said that she did not care about driver's education, but that if they did not let her enroll, she would move away from home and into a friend's apartment?
4. How does the CALM model apply to this case? Discuss how it could be effective.

Many children who exhibit chronic misbehaviour in school display similar behaviours at home. Often, their parents have been frustrated by their own failures in raising their child. Since parents consider their children as extensions of themselves and products of their parenting, they are not anxious to be reminded of how inadequate they have been. Sometimes, there is a history of negative feedback from teachers and administrators that has created a feeling of powerlessness and humiliation. Because these parents feel everyone is blaming them for their child's misbehaviour, they are quite wary of any sort of school contact and react by withdrawing, resisting, or angrily counterattacking and blaming the school for the problems. This does not have to happen. Through careful planning and the use of proper conferencing skills, the school consultative team can gain the needed support and cooperation from parents (Kearney, Turner, and Gauger, 2010; Minke and Anderson, 2003).

A review of research on parental involvement in schools by Hoover-Dempsey and Sandler (1997) suggests that three major factors influence parents' decisions about whether to become involved in their child's education or not. Parents' beliefs about their role as parents as it relates to providing home support for school endeavours is one key factor. A second key factor is parents' sense of efficacy concerning their ability to help their child be successful in school. The third key factor is the parents' perceptions of the general invitation for parental involvement in the school and classroom. Schools can influence parental choice of involvement by engaging in activities that influence these three perceptions. Consistently advocating that parental involvement is a critical factor in school success can have an impact on parental role perception. Conducting workshops, classes, and courses on parental effectiveness can increase parents' sense of efficacy (Hill and Tyson, 2009). Finally, making sure that the general school and individual classroom climates welcome parental involvement can influence parents to become more actively involved in their child's education. Welcoming climates are marked by a variety of factors, including frequent positive parental contact, face-to-face interaction at times that are convenient for parents, and opportunities for parents to influence decisions that will affect their children (Kearney, Turner, and Gauger, 2010).

Conducting Parent Conferences

When the consultative team determines that conditions warrant parental (or caregiver) involvement, the school principal or team coordinator usually makes the first contact. The tone of this initial contact is extremely important in developing a cooperative working relationship. The principal or team coordinator should expect some degree of defensiveness on the part of the parent, especially if the student has had a history of school misbehaviour. This attitude should be understood and not taken personally. The cause of the school's concern should be stated clearly and honestly. The climate of the conversation should be, "How can we work as a team to best meet your child's needs?" rather than "Here we go again!" or "We've done everything we can. Now, it's up to you."

Once a conference has been scheduled, the team must decide who will attend the conference. The answers depend on the particular problem, the amount of expertise needed to explain the situation and the approaches that have been tried, and who will need to be available to answer any questions that may arise. In addition, the conference must be conducted in a positive manner that is least threatening to the parents. This often means the fewer people present, the less threatening the conference appears to parents. In most circumstances, the initial conference is conducted by the team coordinator. Unless the problem includes discussing behaviour or other signs that indicate serious health, emotional, or legal problems, the student may be present.

The conference should begin by introducing all in attendance, thanking the parents for their willingness to attend, and outlining the goal of the conference. Throughout the conference, everyone should have an equal chance to express her viewpoint. School personnel also look for any signs that indicate that the conference is deteriorating into a debate or blaming session and act rapidly to defuse the situation by directing the conference back to the major purpose of how best to meet the student's needs.

Obviously, appropriate interpersonal and conferencing skills must be familiar to and practised by all professionals in attendance (Javed, Eng, Mushag, and Hashim, 2012). Some of these skills include being friendly, being supportive, and using active listening (which includes paraphrasing) to ensure proper understanding by all (see Chapter 10). The teacher should be prepared to include positive characteristics about the student. Information should be elicited through the use of questions rather than directive statements aimed at the student or parents/caregivers. Neither the child nor the parents should be attacked, disparaged, or blamed; however, sometimes parents and the student attack, disparage, and blame the teacher or other school officials. If this occurs, it is important to remember that one does not defend one's professional competence with words, but with behaviour. One of the best means to demonstrate professional competence is through the use of previously collected data that illustrate and demonstrate the concerns of the school and the need for the conference. The data should include a history of objective and specific information about the student's behaviours and the actions taken by the teacher and the school to manage them. Anecdotal records are an excellent source for this data (see Chapter 10). The use of these data reduces the likelihood of the conference turning into a debate, illustrates that the problem is not exaggerated, and defuses any attempt by the parent to suggest that the school did not take appropriate and necessary actions.

Throughout the conference, the parents' and student's feelings, viewpoints, and suggestions should be actively solicited. The outcome of the conference, it is hoped, will be either an agreed-upon course of action or the decision that the school will contact the parents in the near future with a suggested course of action. The meeting ends on an optimistic note with a summary, a show of appreciation, and an encouraging statement that with both the home and school working as a team, a successful outcome is likely.

With some students, additional school and/or classroom strategies that include little additional parental involvement could be tried. This decision is usually a result of new information that allows the school to design additional appropriate strategies or a result of the parents' response to the situation, like Sharon's mother in Case 11.2, which clearly demonstrate their lack of interest. Sharon's mother is atypical, not because she is uninterested but because she openly and honestly admits it. Sometimes, when parents are uninterested, there is a tendency on the part of the school personnel to give up and adopt an attitude that "if they don't care, then we've done what we can." However, children should never be denied access to potentially effective school intervention programs because their parents are uninterested, uncooperative, or unsupportive (Karila and Alasuutari, 2012).

When it is obvious that parental involvement will probably improve the child's behaviour significantly or there is evidence of a deficiency in parenting skills, increased parental involvement may be requested. Some school boards now provide information about parenting classes held in their community.

SYMPTOMS OF SERIOUS PROBLEMS

Some students display symptoms of serious problems that may or may not be accompanied by disruptive and/or academic difficulties. These problems may be related to physical or emotional health or associated with an abusive home or with substance abuse. All of these areas may fall outside the expertise and domain of the school. An alert teacher often recognizes these symptoms and notifies the appropriate school official who then decides on the proper step.

Some of the signs that may be significant include the following:

1. *Changes in physical appearance.* Often, students reveal their underlying problems through sudden changes in their physical appearance. Posture, dress, and grooming habits are reflections of underlying mood and self-image, and a student's deterioration in these habits should be noted with concern. More striking changes such as rapid weight loss or gain, particularly in light of the dramatic increase in eating disorders among high school students, should be investigated. While unusual soreness, bruises, cuts, or scarring are signs of possible neglect or abuse, they may also indicate self-mutilation or other self-destructive tendencies.

CONCENTRIC CASE STUDY KALEIDOSCOPE

CASE 11.2

"I'm Not Much Help to Her"

The Story

Sharon is in grade 10. Her behaviour is excellent. She is of average intelligence, always completes assignments and consistently achieves average marks. In addition, she is rarely absent, is well dressed and has a number of friends. Overall, she appears to be a typical happy grade 10 student; however, she always asks one of her teachers if she can stay in order to help with anything. If there is nothing for her to do, she merely sits and talks. She seems quite content to spend her spare time in this way, and the teachers have become used to her patterns of behaviour. As the term end approaches and her marks are compiled, Sharon's teachers are startled to discover that she will receive all Ds and Fs rather than her usual Cs and Bs.

As Sharon's new slate of marks emerges, her teachers begin to speak to her about the sudden change in her achievement levels. One of them also refers her to the vice-principal for counselling. Throughout all discussions, Sharon maintains that she is happy and that nothing is wrong. In an attempt to help Sharon, extra remedial help is offered but there is no evidence of improved achievement.

Before report cards are issued, the vice-principal schedules a conference with Sharon, her mother, and her teachers. The vice-principal is concerned that Sharon is failing, and she wants to make sure that her mother is apprised of the situation before the report card arrives home.

When Sharon's mother arrives, she appears well dressed, well spoken, and somewhat concerned about Sharon's drop in achievement. As each teacher present talks about Sharon's poor performance in the class,

Sharon's mother appears to listen carefully and looks very serious. When it is her turn to respond she says, "Sharon's dad left us ten years ago. Since then, I have been a single mother devoting myself to raising my daughter. But now that she is older, I need to focus on my own life, look after myself, and get things moving in the right direction. Now I am busy. I have a career and I do a lot of internet dating. To be perfectly honest, I buy Sharon's clothes and make sure that she eats properly, but that is all the time I have. I owe something to myself now and I am not getting any younger." There is a short silence and Sharon's mother continues earnestly, "I would really appreciate anything you can do for Sharon because I know that I'm not much help to her at this time. I have to go now, as I have an important date. Sorry about that."

When she leaves, there is a silence. One of the teachers asks, "What can we do for Sharon?"

Sharon's Perspective

I really like school and I really like my teachers! I know that I am one of the few students who wish that the day would not end. Most of my teachers seem to like me, and if I stay around them after school, they will talk to me. This part of the afternoon is very important for me, and I finally go home feeling good about my day. When I get home, my mother is usually too busy to really talk to me. She always gets dinner and we eat together, but the phone usually rings and she talks to her boyfriends during dinner. I wish she would talk to me more. Sometimes, I think she forgets that I am in the house.

(Continued)

(*Continued*)

I know I have been neglecting my homework and my studying this past term. I am not sure why, but I just don't feel like working hard. It does not seem to be worth the effort at this point. Whether I get good marks or not doesn't seem to matter to anyone, so why should I care? I really don't think my mother would notice one way or the other. In any case, she never asks me about my work and never reminds me to do my homework like she used to.

I miss my old relationship with my mother. We used to talk and laugh and she used to tell me what to do. I didn't always like it but at least she paid attention to me. I know she has been called to the school to talk about the fact that I am not doing very well in my classes. She is going to have to think about me, anyway. In fact, in a way I am glad that the school called her—she seems to have forgotten that I have to do my work if I am going to get good marks.

Sharon's Mother

The school has called to ask me to come and talk about Sharon's marks. I know I should pay more attention to Sharon, but right now I have to think about my own future. I am really tired of struggling as a single mother and feeling so lonely. Sharon is now in high school and I have given her 15 years of my life. I am not getting any younger or more attractive. This may be my last chance to find happiness in a good relationship. I have determined to put my focus there now, and I am going to succeed. I feel good about myself for the first time in years.

At times, I feel a bit guilty about neglecting Sharon, but she is older now and should be able to run her own life and do her homework without constant reminders and interaction with me. I look after the bills; she has a roof over her head and food on the table. She should be fine.

I wonder why she is not doing as well as usual in school. I guess the school will want me to take responsibility for her marks as well. No one really understands how hard it is to be in charge of everything. Am I supposed to sacrifice my whole life for the sake of my daughter? Why is it my fault if a mature child cannot take responsibility for her work? After all, I have taken responsibility for her for most of her life. It is her turn now.

I can sense that the teachers are concerned and that they are being judgmental about my decisions to have fun while I can. I don't care. They are the professionals. They are the ones who are supposed to understand adolescents. It is their job to teach her. I am doing my half and expect them to do theirs. I am glad I was open and honest with them so they will know exactly how I feel.

One of Sharon's Teachers

I like Sharon and I'm disappointed in her marks this term. I know that when she stays behind after school she wants to talk. For some reason, she appears to need attention which did not appear to be her typical behaviour prior to this term. I wonder what has changed in her life. Also, I see that all her marks are lower. Something is certainly going on in her life, which is causing her to react negatively. I'm glad we decided to call her mother in for a talk about this issue.

Now that I see Sharon's mother, I am shocked. She has obviously been paying a very great deal of attention to her appearance. She's trying to look younger than her daughter; instead, she just looks silly. After hearing her talk about her desire to date and find a new relationship, it's obvious that she is paying little attention to Sharon's needs. Although Sharon's physical needs are being met, it is equally clear that there's an emotional hole in her life. I feel bad about that.

I am really too busy with my own issues, my own children, and my own career to take over the kind of relationship that Sharon needs. I believe that parents rely on the school too much to do parenting as well as teaching. I simply do not have the time and I'm not paid to take care of other people's children. If I tried to help all neglected children, I would have no life of my own and my family would suffer. Sharon will have to find another way to cope and perhaps there is someone else she can talk to. I wonder if I should call a counsellor.

Another of Sharon's Teachers

I like Sharon and am sorry to see that she has been less effective as a student this past term. Clearly, something is wrong in her life and I'm really glad that we have called a meeting to address the problem with her mother before it's too late to remedy the problem.

I am shocked by Sharon's mother's appearance, as she's clearly done herself up to look very young and to attract attention. The mother feels she has spent enough time

raising her daughter and now wants to go forward in her own life. I wish her luck, although I am not sure she is going about attaining her goals in a sensible manner. If anything is going to change for Sharon and her emotional needs are to be met, it will clearly have to be by someone other than her mother.

I think that I will have to respond to this situation by trying to help Sharon. I wonder if there is a Big Sister program in the area, and if the school board has a counsellor who can help. Maybe Sharon has a grandmother who is in the area. I wonder what I can do.

Questions to Consider

1. Whose responsibility is it to see that Sharon's emotional needs are met?
2. What specific actions would you take in this case if Sharon were your student?
3. What should the school vice-principal do next?
4. Do you think students such as Sharon are frequently found in our schools? Explain.
5. Set up a role-playing scenario similar to the one discussed in this case and construct a dialogue between the two teachers.

2. *Changes in activity level.* Teachers need to be aware of the significance of changes in activity level. Excessive tardiness, lethargy, absenteeism, and a tendency to fall asleep in class may result from a variety of problems, including depression and substance abuse. Hyperactivity, impulsivity, lowered frustration and tolerance thresholds, and over-aggressiveness also may represent the student's effort to deal with emotional unrest and discomfort.

3. *Changes in personality.* Emotional disturbances in children and adolescents are sometimes reflected in very direct forms of expression and behaviour. The seemingly well-adjusted child who is suddenly sad, easily agitated, or has angry outbursts uncharacteristic of her prior behaviour should be closely observed and monitored.

4. *Changes in achievement status.* A decline in a student's ability to focus on her work, to persist at her studies, or to produce or complete work successfully is often an indication of the draining effects of emotional turmoil or significant changes in the home environment.

5. *Changes in health or physical abilities.* Complaints of not being able to see or hear, when it appears the student is paying attention, should be referred to health professionals for follow-up. Complaints of frequent headaches, stomach aches, dizziness, sores that will not heal, skin rashes, and frequent bathroom use are signs that you should be concerned about the student's health.

6. *Changes in socialization.* Children who spend most of the time by themselves, seem to have no friends, and are socially withdrawn are not often identified as problem students because their symptoms do not have a disturbing impact on the classroom. These students may drift from one grade to another without appropriate attention and concern; however, they often leave a sign of their underlying misery in their behaviour, artwork, and creative writing samples.

In most cases of serious problems, schools are able to arrange for or make referrals to a host of specialized professionals, including psychologists, psychiatrists, nutritionists, medical doctors, social workers, and legal authorities; however, appropriate intervention rests with the aware and concerned teacher who must make the initial observations and referral.

LEGAL ASPECTS OF SEEKING OUTSIDE ASSISTANCE

There are some legal issues that must be considered to protect children's and parents'/caregivers' rights when seeking outside assistance. Most school boards are aware of these laws and have developed appropriate procedures to abide by them. In addition, all provinces have laws that require teachers to report any signs of child abuse. Many of these laws have provisions that impose penalties on school personnel who fail to meet this responsibility.

Summary

Some students simply do not experience the degree of success in the classroom that supports the development and maintenance of appropriate behaviour. Their conduct problems remain unremitting despite the application of appropriate hierarchical strategies, or they show other signs and symptoms indicative of serious underlying disturbances. In these cases, some type of specialized or out-of-school assistance may be required.

A team approach, which may include the student, parents, teacher(s), learning resource teacher, administrator(s), and outside specialists, is an effective means for expanded evaluation and for the development of specific interventions that may extend beyond the normal classroom. The support and cooperation of parents is critical to increase the likelihood of successful intervention. Any negative parental attitudes must be defused. This is best accomplished through careful planning and the skilled use of conferencing techniques when working with parents. Protecting students' rights throughout any process focused on managing misbehaviour is paramount.

Key Terms

consultative team: a team approach that facilitates group problem solving, offers a multidisciplinary perspective, and reduces the possibility that any one individual will become overburdened with a sense of responsibility for "the problem."

outside assistance: needed when a teacher recognizes that a problem is beyond her expertise and outside referral and consultation are necessary.

Exercises

1. The student's success–failure ratio is an extremely important variable that influences student behaviour. There are many areas in which students experience success and failure, including academic, social, and extracurricular areas. List several specific areas in a school setting in which students can experience success or failure.

2. The importance of success in specific areas depends on the student's age. Using the list of specific areas for success developed in the first exercise, rate each area's importance for students in elementary, middle, junior high, and senior high school.

3. Develop a list of symptoms that could be added to the list of potentially serious problems that may warrant outside assistance. Be able to justify why each symptom should be included on the list.

4. Are there any dangers associated with using a list similar to the one developed in the third exercise? Before answering, consider such areas as contextual setting, duration and severity of behaviour, and so on. If there are dangers, what can a teacher do to minimize them?

5. Even when students are not exhibiting behavioural problems, it is important for teachers to gain the support of parents. In what ways can teachers develop such support?

6. Compose a beginning-of-the-school-year letter that you could send to parents. In the letter, be sure to include information about yourself, your classroom, your hopes and goals for the coming year, and ideas about how parents can become involved in supporting their child's success. Also include contact information so parents can reach you. Make sure that the letter is free of educational jargon.

7. Sometimes, teachers may decide to contact the parents before consulting a student's administrators. When should parents be contacted before the administrators?

8. In consultation with your instructor, contact a school (use your own school if you are currently teaching) and identify all the resources available to assist teachers with seriously misbehaving students.

9. Children with ADHD and ODD are in mainstreamed classrooms. Research the behaviours these children exhibit, and suggest or research strategies that are effective in managing these children.

10. It has been said that if a teacher is a good teacher for difficult children, she will be an excellent teacher for all the children in her class. Explain what this means.

Weblinks

The Canadian Home and School Federation

http://www.bccpac.bc.ca/canadian-home-school-federation-chsf
The website describes the role of parents in education today.

Centre for Addiction and Mental Health

www.camh.net
This site has many resources—one article is entitled, "Mischief or a Cry for Help? Disciplining Students Demands Awareness of Underlying Distress."

Children's Mental Health Ontario

http://www.kidsmentalhealth.ca
"Children's Mental Health Ontario (CMHO) represents and supports the providers of child and youth mental health treatment services throughout Ontario."

Edmonton Public Schools Board Policies and Regulations

http://www.epsb.ca/ourdistrict/boardpoliciesadministrativeregulations/h-students/hgbpstudentbehaviourandconduct/
From the Edmonton School Board, this document is entitled "Student behaviour and conduct" and includes policy for issues like "Student rights and responsibilities" and "Student behaviour and conduct."

Fourth Analysis

Considering the concepts discussed in Parts III and IV, reanalyze your third analysis. What has changed and what has stayed the same since your last analysis? Once again, consider why the students may be choosing to behave inappropriately and how you might intervene to influence the students to stop the disruptive behaviour and resume appropriate on-task behaviour.

Elementary School Case Study

During silent reading time in my grade 4 class, I have built-in opportunities to work individually with students. During this time, the students read to me and practice word work with flash cards. One student has refused to read to me but instead wants only to work with the flash cards. After a few sessions, I suggested we work with word cards this time and begin reading the next time. He agreed. The next time we met, I reminded him of our plan, and he screamed, "I don't remember! I want to do word cards!" At this point, I tried to find out why he didn't like reading and he said, "There's a reason, I just can't tell you," and he threw the word cards across the room, some of them hitting other students. What should I do?

Middle School Case Study

I can't stop thinking about a problem I'm having in class with a group of 12-year-old boys. They consistently use profanities toward one another and some of the shyer kids in the class, especially the girls. In addition, they are always pushing and shoving each other. I've tried talking to them about why they keep using bad language when they know it's inappropriate. The response I get is that "'cause my buddies do it." I have implored them to use more appropriate language in the classroom but that has not worked. I haven't even started to address the pushing and shoving. What should I do?

High School Case Study

This past week, I had a student approach me about a problem he was experiencing in our class. The grade 11 student had recently "come out" as being gay. He said he was tired and upset with the three boys who sit near him. These boys frequently call him a "homo" and a "fag" every time they see him, both in and out of class. What should I do?

REFERENCES

Chapter 1

Anderson, S. (2002). Teachers talk about instruction. *Orbit, 32*(4), 22–26.

Bandura, A. (1977). *Social Learning Theory.* New York: General Learning Press.

Bembenutty, H., and Chen, P. P. (2005). Self-efficacy and delay of gratification. *Academic Exchange Quarterly, 9*(4), 78–86.

Berk, L. E. (2014). Development Through the Lifespan, 6/e. Boston: Pearson Education

Boudourides, M. A. (2003). Constructivism, education, science, and technology, *Canadian Journal of Learning and Technology, 29*(3) Fall/automne.

Charles, C. M., and Senter, G. W. (2004). *Building classroom Discipline,* 8th edition. Boston MA: Allyn & Bacon.

Evertson, C. M., and Weistein, C. S. (2006). *Handbook of Classroom Management: Research, Practice and Contemporary Issues. Abingdon.* Oxford: Routledge.

Holt, C., Hargrove, P., and Harris, S. (2011). An Investigation into the Life Experiences and Beliefs of Teachers Exhibiting Highly Effective Classroom Management Behaviors. *Teacher Education and Practice, 24*(1), 96–113.

Horner, R. H., Sugai, G., Lewis-Palmer, T., and Todd, A. W. (2001). Teaching school-wide behavioral expectations. *Report on Emotional and Behavioral Disorders in Youth, 1*(4), 77–79, 93–96.

Lomas, J., and Stough, C. (2012). Improving emotional intelligence in schools-the research project. *TLN Journal, 19*(1), 37–39.

Loughran, J. (2012). *What expert teachers do: Enhancing professional knowledge for classroom practice.* Oxford: Routledge.

Mayer, J. D., Salovey, P., and Carus, D. R. (2004). Emotional intelligence: Theory, findings, and implications, *Psychological Inquiry, 15*(3), 197–215.

McLeskey, J., Rosenberg, M.S., and Westling, D. L. (2013). Inclusion: Effective practices for all students. (2nd ed.). Upper Saddle River, NJ: Pearson Education, Inc.

Miller, R., and Pedro, J. (2006). Creating Respectful Classroom environments. *Early childhood Education Journal, 33*(5), 293–299.

Novak, J. D. (2010). *Learning, creating, and using knowledge: Concept maps as facilitative tools in schools and corporations.* New York: Routledge.

Piaget, J. (1975). *The Development of Thought: Equilibration of Cognitive Structures.* New York: Viking.

Poulou, M. (1995). The prevention of emotional behavioural difficulties in schools: Teachers suggestions. *Educational Psychology in Practice, 21*(10), 37–52.

Prochaska, J. O., and Norcross, J. C. (2013). *Systems of psychotherapy: A transtheoretical analysis.* Pacific Grove, CA: Brooks/Cole Publishing Company.

Shrigley, R. L. (1985). Curbing student disruption in the classroom—teachers need intervention skills. *National Association of Secondary School Principals Bulletin, 69*(479), 26–32.

Sweeney, T. J. (1981). *Adlerian Counseling: Proven Concepts and Strategies* (2nd ed.). Muncie, IN: Accelerated Development.

Vargas, J. S. (2013). *Behavior analysis for effective teaching.* New York: Routledge.

Vygotsky, L. S. (1978). *Mind in Society.* Cambridge, MA: Harvard University Press.

Watts, R. E. (Ed.) (2003). *Adlerian, Cognitive, and Constructivist Therapies. An Integrative Dialogue.* New York: Springer Publishing Company.

Wessler, S., and Preble, W. (2003). *The Respectful School.* Alexandria, VA: Association for Supervision & Curriculum Development.

Zimmerman, B. J., and Schunk, D. H. (Eds.). (2013). *Self-regulated learning and academic achievement: Theoretical perspectives.* New York: Routledge.

Chapter 2

Highbeam Business. (2003). One-quarter of teachers subjected to violence last year (Canada: Nova Scotia). Article from National Post, February 15, 2003. Retrieved July 28, 2014, from http://business.

highbeam.com/435424/article-1G1-98592286/onequarter-teachers-subjected-violence-last-year.

Ahles, P., and Contento, J. M. (2006). Explaining helping behavior in a cooperative learning classroom setting using Attribution Theory. *Community College Journal of Research & Practice, 30*(8), 609–626.

Alderman, M. K. (2013). *Motivation for achievement: Possibilities for teaching and learning.* New York: Routledge.

Allen, J., Murray, M., and Simmons, K. (2013). *Helping Your Pupils to be Resilient.* New York: Routledge.

Angus Reid Group. (1999). Canadian teens voice their opinions on violence in their schools. Retrieved April 15, 2003, from www.angusreid.com/search/pdf/media/pr990503%5F1.pdf.

Arum, R. (2003). *Judging School Discipline: The Crisis of Moral Authority.* Cambridge, MA: Harvard University Press.

Baker, K. (1985). Research evidence of a school discipline problem. *Phi Delta Kappan, 66*(7), 482–488.

Bear, G. (2010). School Discipline and Self-Discipline: *A Practical Guide to Promoting Prosocial Student Behavior.* New York: The Guildford Press.

Bender, D., and Lösel, F. (2011). Bullying at school as a predictor of delinquency, violence and other anti-social behaviour in adulthood. *Criminal Behaviour and Mental Health, 21*(2), 99–106.

Benn, R. (2002). Bullying behaviour not tolerated says school board. Retrieved March 14, 2007, from www.peacefulcommunities.ca/2002/October/oct11.htm.

Bonta, J., and Hanson, R. K. (1994). *Gauging the Risk of Violence: Measurement, Impact and Strategies for Change.* Ottawa, ON: Solicitor General of Canada.

Brendtro, L. K., Brokenleg, M., and Van Bockern, S. (1990). *Reclaiming Youth at Risk: Our Hope for the Future.* Bloomington, IN: National Educational Service.

Brophy, J. (1988). Research on teacher effects: Uses and abuses. *The Elementary School Journal, 89*(1), 3–21.

Canada Education. (2013). What Engages Teachers? A view from the west coast. Retrieved October 25, 2013 from http://www.cea-ace.ca/education-canada/article/what-engages-teachers.

Canadian Teachers' Federation. (2002). National study confirms CTF concerns about teacher recruitment and retention. Retrieved April 15, 2003, from www.ctf-fce.ca/e/press/2002/pr02-2.htm.

Canter, L. (1989). Assertive discipline: More than names on the board and marbles in a jar. *Phi Delta Kappan, 71*(1), 57–61.

Clement, M. C. (2010). Preparing teachers for classroom management: The teacher educator's role. *Delta Kappa Gamma Bulletin, 77*(1), 41–44.

Craig, W. M., and Pepler, D. J. (2007). Understanding bullying: From research to practice. *Canadian Psychology, 48*(2), 86–93.

Crux, S. C. (1993). Why is violence in our schools? *Brock Education, 3*(1), 23–24.

Darling-Hammond, L. (2012). *Powerful teacher education: Lessons from exemplary programs.* New York: John Wiley & Sons.

Department of the Solicitor General of Canada. (2002). School-based violence prevention in Canada: Results of a national survey of policies and programs. Retrieved April 2, 2003, from www.sgc.gc.ca/publications/corrections/199502_e.asp.

Dreikurs, R. (1964). *Children the Challenge.* New York: Hawthorn.

Fang, B. and Dvorak, J. (2013). Using Technology to Increase Quality Time on Task. Retrieved November 26, 2013, from http://www.educause.edu/ero/article/using-technology-increase-quality-time-task.

Feitler, F., and Tokar, E. (1992). Getting a handle on teacher stress: How bad is the problem? *Educational Leadership, 49*, 456–458.

Hawes, J. M. (1971). *Children in Urban Society: Juvenile Delinquency in Nineteenth Century America.* New York: Oxford University Press.

Holt, R. (2007). Edmonton public schools student behaviour and conduct policy. Retrieved March 14, 2007, from www.epsb.ca/datafiles/parents/English_Student_Conduct_Brochure.pdf.

Hong, J. S., and Espelage, D. L. (2012). A review of research on bullying and peer victimization in school: An ecological system analysis. *Aggression and Violent Behavior, 17*(4), 311–322.

Housego, B. E. J. (1990). Student teachers' feelings of preparedness to teach. *Canadian Journal of Education, 15*(1), 37–56.

Huber, J. D. (1984). Discipline in the middle school—parent, teacher, and principal concerns. *National Association of Secondary School Principals Bulletin, 68*(471), 74–79.

Ipsos-Reid. (1999). Canadians' assessment and views of the education system. Retrieved April 15, 2003, from www.ipsos-reid.com/pdf/publicat/RRtoc_9903.pdf.

James, A. (2010). School bullying. Retrieved November 27, 2013 from http://www.nspcc.org.uk/inform/research/briefings/school_bullying_pdf_wdf73502.pdf.

James, J. M. (1993). Conflict resolution: programs and strategies at the secondary level. *Orbit, 24*(1), 26–27.

Janosz, M., Archambault, I., Pagani, L. S., Morin, A. J. S., and Bower, F. (2008). Are there detrimental effects of witnessing school violence in early adolescence? *Journal of Adolescent Health, 43*, 600–608.

Jina, S. Y. (2002). Negative affect and self-efficacy. *Social Behavior & Personality, 30*(5), 485–493.

Johnson, K. (2012). *Building Better Schools not Prisons: A Review of the Literature Surrounding School Suspension and Expulsion Programs and the Implications of Such Programs on the Lives of Racial and Ethinc Minority Students*. Doctoral dissertation, University of Toronto.

Kounin, J. (1970). *Discipline and Group Management in Classrooms*. New York: Holt, Rinehart and Winston.

Leger Marketing. (2002). How Canadians feel about the educational system. Retrieved April 15, 2003, from www.queensu.ca/cora/polls/2002/September16-Perception_of_Education_System.pdf.

Li, Q. (2006). Cyberbullying in schools: A research of gender differences. *School Psychology International, 27*(2), 157–170.

Li, Q. (2007). New bottle but old wine: A research of cyberbullying in schools. *Computers in Human Behavior, 23*(4), 1777–1791.

Lomas, J., and Stough, C. (2012). Improving emotional intelligence in schools—the research project. *TLN Journal, 19*(1), 37.

Looker, E. D., and Theissen, V. (2003). The digital divide in Canadian schools: Factors affecting student access to and use of information technology. *Research Data Centre, Statistics Canada*, Catalogue No. 81-597-XIE.

MacDougall, J. (1993). *Violence in the School: Programs and Policies for Prevention*. Toronto, ON: Canadian Education Association.

Marini, Z., Spear, S., and Bombay, K. (1999). Peer victimization in middle childhood: Characteristics, causes and consequences of school bullying. *Brock Education, 9*, 32–47.

Martin, J. M., Dworet, D. H., and Davis, C. (1997). The secondary student with behaviour disorders: A puzzle worth solving. *Exceptionality Education Canada, 6*(3 and 4), 183–201.

Mennell, R. M. (1973). *Thorns and Thistles: Juvenile Delinquents in the United States 1825–1940*. Hanover, NH: The University Press of New England.

Novak, J. M., and Purkey, W. W. (2001). *Invitational Education*. Bloomington, IN: Phi Delta Kappa Educational Foundation.

O'Connell, P., Pepler, D., and Craig, W. (1999). Peer involvement in bullying: Insights and challenges for intervention. *Journal of Adolescence, 22*(4), 437–452.

Olweus, D. (1991). Bully/victim problems among school children: some basic facts and effects of a school-based intervention program. In D. Pepler and K. Rubin (Eds.), *The Development and Treatment of Childhood Aggression*. Hillsdale, NJ: Erlbaum, 411–438.

Ontario Ministry of Education. (2012). Progressive Discipline and Promoting Positive Student Behaviour. Retrieved October 23, 2013, from http://www.edu.gov.on.ca/extra/eng/ppm/145.pdf.

Ontario Ministry of Labour. (2010). Supporting a Health and Safety Culture in Ontario. Retrieved XXXX, from http://www.labour.gov.on.ca/english/hs/prevention/report/supporting.php.

Palumbo, A., and Sanacore, J. (2007). Classroom management: Help for the beginning secondary school teacher. *Clearing House, 82*(2), 67–70.

Patus, M. (1993). Managing aggressive tendencies in adolescents. *Brock Education, 3*(1), 19–22.

Pepler, D., and Craig, W. (1995). A peek behind the fence: Naturalistic observations of aggressive children with remote audiovisual recording. *Developmental Psychology, 31*, 548–553.

Pepler, D., and Craig, W. (2011). Promoting relationships and eliminating violence in Canada. *International Journal of Behavioral Development, 35*(5), 389–397.

Reinke, W., Lewis-Palmer, T., and Merrell, K. (2008). The classroom check-up: A classwide teacher consultation model for increasing praise and decreasing disruptive behavior. *School Psychology, 37*(3), 315–332.

Reupert, A., and Woodcock, S. (2011). Canadian and Australian pre-service teachers' use, confidence and success in various behaviour management strategies. *International Journal of Educational Research, 50*(5), 271–281.

Rieg, S. A., Paquette, K. R., and Chen, Y. (2010). Coping with stress: An investigation of novice teachers' stressors in the elementary classroom. *Educational Sciences: Theory & Practice, 10*(2), 881–891.

Roher, E. M. (1993). Violence in a school setting. *Brock Education, 3*(1), 1–4.

Romano, M., and Gibson, P. (2006). Beginning teacher successes and struggles: An elementary teacher's reflections on the first year of teaching. *Professional Educator, 28*(1), 1–16.

Roy, I. (1993). Violence is preventable: How some schools are educating students to be peacemakers. *Brock Education, 3*(1), 16–18.

Schlossman, S. L. (1977). *Love and the American Delinquent: The Theory and Practice of "Progressive" Juvenile Justice, 1825–1920*. Chicago: University of Chicago Press.

Seligman, M. E. (2011). *Learned optimism: How to change your mind and your life*. New York: Random House Digital, Inc.

Sharma, U., Loreman, T., and Forlin, C. (2012). Measuring teacher efficacy to implement inclusive practices. *Journal of Research in Special Educational Needs, 12*(1), 12–21.

Skaalvik, E. M., and Skaalvik, S. (2011). Teacher job satisfaction and motivation to leave the teaching profession: Relations with school context, feeling of belonging, and emotional exhaustion. *Teaching and Teacher Education, 27*(6), 1029–1038.

Skaalvik, E. M., and Skaalvik, S. (2010). Teacher self-efficacy and teacher burnout: A study of relations. *Teaching and Teacher Education, 26*(4), 1059–1069.

Smith, O. B. (1969). Discipline. In R. L. Ebel, *Encyclopedia of Educational Research* (4th ed.). New York: Macmillan.

Statistics Canada. (1999). Education indicators in Canada: Report of the Pan-Canadian Education Indicators Program, 1999. Retrieved June 3, 2003, from www.statcan.ca/english/freepub/81-582-XIE/free.htm.

Statistics Canada. (2003). Tech and teens: Access and use. Retrieved February 12, 2003, from www.statcan.ca/english/freepub/11-008-XIE/0010311-008-XIE.pdf.

Statistics Canada. (2009). Self-reported Violent Delinquency and the Influence of School, Neighbourhood and Student Characteristics. Retrieved July 28, 2014, from http://www.statcan.gc.ca/pub/85-561-m/85-561-m2009017-eng.htm

Statistics Canada. (2011). Police-reported crime statistics in Canada, 2011. Ottawa. Retrieved October 23, 2013, from http://www.statcan.gc.ca/pub/85-002-x/2012001/article/11692-eng.htm#a17.

Statistics Canada. (2012). Less than one-half of youth accused are formally charged by police. Ottawa. Retrieved July 31, 2014, from http://www.statcan.gc.ca/pub/85-002-x/2012001/article/11692-eng.htm#a16.

Statistics Canada, (2013). The Daily—Canadian Internet Use Survey, 2012. Ottawa. Retrieved July 31, 2014, from http://www.statcan.gc.ca/daily-quotidien/131126/dq131126d-eng.htm.

Statistics Canada. (2011). Less than one-half of youth accused are formally charged by police. Ottawa. Retrieved October 23, 2013, from http://www.statcan.gc.ca/pub/85-002-x/2012001/article/11692-eng.htm#a16.

Taylor-Butts, A., and Bressan, A. (2006). Youth Crime in Canada, 2006. *Juristat Canadian Centre for Justice Statistics. Statistics Canada-Catalogue no. 85-2002-XIE, 28*(2).

Thomas, G. T., Goodall, R., and Brown, L. (1983). Discipline in the classroom: Perceptions of middle grade teachers. *The Clearinghouse, 57*(3), 139–142.

Walsh, D. (1983). Our schools come to order. *American Teacher, 68*, 1.

Wayson, W. W. (1985). The politics of violence in school: Doublespeak and disruptions in public confidence. *Phi Delta Kappan, 67*(2), 127–132.

Weber, T. R., and Sloan, C. A. (1986). How does high school discipline in 1984 compare to previous decades? *The Clearinghouse, 59*(7), 326–329.

Weiner, B. (1980). A cognitive (attribution)–emotion–action, model of motivated behaviour: An analysis of judgments of help-giving. *Journal of Personality and Social Psychology, 39*, 186–200.

Winzer, M. (2002). *Children with Exceptionalities in Canadian Classrooms* (6th ed.). Don Mills, ON: Prentice Hall.

Yang, K. W. (2009). Discipline of punish? Some suggestions for school policy and teacher practice. *Language Arts, 87*(1), 49–61.

Yoon, J. S. (2002). Teacher characteristics as predictors of teacher-student relationship: Stress, negative affect and self-efficacy. *Social Behavior & Personality: An International Journal, 30*(5), 485–494.

Chapter 3

Active Healthy Kids Canada. (2012). Sedentary Behaviours. Retrieved December 18, 2013, from http://www.activehealthykids.ca/ReportCard/SedentaryBehaviours.aspx.

Adler, I. (1966, December). Mental growth and the art of teaching. *The Mathematics Teacher, 59*, 706–715.

Alphonso, C. (2003, November 19). Schoolyard bullies ape violence on TV, study for teachers finds. *The Globe and Mail*, 1.

Amato, P. R. (2000). The consequences of divorce for adults and children. *Journal of Marriage and Family, 62*(4), 1269–1287.

American Psychiatric Association. (2002). Psychiatric effects of media violence. Retrieved from http://www.pysh.org/public_info/media_violence.cfm.

American Psychological Association. (1993). *Violence and Youth: Psychology's Response*, Vol. 1. Washington, DC.

Anderson, C. A., Gentile, D. A., and Buckley, K. E. (2007). *Violent video game effects on children and adolescents: Theory, research and policy*. New York, NY: Oxford University Press.

Anderson, C. A., Shibuya, A., Ihori, N., Swing, E. L., Bushman, B. J., Sakamoto, A., and Saleem, M. (2010). Violent video game effects on aggression, empathy, and prosocial behavior in eastern and western countries: a meta-analytic review. *Psychological bulletin, 136*(2), 151.

Bandura, A. (1973). *Aggression: A Social Learning Analysis*. Englewood Cliffs, NJ: Prentice Hall.

Banks, J. (2008). Diversity and citizenship education in global times. *Education for citizenship and democracy*, 57–70.

Barton, P. E., and Coley, R. J. (2007). The family: America's smallest school. Princeton, NJ: Educational Testing Services.

Bender, D., and Lösel, F. (2011). Bullying at school as a predictor of delinquency, violence and other anti-social behaviour in adulthood. *Criminal Behaviour and Mental Health, 21*(2), 99–106.

Bornstein, M. H. (Ed.) (2003). *Handbook of parenting Volume 3: Being and becoming a parent*.

Brophy, J. E. (2010). *Motivating students to learn*. New York: Routledge.

Brown, M. R., Higgins, K., Pierce, T., Hong, E., and Thoma, C. (2003). Secondary students' perceptions of school life with regard to alienation: The effects of disability, gender and race. *Learning Disability Quarterly, 26*.

Cameron, C. A., Lau, C., and Tapanya, S. (2009). Passing it on during a day in the life of resilient adolescents in diverse communities around the globe. *Child Youth Care Forum, 38*, 305–325.

Canada says education is key to combating global poverty. (2001, April 29). Department of Finance Canada, 2001–2004. Retrieved May 7, 2003, from www.fin.gc.ca/news01-044e.html.

Canadian Council on Social Development. (2002). Percentage and number of persons in low income/poverty, by age, sex and family characteristics, Canada, 1990 and 1999. Retrieved May 7, 2003, from www.ccsd.ca/factsheets/fs_pov9099.htm.

Canadian Press. (2003). The Roadrunner made me do it. Retrieved April 10, 2007, from www.ctv.ca/servlet/ArticleNews/story/CTVNews/20030309/tv_ciolence_030309?s_name=&no_ads=.

Canadian Radio-television and Telecommunications Commission (CRTC). (2013). *Communications Monitoring Report*. Retrieved July 27, 2014, from CRTC http://www.crtc.gc.ca/eng/com100/2013/r130926.htm.

Canadian Teachers' Federation. (2003). Kids take on media. Retrieved on September 11, 2007, from http://www.ctf-fce.ca/documents/Resources/en/MERP/TeachersandStudentsGuide.pdf.

Cantor, J. (2002 April). The psychological effects of media violence on children and adolescents: Paper presented at colloquium on Television and Violence in Society. Montreal, Canada.

Charles, C. M., Senter, G. W., and Barr, K. B. (1995). *Building Classroom Discipline* (5th ed.). New York: Longman.

Clarizio, H. F., and McCoy, G. F. (1983). *Behaviour Disorders in Children* (3rd ed.). New York: Harper & Row.

Coopersmith, S. (1967). *The Antecedents of Self-Esteem*. San Francisco: W. H. Freeman.

Czubaj, C. A. (1996). Maintaining teacher motivation. *Education*, 116.

Dewey, J. (1916). *Democracy and Education*. New York: Macmillan.

Dreikurs, R., Grundwald, B., and Pepper, F. (1982). *Maintaining Sanity in the Classroom: Classroom Management Techniques* (2nd ed.). New York: Harper & Row.

Dubelle, S. T., and Hoffman, C. M. (1984). *Misbehaving —Solving the Disciplinary Puzzle for Educators*. Lancaster, PA: Technomic.

Egan, K. (2012). *Education and Psychology (RLE Edu E)*. New York: Routledge.

Elliott, A., Bosacki, S., Woloshyn, V., and Richards, M. (2001). Exploring preadolescents' media and literacy choices. *Language and Literacy, 3*(2), 1–13.

Feldhusen, J. F., Thurston, J. R., and Benning, J. J. (1973). A longitudinal study of delinquency and other aspects of children's behaviour. *International Journal of Criminology and Penology, 1*, 341–351.

French, J. R. P., and Raven, B. (1960). In D. Cartwright and A. Zander (Eds.), *Group Dynamics: Research and Theory. Evanston,* IL: Row-Peterson.

Fullan, M. G. (1993). Why teachers must become change agents. *Educational Leadership*, 50(6), 12–17.

Fullan, M. G. (2001). *Leading in a Culture of Change*. San Francisco: Jossey-Bass.

Gelfand, D. M., Jenson, W. R., and Drew, C. J. (1982). *Understanding Child Behaviour Disorders*. New York: Holt, Rinehart & Winston.

Gentile, D. A., and Gentile, J. R. (2008). Video games as exemplary teachers: A conceptual analysis. *Journal of Youth and Adolescence, 37*, 127–141.

Gentile, D. A., Lynch, P. J., Linder, J. R., and Walsh, D. (2004). The effects of violent video games habits on adolescent hostility, aggressive behaviors and school performance. *Journal of Adolescence, 27*(1), 5–22.

Gilbert, R., and Gilbert, P. (1998). *Masculinity goes to school*. Florence, KY: Routledge.

Gilliland, H. (1986). Self-concept and the Indian student. In J. Reyhner (Ed.), *Teaching the Indian Child. Billings,* MT: Eastern Montana College.

Glasser, W. (1978). Disorders in our schools: causes and remedies. *Phi Delta Kappan, 59*(5), 321–333.

Goertzel, V., and Goertzel, M. (1962). *Cradles of Eminence*. Boston: Little, Brown.

Graham, C. R. (2011). Theoretical considerations for understanding technological pedagogical content knowledge (TPACK). *Computers & Education, 57*(3), 1953–1960.

Green, A., Campbell, L., Stirtzinger, R., DeSouza, C., and Dawe, I. (2001). Multimodal school-based intervention for at-risk, aggressive, latency-age youth. *Canadian Journal of School Psychology 17*(1), 27–46.

Health Canada. (2013). Just for You–Youth. Retrieved August 10, 2014 from http://hc-sc.gc.ca/hl-vs/jfy-spv/youth-jeunes-eng.php.

Hord, S. M. (1997). *Professional learning communities: communities of continuous inquiry and improvement*. Austin, TX: Southwest Educational Development Laboratory.

Huesman, L. R. (2002). Understanding aggression requires integrating diverse perspectives. *International Society for the Study of Behavioral Development Newsletter, 42*(2), 15–16.

Jenkins, J., Simpson, A., Dunn, J., Rasbash, J., and O'Connor, T. (2005). Mutual influence of marital conflict and children's behavior problems: Shared and nonshared family risks. *Child Development, 76*(1), 24–39.

Jessor, J., and Jessor, S. L. (1977). *Problem Behaviour and Psychosocial Development*. New York: Academic.

Jull, S. (2000). Youth, violence, schools and the management of zero tolerance and equity in public schooling. *Canadian Journal of Educational Administrative Policy, 17*.

Karplus, R. (1977). *Science Teaching and the Development of Reasoning*. Berkeley: University of California Press.

Kaltiala-Heino, R., Fröjd, S., and Marttunen, M. (2010). Involvement in bullying and depression in a 2-year follow-up in middle adolescence. *European Child & Adolescent Psychiatry, 19*(1), 45–55.

Kindsvatter, R. (1978). A new view of the dynamics of discipline. *Phi Delta Kappan, 59*(5), 322–325.

Kirsh, S. J. (2011). *Children, adolescents, and media violence: A critical look at the research*. Sage.

Kohlberg, L. (1969). *Stages in the Development of Moral Thought and Action*. New York: Holt, Rinehart & Winston.

Kohlberg, L. (1975). The cognitive-developmental approach to moral education. *Phi Delta Kappan, 56*(10), 610–677.

Kounin, J. S. (1970). *Discipline and Group Management in Classrooms*. New York: Holt, Rinehart & Winston.

Kuperminc, G. P., Leadbeater, B. J., and Blatt, S. J. (2001). *Society for the study of school psychology*. Elsevier Science Ltd.

Legault, L., Anawati, M., and Flynn, R. (2005). Factors favoring psychological resilience among fostered young people. *Children and Youth Services Review, 28*(9), 1024–1038.

Leithwood, K., Day, C., Sammons, P., Hopkins, D., and Harris, A. (2006). *Successful school leadership: What it is and how it influences pupil learning*. London, UK: Department of Education & Skills.

Levin, J., and Shanken-Kaye, J. (2002). From distruster to achiever: Creating successful learning environments for the self-control classroom. Dubuque, IA: Kendall-Hunt.

MacDonald, I. (1997). Violence in school: Multiple realities. *Alberta Journal of Educational Research, 43*(2–3), 142–156.

Mahoney, J. (2007, March 14). Population growth will likely be all immigration by 2030. *The Globe and Mail.*

Marini, Z., Fairbain, L., and Zuber, R. (2001). Peer harassment in individuals with developmental disabilities: Towards the development of a multi-dimensional bullying identification model. *Developmental Disabilities Bulletin, 29*(2), 170–195.

Marini, Z., Spear, S., and Bombay, K. (1999). Peer victimization in childhood: Characteristics, causes and consequences of school bullying. *Brock Education, 9*, 32–47.

Maslow, A. (1968). *Toward a Psychology of Being.* New York: D. Van Nostrand.

McMillan, S. J., and Morrison, M. (2006, February). Coming of age with the internet: A qualitative exploration of how the internet has become an integral part of young people's lives. *New Media Society, 8*(1), 73–95.

McNamara, L. (2013). What's getting in the way of play? An analysis of the contextual factors that hinder recess in elementary schools. *The Canadian Journal of Action Research, 14*(2), 3–21.

Morgan, M., Shanahan, J., and De-Guise, J. (2001). Television and its viewers: Cultivation theory and research. *Canadian Journal of Communication, 26*(4), 568–570.

Muscott, H. S., and Mann, E. L. (2010). Positive behavioral interventions and supports in New Hampshire. *Journal of Positive Behavior, 10*, 190–205.

Ng, S. M. (2006). Literacy and diversity: Challenges of change. In A. McKeough, L. Phillips, V. Timmons, and J. L. Lupart (Eds.) *Understanding Literacy Development*. Mahwah, NJ: Lawrence Erlbaum Associates, Publishers.

Noddings, N. (1988). Schools face crisis in caring. *Education Week,* December 7.

Novak, J. M., and Purkey, W. W. (2001). *Invitational Education*. Bloomington, IN: Phi Delta Kappa Educational Foundation.

Olson, C. K., Kutner, L. A., Warner, D. E., Almerigi, J., Baer, L., and Nicholi, M. (2007). Factors correlated with violent video game use by adolescent boys and girls. *Journal of Adolescent Health, 41*, 77–83.

Ontario: Where everyone looks the same? (1999, February 2). Canadian Press Newswire. Retrieved. Apr. 27, 2003, from Canadian Business and Current Affairs (CBCA) database through www.brocku.ca/library/databases. (While only those with access to Brock's online library can gain access to the CBCA through this URL, many libraries offer access to the CBCA database.)

Orenstein, P. (2013). *Schoolgirls: Young women, self esteem, and the confidence gap*. Random House Digital, Inc.

Paquette, G. (2004). Violence on Canadian Television Networks. *The Canadian Child and Adolescent Psychiatry Review,* 13(1), 13.

Parents Television Council (2007). www.parentstv.org.

Pearl, D. (1984). Violence and aggression. *Society,* *21*(6). 15–16.

Pearl, D., Bouthilet, L., and Lazar, J. (Eds.). (1982). *Television and Behaviour: Ten Years of Scientific Progress and Implications for the Eighties*, Vol. 2. Washington, DC: U.S. Government Printing Office.

Piaget, J. (1965). *The Moral Judgment of the Child.* Glencoe, IL: Free Press.

Piaget, J. (1970). Piaget's theory. In P. H. Mussen (Ed.), *Carmichael's Manual of Child Psychology,* Vol. 1. New York: John Wiley & Sons.

Rice, M. L., Huston, A. C., and Wright, J. C. (1982). The forms and codes of television: Effects on children's attention, comprehension and social behaviour. In D. Pearl, L. Bouthilet, and J. Lazar (Eds.), *Television and Behaviour: Ten Years of Scientific Progress and Implications for the Eighties*, Vol. 2. Washington, DC: U.S. Government Printing Office.

Rice, P. F. (1981). *The Adolescent Development, Relationships, and Culture* (3rd ed.). Boston: Allyn & Bacon.

Robinson, L. M., McIntyre, L., and Officer, S. (2005). Welfare babies: Poor children's experiences in forming healthy peer relationships in Canada. *Health Promotion International, 20*(4).

Rosenberg, J., and Barbara, J. S. (2007). Media and entertainment violence and children. Retrieved April 1, 2007, from www.Fradical.Com/Physicians_ For_Global_Survival_Canada.htm.

Ruck, M. D., and Wortley, S. (2002). Racial and ethnic minority high schools students' perceptions of school disciplinary practices: A look at some Canadian findings. *Journal of Youth and Adolescence, 31*(3), 185–195.

Salmivalli, C. (2001). Aggression and Violent Behavior. *Elsevier Science Ltd. 6*(4), 375–393.

Seeds of violence, The. (2001, October). *Canada and the World Backgrounder, 67*(2), 17, Retrieved April 27, 2003, from the Canadian Business and Current Affairs (CBCA) database through www.brocku.ca/library/databases. (While only those with access to Brock's online library can gain access to the CBCA through this URL, many libraries offer access to the CBCA database.)

Schunk, D. H., and Mullen, C. A. (2012). Self-efficacy as an engaged learner. In *Handbook of research on student engagement.* Springer US. 219–235.

Singer, J. L., Singer, D. G., and Rapaczynski, W. S. (1984). Family patterns and television viewing as predictors of children's beliefs and aggression. *Journal of Communications, 34*(2), 73–89.

Statistics Canada. (2002). Divorce. *The Daily.* Retrieved May 4, 2003, from www.statcan.ca/Daily/English/021202/d021202f.htm.

Statistics Canada. (2010). Internet use by individuals, by type of activity. Retrived December 18, 2013, from http://www.statcan.gc.ca/tables-tableaux/sum-som/l01/cst01/comm29a-eng.htm.

Statistics Canada. (2011). Marital Status: Overview, 2011. Retrieved August 6, 2014, from http://www.statcan.gc.ca/pub/91-209-x/2013001/article/11788-eng.htm.

Statistics Canada. (2013). Individual Internet use and e-commerce, 2012. Retrieved August 5, 2014, from http://www.statcan.gc.ca/daily-quotidien/131028/dq131028a-eng.htm.

Statistics Canada. (2013). Persons in low income before tax (In percent, 2007 to 2011). Retrieved December 18, 2013, from http://www.statcan.gc.ca/tables-tableaux/sum-som/l01/cst01/famil41a-eng.htm?sdi=low%20income.

Statistics Canada. (2014). Canada's population estimates: Subprovincial areas, July 1, 2013. Retrieved August 5, 2014, from http://www.statcan.gc.ca/daily-quotidien/140226/dq140226b-eng.htm.

St. Thomas University, (2013). CENTRE FOR RESEARCH ON YOUTH AT RISK. Retrieved December 18, 2013, from http://www.stthomasu.ca/research/youth/index.htm.

Stinchcombe, A. L. (1964). *Rebellion in a High School.* Chicago: Quadrangle.

Stipek, D. J. (1993). *Motivation to Learn, from Theory to Practice* (2nd ed.). Boston: Allyn & Bacon.

Subrahmanyam, K., Kraut, R. E., Greenfield, P. M., and Gross, E. F. (2000). The impact of home computer use on children's activities and development. *Children and Computer Technology, 10*(2), 123–145.

Swing, E. L., Gentile, D. A., Anderson, C. A., and Walsh, D. A. (2010). Television and video game exposure and the development of attention problems. *Pediatrics, 126*(2), 214–221.

Sylva, K., Melhuish, E., Sammons, P., Siraj-Blatchford, I., and Taggart, B. (Eds.). (2010). *Early childhood matters: Evidence from the effective pre-school and primary education project*. Routledge.

Tanner, L. N. (1978). *Classroom Discipline for Effective Teaching and Learning*. New York: Holt, Rinehart & Winston.

Toffler, A. (1970). *Future Shock*. New York: Random House.

Totten, M., Quigley, P., and Morgan, M. (2004). *CPHA safe school survey for students in Grades 4-7*. Ottawa: Canadian public Health Association and Department of Justice Canada. http://acsp.cpha.ca/antibullying.english/surveys/4-7_survey.html.

Thompson, K. M. (2005). Addicted media: substances on screen. *Child and Adolescent Psychiatric Clinics of North America, 14*(2), 473–489.

Turkel, S. (1996). *Life on the Screen*. New York: Simon & Schuster.

Ungar, M. (Ed.) (2012). *The social ecology of resilience: A handbook*. New York, NY: Springer.

Volk, A., Craig, W., Boyce, W., and King, M. (2003). Adolescent risk correlates of bullying and different types of victimization. Poster presented at the World congress on child and Youth Health, Vancouver, May, 2003.

Wagner, R. D. (2007). Balanced school day. Retrieved April 1, 2007, from www.wrdsb.on.ca/balanced_school.php.

Wentzel, K. R. (2010). Students' relationships with teachers. *Handbook of research on schools, schooling, and human development*, 75–91.

Williams, C. (2001, Fall). Family disruptions and childhood happiness. Canada Social Trends, Statistics Canada. Retrieved May 4, 2003, from 0-www.statcan.ca.brain.biblio.brocku.ca/english/indepth/11-008/feature/star2001062000s3a01.pdf.

Willoughby, T., Adachi, P. J., and Good, M. (2012). A longitudinal study of the association between violent video game play and aggression among adolescents. *Developmental psychology, 48*(4), 1044.

Withall, J. (1969, March). Evaluation of classroom climate. *Childhood Education, 45*(7), 403–408.

Withall, J. (1979). Problem behaviour: Function of social–emotional climate? *Journal of Education, 161*(2), 89–101.

Zolkoski, S. M., and Bullock, L. M. (2012). Resilience in children and youth: A review. *Children and Youth Services Review.*

Chapter 4

Affan, I. (2013). Bystanders in cyberbullying. *Define the Line*, April 17. 2013. Retrieved August 9, 2014, from: http://definetheline.ca/bystnaders-in-cyberbullying/.

Bandura, A. (2011). Social cognitive theory. *Handbook of Theories of Social Psychology:* Volume One, 1, 349.

Bandura, A. (2001). Social cognitive theory: An agentic perspective. *Annual Review of Psychology, 52*(1), 1–26.

Bandura, A. (1991). Social cognitive theory of self-regulation. *Organizational Behavior and Human Decision Processes, 50*(2), 248–287.

Battey, G. L., and Ebbeck, V. (2013). A qualitative exploration of an experiential education bully prevention curriculum. *Journal of Experiential Education, 36*(3), 203–217.

Bazelon, E. (2013). *Sticks and stones: Defeating the culture of bullying and rediscovering the power of character and empathy*. Random House Digital, Inc.: New York, NY.

Beran, T. N., Hughes, G., and Lupart, J. (2008). A model of achievement and bullying: analyses of the Canadian National Longitudinal Survey of Children and Youth data. *Educational Research, 50*(1), 25–39.

Berkowitz, M., and Bier, M. (2005). *What works in character education: A report for policy makers and opinion leaders*. Character Education Partnership.

Bosaki, S. L., Marini, Z A., and Dane, A. V. (2006). Voices from the classroom: Pectoral and narrative representations of children's bullying experiences. *Journal of Moral Education, 35*(2), 231–245.

Bolton, J., & Graeve, S. (2005). *No Room for Bullies: From the Classroom to Cyberspace*. Boys Town, Neb.: Boys Town Press.

Rubin, S. (2014). The need to address cyberbullying in Canada. Canadian Resource Centre for Victims of Crime, March 17, 2014. Retrieved August 8, 2014, from http://crcvc.ca/2014/03/17/francais-cyberbullying/

Canadian Council on Learning: Lessons in learning. (2008). *Bullying in Canada: How intimidation affects learning*. Retrieved January 16, 2014, from http://www.ccl-cca.ca/pdfs/LessonsInLearning/Mar-20-08-Bullying-in-Canad.pdf.

Canadian Red Cross. (2014). *Bullying and Harassment Prevention Program*. Retrieved January, 22, 2014, from http://www.redcross.ca/what-we-do/violence-bullying-and-abuse-prevention/educators/bullying-and-harassment-prevention/cyberbullying.

The Canadian Teachers' Federation. (2008). *Cyberbullying in schools national survey*. Retrieved January 18, 2014 from http://www.erinresearch.com.

Carney, J. L., Hazler, R. J., Hibel, L. C., and Grander, D. A. (2010). The relations between bullying exposures in middle childhood, anxiety and adrenocortical activity. *Journal of School Violence, 9*(2), 194–211.

Centre for the Study and Prevention of Violence. (2006). Blueprints Model Programs Fact Sheet: Olweus Bullying Prevention Program. Retrieved January 28, 2014, from http://www.colorado.edu/cspv/publications/factsheets.blueprints/pdf/FS-BPMO9.pdf.

Dauvergne, M., and Brennan, S. (2009). Police-reported hate-crime in Canada. Component of Statistics Canada catalogue no. 85-002-X juristat. Retrieved January 22, 2014, from http://www.statcan.gc.ca/pub/85-002-x/2011/article/11469-eng.pdf.

Durlak, J. A., Weissberg, R. P., Dymnicki, A. B., Taylor, R. D., and Schellinger, K. B. (2011). The impact of enhancing students' social and emotional learning: A meta-analysis of school-based universal interventions. *Child development, 82*(1), 405–432.

Gini, G. (2008). Associations between bullying behaviour, psychosomatic complaints, emotional and behavioural problems. *Journal of Pediatrics and Child Health, 44,* 492–497.

Hamilton, V., and Reati, J. (2010). *Bullying Awareness: Reclaiming our schools*. Info@bullyingAwarenss.ca. Ontario Teachers Federation.

Hargrove, L. (2013). *Family Online Safety Guide*. Symantec Corporation.

Hinduja, S., and Patchin, J. W. (2010). Bullying, cyberbullying and suicide. *Archives of Suicide Research, 14,* 206–221.

Hirsch, L., Lowen, C., and Santorelli, D. (2012). *Bully: An Action Plan for Teachers, Parents and Communities to Combat the Bullying Crisis*. Philadelphia, PA: Weinstein Books.

Holfeld, B. (2014). Perceptions and attributions of bystanders to cyber bullying. *Computers in Human Behavior, 38,* 1–7.

Janosz, M., Archambault, I., Pagani, L. S., Pascal, S., Morin, A. J. S., and Bowen, F. (2008). Are there detrimental effects of witnessing school violence in early adolescence? *Journal of Adolescent Health, 43,* 600–608.

Jones, S., Weissbourd, S. B., and Ross, T. (2012). Creating just and caring communities. In L. Hirsch, C. Lowen, and D. Santorelli (Eds.), *Bully: An Action Plan for Teachers and Parents to Combat the Bullying Crisis*. Philadelphia, PA: Weinstein Books.

Knighton, K. (2011). Cyberbullying: Reality Check. *Kids Help Phone. 2011 Research Update.*

Knoff, H. M. (2007). Teasing, taunting, bullying, harassment and aggression: A school wide approach to prevention, strategic intervention and crisis management. In J. E, Sins, M. J. Elias, and C. A. Maher (Eds.), *Bullying, Victimization and Peer Harassment* (389–412). New York: Hawthorn Press.

Larochette, A., Murphy, A., and Craig, W. (2010). Racial bullying and victimization in Canadian school - aged children. *School Psychology International, 31,* 389–408.

Li, Q. (2007). New bottle but old wine: A research of cyberbullying in schools. *Computers in Human Behavior, 23*(4), 1777–1791.

Limber, S. P. (2012). *Cyberbullying: Bullying in the digital age*. Wiley.com.

MacKay, W. (2012). Respectful and responsible relationships: There's no app for that. *The Report of the Nova Scotia Task Force on Bullying and Cyberbullying*. Retrieved January 23, 2014, from http://novascotia.ca/news/release/?id=20120322002.

Mandela, N. (1995). *Long Walk to Freedom*. New York: Little, Brown & Company.

Marini, Z., Spear, S., and Bombay, K. (1999). Peer victimization in middle childhood: Characteristics, causes, and consequences of bullying. *Brock Education, 9,* 32–47.

Mason, K. L. (2013). *Bullying No More: Understanding and Preventing Bullying*. New York: Barrons Educational Series, Inc.

McCready, A. (2012). A little "I'm sorry" goes a long way. In L. Hirsch, C. Lowen, and D. Santorelli (Eds.), *Bully: An Action Plan for Teachers, Parents and Communities to Combat the Bullying Crisis*. Philadelphia, PA: Weinstein Books.

Michael, S. L. (2007). *Stop the Bullying Now! An Easy-to-use-Technique that gives the Victim a Voice*. Nashville, TN: Incentive Publications.

Mishna, F., Cook, C., Gadalla, T., Daciuk, J., and Solomon, S. (2010). Cyberbullying behaviors among middle and high school students. *American Journal of Orthopsychiatry, 80*, 362–374.

Mitchell, P. J. (2012). The limits of anti-bullying legislation. *Institute of Marriage and Family Canada*. Retrieved January 28, 2014, from http://www.imfcanada.org/sites/default/files/IMFCPublicationMay2012FINAL-WEB.pdf

Nagin, D., and Tremblay, R. E. (2001). Parental and early childhood predictors of persistent physical aggression in boys from Kindergarten to high school. *Archives of General Psychiatry, 58*, 389–394.

O'Connell, P., Pepler, D. J., and Craig, W. M. (1999). Peer involvement in bullying: Insights and challenges for intervention. *Journal of Adolescence, 22*, 437–452.

Pepler, D. J. and Craig, W. M. (2011). Promoting relationship and eliminating violence in Canada. *International Journal of Behavioural Development, 35*, 389–397.

Piquero, A. R., Connell, N. M., Piquero, N. L., Farrington, D. P., and Jennings, W. G. (2013). Does adolescent bullying distinguish between male offending trajectories in late middle age? *Journal of Youth and Adolescence, 42*(3), 444–453.

Pozzoli, T., and Gini, G. (2012). Why do bystanders of bullying help or not? A multidimensional model. *Journal of Early Adolescence, 33*(3), 315–340.

Public Safety Canada. (2014). *Bullying Prevention: Nature and Extent of Bullying in Canada*. Ottawa: National Crime Prevention Centre. Retrieved January, 16, 2014, from http://www.publicsafety.gc.ca/cnt/rsrcs/pblctns/bllng-prvntn.index-eng.aspx.

Novak, J. M., and Purkey, W. W. (2001). *Invitational Education*. Bloomington, IN: Phi.Delta Kappa Education Foundation.

Raising Children Network. Retrieved March 5, 2014 from http://raisingchildren.net.au/

Santos, R. G., Chartier, M. J., Whalen, J. C., Chateau, D., and Boyd, L. (2011). Effectiveness of school-based violence prevention for children and youth: Cluster randomized controlled field trial of the Roots of empathy program with replication and three-year follow-up. *Healthcare Quarterly, 14*, 80–91.

Smith, P. K., Salmivalli, C., and Cowie, H. (2012). Effectiveness of school-based programs to reduce bullying: A commentary. *Journal of Experimental Criminology*, e-print ahead of publication, DOI: 10.1007/s11292-012-091420-3.

Smokowski, P. R., and Kopasz, K. H. (2004). Bullying in school: An overview of types, effects, family characteristics, and intervention strategies. *Children & Schools, 27*(2), 101–110.

Sontag, L. M., Clemans, K. H., Grabe, J. A., and Lyndon, S. T. (2011). Traditional and cyber aggressors and victims: A comparison of psychosocial characteristics. *Journal of Youth and Adolescence. 40*, 392–404.

Statistics Canada (2013). *Canadian Bullying Statistics*. Retrieved January 7, 2014, from http://www.cihr-irsc.gc.ca/e/45838.html.

Toblin, R. L., Schwartz, D., Hopmeyer Gorman, A., and Abou-ezzeddone, T. (2005). Social-cognitive and behavioral attributes of aggressive victims of bullying. *Journal of Applied Developmental Psychology, 26*(3), 329–346.

Tokunaga, R. S. (2010). Following you home from school: A critical review and synthesis of research on cyberbullying victimization. *Computers in Human Behavior, 26*(3), 277–287.

Ttofi, M. M., Farrington, D. P., Losel, F., and Loeber, R. (2009). Do the victims of school bullies tend to become depressed later in life? A systematic review and meta-analysis of longitudinal studies. *Journal of Aggression, Conflict and Peace Research, 3*(2), 63–73.

Ttofi, M. M., Farrington, D. P., Losel, F., and Loeber, R. (2011). The predictive efficiency of school bullying versus later offending: A systematic/meta-analysis of longitudinal studies. *Criminal Behaviour and Mental Health, 21*(92), 80–89.

Wang, J., Nansel, T. R., and Iannotti, R. J. (2011). Cyber bullying and traditional bullying: Differential association with depression. *The Journal of adolescent health: official publication of the Society for Adolescent Medicine, 48*(4), 415.

Ziv, N., and Dolev, E. (2013). The effect of background music on bullying: A pilot study. *Children & Schools*. Retrieved January 29, 2014, from http://cs.oxfordjournals.org.

Chapter 5

Alberta Department of Education. (2010). Curriculum. Retrieved, December 27, 2010, from http://education.alberta.ca.

Alberto, P. A., and Troutman, A. C. (2012). *Applied behavior analysis for teachers* (9th ed.). Upper Saddle River, NJ: Pearson Chapter 4 Education Inc.

Aultman, L. P., Williams-Johnson, M. H., and Schutz, P. A. (2009). Boundary dilemmas in teacher-student relationships: Struggling with "the line". *Teaching and Teacher Education, 25*(5), 636–646.

Beltman, S., Mansfield, C., and Price, A. (2011). Thriving not just surviving: A review of research on teacher resilience. *Educational Research Review, 6*(3), 185–207.

Berne, E. (1964). *Games People Play: The Psychology of Human Relations.* New York: Avon.

Brookhart, S., Moss, C., and Long, B. (2008). Formative assessment that empowers. *Educational Leadership, 66*(3), 52–57.

Cangelosi, J. (2008). *Classroom Management Strategies: Gaining and Maintaining Students' Cooperation (6th ed.).* New York: Wiley.

Canter, L., and Canter, M. (2007). *Assertive Discipline: Positive Behaviour Management for Today's Classrooms* (rev. ed.). Santa Monica, CA: Canter Associates.

Charles, C. M. (2007). *Building classroom discipline (9th ed.).* Boston, MA: Allyn & Bacon.

Charney, R. (2002). *Teaching Children to Care: Classroom management for ethical and academic growth,* (K-8 Revised ed.). Greenfield, MA: Northeast Foundation for Children.

Clunies-Ross, P., Little, E., and Kienhuis, M. (2008). Self reported and actual use of proactive and reactive classroom manangement strategies and their relationship with teacher stress and student behaviour. *Educational Psychology: An International Journal of Experimental Educational Psychology. 28*(6), 693–710.

Davis, D. H., Fredrick, L. D., Alberto, P. A., and Gama, R. (2012). Functional communication training without

extinction using concurrent schedules of differing magnitudes of reinforcements in classrooms. *Journal of Positive Behavior Interventions, 14*(3), 162–172.

Deci, E. L., and Ryan, R. M. (2012). Motivation, personality, and development within embedded social contexts: An overview of self-determination theory. In Edward, L. Deci and Richard M Ryan (Eds.), *The Oxford Handbook of Human Motivation,* 85–107.

Depres, S., Kuhn, S., Ngirumpatse, P., and Parent, M. (2013). Real accountability or an illusion of success? Action Canada Task Force Report. Retrieved on August 10, 2014 from http://testingillusion.ca/wp-content/uploads/2013/01/illusions.

Doyle, W. (2009). Situated practice: A reflection on person-centered classroom management. *Theory into Practice, 48,* 156–159.

Drake, S. M. (2012). *Creating Standards-Based Integrated Curriculum* (3rd ed.). Thousand Oaks, CA: Corwin.

Dreikurs, R., Grundwald, B., and Pepper, F. (1998). *Maintaining Sanity in the Classroom: Classroom Management Techniques* (2nd ed.). Washington, DC: Taylor and Francis.

Earl, L. M. (2013). *Assessment as Learning: Using Classroom Assessment to Maximize Student Learning.* Thousand Oaks, CA: Sage.

Elias, S. (2008). Fifty years of influence in the workplace: The evolution of the French and Raven power taxonomy. *Journal of Management History, 14*(3), 267–283.

Forton, M. B. (1998). Apology of action. *Responsive Classroom, 10*(1), 6–7.

Freiberg, H. J., and Lamb, S. M. (2009). Dimensions of person-centered classroom management. *Theory into Practice, 48,* 99–105.

French, J. R. P., and Raven, B. (1960). The bases of social power. In D. Cartwright and A. Zander (Eds.), *Group Dynamics: Research and Theory.* Evanston, IL: Row-Peterson.

Ginott, H. (1972). *Between Teacher and Child.* New York: Wyden.

Glasser, W. (1992). *The Quality School: Managing Students without Coercion.* New York: HarperCollins.

Glick, M. (2011). *The instructional leader and the brain: Using neuroscience to inform practice.* Thousand Oaks, CA: Corwin Press.

Gootman, M. E. (2008). *The Caring Teacher's Guide to Discipline* (3rd ed.). Thousand Oaks, CA: Corwin Press.

Gordon, T. (1989). *Teaching Children Self-Discipline at Home and in School*. New York: Random House.

Guay, F., Ratelle, C. F., and Chanal, J. (2008). Optimal learning in optimal contexts: the role of self-determination in education. *Canadian Psychology*, *49*(3), 233–240.

Harris, T. (1969). *I'm O.K., You're O.K.: A Practical Guide to Transactional Analysis*. New York: Harper & Row.

Klassen, R. M., and Chui, M. M. (2010). Effects on teachers' self-efficacy and job satisfaction: Teacher gender, years of experience, and job stress. *Journal of Educational Psychology*, *102*(3), 741–756.

Kohn, A. (2006). *Beyond Discipline: From Compliance to Community*. Alexandria, VA: Association for Supervision and Curriculum Development.

Martella, R., Nelson, J., Marchand-Martella, N., and O'Rilley, M. (2011). *Comprehensive behavior management: Individualized, classroom and school-wide approaches*. Thousand Oaks, CA: Sage Publications.

Martin, J., Sugarman, J. H., and Hichinbottom, S. (2009). *Persons: Understanding Psychological Selfhood and Agency*. New York: Springer.

Murray, S., Ma, X., and Mazur, J. (2009). Effects of peer coaching on teachers' collaborative interactions and students' mathematics achievement. *The Journal of Educational Research*, *102*(3), 203–212.

Ng, J. Y. Y., Ntoumanis, N., Thogersen-Ntoumanic, C., Deci, E. L., Ryan, R. M., Duda, J. L., and Williams, G. C. (2012). Self-determination Theory applied to health cntexts: A meta analysis. Perspectives on *Psychological Sciences*, *7*(4), 325–340.

Newfoundland and Labrador Department of Education. (2010). Education. Retrieved December 27, 2010, from www.gov.nf.ca/edu/sp/main.htm.

Novak, J. (2005). *Experiencing Dewey: Insights for Today's Classrooms*. Kappa Delta Pi, International Honor Society in Education.

Ontario Ministry of Education. (2006). Curriculum and policy. Retrieved December, 27, 2010, from www.edu.gov.on.ca/eng/document/curricul/curricul.html.

Poduska, J. M., Kellam, S. G., Wang, W., Brown, C. H., Ialongo, N. S., and Toyinbo, P. (2008). Impact of the good behavior game, a universal classroom-based behavior intervention, on young adult service use for problems with emotions, behavior, or drugs or alcohol. *Drug and Alcohol Dependence*, *95*(1), 829–844.

Reupert, A., and Woodcock, S. (2010). Success and near misses: Pre-service teachers' use, confidence and success in various classroom management strategies. *Teaching and Teacher Education*, *26*(6), 1261–1268.

Riley, P. (2009). An adult attachment perspective on the student-teacher relationship and classroom management difficulties. *Teaching and Teacher Education*, *25*(5), 626–635.

Schwartz, S., and Pollishuke, M. (2002). *Creating the Dynamic Classroom*. Toronto, ON: Irwin.

Soller, A., Martinez, A., Jermann, P., and Muehlenbrock, M. (2005). From mirroring to guiding: A review of state of the art technology for supporting collaborative learning. *International Journal of Artificial Intelligence in Education*, *15*(4), 261–290.

Strachota, R. (1996). *On Their Side: Helping Children Take Charge of Their Learning*. Greenfield, MA: Northeast Foundation for Children.

Sumerall, W. J. and Schillinger, D. N. (2004). A student-directed model of designing a science/social studies curriculum. *The Social Studies*, *95*(1).

Volante, L. (2010). Assessment of, for, and as learning within schools: Implications for transforming classroom practice. *Action in Teacher Education*, *31*(4), 66–75.

Volante, L. (2004). Teaching to the test: What every educator and policy-maker should know. Canadian Journal of Educational Administration and Policy, 35.

Walker, J. M. T. (2009). Authoritative classroom management: How control and nurturance work together. *Theory into Practice*, *48*, 122–129.

Wodzicki, K., Schewammlein, E., and Moskaliuk, I. J. (2012). "Actually, I wanted to learn: Study-related knowledge exchange on social networking sites. *The Internet and Higher Education*, *15*(1), 914.

Wolfgang, C. (2008). *Solving discipline problems: Methods and models for today's teachers (7th ed.)*. New York: Wiley & Sons.

Wolfgang, C., and Glickman, C. (1995). *Solving Discipline Problems: Methods and Models for Today's Teachers* (2nd ed.). Boston: Allyn & Bacon.

Chapter 6

Akey, T. M. (2006). School context, student attitudes and behavior, and academic achievement: An exploratory analysis. Retrieved May 22, 2007, from www.mdrc.org/publications/419/full.pdf#search=%22School%20Context%2C%20Student%20Attitudes%20and%20Behavior%2C%20and%20Academic%20Achievement%3A%20An%20Exploratory%20Analysis%22.

Allum, J. (2014). Smaller Classes. Minister's message. Retrieved August 16, 2014 from http://www.edu.gov.mb.ca/k12/smclass/index.html.

Almesi, J. F., and Fullerton, S. K. (2012). *Teaching Strategic Processes in Reading Second Edition.* New York: The Guilford Press.

Anderson, L. M. (1989). Classroom instruction. In M. C. Reynolds (Ed.), *Knowledge Base for the Beginning Teacher.* New York: Pergamon.

Armstrong, T. (1994). *Multiple Intelligences in the Classroom.* Alexandria, VA: Association for Supervision and Curriculum Development.

Auditor General of Canada. (2010). *2010 May Report of the Auditor General. Education in the Northwest Territories–Department of Education, Culture and Employment.* Retrieved August 11, 2014, from http://www.oag-bvg.gc.ca/internet/english/nwt_201005_e_33873.html.

Baker, E. L., and Linn, R. L. (2004). Validity issues for accountability systems. In S. Fuhrman and R. F. Elmore (Eds.), *Redesigning accountability systems for education.* New York:Teachers College Press, 47–72.

Bajovic, M., and Elliott, A. (2011). The Intersection of Critical Literacy and Moral Literacy: Implications for Practice. *Critical Literacy: Theories and Practices, 5*(1).

Bandura, A. (1997). *Self-efficacy: The Exercise of Control.* New York: W. H. Freeman & Company.

Brophy, J. E. (1987). Synthesis of research strategies on motivating students to learn. *Educational Leadership, 45*(2), 40–48.

Brophy, J. E. (2010). *Motivating Students to Learn* (3rd ed.). New York: Routledge.

Brophy, J. E., and Good, T. L. (1974). *Teacher–Student Relationships: Causes and Consequences.* New York: Holt, Rinehart & Winston.

Cope, B., and Kalantzis, M. (2000). *Multiliteracies: Literacy Learning and the Design of Social Futures.* New York: Routledge.

Council of Ministers of Education Canada. (1997). Pan Canadian Common Framework of Learning Outcomes K-12. Retrieved on August 13, 2014 from http://racerocks.ca/metcnosinmovine/sustainability/curricul.

Darling-Hammond, L. and Bransford, J. (2005). *Preparing Teachers for a Changing World.* San Francisco, CA: Jossey-Bass.

Denham, S. A. and Brown, C. (2010). "Plays nice with others": Social-emotional learning and academic success. *Early Education & Development, 21*(5) 652–680.

Drake, S. M. (2007). *Creating Standards-Based Integrated Curriculum: Aligning Curriculum, Content, Assessment, and Instruction.* Thousand Oaks, CA: Corwin Press Inc.

Dreikurs, R. (2004). *Discipline Without Tears: How to Reduce Conflict and Establish Cooperation in the Classroom.* New York: Wiley.

Earl, L. M. (2013). *Assessment as Learning: Using Classroom Assessment to Maximize Student Learning* (2nd ed.). Thousand Oaks, CA: Corwin.

Edwards, C. H., and Watts, V. J. (2010). *Classroom Discipline & Management* (2nd ed.). Milton, Qld: John Wiley & Sons.

Elliott, A., Woloshyn, V., Bajovic, M., and Ratkovic, S. (2007 July). Promoting teacher candidates' awareness of the role of critical literacy in the curriculum: Lunchtime conversations. *The Reading Professor,* July.

Erwin, J. O., and Worrell, F. C. (2012). Assessment practices and the under-representation of minority students in gifted and talented education. *Journal of Psychoeducational Assessment, 30*(10), 74–87.

Fisher, E. (2013). Aboriginal graduation rates drop in North Peace, skyrocket in Fort Nelson (B.C. Ministry of Education). *Energeticcity.ca,* December 22, 2013. Retrieved August 11, 2014, from http://energeticcity.ca/article/news/2013/11/22/aboriginal-graduation-rates-drop-in-north-peace-skyrocket-in-fort-nelson.

Fleming, T., and Raptis, H. (2004). *School Improvement in Action: Case Studies from British Columbia.* Kelowna, BC: Society for the Advancement of Excellence in Education.

Fullan M., Hill, P., and Crevola, C. (2006). *Breakthrough.* Thousand Oaks, CA: Corwin Press.

Gardner, H. (2006 a). *Frames of Mind: The Theory of Multiple Intelligences_* (rev. ed.). Philadelphia, PA: Basic Books.

Gardner, H. (2006 b). *Multiple Intelligences: New Horizons* (rev. ed.). New York: Basic Books.

Gilles, R. M., and Boyle, M. (2010). Teachers' reflections on cooperative learning: Issues of implementation. *Teaching and Teacher Education, 26*(4), 933–940.

Goeke, J. L. (2008). *Explicit Instruction: Strategies for Meaningful Direct Teaching*. Princeton, NC: Merrill.

Gonzalez-DeHass, A. R., Willems, P. P. and Holbein, M. F. D. (2005. Examining the relationship between parental involvement and student motivation. *Educational Psychology Review, 17*(3), 99–123.

Good, T. L., and Brophy, J. E. (2008). *Looking in Classrooms* (10th ed.). Boston: Allyn & Bacon.

Hallett, D., Want, S. C., Chandler, M. J., Koopman, L. L., Flores, J. P., and Gehrke, E. C. (2008). Identity in flux: Ethnic self-identification and school attrition in Canadian Aboriginal youth. *Journal of Applied Developmental Psychology, 29*(1), 62–75.

Hansen, D. T. (2006). Epilogue: The sources and expressions of classroom authority in classroom discipline. In J. L Pace and A. Hemmings (Eds.), *Classroom authority*. Mahwah, NJ: Erlbaum, 175–185.

Hattie, J. C. (2009). *Visible Learning: A Synthesis of over 800 Meta-Analyses Relating to Achievement*. New York: Routledge.

Hawley, W. D., and Rollie, D. L. (2007). *The Keys to Effective Schools* (2nd ed.). Thousand Oaks, CA: Corwin.

Henderson, J., and Wakeham, P. (2009). Colonial reckoning, national reconciliation? Aboriginal peoples and the cultural redress in Canada. *ESC: English Studies in Canada, 35*(1), 1–26.

Huber, M. T., and McKinney, K. (2013). *The Scholarship of Teaching and Learning Across the Disciplines*. Indiana: Indiana University Press.

Hunter, M. (1982). *Mastery Teaching*. El Segundo, CA: TIP Publications.

Huntly, H. (2008). Teachers' work: beginning teachers' conceptions of competence. *The Australian Educational Researcher, 35*(1), 125–147.

Johnson, D. W., Johnson, R. T., and Holubec, E. J. (1993). *Cooperation in the Classroom* (rev. ed.). Edina, MN: Interaction Book Company.

Jones, V., and Jones, L. (2006). *Comprehensive Classroom Management: Creating Committees of Support and Solving Problems (6th ed.)*. Boston, MA: Allyn & Bacon.

Jones, K. A., Vermette, P. J., and Jones, J. L. (2009). An integration of "backwards planning" unit design with the "two-step" lesson planning framework. *Education, 130*(2), 357–360.

Jennings, J. L., and DiPrete, A. (2010). Teacher effects on social and behavioural skills in early elementary school. *Sociology of Education, 83*(2), 135–159.

Jussim, L., and Harber, K. D. E. (2005). Teacher expectations and self-fulfilling prophecies: Knowns and unknowns, resolved and unresolved controversies. *Personality and Social Psychology Review, 9*(2), 131–155.

Kagan, S. (1994). *Cooperative Learning: Resources for Teachers*. San Juan Capistrano, CA: Resources for Teachers.

Kessler, G., and Bikowski, D. (2010). Developing collaborative autonomous learning abilities in computer mediated language learning: Attention to meaning among students in wiki space. *Computer Assisted Language Learning, 23*(1), 41–58.

Kitagawa, K. (2001). SchoolNet GrassRoots Program building Innovative Capacity in the Classroom. Retrieved August 16, 2014 from http://www.conferenceboard.ca-library/abstract.aspx?did=324.

Laboucane, R. (2010). Canada's Aboriginal education crisis. *Windspeaker, 28*(7).

Lieberman, A., and Denham, C. (1980). *Time to Learn*. Sacramento, CA: California Commission for Teacher Preparation and Licensing.

Lytton, H., and Pyryt, M. C. (1998). Predictors of achievement in basic skills: A Canadian effective schools study. *Canadian Journal of Education, 23*(3), 281–301.

MaaB, K., and Artigue, M. (2013). Implementation of inquiry-based learning in day-to-day teaching; A synthesis. *ZDM Mathematics Education, 45*(96), 779–795.

Mamde'awt Aboriginal Education. (2013). Retrieved August 16 2014 from http://start.sd34.bc.ca/aboriginal/community-programs/strong-start/

Manitoba Education Safe and Caring Schools. (2014). Retrieved August 16, 2014 from http://www.edu.gov.mb.ca/K12/safe_schools/indexhtp

Martin, J., Sugarman, J. H., and Hichinbottom, S. (2009). *Persons: Understanding Psychological Selfhood and Agency*. New York: Springe

Marks, H. M. (2000). Student engagement in instructional activity: Patterns in the elementary, middle, and high school years. *American Educational Research Journal, 37*(1), 153–184.

Marin, L. M., and Halpern, D. F. (2011). Pedagogy for developing critical thinking in adolescents: Explict instruction prduces greatest gain. *Thinking Skills & Creativity, 6* (1), 1–13.

Marsh, H. W., and Seaton, M. (2013). Academic Self-Concept. In J. Hattie and E. M. Anderson (Eds.), *International Guide to Student Achievement*. New York: Routledge, 62–64.

Marzano, R., Frontier, T., and Livingston, D. (2011). *Effective Supervision: Supporting the Art and Science of Teaching*. Alexandria, VA: Association for Supervision and Curriculum Development.

Marzano, R. (2007). *The art and science of teaching: A comprehensive framework for effective instruction*. Alexandria, VA: Association for Supervision and Curriculum.

Maslow, A. (1968). *Toward a Psychology of Being*. New York: D. Van Nostrand.

Mastropieri, M. A., and Scruggs, T. (2005). *Effective Instruction for Special Education* (3rd ed.). Austin, TX: Allyn & Bacon.

Matsumura, L. Cl., Slater, S. C., and Crosson, A. (2008). Classroom climate, rigorous instruction and curriculum, and students' interactions in urban middle schools. *The Elementary School Journal, 108*(4), 293–312.

Morgan, D. (2014). Saskatchewan Government Supports Province-Wide Access to Online Learning Resources. Retrieved August 17, 2014 from http://www/saksatchewan.ca/government/news-and-media2014/august/08/online-learningresources.

McCoog, I. J. (2010). The existential learner. *The Clearing House: A Journal of Educational Strategies, Issues and Ideas, 83*(4).

Morgan, N., and Saxton, J. (2006). *Teaching Questioning and Learning* (2nd ed.). Markham, Ontario: Pembroke Publishers.

Nazir, J., Pedretti, E.,Wallace, J., Montemurro, D., and Inwood, H. (2009). Climate Change and sustainable Development: The Response form Education. The Canadian Perspective. Retrieved August 14, 2014 from http://www.oise,utoronto.ca/eseofuswfiles/File.esinpractice_file/IAEL1%2002SE%20report%20 2009.pdfNelson, R. M., Martella, R. M., and Marchand-Martella, N. (2002). Maximizing Student Learning. *Journal of Emotional and Behavioral Disorders, 10*(3), 136–148.

Newmann, F., and Wehlage, G. (1993). Five standards of authentic instruction. *Educational Leadership, 50*(7), 8–12.

Nye, B., Konstantopoulos, S., and Hedges, L. V. (2004). How large are teacher effects? *Educational Evaluation and Policy Analysis, 26*(3), 237–257.

Ontario Ministry of Education. (2014). *Achieving excellence: a renewed vision for education in Ontario*. Retrieved Aug 16, 2014 from http://www.edu.gov.on.ca/eng/about/excellent.html.

Pace, J. L., and Hemmings, A. (2006). Understanding classroom authority as a social construction. In J. L. Pace and A. Hemmings (Eds.), *Classroom authority*. Mahwah, NJ: Erlbaum, 1–31.

Palardy, G. J., and Rumberger, R. W. (2008). Teacher effectiveness in first grade: The importance of background qualifications, attitudes and instructional practices for student learning. *Educational Evaluation and Policy Analysis, 30*(2), 111–140.

Parker, M., and Hurry, J. (2007). Teachers' use of questioning and modelling comprehension skills in primary classrooms. *Educational Review, 59*(3), 299–314.

Pelegrino, A. M. (2010). Pre-service teachers and classroom authority. *American Secondary Education, 38*(93), 62–79.

Preston, J. P. (2008). The urgency of postsecondary education for Aboriginal peoples. *Canadian Journal of Educational Administration and Policy, 86*, 1–22.

Purkey, W. W., Schmidt, J. J., and Novak, J. M. (2010). *Conflict to Conciliation*. Thousand Oaks, CA: Corsin.

Putman, M. S. (2009). Grappling with classroom management: The orientations of preservice teachers and impact of student teaching. *Teacher Educator, 44*(4), 232–247.

Rasmussen, C., Birch, J., Sherman, J., Wikman, E., Charchun, J., Kennedy, M., and Bisanz, J., (2009). Self-beliefs and behavioural development as related to academic achievement in Canadian Aboriginal children. *Canadian Journal of School Psychology, 24*(1), 10–33.

Reeve, J. M. (2009). Why teachers adopt a controlling motivating style toward students and how they can become more autonomy supportive. *Educational Psychologist, 44*(3) 159–175.

Ritchhart, R., Church, M., and Morrison, K. (2011). *Making Thinking Viable*. San Francisco, CA: Jossey-Bass.

Roorda, D. L., Kooman, H. M. Y., Spilt, J. L., and Oort, F. J. (2011). The influence of affective teacher-student relationships on student's school engagement and achievement. A Meta-analytic approach. *Review of Educational Research, 81*(4), 493–529.

Rosenshine, B., and Stevens, R. (1986). Teaching functions. In M. C. Wittrock (ed.). *Handbook of Research on Teaching* (3rd ed.). New York: Macmillan.

Rosenthal, R., and Jacobson, L. (1968). *Pygmalion in the Classroom: Teacher Expectations and Pupils' Intellectual Development*. New York: Holt, Rinehart & Winston.

Rowsell, J., and Lapp, D. (2011). New Literacies and Literacy Instruction. In L. Morrow and L. Gambrell (Eds.), *Best Practices in Literacy Instruction* (4th ed.). New York: Guildford.

Schwartz, S. H. (2012). An Overview of the Schwartz Theory of Basic Values. *Online Readings in Psychology and Culture, 2*(1). http://dx.doi.org/10.9707/2307-0919.1116.

Shepard, L., Hammerness, K., Darling-Hammond, L., and Rust, F. (2005). Assessment. In L. Darling-Hammond and J. Bransford (Eds.). *Preparing Teachers for a Changing World: What Teachers Should Learn and Be Able to Do*. San Francisco, CA: Jossey-Bass.

Slavin, R. E. (1989–90). Research on cooperative learning: consensus and controversy. *Educational Leadership, 47*(4), 52–54.

St. Denis, V. (2007). Aboriginal Education and anti-racist education: Building alliances across cultrue and racial identity. *Canadian Journal of Education, 30*(4), 1068–1092.

StrongStart BC. (2009). Early Learning Programs. Operations Guide. Retrieved Aug 17, 2014 from http://www2.gov.bc.ca/gov/DownloadAsset?assetId=B4DCE0695E104C79903F6E17D9DBE33D.

Statistics Canada. (2005). Characteristics of individuals using the internet. Retrieved May 24, 2007, from www40.statcan.ca/l01/cst01/comm15.htm.

Stipek, D. (2002). *Motivation to Learn: Integrating Theory and Practice* (4th ed.). Boston, MA: Allyn & Bacon.

Tollefson, N. (2000). Classroom applications of cognitive theories of motivation. *Educational Psychological Review, 12*(1) 63–983.

Tomlinson, C. A. (2005). Travelling the road to differentiation and staff development. *Journal of Staff Development, 26*, 8–19.

Toulouse, P. R. (2008). Integrating Aboriginal teaching and values into the classroom. What works? *Research into Practice 11*. Retrieved November 12, 2010 from www.edu.gov.on.ca/eng/literacy/numeracy/inspire/whatworks.html.

Volante, L. (2010). Assessment of, for, and as learning within schools: Implications for transforming classroom practice. *Action in Teacher Education, 31*(4), 66–75.

Vygotsky, L. S. (1978). *Mind and Society*. Cambridge, MA: Harvard University Press.

Wang, M., and Holcombe, R. (2010). Adolescents' perceptions of school environment, engagement and academic achievement in middle school. *American Educational Research Journal, 47*(3), 633–662.

Wang, M. C., and Palinscar, A. S. (1989). Teaching students to assume an active role in their learning. In M. C. Reynolds (Ed.), *Knowledge Base for the Beginning Teacher*. New York: Pergamon.

Wilson, J. B. (2007). First Nations Education: The need for legislation in the jurisdictional gray zone. *Canadian Journal of Native Education, 30*, 248–256.

Wineburg, S. (1987). The self-fulfillment of the self-fulfilling prophecy. *Educational Researcher, 16*(9), 28–36.

Wiske, M. (1998). What is teaching for understanding? In M. S. Wiske (Ed.). *Linking Research with Practice*. San Francisco, CA: Jossey-Bass.

Zins, J. E., Bloodworth, M. R., Weissberg, R. P., and Walberg, H. J. (2007). The scientific base linking social and emotional learning to school success. *Journal of Educational and Psychological Consultation, 17*(2/3), 191–210.

Young, K. K., and Talanquer, V. (2013). Effect of different types of small-group activities on students' conversations. *Chemical Educational Research, 90*(9), 1123–1129.

Chapter 7

Abi-Nader, J. (1993). Meeting the needs of multicultural classrooms: Family values and the motivation of minority students. In M. J. O'Hair and S. J. Odell (Eds.), Diversity and Teaching: Teacher Education Yearbook 1. Fort Worth, TX: Harcourt, Brace, Jovanovich College Publications.

Alvarez, H. K. (2007). The impact of teacher preparation on responses to student aggression in the classroom. *Teaching and Teacher Education*, *23*(7), 113–126.

Andrews, J., and Lupart, J. (2000). *The Inclusive Classroom (2nd ed.)*. Scarborough, ON: Nelson.

Arora, K. S. K. (2013). Reflections on the Experiences of Turbaned Sikh Men in the Aftermath of 9/11. *Journal of Social Action in Counseling and Psychology, 5*(1), 116–121.

Ateah, C. A., Secco, M. L., and Woodgate, R. L. (2003). The risks and alternatives to physical punishment use with children. *Journal of Pediatric Health Care, 17*(3), 126–132.

Axelrod, P. (2010). No longer a "Last resort": The end of corporal punishment in the schools of Toronto. *Canadian Historical Review, 91*(2), 261–285.

August, D., and Shanahan, T. (2006). *Developing Literacy in Second-Language Learners: Report of the National Literacy Panel on Language-Minority Children and Youth*. Mahwah, NJ: Lawrence Erlbaum Associates Publishers.

Bear, G. G. (2011). *School Discipline and Self-Discipline: A Practical guide to Promoting Prosocial student behavior*. New York: The Guilford Press.

Belfiore, P. J., Basile, S. P., and Lee, D. L. (2008). Using a high probablility command sequence to increase classroom compliance: The role of Behavioral momentum. *Journal of Behavioral Education, 17*, 160–171.

Blades, D., Johnston, I., and Simmt, E. (2000, June). Cultural diversity and secondary school curricula. Canadian Race Relations Foundation, Toronto. Retrieved July 4, 2003, from www.crr.ca/en/Publications/ResearchReports/doc/ePub_FinalBladesRpt.pdf.

Brady, K., Forton, M., Porter, D., and Wood, C. (2003). *Rules in school*. Greenfield, MA: Northeast Foundation for Children.

Brock University. (2010). Code of Student Conduct and Disciplinary Procedures in Non-Academic Matters. Retrieved July 14, 2010, from www.brocku.ca/webcal/undergrad/code.html.

The Canadian Press. (2010). Schools should be open to cellphones in class: McGuinty. The Globe and Mail. Retrieved January 11, 2011, from www.theglobeandmail.com at www.theglobeandmail.com/news/national/ontario/schools-should-be-open-to-cellphones-in-class-mcguinty/article1708313.

Carter, M. (2005). The constitutional validity fo the corporal punishment defense in Canada: A critical analysis of Canadian Foundation for Children, Youth and the Law versus Canada (Attorney General). *International Review of Victimology, 12*(2), 189–211.

Cihak, D., Kirk, E., and Boon, R. (2009). Effects of classwide positive peer "tootling" to reduce the disruptive classroom behaviors of elementary students with and without disabilities. *Journal of Behavioral Education, 18*(4), 267–278.

Collet, B. A. (2007). Islam, national identity and public secondary education: Perspectives from the Somali diaspora in Toronto, Canada. *Race Ethnicity and Education, 10*(2), 131–153.

Cummins, J. (1986). Empowering minority students. *Harvard Educational Review, 17*(4), 18–36.

Dreikurs, R. (1964). *Children the Challenge*. New York: Hawthorne.

Dreikurs, R., Grundwald, B. B., and Pepper, F. C. (1998). *Maintaining Sanity in the Classroom: Classroom Management Techniques* (2nd ed.). New York: Taylor and Francis.

Dreikurs, R., Cassel, P., Ferguson, E. D. (2004). *Discipline without Tears: How To Reduce Conflict and Establish Cooperation in the Classroom*. Toronto: John Wiley & Sons.

Durrant, J. E., Trocme, N., Fallon, B., Milne, C., and Black, T. (2009). Protection of children from physical maltreatment in Canada: An evaluation of the Supreme Court's definition of reasonable force. *Journal of Aggression, Maltreatment & Trauma, 18*(1), 64–87.

Durrant, J. E. (2007). Corporal Punishment: A violation of the rights of the child. In K. Covell and R, Brian (Eds.), *A Question of Commitment: Children's Rights in Canada*. Waterloo, ON: Wilfred Laurier University Press, 99–125.

Elementary Teachers' Federation of Ontario. (2000). *Classroom Beginnings*. Toronto, ON: Elementary Teachers' Federation of Ontario.

Elliott, A., and Woloshyn, V. (2013). *Language Arts in Canadian Classrooms*. Toronto, ON: Pearson Education.

Emmer, E. T., and Evertson, C. M. (2008). *Classroom management for secondary teachers* (8th ed.). Boston: Allyn & Bacon.

Erford, B. (2012). *Assessment for Counselors* (2nd ed.). Belmont, CA: Brooks/Cole.

Flint, T. K. (2010). Making meaning together: Buddy reading in first grade classrooms. *Early Childhood Education Journal*, *38*(4), 289–297.

Gregson, S. A. (2013). Negotiating justice in teaching: One full-time teacher's practice viewed from the trenches. *Journal for Research in Mathematics Education*, *44*(1), 164–198.

Good, T., and Brophy, J. (1997). *Looking in Classrooms* (5th ed.). New York: Longman.

Harris, J. R. (1998). *The Nurture Assumption*. New York: Simon & Schuster.

Hollins, E. R. (2008). *Culture in School Learning: Revealing the Deep Meaning* (2nd ed.). New York: Routledge.

Jankowska, M., and Atley, M. (2008). Use of creative space in enhancing students' engagement. *Innovations in Education & Teaching International*, *45*(3), 271–279.

Johnson, D. W., Johnson, R. T., and Holubec, E. J. (1993). *Cooperation in the Classroom* (6th ed.). Edina, MN: Interaction Book Company.

Jones, V. F., and Jones, L. S. (2012). *Comprehensive Classroom Management: Creating Communities of Support and Solving Problems* (10th ed.). Boston: Allyn & Bacon.

Kern, L., and Clemens, N. H. (2007). Antecedent strategies to promote appropriate classroom behavior. *Psychology in the Schools*, *44*(1), 65–75.

Modood, T. (2013). *Multiculturalism*. Cambridge, UK: Polity Press.

Manitoba Human Rights Commission. (2007). Human rights in the school. Retrieved February 12, 2007, from www.gov.mb.ca/hrc/english/publications/school/chap1.html.

McGillivary, A. (2011). Children's rights, paternal, power and fiduciary duty: From Roman law to the Supreme Court of Canada. *International Journal of Children's Rights*, *19*(1), 21–54.

McGillivary, A. E., and Durrant, J. E. (2006). Child corporal punishment, violence, law and rights. In R. Alaggia and C. Vine (Eds.), *Cruel but Not Unusual: Violence in Canadian Families*. Waterloo, ON: Wilfred Laurier University Press.

McIntosh, J. (2009). Classroom management, rules, consequences, and rewards! Oh, my! *Science Scope*, *32*(9), 49–51.

Myers, J. (2010). Creating a Positive Classroom Environment. Retrieved July 14, 2010, from www.etfo.ca/Publications/Voice/Documents/Creating%20a%20Positive%20Classroom%20Environment.pdf.

NCEF (National Clearinghouse of Educational Facilities). (2010). *Classroom design*. Retrieved August 22, 2014, from http://www.ncef.org/rl/classroom_design.cfm#860.

National Post. Spanking is not abuse (editorial). Retrieved August 6, 2003, from http://proquest.umi.com/pqdweb?index=2&did=000000347477191&SrchMode=1&sid=1&Fmt=3&VInst=PROD&VType=PQD&RQT=309&VName=PQD&TS=1060198475&clientId=17280.

O'Brien, A., and Pietersma, E. G. (2000). The Section 43 debate: The teacher's perspective. *Education Canada*, *40*(2), 44–45.

Osher, D., Bear, G. G., Sprague, J. R., and Doyle, W. (2010). How can we improve school discipline? *Educational Researcher*, *39*(1), 48–58.

Ritchie, P. J., Rinholm, J., Flewelling, R., Kelly, M. J., and Sammon, J. (1999). The fine art of teaching and behaviour management. *Education Forum*, *25*(3), 19–22.

Rotheram-Borus, M. J., Swendeman, D., and Becker, K. D. (2014). Adapting evidence-based interventions using a common theory, practice, and principles. *Journal of Clinical Child & Adolescent Psychology*, *43*(2), 229–243. DOI: 10.1080/15374416.2013.836453.Sanghera, B. (2013). *Celebrating Punjabi Language in Canada*. Retrieved August 21, 2014 from http://plea4punjabi1.wordpress.com/

Scornavacca, E., Huff, S., and Marshall, S. (2009). Mobile phones in the classroom: If you can't beat them, join them. *Communications of the ACM, 52*(4), 142–146.

Schwartz, S., and Pollishuke, M. (2002). *Creating the Dynamic Classroom*. Toronto, ON: Irwin.

Simonsen, B., Fairbanks, S., Briesch, A., Myers, D., and Sugai, G. (2008). Evidence-based practices in classroom management: Considerations for research to practice. *Evaluation and Treatment of Children, 31*(3) 351–380.

Smith, A. B., Gollop, M. M., Taylor, N. J., and Marshall, K. A. (2003). The discipline and guidance of children: Messages from research. Retrieved December 22, 2006, from www.occ.org.nz/childcomm/content/download/840/4422/file/discipline.pdf.

Stoughton, E. H. (2007). "How will I get them to behave": Pre-service teachers reflect on classroom management. *Teaching and Teacher Education, 23*(7), 1024–1037.

Sweeney, T. J. (1981). Adlerian Counseling, Proven Concepts and Strategies (2nd ed.). Muncie, IN: Accelerated Development.

Technology and Instruction: Educ 204/504/531. (2006). Learning environment design. Retrieved December 20, 2006, from www.coastal.edu/education/ti/environment.html.

Uusiautti, S. (2014). On the positive connection between success and happiness. *International Journal of Research Studies in Psychology*, 3(1).

Vinciarelli, A., Pantic, M., and Bourland, H. (2009). Social signal processing: Survey of an emerging domain. *Image and Vision Computing, 27*(12), 1743–1759.

Walker, H. M. (1979). *The Acting-Out Child: Coping with Classroom Disruption*. Boston: Allyn & Bacon.

Watkinson, A. M. (2011). Constructing the "criminal"—deconstructing the "crime". *International Journal of Human Rights, 16*(3), 517–532.

Windahl, S., Signitzer, B., and Olson, J. (2009). *Using Communication Theory: An Introduction to Planned Communication*. Thousand Oaks, CA: Sage Publications.

Wolfgang, C. N. (2009). Managing Inquiry-Based Classrooms. *Science Scope, 32*(9), 14–17.

Zine, J. (2003). Dealing with September 12th: The chapters with anti-Islamophobia education. *Orbit, 33*(3), 39–41.

Chapter 8

Brophy, J. E. (2010). *Motivating students to learn*. New York: Routledge.

Canter, L., and Canter, M. (2001). *Assertive Discipline: Positive Behaviour Management for Today's Classrooms* (rev. ed.). Los Angeles, CA: Canter Associates.

Dhaem, J. (2012). Responding to minor misbehavior through verbal and nonverbal responses. *Beyond Behavior, 21*(3), 29–34.

Emmer, E. T., and Evertson, C. M. (2009). *Classroom management (8th ed.)*. Upper Saddle River, NJ: Pearson Education, Inc.

Hester, P. P., Hendrickson, J. M., and Gable, R. A. (2009). Forty years later—The value of praise, ignoring, and rules for preschoolers at risk for behavior disorders. *Education & Treatment of Children, 32*(4), 513–535.

Kerr, M. M., and Nelson, C. M. (2002). *Strategies for Addressing Behaviour Problems in the Classroom* (4th ed.). Don Mills, ON: Prentice Hall.

Kounin, J. (1970). *Discipline and Group Management in Classrooms*. New York: Holt, Rinehart & Winston.

Leflot, G., Lier, P. A., Onghena, P., and Colpin, H. (2010). The role of teacher behavior management in the development of disruptive behaviors: An intervention study with the good behavior game. *Journal of Abnormal Child Psychology, 38*(6), 869–882.

Redl, F., and Wineman, D. (1952). *Controls from Within*. New York: Free Press.

Reinke, W. M., Herman, K. C., and Sprick, R. S. (2011). *Motivational interviewing for effective classroom management: The classroom check-up*. New York: Guilford Press.

Sayeski, K. L., and Brown, M. R. (2011). Developing a classroom management plan using a tiered approach. Teaching Exceptional Children, 44(1), 8–17.

Schwartz, S., and Pollishuke, M. (2002). *Creating the Dynamic Classroom*. Toronto, ON: Irwin.

Shrigley, R. L. (1985). Curbing student disruption in the classroom—Teachers need intervention skills. *National Association of Secondary School Principals Bulletin, 69*(479), 26–32.

Skinner, B. F. (1938). *The Behavior of Organisms: An Experimental Analysis*. New York: Appleton-Century.

Tsouloupas, C. N., Carson, R. L., Matthews, R., Grawitch, M. J., and Barber, L. K. (2010). Exploring the association between teachers' perceived student misbehaviour and emotional exhaustion: The importance of teacher efficacy beliefs and emotion regulation. *Educational Psychology, 30*(2), 173–189.

Chapter 9

Bandura, A. (1977). *Social Learning Theory.* Englewood Cliffs, NJ: Prentice Hall.

Brophy, J. E. (2010). *Motivating students to learn.* New York: Routledge.

Booth-Butterfield, M., and Wanzer, M. B. (2010). Humor and Communication. *The SAGE Handbook of Communication and Instruction, 221.* Thousand Oaks, CA: Sage.

Canter, L., and Canter, M. (2001). *Assertive discipline: Positive behavior management for today's classrooms* (3rd ed.). Los Angeles, CA: Canter Associates.

Dhaem, J. (2012). Responding to minor misbehavior through verbal and nonverbal responses. *Beyond Behavior, 21*(3), 29–34.

Emmer, E. T., and Evertson, C. M. (2009). *Classroom management* (8th ed.). Upper Saddle River, NJ: Pearson Education, Inc.

Gatongi, F. (2007). Person-centred approach in schools: Is it the answer to disruptive behaviour in our classrooms? *Counselling Psychology Quarterly, 20*(2), 205–211.

Ginott, H. G. (2009). *Between parent and child: The best-selling classic that revolutionized parent-child communication.* New York: Random House Digital, Inc.

Glasser, W. (2010). *Choice theory in the classroom.* New York: Harper Collins.

Gordon, T. (1989). *Teaching Children Self-Discipline at Home and in School.* New York: Random House.

Hue, M. T., and Li, W. S. (2008). *Classroom Management: Creating a Positive Learning Environment.* Hong Kong: Hong Kong University Press.

Levin, J., and Nolan, J. F. (2007). *Principles of classroom management: a professional decision-making model* (5th ed.). United States: Pearson Education, Inc.

Mackenzie, R. J., and Stanzione, L. (2010). *Setting limits in the classroom: A complete guide to effective classroom management with a school-wide discipline plan.* New York: Random House Digital, Inc.

Moore, K. D. (2011). *Effective instructional strategies: From theory to practice.* Thousand Oaks, CA: Sage.

Pagliaro, M. (2011). *Educator or bully?: managing the 21st century classroom.* Lanham, MD: Rowman and Littlefield Education.

Sheffield, K., and Waller, R. J. (2010). A review of single-case studies utilizing self-monitoring interventions to reduce problem classroom behaviors. *Beyond Behavior, 19*(2), 7–13

Shrigley, R. (1985). Curbing student disruption in the classroom: Teachers need intervention skills. *National Association of Secondary School Principals Bulletin, 69*(7), 26–32.

Zimmerman, B. J., and Schunk, D. H. (Eds.). (2013). *Self-regulated learning and academic achievement: Theoretical perspectives.* New York: Routledge.

Chapter 10

Bailey, J. A, Hill, K. G. Guttmannova, K., Oesterle, S., Hawkins, J. D., Catalano, R. F., and McMahon, R. J. (2013). The association between parent early adult drug use disorder and later observed parenting practices and child behavior problems: Testing alternate models. *Developmental Psychology, 49*(5), 887–899.

Brendtro, L., Brokenleg, M., and Van Bockern, S. (2002). *Reclaiming Youth at Risk: Our Hope for the Future* (2nd ed.). Bloomington, IN: National Educational Services.

Byers, D. L., Caltabiano, N. J., and Caltabiano, M. L. (2011). Teachers' Attitudes Towards Overt and Covert Bullying, and Perceived Efficacy to Intervene. *Australian Journal of Teacher Education, 36*(11), 8–18.

Canter, L., and Canter, M. (2001). *Assertive discipline: Positive behavior management for today's classrooms* (3rd ed.). Los Angeles, CA: Canter Associates.

Charney, R. S. (2002). *Teaching children to care: Classroom management for ethical and academic growth, K-8.* Greenfield, MA: Northeast Foundation for Children.

Cummins, K. K. (1998). *The Teacher's Guide to Behavioral Interventions: Intervention Strategies for Behavioral Problems in the Educational Environment.* Columbia, MO: Hawthorne Educational Services.

Dunlap, G., Iovannone, R., Wilson, K. J., Kincaid, D. K., and Strain, P. (2010). Prevent-Teach-Reinforce: A Standardized Model of School-Based Behavioral Intervention. *Journal of Positive Behavior Interventions, 12*(1), 9–22.

Emmer, E. T., and Evertson, C. M. (2009). *Classroom management* (8th ed.). Upper Saddle River, NJ: Pearson Education, Inc.

Ginott, H. G. (1972). *Teacher and Child*. New York: Macmillan.

Glaser, C., Palm, D., and Brunstein, J. C. (2012). Writing Strategies Instruction for Fourth Graders with and without Problem Behavior: Effects of Self-Monitoring and Operant Procedures on Compositional Achievements and on-task Behavior. *Zeitschrift fur Padagogische Psychologie, 26*(1), 19–30.

Hall, P. S., and Hall, N. D. (2003). *Educating oppositional and defiant children*. Alexandria, VA: Association for Supervision and Curriculum Development.

Jennings, P. A., and Greenberg, M. T. (2009). The prosocial classroom: Teacher social and emotional competence in relation to student and classroom outcomes. *Review of Educational Research, 79*(1), 491–525.

Jones, V. F. (1980). *Adolescents with Behavioural Problems*. Boston: Allyn & Bacon.

Koshik, I. (2010). Questions that convey information in teacher–student conferences. In Alice F. Freed and Susan Ehrlich (Eds.), *Why do you ask? The function of questions in institutional discourse,* 159–86.

Leitao, N., and Waugh, R. W. (2007). Teachers' views of teacher-student relationship in primary school. *Annual International Educational Research*. Freemantle, Western Australia.

Levin, J., and Nolan, J. F. (2007). *Principles of classroom management: a professional decision-making model* (5th ed.). United States: Pearson Education, Inc.

Malti, T., Perren, S., and Buchmann, M. (2010). Children's peer victimization, empathy, and emotional symptoms. *Child Psychiatry & Human Development, 41*(1), 98–113.

Marzano, R., Frontier, T., and Livingston, D. (2011). *Effective Supervision: supporting the art and science of teaching*. Alexandria VA: ASCD.

Miltenberger, R. G. (2011). *Behavior Modification: Principles & Procedures* (5th ed). Belmont, CA: Wadsworth, Cengage Learning.

Moore, D. W., Anderson, A., Glassenbury, M., Lang, R., and Didden, R. (2013). Increasing On-Task Behavior in Students in a Regular Classroom: Effectiveness of a Self-Management Procedure Using a Tactile Prompt. *Journal of Behavioral Education, 22*(4), 302–311.

Narvaez, D. (2010). The emotional foundations of high moral intelligence. *New directions for child and adolescent development, (129),* 77–94.

Pattan. (2008). Functional Behavior Assessment Mini-Module Training Materials. Pennsylvania Technical Training and Assistance Network. Retrieved July 29, 2008, from www.pattan.k12.pa.us/resources/request.aspx?UniqueID=04525.

Pianta, R. C., Hamre, B., and Stuhlman, M. (2003) Relationships between teachers and children. In Reynolds, WM, Miller, GE (Eds.). *Handbook of psychology: Vol. 7*. Educational psychology. New York: Wiley, 199–234.

Poole, I. R., and Vertson, C. M. (2012). *Elementary Classroom Management. International Guide to Student Achievement*. Routledge: New York.

Rathvon, N. (2008). *Effective school interventions: Evidence-based strategies for improving student outcomes* (2nd ed.). New York: The Guilford Press.

Schaubman, A., Stetson, E., and Plog, A. (2011). Reducing teacher stress by implementing collaborative problem solving in a school setting. *School Social Work Journal, 35*(2), 72–93.

Shrigley, R. L. (1980). *The Resolution of 523 Classroom Incidents by 54 Classroom Teachers Using the Six-Step Intervention Model*. University Park: Pennsylvania State University, College of Education, Division of Curriculum and Instruction.

Strachota, R. (1996). *On Their Side: Helping Children Take Charge of Their Learning*. Greenfield, MA: Northeast Foundation for Children.

Sweeney, T. J. (1981). *Adlerian Counseling: Proven Concepts and Strategies*. Muncie, IN: Accelerated Development.

Tillson, T. (2000). Mischief or a cry for help? Disciplining students demands awareness of underlying distress. *The Journal of Addiction and Mental Health*. Retrieved September 19, 2003, from www.cfcefc.ca/docs/cccf/00009_en.htm.

Tsouloupas, C. N., Carson, R. L., Matthews, R., Grawitch, M. J., and Barber, L. K. (2010). Exploring the association between teachers' perceived student misbehaviour and emotional exhaustion: the importance of teacher efficacy beliefs and emotion regulation. *Educational Psychology, 30*(2), 173–189.

Chapter 11

Bailey, J. A., Hill, K. G., Guttmannova, K., Oesterle, S., Hawkins, J. D., Catalano, R. F., and McMahon, R. J. (2013). The association between parent early adult drug use disorder and later observed parenting practices and child behavior problems: Testing alternate models. *Developmental Psychology, 49*(5), 887–899.

Canter, L., and Canter, M. (2001). *Assertive Discipline: Positive Behaviour Management for Today's Classrooms* (rev. ed.). Los Angeles, CA: Canter Associates.

Durlak, J. A., Weissberg, R. P., Dymnicki, A. B., Taylor, R. D., and Schellinger, K. B. (2011). The impact of enhancing students' social and emotional learning: A meta-analysis of school-based universal interventions. *Child development, 82*(1), 405–432.

El Nokali, N. E., Bachman, H. J., and Votruba-Drzal, E. (2010). Parent involvement and children's academic and social development in elementary school. *Child development, 81*(3), 988–1005.

Glaser, C., Palm, D., and Brunstein, J. C. (2012). Writing Strategies Instruction for Fourth Graders with and without Problem Behavior: Effects of Self-Monitoring and Operant Procedures on Compositional Achievements and on-task Behavior. *Zeitschrift für Pädagogische Psychologie, 26*(1), 19–30.

Hill, N. E., and Tyson, D. F. (2009). Parental involvement in middle school: a meta-analytic assessment of the strategies that promote achievement. *Developmental psychology, 45*(3), 740.

Hoover-Dempsey, K., and Sandler, H. (1997). Why do parents become involved in their children's education? *Review of Educational Research, 67*(1), 3–42.

Javed, M., Eng, L. S., Mushtaq, I., and Hashim, N. H. (2012). Analysis of the role of parent-teacher meeting in enhancing the quality of education at school level. *Language in India, 12*(5).

Jones, V. F., and Jones, L. S. (2010). *Comprehensive Classroom Management: Creating Communities of Support and Solving Problems* (9th ed.). Boston: Allyn & Bacon.

Karila, K., and Alasuutari, M. (2012). Drawing partnership on paper: how do the forms for individual educational plans frame parent-teacher relationship? *International Journal about Parents in Education, 6*(1).

Kearney, C. A., Turner, D., and Gauger, M. (2010). School refusal behavior. In I. Weiner & E. Craighead (Eds.), *Corsini's Encyclopedia of Psychology* (4th ed.) New York: Wiley, 1517–1519.

Koshik, I. (2010). Questions that convey information in teacher–student conferences. In *"Why do you ask? The function of questions in institutional discourse"*, ed. Alice F. Freed and Susan Ehrlich, 159–86.

Marini, Z., Fairbain, L., and Zuber, R. (2001). Peer harassment in individuals with developmental disabilities: Towards the development of a multi-dimensional bullying identification model. *Developmental Disabilities Bulletin, 29*(2), 170–195.

Miltenberger, R. G. (2011). *Behavior Modification: Principles & Procedures.* (5th ed.). Belmont, CA: Wadsworth, Cengage Learning.

Minke, K., and Anderson, K. (2003). Restructuring Routine Parent–Teacher Conferences: The Family–School Conference Model. *The Elementary School Journal, 104*(1), 49–69.

Rogers, M. A., Wiener, J., Marton, I., and Tannock, R. (2009). Parental involvement in children's learning: Comparing parents of children with and without Attention-Deficit/Hyperactivity Disorder (ADHD). *Journal of School Psychology, 47*(3), 167–185.

Smith, B. N., and Hains, B. J. (2012). Examining administrators' disciplinary philosophies. A conceptual model. *Educational Administration Quarterly, 48*(3), 548–576.

Turecki, S., and Tonner, L. (2012). *The difficult child: Expanded and revised edition.* Random House Digital, Inc.

Whannell, R., and Allen, W. (2011). High school dropouts returning to study: The influence of the teacher and family during secondary school. *Australian Journal of Teacher Education, 36*(9), 3.

Wolfgang, C. H. (2008). *Solve discipline problems* (7th ed.). Boston: Allyn & Bacon.

Zentall, S. S., and Beike, S. M. (2012). Achievement and Social Goals of Younger and Older Elementary Students Response to Academic and Social Failure. *Learning Disability Quarterly, 35*(1), 39–5.

INDEX